How Ottawa Spends 1997-98

How Ottawa Spends 1997-98

Seeing Red: A Liberal Report Card

Edited by
Gene Swimmer

CARLETON UNIVERSITY PRESS

Printed and bound in Canada

National Library of Canada cataloguing

How Ottawa Spends

1983-
Annual.
1997-98 ed.: Seeing Red
Each vol. also has a distinctive title.
Prepared at the School of Public Administration
        Carleton University
includes bibliographical references.
ISSN 0822-6482
ISBN 0-88629-326-x (1997-98 ed.)

1. Canada-Appropriations and expenditures-Periodicals.
1. Carleton University. School of Public Administration.

HJ7663.S6   354.7100722   C84-030303-3

Cover design: Xpressive Designs

Carleton University Press gratefully acknowledges the support extended to its
publishing program by the Canada Council and the Ontario Arts Council.
The Press would also like to thank the Department of Canadian Heritage,
Government of Canada, and the Government of Ontario through the
Ministry of Culture, Tourism and Recreation, for their assistance.

W. Irwin Gillespie
(1937 - 1997)

This edition of *How Ottawa Spends* is dedicated to the memory of Irwin Gillespie. Professor Gillespie joined the Department of Economics at Carleton University in 1963. He was a brilliant teacher and a superb instructor, advisor, and trainer of research students. Professor Gillespie was one of Canada's foremost authorities in the fields of taxation, public finance and fiscal policy, and contributed to *How Ottawa Spends* on several occasions. Students, colleagues and friends will miss this distinguished scholar and remarkable person.

CONTENTS

PREFACE

This is the eighteenth edition of *How Ottawa Spends*. Over the years, we have attempted to provide timely and constructive analyses of federal government spending and policy in the hope of stimulating debate about public priorities and options. This year's edition provides a comprehensive assessment of the Liberal government's performance, using its pre-election blueprint for governance (known as the Red Book) as a point of departure. Eleven areas of government policy are analyzed, including aspects of economic management, national unity, social policy, and ethics.

The School of Public Administration at Carleton University could not produce *How Ottawa Spends* without the contributions and collaboration of many people. First and foremost, I want to thank the authors, who worked under extremely tight deadlines to ensure that the book would be published on time. I am especially pleased that four chapters were each co-written by a faculty member and doctoral candidate from the School of Public Administration. As a peer-reviewed publication, we also rely heavily on the assistance of many other academic colleagues to provide comments, criticism, and advice to the contributors and to the editor. Thanks to all those individuals who provided helpful comments. I particularly want to express my gratitude to Sandra Bach, who did double duty as both co-contributor of one chapter and my research assistant. She provided excellent comments to all of the authors, in addition to compiling the tables and charts that appear in the appendix, *Fiscal Facts and Trends*.

As always, we are indebted to the staff at the School of Public Administration, without whom this annual publication would not appear. In particular, Jackie Carberry did a superb job of organizing the editing process and transforming the original manuscripts into photo-ready page proofs, and Martha Clark served as copy editor for the final version of the volume. We also want to thank Douglas Campbell for his impeccable copy editing at various stages of this project, as well as John Flood and Pauline McKillop of Carleton University Press for their invaluable support. We are grateful to Sinclair Robinson and Nandini Sarma for French translation.

Given that this is my final year as editor of *How Ottawa Spends*, I would like to express my special thanks to Susan Phillips, Katherine Graham, and Allan Maslove, and to Martha Clark, for their assistance and encouragement during the last two years. I will do my best to be as helpful to my successor as they have been to me. Finally, I must acknowledge the understanding and support of Carol Silcoff, my lifetime partner, despite the many weekends I spent in my office working on this project.

Gene Swimmer
Ottawa
April 1997

The opinions expressed by the contributors to this volume are the personal views of the authors of the individual chapters and do not necessarily reflect the views of the Editor or the School of Public Administration of Carleton University.

1

Seeing Red:
A Liberal Report Card

GENE SWIMMER

In the run-up to the 1993 federal election, the Liberals embarked on the novel strategy of producing and widely distributing a document with the party's detailed blueprint for how it would govern if elected. In addition to harsh criticism of the past nine years of Conservative rule, the publication, which has become known as the Red Book, included about 200 specific commitments.[1] Often during the campaign Jean Chrétien stated that the promises were put in writing so that the public (and the media) would be in a better position to hold his government accountable. Three years into their current mandate, the Liberals issued a self-assessment of their record that indicated that 153 of the 197 Red Book commitments (78 percent) have been fulfilled and another 24 (12 percent) are in progress.[2] Not surprisingly, what constitutes living up to a promise is very much in the eye of the beholder. For example, the Reform party issued its own Red Book assessment, which states that only 50 of the 197 promises (25 percent) were kept, and that the Liberals conveniently omitted 27 Red Book commitments from their analysis, of which only three were kept.[3] Similarly, the Conservatives identified 60 broken commitments.[4] Although these counting exercises may make for interesting public relations, it is questionable whether they represent an effective evaluation of the Liberal government's first term in office. All 200 commitments were not of equal importance to the government or the public, and the Red Book was silent on many crucial public policy areas.

Given the imminent federal election, this edition of *How Ottawa Spends* attempts a more comprehensive assessment of the government, using the Red Book only as a point of departure. In the following chapters, eleven areas of government policy, ranging from economic management and national unity to social policies, are analyzed. When applicable, the authors compare Liberal actions with Red Book commitments. A fairly consistent picture emerges across the chapters. Despite the Red Book's attempt to distinguish Liberal ideals from those of previous Conservative governments, Liberal policies, once in office, bear a much stronger resemblance to Tory Blue philosophy than to the Red Book. The Liberals have performed well in economic management areas, like deficit control and trade promotion, with the important exception of employment policies. In the national unity field, they are barely passing, with another major test yet to come. Their record is weak in social areas, such as child care, communications, and social housing, where the twin obsessions of deficit control and response to decentralist pressures are driving the policy agenda. Finally, in environmental protection and integrity agendas, Liberal performance has been mixed, but falls far short of the expectations created by the Red Book.

The remainder of this chapter is divided as follows. After a discussion of evidence about governments living up to campaign promises, there is a detailed overview of the eleven chapters in the book. The 1997 pre-election Budget is then discussed, after which, in the conclusion, final grades are assigned to the Liberals in relation to their current mandate.

PROMISES TO KEEP?

The introduction to the Red Book speaks of the Canadian dream to build "an independent country that is economically strong, socially just, proud of its diversity, and characterized by integrity, compassion, and competence."[5] It is argued that after nine years of Conservative government the dream had turned into a nightmare.

The Liberals identify two aspects of their philosophy that distinguish them from the Conservatives. First, the Liberal agenda is based on an integrated approach to economic, environmental, and social policy: "One of the greatest failings of the Conservative government has been a tendency to focus on one problem, such as the deficit or inflation, without understanding or caring about the consequences of their policies in other areas such as lost jobs, increased poverty, and dependence on social assistance."[6] Secondly, Liberals fundamentally believe that it is not enough simply to rely on market forces; that "governments can be a force for good in society"[7] with respect to jobs, health care, gender equality, the environment, caring for the children and the aged, and alleviation of poverty. Ironically, the criticisms with respect to being obsessed with the deficit and relying on market forces are used by several authors in this volume to describe specific aspects of the Liberal government since it took power in 1993.

Although the Red Book represents an uncommonly explicit statement of commitments, political parties often issue and campaign on platforms that embody their ideology and policy priorities. As a result, the question of whether voters can rely on a party to live up to its election promises is hardly new for researchers. Empirical studies have been conducted in several countries, including Canada, to determine whether there is a relationship between the victorious party's pre-election platform priorities and its post-election expenditure in policy areas. Focusing on spending provides a way to assign relative values to various commitments. Results for Great Britain and the United States generally support the view that post-election spending priorities reflect the winning party's platform. The result for the United States is particularly surprising, given both the separation of powers and the fact that the party that controls the presidency often does not control

Congress.[8] To judge by a recent study by Pétry,[9] Canada appears to be an anomaly. During the period 1949-1988, the spending priorities of Canadian governments in economic development policies tended to be a hybrid of the platforms of the governing party and the major party in opposition (the Liberals or Conservatives). On these issues the governing party attempted to compromise with its major opponent. By contrast, spending in many social policy areas contradicted both the Liberal and Conservative platform priorities, but was consistent with the New Democratic Party (NDP) platform. Both major parties, once in office, expropriated NDP policies, apparently to remove a potential electoral threat.

The Chrétien government appears to continue the trend. On economic development issues, such as deficit control and unemployment, its policies reflect much of the ideology of the Conservatives and the current major opposition, the Reform party.[10] With very little NDP presence in the House of Commons, there is no potential for a contagion from the left. As a result, even on social policy issues, such as child care and social housing, Liberal spending decisions and actions are more consistent with Reform and Conservative party platforms than with their own Red Book.

AN OVERVIEW OF THE VOLUME: PROMISES FULFILLED?

The following chapters assess the Chrétien government with respect to eleven different policy areas. The analysis begins with a consideration of the two mega-problems the government has faced: the deficit and national unity. Liberal decisions on how to attack these issues have created the backdrop for the approach to other policy areas. The next three chapters focus on other aspects of economic management: labour markets, and internal and foreign trade. This is followed by discussions of communications and environmental policy, which have both economic and social components. Three social policies are then evaluated: elderly benefits, child care, and housing. The book concludes with a discussion of a matter of process as opposed to content, the Liberals' ability to govern with integrity.

Nowhere is the difference between Red Book rhetoric and government policy more evident than in deficit reduction. This is also the area where Liberal actions most mirror the platform of their Conservative predecessors, though they have achieved far superior results.

- **Allan Maslove** and **Kevin Moore** focus on the Chrétien government's success in "getting its fiscal house in order." Unlike the Mulroney Conservatives' monolithic approach to cutting deficits and inflation, the Red Book proposed an integrated two-track strategy to reduce the deficit to 3 percent of Gross Domestic Product by 1996, through both spending restraint and direct government intervention to spur economic growth. Once in office the Liberals instituted major program spending cuts, reducing the deficit further and faster than originally envisioned, though the task was simplified by greater public concern about the deficit and the lack of an effective left-of-centre opposition in Parliament. Nonetheless, the Liberals must be credited for demonstrating unusual determination in controlling expenditures, only allowing new spending initiatives when there were equivalent reductions elsewhere. In the process they have restored confidence in the Department of Finance budget forecasts by setting modest goals and consistently achieving them. If anything, the Liberals have become victims of their own success, with calls now coming (from the right) to cut taxes or (from the left) to restore some social program spending. Finance Minister Paul Martin has so far resisted the pressure from both groups.

   On the down side, the Liberals have largely abandoned their other track, believing that deficit reduction will create the low interest rates required for economic growth and job creation. Canada's unemployed are still waiting for these promised effects to materialize.

National unity, Canada's other major issue, is not mentioned in the Red Book. The omission was both deliberate and integral to the Liberals' pre-referendum strategy of neither threatening nor offering inducements to Quebec. This was a reasonable approach as long as the polls showed the "No" (to sovereignty) side ahead. However, in the final weeks of the campaign polls indicated a swing to Lucien Bouchard (who took over leadership of the sovereignty campaign) and the "Yes" side. The Liberals scrambled to come up with alternatives, which ranged from raising fears of massive job loss in a separate Quebec to hinting at constitutional benefits for Quebec following a "No" victory. As a result of the federalist forces having achieved the narrowest of victories, the Liberals have been forced to change the game plan regarding Quebec.

- **Reg Whitaker** likens the national unity issue to a missing engine on the Liberals' otherwise smoothly running airplane. Since the referendum, the Liberals have been balancing two political strategies toward Quebec. Plan A is based on positive initiatives to change the status quo by House of Commons resolutions that recognize Quebec as a distinct society and grant regional vetoes (including one for Quebec) on constitutional amendments, and by a commitment to transfer labour market training to the provinces. Plan B focuses on the creation of ground rules for negotiations between Quebec and Canada following a successful vote for sovereignty. Issues include what kind of referendum question and what size of majority would trigger negotiations, what laws would govern the transition, and what Canada's bottom line would be at the negotiating table. The Liberals have been ambiguous about this strategy, hinting that a simple majority would not be enough, and that a partition of Quebec could be required to ensure the right of Aboriginal peoples to remain in Canada. The best-defined part of Plan B is the government's reference to the Supreme Court on whether Canadian law allows Quebec to secede unilaterally and whether Canadian law would take precedence over international law following a "Yes" vote.

  In the run-up to the federal election, the Liberals are shrewdly stressing Plan A, shunting aside the potentially divisive Plan B. However, the crunch is going to come before the next referendum, and the Liberals (assuming they remain in power) will have to spell out the ground rules for dealing with a Quebec that has voted for sovereignty.

The Liberal decisions to control deficits primarily by means of spending cuts and to respond to the referendum by agreeing to devolve training programs have had a substantial impact on attempts to reduce unemployment. Once again the Chrétien government's policies look more like those of their predecessors, but they have not been more successful than the Conservatives in controlling unemployment, leaving the high unemployment rate as their "Achilles' heel" in the upcoming election.

- **Peter Stoyko** investigates another keynote of the Red Book, labour market policy. The Liberals decried the Conservative government's laissez-faire approach to creating jobs, and committed themselves to active measures to invest in people. Their proposals included increased apprenticeship and training programs, and the creation of a Youth Service Corps to foster career development for young workers. These active measures would be better integrated with the existing unemployment insurance system in order to reduce dependence on government transfers. The Liberals also promised to generate new jobs through a technologically inclined public infrastructure program as well as by reducing the regulatory burden on businesses and fostering greater co-operation between labour and management. The lion's share of these commitments has not been fulfilled. Attempts to better target unemployment insurance to those in greater need have been neutralized by overall reductions in benefits. Active measures such as training and apprenticeship programs have been devolved to the provinces, with little assurance that spending will be maintained. Youth career development initiatives have received less funding than promised and have become focused on university-educated young people, who already have above-average employment prospects. With respect to the infrastructure program, about one-third of the money went to finance initiatives that would have proceeded anyway, and a large share of the remaining money was spent on low-tech politically-inspired projects.

Though labour regulations have been streamlined, there is little evidence that labour relations have been depoliticized. The Liberals now justify the fact that unemployment rates remain above 9 percent by suggesting that governments cannot create jobs, they can only develop an environment conducive to job growth.

Concerns about stimulating economic growth in order to create jobs have led the Liberals to move export promotion to centre stage within its foreign affairs portfolio. Though there have been real payoffs from this decision, it has also had questionable effects upon aspects of foreign policy.

• **Claire Turenne Sjolander** focuses on the new role of international trade and its relationship to Canadian foreign policy. Aside from the Liberal pledge to renegotiate certain provisions of the North American Free Trade Agreement (NAFTA), the only Red Book trade commitment is to enhance export opportunities for Canadian business. Philosophically, the Red Book treats trade policy as a natural extension of industrial, rather than foreign, policy. The Liberal pre-election foreign policy agenda concentrated on the need to distinguish Canada's international presence from that of the United States (unlike the Conservatives), and re-commited the party to its "internationalist" heritage, including peacekeeping and foreign aid. Once taking office, the Liberals have accepted the NAFTA, subject to the establishment of working groups to discuss problem issues. Simultaneously, the Liberals pushed trade with countries other than the United States to the forefront. The "Team Canada" trade missions to Asia and Latin America, which included the Prime Minister, provincial premiers, and business leaders, have become the centre of a successful multi-department strategy to create new export opportunities. On the negative side, trade has become the "tail that wags the foreign policy dog," inevitably compromising the internationalist values heralded in the Red Book. In particular, the Liberal government will not make better trade relations with undemocratic regimes dependent upon improvements in the protection of human rights, a policy decision determined without any public debate. It is ironic that a distinguishing feature of current Canadian foreign policy is that human rights play a far less visible role than they did under the Mulroney Conservative government.

Despite their original scepticism about the NAFTA, the Liberals included a commitment in the Red Book to negotiate with the provinces to eliminate interprovincial trade barriers. A reduction in the estimated $6 billion annual cost associated with these barriers was no doubt a factor in the decision to adopt a policy from the governing Conservatives.

• **Bruce Doern** and **Mark MacDonald** examine the Agreement on Internal Trade, the negotiation of which by the Liberals in July 1994 was no small feat, given the federal-provincial experiences with the Meech Lake and Charlottetown accords. The Agreement sets out general rules, including those concerning reciprocal non-discrimination and the right to entry and exit, but allows provinces to practise certain policies that may contradict the general rules for "legitimate objectives." Dispute-resolution procedures modelled on international trade practices are also included. Although many commentators characterize the Agreement as weak and contradictory, Doern and MacDonald argue that the deal will enhance internal trade as well as constrain governmental policy instruments, particularly at the provincial level. For that reason, it can implicitly be considered a "side-deal to the constitution." They give the Liberals more than a passing grade for keeping their Red Book promise to establish an agreement, but it will take subsequent rounds of negotiation before interprovincial trade barriers are eliminated.

Given the general Liberal philosophy that governments should become involved in private markets to ensure the public interest, two areas where they would be expected to actively intervene are culture and the environment. Though there certainly were specific Red Book commitments consistent with this view, concerns of deficit reduction and the adverse effects of regulation upon employment have led the government to adopt a more laissez-faire approach.

- **Vincent Mosco** focuses on the contradictions between the domestic and the international aspects of the Liberals' communications policy. His assessment begins with the explicit Red Book commitment to maintain stable, multi-year funding for the CBC and other national cultural institutions. Despite attacking the Conservative government for undermining Canadian culture by funding cuts, in the end the Liberals conceded that fiscal restraints required this industry to make do with greatly reduced federal financing. The government has perpetuated the Tory view that information and culture are simply marketable products, rather than resources vital to citizenship and nationhood. Other examples of treating communications as just another industry include the Liberals' ignoring increased concentration in the newspaper and cable television industries, their allowing huge increases in local phone service rates, and their pursuing initiatives to commercialize federal information and cultural agencies.

  In contrast, the Liberals' international policy continues to stress the special status required for culture and communication. This policy of protection, in the form of excise taxes on split-run magazines and the limitations on foreign ownership of communications companies, is becoming untenable, given their domestic policy thrust. A recent World Trade Organization decision supporting the U.S. protest against the split-run magazine tax will force the government to fundamentally rethink its cultural and communication policy, as it attempts to reduce the short-run political damage of its policy failures.

- **Luc Juillet** and **Glen Toner** find a substantial gap between the Liberals' environmental promises and their subsequent actions. The Red Book devoted an entire chapter to the Liberal vision of a fundamental shift in values and public policy to reconcile economic growth with the preservation of the environment by means of strict standards, and by building environmental

concerns into government decision-making. Pollution prevention would replace pollution management and clean-up as the
philosophy underpinning public intervention. On the basis of
an evaluation of its record in five problem areas (toxic substances, environmental assessment, biodiversity, global warming, and sustainable development in public administration),
Juillet and Toner conclude that the government's actions
amount to cautious incremental steps toward a solution, in
contrast with the aggressive rhetoric of the Red Book. This is
reminiscent of the record of the Conservatives, who made
strong environmental pronouncements but were guilty of "eco-
backtracking" throughout their mandate.

The Liberal government has allowed environmental policy
to be sideswiped by concerns about the deficit, job-creation,
and national unity. These preoccupations have given greater
credibility to arguments made by businesses and resource
departments that mandatory environmental regulations kill
jobs, and have led to negotiations about devolving federal
environmental responsibilities, despite scepticism about the
capacity and motivation of some provinces to accept this
jurisdiction.

The next three chapters focus on different aspects of social policy,
where the Liberals were deliberately vague or included provisos in
their Red Book promises. Liberal post-election actions in these policy
fields were also driven by the need to cut spending and/or to placate
Quebec through decentralist policies. Although the Red Book criticized the Mulroney government for cutting elderly benefit programs, it
was silent on expenditure priorities with respect to senior citizens.

• **Michael Prince** traces the Chrétien government's modifications to retirement benefits that resulted in the creation of the
Seniors Benefit. These changes built on the Conservative
legacy, particularly the "clawback" of Old Age Security from
high-income seniors, which essentially ended universality. The
Liberal approach has been to impose losses on middle- and
higher-income seniors in order to provide modest increases for

low-income seniors, and to ensure that these programs are sustainable in the long term, once "baby-boomers" are potential recipients. The new Seniors Benefit, which comes into effect in 2001, will be tax-free and fully indexed to inflation, but will be reduced once the threshold family income (also indexed to inflation) has been reached. It replaces and incorporates Old Age Security, the Guaranteed Income Supplement, and age and pension income tax credits, although everyone 60 years of age or more in 1996 will have the choice of the old or the new regime.

Although the Liberals trumpet the Seniors Benefit as breaking new ground, Prince argues that it is more incremental than innovative, and that it represents the driving role of the Department of Finance in determining social policy. The Liberals must be commended for combining four programs into one, with complete indexation. However, they lose marks for failing to redistribute benefits taken away from rich seniors: they will provide a miserly increase of 17 cents a day to the poorest seniors, while keeping the rest. Even this minuscule improvement for the poorest seniors will be negated once the effect of lower Canada Pension Plan benefits comes on stream.

The major unfulfilled social policy promise in the Red Book was to expand child care spaces by means of a federal-provincial shared-cost program. The original commitment was predicated on obtaining an annual economic growth rate of at least 3 percent, and provincial agreement. According to the Liberals' self-assessment, the program was not introduced because the economic growth threshold was achieved in only one year, and because an insufficient number of provinces expressed interest in proceeding.

• **Sandra Bach** and **Susan Phillips** reject the Liberals' explanation, arguing that child care is the first fatality of a New Social Union constructed by the federal and provincial governments, which has resulted in a shift toward greater private provision and provincial control over social services, and a greater emphasis placed on the tax system to redistribute income at the

expense of direct state funding of services. This new environment has been shaped by the Liberals' responses to fiscal and
decentralist political pressures, rather than by an electoral
mandate or public consultation. The Canada Health and Social
Transfer (CHST) dramatically reduced federal transfer payments to provinces and simultaneously increased provincial
discretion on how this money could be used. Under these
circumstances, provinces were much less likely to agree to a
new shared-cost child care program. The long-term fate of
child care was sealed by the Liberals' post-referendum decision
that the federal government would not create new shared-cost
programs in areas of provincial jurisdiction without the consent
of a majority of provinces.

As part of the New Social Union, the federal and provincial
governments plan to integrate their respective tax assistance
and welfare benefits for children into a National Child Benefit
System. Although the system will redistribute income primarily
to working-poor families, it will do little to help parents access
affordable and high quality child care in a largely private and
unregulated market.

There are few references to federal housing initiatives in the Red Book,
and this policy field appears to be another victim of this new social
union.

- **Fran Klodawsky** and **Aron Spector** find that the Liberal
  government has continued the Mulroney Conservatives' policy
  of devolving existing social housing programs to provincial
  and territorial governments, except for housing on Aboriginal
  reserves. Although the Liberals justify the policy as being
  responsive to regional and individual needs, social housing
  provides the government with a convenient pawn for its goals
  of cutting the deficit and promoting flexible federalism. The
  new strategy implicitly relies more heavily on the private sector
  housing market, despite the fact that in the 1990s lower-income
  Canadians have experienced a sharp increase in the proportion
  of their incomes that must be spent on shelter. The Liberals

have also allowed housing issues to become segregated from social policy debates. Not only are the "bricks and mortar" of the current federal housing stock in jeopardy of being abandoned, but also it is likely that significant achievements in management structure and expertise in the field of non-profit housing fostered by the Federal government over the past 25 years will be wasted.

A final cornerstone of the Liberals' pre-election platform was the pledge to govern with integrity. They were determined to capitalize on the Mulroney government's poor ethical record, which included fourteen conflict of interest accusations affecting cabinet ministers or their senior advisors. In 1996, Chrétien stated that he was especially proud that his government had fulfilled this pledge.[11]

- **Ian Greene** focuses on the Red Book promises to restore honesty and integrity in our political institutions. Using the principle of mutual respect, he evaluates the Liberals with respect to the major ethical issues present when they assumed power, including conflict of interest, patronage, party discipline, and the influence of lobbyists. The Liberals have at least partially fulfilled their commitments by appointing an Ethics Counsellor and strengthening the Lobbyist Registration Act, and must be given credit for putting election promises in writing to increase their accountability. Nonetheless, their performance is disappointing. The government had a golden opportunity to enhance integrity in government by demanding real transparency in lobbyist registration, by limiting financial contributions from single sources to prevent undue influence, by eliminating patronage appointments, and by legislating codes of conduct to address conflict of interest. Unfortunately, the Liberals' old partisan habits die hard, and they paid little attention to the public's higher expectations for democratic government.

THE 1997 PRE-ELECTION BUDGET

Paul Martin's fourth budget, issued on February 18, 1997, was apparently calculated by the Liberals to be a "non-event." Compared to previous pre-election budgets, there are very few new initiatives, and those had been announced or leaked to the media in advance. Martin's overwhelming theme is that the government must "stay the course of deficit reduction,"[12] despite its substantial success in the past years. He goes to great lengths to argue that despite bettering his deficit target of $24.3 billion by more than $5 billion, and projecting that by 1998-99 the government will be able to finance its $9 billion deficit internally, the fiscal battle is not over. With a balanced budget on the horizon, the Liberals' goal has shifted to reducing the federal debt-to-Gross Domestic Product (GDP) ratio, from its current level of 74 percent. Martin rejects a broad-based tax cut at this time, because it would only lead to higher deficits in the future or require further cuts to government spending, which would have serious ramifications for program delivery.[13] Instead, some strategic tax changes and new programs are introduced, amounting to about $.8 billion in 1996-97 and $1.2 billion in 1997-98.[14]

Before examining specifics, we should address the general philosophy underlying the Budget. Faced with the conflict between currying favour with financial markets and satisfying their traditional constituency, which expects an activist government, the Liberals have chosen to move to the right. First of all, the deficit projections for 1996-97 through 1998-99 are extremely high. Most non-government forecasters are predicting a deficit of $15 to 18 billion for 1996-97 ($1 to 4 billion below Martin's figure), $10 billion for 1997-98, and a balanced budget for 1998-99 ($7 to 9 billion below Martin in each year).[15] This weakens the argument for continued restraint.

Although the government admits that the unemployment rate remains too high, few new resources are being made available to ameliorate the problem. Martin argues that declining interest rates, a product of the government's success in reducing the deficit, will stimulate consumer demand and business investment, which will in turn create jobs. He points to the fact that 85,000 private sector jobs have been created in the four months leading up to the Budget, and that most forecasters expect 300,000 to 350,000 jobs to be created this year.[16] It is interesting that while the finance minister refuses to rely on private forecasts for the deficit, he is content to do so for job-creation. The Budget does not provide an estimate of unemployment for the upcoming year, probably because the pessimistic economic assumptions used to obtain high deficit projections would generate a double-digit unemployment rate forecast.

The employment situation has not improved appreciably since the Budget. Although 42,300 new jobs were created in February and March 1997, and the unemployment rate fell to 9.3 percent, March 1997 marked the 78th consecutive month that the unemployment rate exceeded 9 percent. Indeed, without a drop in the labour force since October 1996 (those who are working, or looking for work), the unemployment rate would have been 10 percent for March 1997. [17]

Martin also made it clear that the Liberals eventually plan to use the moneys gained from the taming of the debt to lower personal income taxes.[18] The alternative of restoring spending to various government social programs is never mentioned. This contrasts with the findings of the February 1997 Southam News-Angus Reid poll, which reports that 68 percent of respondents would spend the savings above the current deficit targets on health care, education, and job creation, 21 percent would cut the deficit further, and only 9 percent would reduce taxes.[19]

Finally, Martin portrays this budget as reasonably progressive because there are no further cuts to government programs and there are significant investments of about $1 billion in 1996-97 and 1997-98 in the priority social policy areas of post-secondary education, medicare, and the needs of children.[20] What he neglects to mention is that as a result of his earlier budgets, transfers to provinces for social programs (under the CHST) have been reduced by $6 billion annually between 1995-96 and 1997-98, which dwarfs any new funding.

The Budget can be divided into employment and social policy initiatives. There are programs aimed at immediately helping the private sector to create jobs, until the hoped-for effects of lower interest rates and higher economic growth take effect.[21] The Canada Infrastructure Works Program will receive $425 million in new money to support local infrastructure projects in 1997-98. Since these federal funds must be matched by provincial and municipal contributions, a total of $1.275 billion in new projects could potentially be supported. However, as Stoyko points out, given the many problems that plagued the original program, the job impact will probably be small. The government has also reduced Employment Insurance (EI) premium rates slightly and introduced a New Hires Program, which exempts employers from EI premiums on jobs created in 1997. The government does not mention that Canada Pension Plan contributions are rising at a faster rate, effective January 1997, so that it is extremely unlikely that EI payroll savings will create new jobs (as opposed to protecting existing ones).[22] Finally, there is the $255 million Youth Employment Strategy to support 120,000 summer placements and 19,000 internships. This does not represent any new money (funds were provided in the 1996 Budget), and it is aimed at post-secondary students, who are the elite of the youth labour force.

The Budget also attempts to improve long-term employment performance by increasing the availability and quality of post-secondary education.[23] There are several tax changes designed to make university more affordable. These include doubling the education tax credit from $100 to $200 per month by 1998, making post-secondary mandatory fees eligible for the tuition credit, lengthening the post-graduate deferral of student loan payments from 18 to 30 months, and increasing the maximum contribution on registered education savings plans to $4,000 per year. While these changes will be welcomed by most middle-class parents, the savings are marginal, and therefore unlikely to affect individual educational choices. Almost all those who could not previously afford post-secondary education will still be unable to attend.

To ensure that educational institutions have up-to-date equipment, the Budget provides an $800 million endowment (paid out of 1996-97 funds) to establish the Canada Foundation for Innovation. This independent corporation will distribute $180 million annually in research infrastructure grants to Canadian universities and research hospitals for five years. This money must be levered by partnerships with the private, voluntary, and public sectors, so that the total impact on infrastructure will be at least double the Foundation's grant. The program is good news for universities, which have experienced substantial funding cuts from provinces, often justified on the basis of the recent federal reductions to transfer payments.

The Budget's new social programs are aimed at health care, children, and the disabled.[24] In line with recommendations of the National Forum on Health, the government is providing $300 million over three years for new initiatives. Half the money will go to a Health Transition Fund to support provincial pilot projects aimed at better health care delivery. The remainder is allocated to create a national health information system and to expand two existing federal programs that fund community groups providing assistance for the developmental needs of young children and the improvement of prenatal nutrition of high-risk pregnant women. While these are all worthwhile programs, the amount of money involved ($0.1 billion per year) is minute compared to the annual CHST reduction of $1.8 billion between now and the end of the three-year period.

The Budget also announced plans to institute a joint federal-provincial program aimed at increasing the incentives for low-income families with children to enter the work force and leave welfare. The federal government would enrich the existing child tax benefits for all low-income families, and individual provinces would then reallocate the social assistance benefits to the working poor, negating the current situation, where a low-income family is better off remaining on social assistance than working. The federal contribution will start at $800 million annually, beginning in July 1998. But as Bach and Phillips point out, $630 million was saved by not fulfilling the child care pledge. In addition, the amount of money allocated is far below the $2 billion needed to remove the welfare trap, and the program presumes that there will be jobs available for those who want to work.[25]

The government has attempted to provide help for Canadians with disabilities. A number of tax changes will allow for greater tax deductibility of medical expenses, attendant care, and adapting vans for wheelchair access. In addition, an Opportunities Fund will be established to develop projects aimed at reducing the barriers faced by the disabled who want to work. The main problem with tax credits is that they only benefit the disabled who have income (usually through a job). The proposals do little for those who are unemployed.

Taken together, the Budget is much longer on rhetoric than action, with respect to both job creation and social policy. Nonetheless, it seems to be a winner with the public. According to a recent poll, 58 percent of those responding agreed that the 1997 Budget puts the government on the right track, compared to only 25 percent who think it is on the wrong one. Immediately following the presentation of the Budget, the Liberals' popularity stood at 46 percent of decided voters, up one percentage point from January 1997.[26] Though Liberal popularity has since slipped to 41 percent, it should still generate a healthy electoral majority.[27]

CONCLUSION: A LIBERAL REPORT CARD

Since the Liberals graded themselves on their Red Book commitments, and no report card would be complete without final grades, I will attempt to translate my colleagues' analyses into letter grades. It should come as no surprise that the Liberals deserve an "A" for their handling of the deficit. Although they were helped by a change in public opinion and unexpectedly low interest rates (at the beginning of the crusade), their achievement in reducing the deficit from $42 billion to less than $19 billion in three years and setting a course for a balanced budget within the next two years is impressive by international as well as Canadian standards.

Unfortunately, the rest of their record pales in comparison, perhaps an inevitable consequence of being obsessed with fiscal concerns. With an unemployment problem not much better than when they took office, and recent attempts to abdicate any responsibility for creating jobs, the Liberals deserve no more than a "D" grade for their labour market (employment) policy.

With respect to the promotion of trade within Canada and internationally, the Liberals have done a credible job. They were able to negotiate the first agreement on interprovincial trade, and have generated numerous foreign trade opportunities for Canadian firms. Still, there is a long way to go before internal trade barriers are removed, and foreign policy has been forced to take a back seat to international trade concerns. On balance a grade of "B" is appropriate in these areas.

The verdict on their performance with respect to Quebec and national unity is still in doubt. The Liberals barely passed the mid-term test of the 1995 Quebec referendum, and right now their grade must be recorded as "Incomplete."

In the areas of environment policy and governing with integrity, the Liberals' record has been mixed, though it definitely represents an improvement over that of their predecessors in the latter area. Given their stated commitment to these issues, they did not live up to expectations. Nonetheless, in terms of results, they have done a satisfactory job, and are entitled to grades of "C" for environmental policy and "C+" for integrity.

In the area of communications and cultural policy the Liberals' performance can only be portrayed as inconsistent and replete with failures, particularly their espousal of the view that communications is just another industry domestically, but crucial to Canadian identity internationally. If this were a university course, they would receive an "F" and be required to repeat it.

The Liberals' performance in the remaining social policy areas has been hurt by their preoccupation with responding to Quebec and restraining spending. With respect to the elderly, they have exhibited some innovation in their development of the new Seniors Benefit, though their main preoccupation was to reduce spending. As it is doubtful that this program represents a significant step forward for low-income seniors, only a grade of "C" is warranted. In comparison, there is nothing positive about the decisions to abandon the federal role in child care and in social housing, and the Liberals are therefore awarded two grades of "D."

Given our assessment, it is obvious that the Liberals will emphasize their success at fiscal management in the upcoming election. At the time of writing, their popularity seems insurmountable, but they face the danger of being a "one-trick pony." Though they have performed that trick exceptionally well, sooner or later the public will focus on the rest of their record, now that the deficit has been tamed. Although it may not happen before the country goes to the polls, the Liberals will eventually have to answer for their less than stellar performance in other policy fields.

NOTES

The author would like to thank Sandra Bach, Susan Phillips, and Allan Maslove for their comments on the first draft.

1 Liberal Party of Canada, *Creating Opportunity: The Liberal Plan for Canada* (Ottawa, 1993).
2 Liberal Party of Canada, *A Record of Achievement: A Report on the Liberal Government's 36 Months in Office* (Ottawa, 1996), 9.
3 Reform Party of Canada, "Creative Opportunism: The Liberal Dead Book," October 23, 1996.
4 The Conservatives identified sixty broken or unfulfilled promises from the Red Book and other campaign statements, while the NDP issued a document that focused on major broken promises. See Progressive Conservative Party "Charest Denounces Liberal's Broken Promises," Press Release, October 23, 1996, and Canada's New Democrats, "McDonough Discloses $17.11 Billion in Corporate Profits Going Untaxed," Communiqué, October 31, 1996.
5 Liberal Party, *Creating Opportunity*, 9.
6 Ibid., 10.
7 Ibid., 11.
8 See Ian Budge and Richard Hofferbert, "Mandates and Policy Outputs: US Party Platforms and Federal Expenditures 1948-1985," *American Political Science Review*, 84, 1 (March 1990), 111-31, and Richard Hofferbert and Ian Budge, "The Party Mandate Model and the Westminster Model: Election Programmes and Government Spending in Britain 1948-1985," *British Journal of Political Science*, 22 (1992), 151-82.
9 François Pétry, "The Party Agenda Model: Election Programmes and Government Spending in Canada," *Canadian Journal of Political Science*, 28,1 (March 1995), 51-84.
10 Although the Bloc Québécois is the Official Opposition, it is essentially a one-issue (sovereignty) party with no influence outside of Quebec. However, it has forged temporary alliances with the Reform party over decentralization of federal powers that have greatly increased the pressure on the Liberals to adjust their policies.
11 Liberal Party, *A Record of Achievement*, 9.
12 Paul Martin, Minister of Finance, *Budget Speech* (Ottawa: Public Works and Government Services Canada, 1997), 3.
13 Ibid., 6-7, 26-27.
14 Paul Martin, Minister of Finance, *Budget Plan* (Ottawa: Public Works and Government Services Canada, 1997), 19.

15 Bruce Little, "Balanced Budget on Horizon, Analysts Predict," *The Globe and Mail* [Toronto], February 19, 1997, A10.

16 Martin, *Budget Speech*, 8-9.

17 Bruce Little, "Jobs Figures Don't Tell Full Story," *The Globe and Mail* [Toronto], April 5, 1997, A1, A7.

18 Martin, *Budget Speech*, 26.

19 Eric Beauchesne, "Martin Budget a Hit With Taxpayers, Poll Finds," *The Ottawa Citizen*, February 27, 1997, A3.

20 Martin, *Budget Speech*, 4.

21 Martin, *Budget Plan*, 80-83.

22 In addition, the link between payroll taxes and employment is not clear-cut. Dahlby found that the incidence of payroll taxes falls overwhelmingly on employees, who are obliged to accept lower wages. In this scenario, lower payroll taxes would not provide employers with any incentive to hire more employees. See Bev Dahlby, "Payroll Taxes," in Allan Maslove, ed., *Business Taxation in Ontario* (Toronto: University of Toronto Press, 1993), 96-133.

23 Martin, *Budget Plan*, 93-99.

24 Ibid., 102-11.

25 See Edward Greenspon, "Child Benefit Boosted by $600-million," *The Globe and Mail* [Toronto], February 19, 1997, A9.

26 Beauchesne, "Martin Budget a Hit."

27 Joan Bryden, "Liberals Hit Four-year Low," *The Ottawa Citizen*, April 3, 1997, A1, A2.

2

From Red Books to Blue Books: Repairing Ottawa's Fiscal House

ALLAN M. MASLOVE

KEVIN D. MOORE

We have set for ourselves four challenges: first, to put our own fiscal house in order so that we can limit, and ultimately reverse, the massive build-up in public debt and the damaging impact this has on confidence and growth.

Michael Wilson, Minister of Finance, *Economic and Fiscal Statement,*
November 8, 1984

It is now time for government to get its fiscal house in order.... We will achieve this by using reasonable economic assumptions, not rosy fore-casts. We believe it is more important to meet a target than declare an illusion and then fall far short.

Paul Martin, Minister of Finance, *Budget Speech,*
February 22, 1994

These statements, delivered a decade apart by two finance ministers on behalf of their governments in their first few months in office, are remarkably similar. Both accord first priority to getting the "fiscal house in order." The records of success in deficit reduction of the two governments, however, have been quite different, partly as a product of the different approaches adopted by the two ministers and the governments of which they were members.

The Liberal government was elected on a platform that clearly attempted to differentiate its proposed macroeconomic policy from that of the previous Tory regime. The Red Book[1] strongly criticized the previous Tory government's macroeconomic policy performance. It argued that the Tories had focused obsessively on reducing the deficit and inflation, while paying insufficient attention to the related problems of unacceptably low levels of economic growth and high rates of unemployment. Not only did this single-minded approach result in high interest rates and unacceptably high social costs measured in unemployment and poverty, but it also reflected a lack of understanding of the determinants of the deficit. The Red Book asserted that faster economic growth and the accompanying reductions in unemployment were prerequisites for making substantial progress in reducing the deficit.[2]

The Red Book laid out a proposed economic policy framework, which was envisaged as a balanced, integrated set of policies to address these interrelated problems simultaneously. First, a deficit target of 3 percent of GDP was to be attained after the Liberals' third year in office. No further indication of what would happen beyond that point either in terms of the deficit or the debt-to-GDP ratio was provided. Second, a Liberal government would be ready to intervene in the economy to spur economic growth and create jobs. These two courses of action were considered mutually reinforcing. Economic growth and reduced unemployment would increase government revenue and reduce social spending. In turn, making substantial headway against the deficit would foster economic growth.

The Red Book also suggested that a Liberal government would pursue a more "balanced" monetary policy. Presumably, this would consist of a monetary policy with broader goals than the Bank of Canada's existing single goal of price stability, and would incorporate concerns for economic growth and employment. The Red Book was less explicit about monetary policy than about fiscal policy, which is understandable given the important role the Bank of Canada plays in this policy area.

In this chapter, we highlight the differences between the two governments with respect to deficit fighting and begin to probe the reasons for and the nature of those differences. Following a brief description of the deficit trends under the two governments, the chapter turns to a discussion of some of the primary factors that lie behind the Chrétien government's successful drive toward eliminating the deficit. We also note budget process and fiscal forecasting differences, not because they "explain" this success, but as evidence of the resolve of the government in general, and the minister of finance in particular, to reduce the deficit. We then briefly review the debate of the past several years about whether, from a macroeconomic perspective, this ardent deficit reduction policy was necessary or even desirable. The chapter concludes with a more speculative discussion of the fiscal debates and fiscal policies to be expected during the term of the next government.

THE FISCAL RECORD

In broad terms, despite numerous statements on the record stressing the importance of reducing the deficit, the Mulroney Tory governments, over nine years, achieved only sporadic and unsustained deficit reduction. Throughout their years in office the deficit hovered in the neighbourhood of $30 billion annually, and ballooned to more than $40 billion in their last year. The Chrétien Liberal government, in contrast, has sustained a clear deficit reduction trend, and thus far has managed to surpass its stated targets. By 1996-97 the deficit had declined to less than $19 billion (Table 2.1 and Figure 2.1).[3]

At least some of the reasons behind these differences are suggested by an examination of Tables 2.2 and 2.3. In the first three years of the Tory government, the deficit declined. This happened as a result of the higher revenues generated by strong economic growth, not because of any sustained expenditure reductions. Thereafter progress was stalled, and over its second term of office the deficit steadily climbed again. During the Liberal years, the progress in deficit reduction has been steady and, judged comparatively, quite dramatic.[4] The Liberal record reflects large cuts in expenditures, as well as revenue increases (which are partially due to tax structure changes introduced by the Mulroney

Table 2.1

Federal Government Deficits, Debt, and Financial Requirements

Fiscal Year	Forecast Deficit ($billion)	Actual Deficit ($billion)	Deficit/ GDP Ratio (%)	Net Public Debt/ GDP Ratio (%)	Financial Require- ments ($billion)	Financial Require- ments/ GDP Ratio (%)
1984-85	29.6	38.4	8.6	46.8	29.8	6.7
1985-86	33.8	34.6	7.2	50.8	30.5	6.4
1986-87	29.5	30.7	6.1	54.1	22.9	4.5
1987-88	29.3	27.8	5.0	54.6	18.8	3.4
1988-89	28.9	28.8	4.7	54.4	22.4	3.7
1989-90	30.5	28.9	4.4	55.1	20.5	3.2
1990-91	28.5	32.0	4.8	58.4	24.5	3.7
1991-92	30.5	34.4	5.1	62.9	31.8	4.7
1992-93	27.5	41.0	5.9	67.6	34.5	5.0
1993-94	32.6	42.0	5.9	71.3	29.9	4.2
1994-95	39.7	37.5	5.0	73.0	25.8	3.5
1995-96	32.7	28.6	3.7	74.0	17.2	2.2
1996-97	24.3	19.0	2.4	74.4	6.0	0.8
1997-98	17.0	n/a	2.0	73.1	6.0	0.7
1998-99	9.0	n/a	1.0	71.2	-1.0	-0.1

Notes:

a Figures for fiscal years after 1995-96 are based on forecasts.

b The "Forecast Deficit" is the forecast made near the beginning of the fiscal year in the Budget Speech.

c The "Actual Deficit" for 1996-97 is the estimate presented in the February 1997 Budget. It is not final.

d Ratios for deficit, net public debt, and financial requirements to GDP are derived from the "Actual Deficit" up to 1996-97, and the "Forecast Deficit" subsequently.

e Financial requirements exclude foreign exchange requirements.

Sources: Canada, Department of Finance, *Fiscal Reference Tables* (Ottawa, October 1996); Paul Martin, Minister of Finance, *Budget Plan* (Ottawa: Public Works and Government Services Canada, 1997).

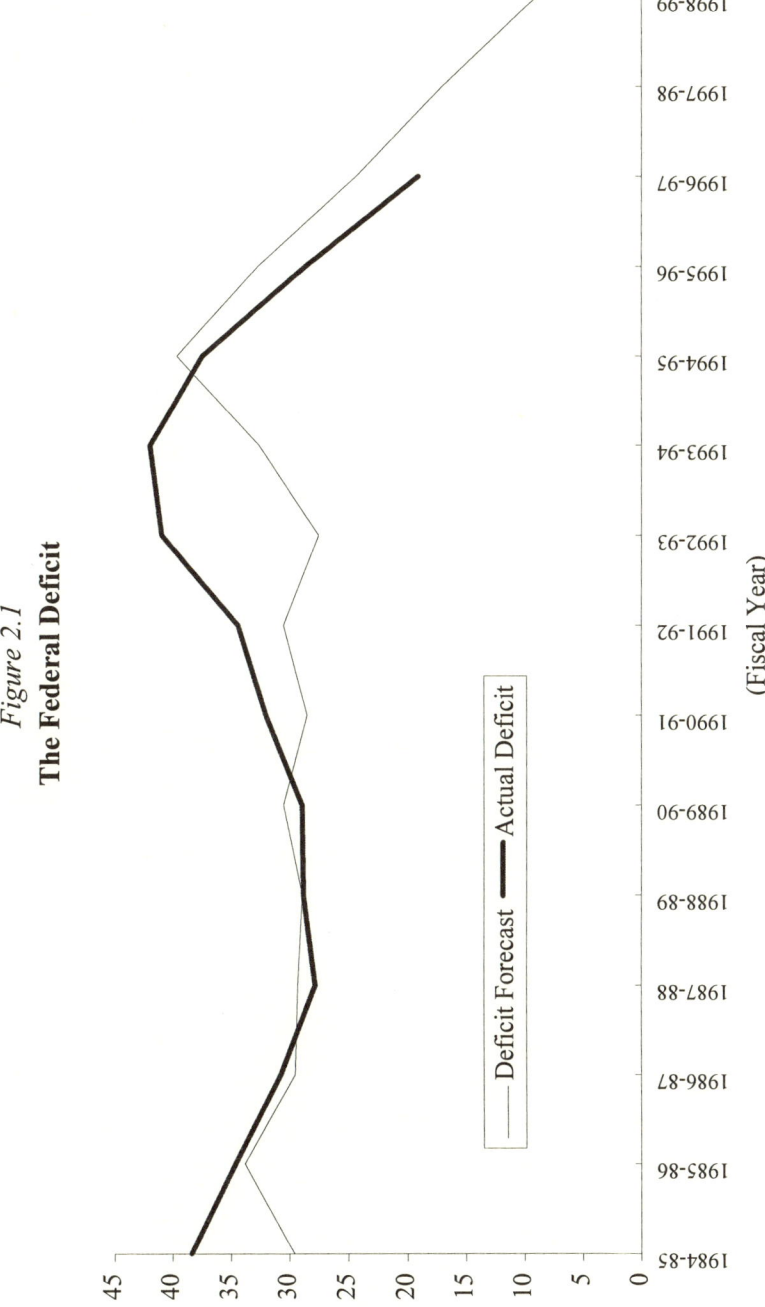

Figure 2.1
The Federal Deficit

45
40
35
30
25
20
15
10
5
0

($ Billions)

1984-85
1985-86
1986-87
1987-88
1988-89
1989-90
1990-91
1991-92
1992-93
1993-94
1994-95
1995-96
1996-97
1997-98
1998-99

(Fiscal Year)

Deficit Forecast   Actual Deficit

Source: Table 2.1

government). These general characterizations are true even if one allows for some of the "artful accounting" in which governments engage in order to overstate the deficit in the year in which they take office (1984-85 and 1993-94, respectively), so as to emphasize the distinction between their policies and the fiscal imprudence of the previous government.[5]

Turning to the broad components of the fiscal picture, only in their final (partial) year in office did the Mulroney government succeed in reducing program expenditures (nominal dollars). In all other years, the rhetoric of restraint notwithstanding, actual program spending increased (albeit usually by less than the rate of inflation). In contrast, in each year of the Liberal period absolute program spending has declined. Public debt charges, which depend upon the amount of outstanding debt and upon interest rates, generally rose during the first Tory mandate, and declined during the latter years of the second. After initial increases, over the course of the Liberal years these costs remained roughly steady. Since the stock of outstanding debt continued to increase throughout, the periods of decline and stability reflect declining interest rates during these years. On the revenue side, with the exception of the years 1992-93 and 1993-94, which were influenced by the recession, federal revenues grew throughout the period. Table 2.2 shows that within this overall pattern there was considerably volatility in income tax collections, both corporate and personal.

The pattern of program spending cuts (Table 2.3) under the Chrétien Liberals is noteworthy. Major transfers to individuals have declined throughout the Liberal years. Two programs account for the bulk of this spending. Payments to seniors (Old Age Security, Guaranteed Income Supplement, and Spouses Allowance) have continued to increase from year to year, reflecting the growth in the population of seniors and no significant reductions in benefits. These increases have been more than offset by major declines in (Un)Employment Insurance program payouts as a result of major cuts in benefits. Transfers to provincial governments, after many years of steady growth, flattened out, in part because of decisions made by the previous government to restrain the former Established Programs Financing (EPF) and Canada Assistance Plan (CAP) programs, but also because of additional restraint imposed by the Liberals as they implemented the Canada Health and Social Transfer (CHST).

Table 2.2

Annual Percentage Change in the Components of Federal Government Revenue (nominal change [%], measured in current dollars)

Fiscal Year	Personal Income Tax	Corporate Income Tax	U.I. Premiums	Excise Tax and Duties	Other Tax Revenue	Total Non-Tax Revenue	Total Budgetary Revenue
1984-85	8.5	28.7	4.1	12.1	9.1	2.9	10.7
1985-86	12.8	-1.8	15.4	7.2	4.5	-4.3	8.3
1986-87	14.8	7.3	9.6	8.0	27.1	13.8	11.7
1987-88	19.1	10.0	9.1	9.0	-8.7	13.4	13.6
1988-89	2.0	7.8	8.1	12.3	34.6	8.1	6.6
1989-90	12.8	11.0	-4.7	9.3	-13.9	11.9	9.3
1990-91	11.0	-9.9	18.3	-7.3	4.0	15.0	5.0
1991-92	6.3	-20.2	21.1	-3.5	-7.1	-2.4	2.2
1992-93	-4.8	-23.0	13.9	3.5	-4.7	5.2	-1.4
1993-94	-11.8	31.1	4.0	2.1	9.0	-11.8	-3.7
1994-95	9.5	22.9	3.8	1.7	11.0	-12.1	6.3
1995-96	6.8	37.5	-2.2	-1.4	19.0	-8.5	5.7
1996-97	5.2	-1.0	5.9	1.1	-0.2	10.6	4.0
1997-98	5.1	2.5	-1.5	2.6	0.0	-20.8	1.7
1998-99	5.9	5.6	2.1	3.2	-4.8	3.3	4.5

Note:
Figures for fiscal years after 1995-96 are estimates.

Sources: Canada, Department of Finance, *Fiscal Reference Tables* (Ottawa, October 1996); Paul Martin, Minister of Finance, *Budget Plan* (Ottawa: Public Works and Government Services Canada, 1997).

Table 2.3

Annual Percentage Change in the Components of Federal Government Expenditure
(nominal change [%], measured in current dollars)

Fiscal Year	1984-85	1985-86	1986-87	1987-88	1988-89	1989-90	1990-91	1991-92	1992-93	1993-94	1994-95	1995-96	1996-97[a]	1997-98[a]	1998-99[a]
Major Transfers to Persons															
Elderly Benefits	9.7	9.7	7.3	6.7	5.9	6.3	6.1	7.4	3.9	4.2	3.1	2.5	2.7	3.2	2.7
Family Allowance	4.0	3.4	1.3	1.2	1.6	1.8	3.1	-22.2	-99.7	n/a	n/a	n/a	n/a	n/a	n/a
U.I. Benefits	2.8	-0.2	4.1	0.4	4.6	6.6	25.4	23.6	5.2	-7.5	-15.9	-9.0	-2.8	3.1	4.4
Major Transfers to Other Levels of Government															
Fiscal Transfers	1.2	0.2	6.0	11.8	15.6	6.3	-3.2	7.4	-11.4	15.8	-11.9	5.7	-1.1	-3.1	1.1
Insurance and Medical Care[b]	13.8	1.1	3.2	-0.7	1.8	-0.2	-9.5	10.9	24.2	-12.9	6.3	-7.5	n/a	n/a	n/a
Education Support[b]	9.7	0.5	-2.0	0.4	-0.7	-2.7	-14.0	15.0	34.8	-17.6	4.5	-4.9	n/a	n/a	n/a
CAP[b]	13.9	4.6	3.4	4.8	7.3	9.9	15.6	5.4	9.6	8.2	0.4	-1.0	n/a	n/a	n/a
CHST[b]	n/a	n/a	n/a	n/a	n/a	n/a	n/a	n/a	n/a	n/a	n/a	-22.6[c]	-19.4	-7.7	

Other Transfer Payments	18.2	-7.1	-1.0	13.9	-0.2	-2.8	-3.7	13.6	4.0	1.8	8.3	-9.2	0.8	-9.8	-12.1
National Defence	12.5	2.9	9.1	6.6	3.5	5.1	2.4	-5.4	0.3	3.1	-5.2	-7.1	-3.4	-6.3	-5.6
Other Depts. and Agencies	3.6	0.8	5.2	6.1	6.2	5.6	7.0	-7.2	16.7	0.5	4.7	-11.4	4.7	6.7	-0.5
Crown Corps.	29.4	-27.3	10.2	19.0	-18.7	9.7	9.1	-8.1	18.4	-14.8	-5.6	-13.6	-0.5	-9.3	-2.6
Total Program Spending	10.3	-1.1	4.5	7.2	3.4	4.2	4.7	5.9	6.4	-2.1	-1.1	-5.7	-2.7	-2.9	-2.2
Gross Public Debt Charges	23.9	13.5	4.9	8.6	14.5	17.0	9.8	-3.3	-5.7	-2.2	10.7	11.6	-3.0	1.1	1.1
Total Expenditure	12.8	1.9	4.6	7.5	5.9	7.4	6.1	3.3	3.2	-2.1	1.8	-1.2	-2.8	-1.7[d]	-1.1[d]

Notes:

a Figures for fiscal years after 1995-96 are estimates.

b The amounts spent on Insurance and Medical Care, Education Support, CAP, and CHST are reported "net" of the recovery of federal tax point abatements made to Quebec under the Alternative Payments for Standing Programs.

c The percent change in the CHST for 1996-97 is measured relative to the sum of the amounts spent on Insurance and Medical Care, Education Support, and CAP in 1995-96.

d The figures for Total Expenditure in 1997-98 and 1998-99 assume that the contingency reserves will not be spent.

Sources: Canada, Department of Finance, *Fiscal Reference Tables* (Ottawa, October 1996); Paul Martin, Minister of Finance, *Budget Plan* (Ottawa: Public Works and Government Services, 1997).

In other program areas, the decline in defence spending that was initiated under the former government continued under the Liberals, and other departmental spending, which (in the aggregate) the Tories had not succeeded in reducing, began to show evidence of significant cutbacks under the Liberals. Other than seniors' benefits, the only significant spending area to be spared cuts over the Liberal years has been Aboriginal affairs.

In summary, then, while both governments focused intensely on deficit reduction, it was not until the Chrétien Liberals assumed office that substantive progress was made. Moreover, their success has been so pronounced that they are on course essentially to eliminate annual deficits by the end of the decade and possibly sooner. For the most part, this has been accomplished by altering the structure of government spending,[6] though the impact of lower interest rates on debt servicing costs must be noted as well.

WHAT LIES BEHIND THE DIFFERENCES?

One has to wonder why the Liberal government has been so much more successful in reducing the deficit than the Conservatives were. The question becomes more pointed when one considers that, initially at least, the Tories were much more ideologically predisposed to lowering the deficit and reducing the role of government than the Liberals. In particular, stark differences in the willingness of the two governments to implement significant and visible reductions in program spending are evident. The Liberals have largely maintained their popularity with the electorate despite cutting program spending on a scale that the Conservatives never seriously contemplated. Several political and managerial factors that might shed some light on this puzzle are worth exploring.

Public Opinion and Politics
If governments are concerned with being re-elected, then public opinion serves as a significant constraint on their policy choices. Polling data show that the Canadian public has been more troubled about public deficits and debt during the Liberal mandate than under the previous Tory government. In a series of polls done by Angus Reid from 1988 to 1992, the proportion of respondents who believed that

reducing the deficit should be an important priority of the federal government ranged from 4 percent to 13 percent. Polls taken from the summer of 1993 until the present have consistently indicated greater support for deficit reduction, typically in the range of 20 to 30 percent of respondents, reaching a high of 48 percent just prior to the February 1995 Budget.[7]

This is an indication that the electorate has been significantly more supportive of deficit reduction under the Liberal mandate than it was under the Tories, with the result that substantive deficit reduction became more politically feasible. What these data do not reveal is the extent to which the Liberal government is responsible for actively shaping this change in public opinion, rather than responding to an "external" change in the political environment. Nonetheless, it appears that Paul Martin's rhetoric on deficit fighting has been received more favourably than Michael Wilson's was.

The position of the Liberal party on the ideological spectrum and the composition of the current Parliament can be seen as related factors underpinning the government's current success in reducing the deficit. The fact that the Liberal party is generally considered somewhat "left" of the ideological centre, and supports the idea of an active, interventionist state added credibility to its claim that the deficit had to be reduced. Deficit reduction is, therefore, perceived by the public as something that the Liberals would much rather avoid, but that is urgent and inescapable. In contrast, for many people, the Tory government's exhortations about the necessity of reducing the deficit were less credible, tainted by the Tories' obvious desire to reduce the role of government.

In addition, the current Parliament has little opposition to the left of the Liberals. The Reform party and the Tories have advocated even more severe expenditure cuts than those delivered by the current government. It can be argued that the NDP has not really established a tangible presence in this Parliament, and that the Bloc Québécois is not taken seriously on fiscal issues by very many Canadians outside of Quebec. The Mulroney Tories faced much more concrete opposition from the Liberals and the NDP in their desire to reduce the deficit. Given the political vacuum to their left, the Chrétien Liberals can be seen to have moved their platform sharply to the right to maximize voter support, effectively creating a new ideological "centre." These factors have assisted in creating a political climate in which the Liberal government has been able to maintain its popular support while making unprecedented cuts in program spending.

In contrast to the Mulroney Tories, the Liberal government has also shown an unusual clarity of purpose in its determination to meet its deficit targets. This may be partially explained by the different governing styles of Mulroney and Chrétien. A common perception is that Mulroney preferred to play a relatively active role in fiscal policy. As a result, spending ministers were able to perform end-runs around the Finance Minister, Michael Wilson, by appealing directly to the Prime Minister, whose political instincts were more conducive to spending than to restraint. This was particularly evident during the Tories' second term in office, and seemed to play a significant role in forestalling significant deficit reduction by the Tories.

On the other hand, Chrétien appears to have invested his ministers, particularly Finance Minister Paul Martin, with much more autonomy, and has made clear his support for the Finance Minister's policies.[8] Accordingly, the Liberal government's fiscal policy has been characterized by a single-minded focus on reducing the deficit. As a result, the government continues to meet and exceed its deficit reduction goals, and the credibility of its fiscal policy has been greatly enhanced.

The Expenditure Management System
The "expenditure management system" (EMS) introduced by the Liberals in 1995 has significantly contributed to the government's ability to control program spending. It has done so largely by consolidating budgetary power in the hands of the "guardian" central agencies, particularly the Department of Finance. There are no longer any policy reserves. The Minister of Finance controls the contingency reserve and has made it very clear that it will not be used to fund program spending.[9] Treasury Board controls a small operating reserve for existing programs, but any such funds received by departments are treated as short-term, repayable, interest-bearing loans. There is no new money available for any new spending initiatives. These must be funded through reallocation of existing resources. Spending ministers have very little room to manoeuvre under the EMS.

The new EMS is probably best understood not as being an independent factor in the Liberals' ability to restrain program spending, but rather as a reflection of the government's willingness to make the tough decisions in order to reduce the deficit. The Mulroney government certainly had the technical ability to implement such a system. They made the political choice not to do so. Any budget management system is effective only to the extent that it reflects the government's continuing determination to control spending. Thus, a crucial factor in the success of the current EMS is the power of the Finance Minister, and the evident consistent support of the Prime Minister to prevent "end-runs."

The Department of Finance Forecasts
One, perhaps arcane, area where there are notable differences between the two governments is the forecasting of key fiscal variables by the Department of Finance. To generalize, under the Tories forecasts tended to underestimate actual deficits; under the Liberals, deficit reduction has actually proceeded more rapidly than forecast. Discounting the transition years (1984-85 and 1993-94), the Tory government underestimated the federal deficit in five out of eight years, sometimes by very large amounts.[10] The Liberal forecasts for the three fiscal years completed under their mandate have all been overestimates; that is, the actual deficits have been lower than forecast (Table 2.4).[11]

The deficit, of course, is a residual, the difference between spending and revenues. An examination of those components shows that the Tory underestimates of the deficit were primarily due to underestimates of expenditures rather than overestimates of revenue. Interestingly, it is in the area of program expenditures, arguably the most controllable of the aggregate fiscal variables, that the Tories' plans were most often thwarted and where the Liberals have had consistent success in holding expenditures to planned (forecast) levels.

In the areas of revenue and debt service charges, distinctions between the two governments cannot be drawn as readily. Debt charges tended to be underestimated by both governments in the earlier years (one-year forecast), when interest rates were high and/or rising, and overestimated in the latter years, when rates have, for the most part, been decreasing. Revenues have been consistently overestimated since 1991-92, which roughly coincides with the onset of the severe recession, and the generally slower-than-predicted recovery.

A clear difference underlying these forecasting performances is the approach taken by the two governments. Under the Mulroney Tories,

Table 2.4

Forecasting Errors for Major Fiscal Variables
Defined as ([forecast-actual/actual])*100

Fiscal Year	Revenue		Total Expenditure		Program Expenditure		Debt Charges		Deficit	
	2 year (%)	1 year (%)	2 year (%)	1 year (%)	2 year (%)	1 year (%)	2 year (%)	1 year (%)	2 year (%)	1 year (%)
1984-85	-7.6	-5.2	-13.8	-11.5	-12.1	-10.6	-13.8	-9.1	-25.3	-23.0
1985-86	-3.6	-7.4	-8.5	-5.9	-6.1	-8.2	-11.9	2.1	-19.2	-2.4
1986-87	-10.5	1.6	-6.0	0.1	-10.2	-0.7	8.2	2.7	6.4	-4.2
1987-88	-3.7	-4.5	-4.3	-2.3	-6.1	-2.2	1.4	-2.6	-6.7	5.5
1988-89	n/a	-0.7	n/a	-0.4	n/a	0.5	n/a	-3.3	n/a	0.6
1989-90	-6.5	-1.1	-5.4	-0.2	-1.9	-0.3	-14.8	1.6	-1.2	5.4
1990-91	1.2	-0.1	-1.7	-2.4	0.2	-2.0	-6.5	-304.0	-12.5	-10.9
1991-92	3.2	5.3	-2.3	1.7	-3.4	0.5	0.8	4.9	-21.8	-11.2
1992-93	16.0	9.7	1.4	-1.1	-2.4	-2.6	13.2	3.5	-41.5	-33.0
1993-94	19.7	9.4	2.1	1.0	-0.1	0.0	9.1	4.0	-46.4	-22.4
1994-95	10.2	0.5	2.5	1.8	3.7	3.3	-0.6	-2.5	-22.6	6.0
1995-96	1.3	2.2	3.6	2.9	9.5	1.8	-10.5	5.5	14.3	14.3
1996-97a	1.4	0.0	2.7	1.5	-1.0	0.0	11.4	5.1	27.9	27.9

Note:

a 1996-97 forecast errors are based on "actual" values as reported in the February 1997 Budget.

Source: Calculations by authors based on figures presented in various federal budget documents.

the strategy appeared to be to emphasize long-run progress, highlighting the significant achievements waiting just over the horizon, three or more years hence. Proposed spending cuts, because they were often intended to occur two or three years hence, were often unspecified. Despite all the tough deficit reduction rhetoric, few hard decisions were made in the short term, and the government relied upon spending freezes and inflation erosion to restrain expenditures. Absolute cuts, which carried higher risks of political confrontation, were much less likely. The Tory government found itself having to revise its longer-term forecasts in the direction of higher deficits as time moved on and they became short-term forecasts.

In contrast, the Chrétien Liberals, and Finance Minister Martin in particular, have set modest short-run targets (two years at most), and exceeded them. In most cases, they immediately embarked upon the restraint measures required to achieve these targets, though the full cuts were to be phased in over two or three years. (The planned Seniors Benefit, announced in the 1996 Budget for implementation in 2001, is a notable exception.) Through the Program Review Process[12] they opened the attack on spending on many fronts simultaneously. In this regard, one can see a similarity to the "Klein/Harris" strategy—cut hard, cut everywhere—which makes it difficult for program defenders to respond effectively.

Further, Mr. Martin has consistently resisted the immediate temptation to score political points. He has not trumpeted his successes in deficit reduction, but, in fact, has tended to reveal the better than predicted results only when absolutely necessary, and then as obliquely as possible. By so doing, Martin has enhanced his efforts to reduce the deficit further, because he has kept the focus of discussion on the modest deficit targets rather than on the more impressive achievements. This has helped in maintaining public support for the deficit reduction agenda and expenditure reductions, and forestalled pressures that might otherwise have arisen for new spending, lesser cutbacks, or tax cuts. In this, Martin appears to have largely succeeded. Only in recent months, as the deficit reduction record has become increasingly known, have pressures started to emerge for other fiscal strategies. We return to this point at the end of the chapter.

In somewhat modified form, this "modesty" characterized the February 1997 Budget as well. Mr. Martin reported that the 1996-97 deficit would be "no higher than $19 billion," compared to the target of $24.3 billion set at the start of the fiscal year. In fact, it is likely to be well below $19 billion. Moreover, Martin chose not to adjust his target deficit levels for 1997-98 ($17 billion) and 1998-99 ($9 billion). This is despite the fact that a large portion of the deficit reduction to date is structural, and not the result of one-time events. This suggests that targets should be lowered accordingly, but Martin has chosen not to do this, thereby continuing to post targets that overstate the actual deficit.

Finally, we should note that Martin's strategy of modest goals and his success in achieving them have clearly restored the credibility of the Department of Finance as a forecaster. They have also considerably enhanced the department's power within the government as well as its stature in the business and financial communities. The Tory years, which seemed to be a continuing story of missed deficit targets, clearly damaged the credibility of the department. By the end of the Tory regime, stated targets were ignored or heavily discounted as soon as they were announced. That damage has been repaired. If anything, there is a danger of creating an impression among observers that the department is "sandbagging"; there is a reluctance to admit how rapidly the deficit is, in fact, declining.

LINKING LIBERAL FISCAL/MONETARY POLICY
TO IDEAS ABOUT THE MACROECONOMY

There is no doubt that the Liberals have been much more successful deficit-busters than their predecessors. There is some question, however, whether what they did so well was the right thing. Critics of the government's macroeconomic policy have argued that the severe restraint in fiscal policy and the accompanying tight monetary policy have not only been unnecessary, but have actually harmed the economy.

The Liberal Record and Performance
The Liberal government has implemented a number of initiatives, including its infrastructure spending program, that have been aimed at encouraging economic growth and creating jobs. In general, however, both its attempts and the success it has achieved on this front must be

seen to have been very modest. Unemployment has remained "unacceptably high" as judged by the standards of the Liberals' own Red Book.[13] Many would suggest that the economic growth and job creation plank of the Liberals' platform has been essentially abandoned. Instead, reducing the deficit and "putting the fiscal house in order" has become the Liberals' main focus, and has served as the foundation of their macroeconomic policy. As noted, the Liberals' action on the deficit has been more drastic than that envisioned in the Red Book. In addition, the Liberal government has supported the Bank of Canada's monetary policy, with its primary emphasis on price stability.

In sharp contrast to the Red Book promise of a "two-track" economic policy, the Liberals have largely narrowed the thrust of their macroeconomic policy to an attempt to establish the "economic fundamentals" necessary for low and stable interest rates. Their budgets and other economic policy documents[14] assert that such rates are the preconditions for sustained job creation and economic growth. Low and stable interest rates are characterized as creating an economic climate that encourages consumer demand and new capital investment, which in turn spur growth and job creation.

The Liberal government has identified two prerequisites for low and stable interest rates. First, the fiscal situation of Canadian governments, particularly the federal government, must become sustainable. Deficits must be eliminated or at least decreased sufficiently so that the size of the public debt relative to the economy stops increasing, and instead starts on a downward track. It is argued that interest rates are higher in countries with high public debt/GDP ratios, such as Canada. Lenders demand a risk premium from highly-indebted governments, reflecting their concerns about the ability of such governments to meet their financial commitments. Once the federal government gets its deficits and debt under better control, significantly lower interest rates should be possible for all Canadian borrowers. The second prerequisite for low and stable interest rates is low inflation. The Liberal government has continued to support the Bank of Canada's efforts to keep inflation down to between 1 and 3 percent per annum.[15]

The Liberal government has delivered what it claims is necessary for low and stable interest rates, and, therefore, for sustained growth and job creation. This chapter has described the fiscal measures, notably expenditure reductions, that should put the federal public debt/GDP ratio on a downward track starting in 1997-98. The enhanced fiscal credibility created by this government is significant in itself, given the importance of expectations in determining interest rates and other macroeconomic variables. Inflation has remained well within its target range since 1992. It remains to examine whether interest rates have responded as expected. Figure 2.2 tracks short-term interest rates in Canada and the United States from 1984 to December 1996. The Canada-U.S. rate differential is probably the best indicator of interest rate changes in Canada, as it controls for world-wide fluctuation in rates. Of particular note is the steady drop in the differential between March 1995 and February 1997, with Canadian rates moving from 240 basis points above comparable U.S. rates to 230 basis points below, a relative decrease of almost 5 percentage points. Many observers believed that it was not possible for Canadian rates to fall below U.S. rates.

It may be argued that it is no coincidence that the Liberals delivered their "landmark" budget in February, 1995, just before this interest rate trend was established, and that the decline became more rapid as the credibility of the Liberals' deficit forecasts became widely accepted. A much better test of the efficacy of the Liberal government's macroeconomic policy choices, however, will be whether these low interest rates can be sustained over time and how well the economy responds with robust growth and job creation, the ultimate goals.

Alternative Perspectives

All areas of public policy serve as arenas for conflict between different sets of ideas. Macroeconomic policy is particularly contentious in this regard. There are a number of fundamentally divergent views about how the macroeconomy operates, each with different prescriptions regarding the capability and desirability of government intervention in the economy. A number of these directly challenge the viewpoint of the Department of Finance and the Liberal government. The most prominent of these is closely associated with the work of Pierre Fortin, although the work of a number of other authors is also notable.[16] Paradoxically, this perspective has much in common with the ideas expressed in the Red Book; its prescriptions bear more resemblance to the Red Book than does the Liberal government's actual macroeconomic policy performance.

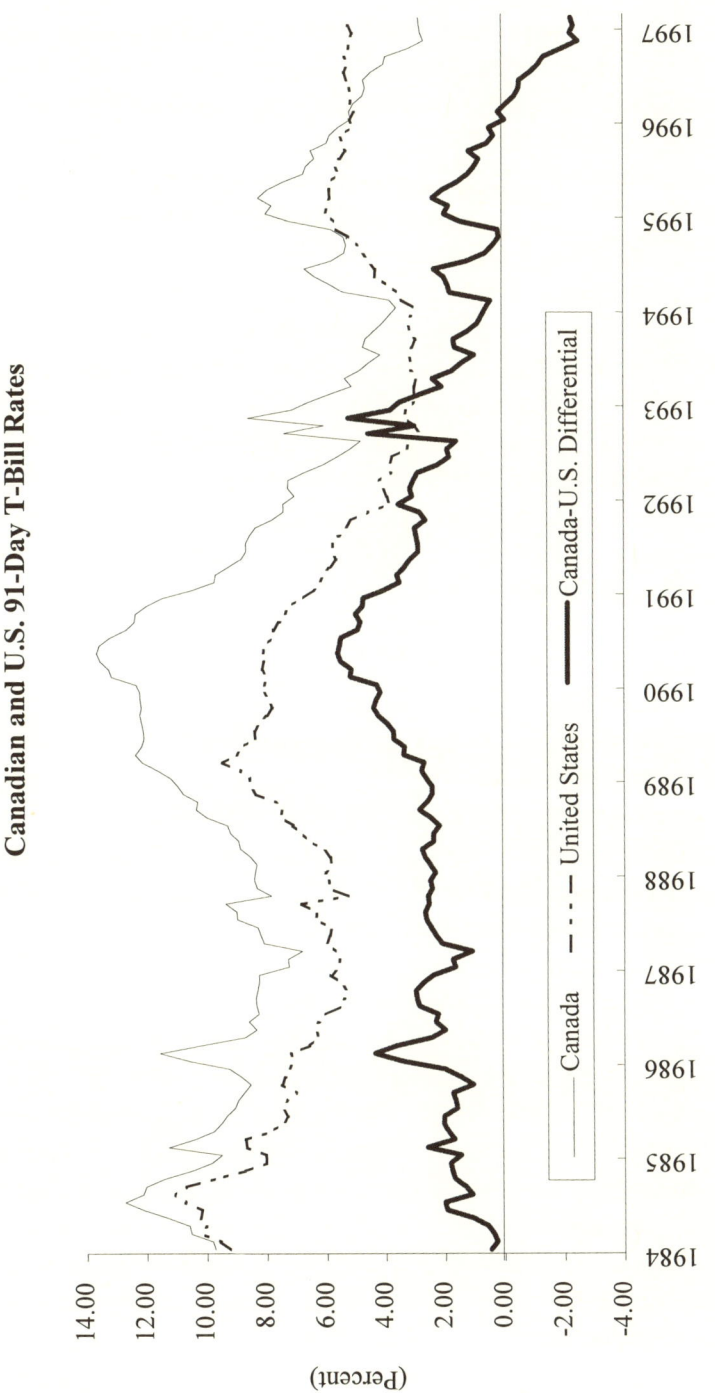

Figure 2.2
Canadian and U.S. 91-Day T-Bill Rates

Canada — United States — · — Canada-U.S. Differential ——

Source: Cansim Matrices B14007, B54409

These authors tend to be highly critical of recent macroeconomic policy in Canada. In general, they believe that the federal government's approach to handling the federal public debt by sharply reducing program spending has been misguided. The federal government's debt problems in the last decade are attributed not to high program spending, but rather primarily to the effect of high interest rates, which have significantly increased the size of the federal government's debt charges, and, by restricting economic growth and employment, have impaired the ability of the economy to support the public debt. Supporters of these views turn the macroeconomic ideas presented in the Liberal budgets on their heads. Large deficits and debt/GDP ratios are seen as the result of high interest rates, not as the cause of them. This perspective is most critical of the Bank of Canada, and in particular of monetary policy since the late 1980s. At that time the Bank chose price stability (zero inflation) as its pre-eminent goal. In general, the pursuit of such a goal requires higher interest rates, at least temporarily, than would be necessary if a moderate level of inflation were tolerated.

It is argued that Canadians have paid a very high price for the low levels of inflation it has "enjoyed" since 1992. The price includes very high public debt charges, high interest rates charged to consumers and businesses, lower income for Canadians and lower revenue for governments, high levels of unemployment (that have continued well after interest rates have declined), and, subsequently, high social policy expenditures. This price is much too high, particularly when the benefits of extremely low inflation have yet to be demonstrated, or even convincingly described. These authors argue that a strategy of more modest cuts in program spending, coupled with a "looser" monetary policy (i.e. lower interest rates), was and continues to be a superior way of confronting Canada's deficit and debt problems, even if accompanied by somewhat higher levels of inflation. Ironically, the Red Book itself argues that "cutting expenditures alone ... will not be sufficient. Faster growth and reduction of unemployment is a prerequisite for sustained deficit reduction."[17]

On balance, this alternative perspective presents a credible and convincing challenge to those macroeconomic policy ideas underlying the policy choices made over the last decade, including those choices made by the Liberal government during its current mandate. One suspects that the derailment of the Red Book's "two-track" economic policy, i.e. reducing the deficit while simultaneously actively intervening to foster growth and create jobs, can be largely attributed to the prevailing orthodoxy and influence of the Bank of Canada and the Department of Finance. The policy that has been pursued over the last decade, even if it results in a healthier economy in the coming years, has imposed an enormous cumulative cost on Canadians. The magnitude of the costs associated with this policy may very well dwarf any resulting benefits.

MAINTAINING CONTROL OF THE AGENDA

Earlier it was suggested that Mr. Martin declined, perhaps deliberately, to claim credit for his short-term success in bringing down the deficit, in order to maintain the focus of fiscal attention on the deficit fight. As 1996 drew to a close, and the faster than projected decline in the deficit became apparent to more observers, this strategy inevitably became more difficult. In a real sense, the Liberal deficit fighters became victims of their own success, although, as suggested above, the February 1997 Budget can be seen as a continuation of the same strategy.

More or less simultaneously, several alternatives were being advanced for the now foreseeable time when the deficit would essentially be eliminated. In these alternatives, one can see the sides in the debate that are likely to become prominent features of the 1997 election and shape the mandate of the new government. Basically, three options have been proposed.

The "establishment" conservative argument, promoted by some business interest groups among others, is that Ottawa's fiscal restraint should continue beyond balancing the budget and generate surpluses to reduce the stock of outstanding debt. This position follows from an argument that Ottawa's debt load is too large, that it restricts the government's fiscal room to manoeuvre and leaves its fiscal security vulnerable to the uncertainties of international money markets, particularly when a future recession again forces Ottawa into a cyclical deficit.[18] However, in this regard, the absolute debt is less meaningful than the debt to GDP ratio. In 1996-97, this ratio will peak at 75 percent; assuming modest growth[19] and balanced budgets starting in 1999-2000, the ratio will fall to about 50 percent within a decade.

That is, even without running surpluses to pay down the outstanding debt, its size relative to the economy will decline quite quickly.

In some cases, this "pay off the debt" argument reflects a philosophic position that government's role in the economy and society, which has been pared down substantially over the last decade, should not be allowed to increase again. It is consistent with the values long held by the groups advocating this policy and that underly the strong anti-deficit arguments advanced by them over most of the past two decades.

The second argument is a "populist" conservative argument that has recently become a plank in the election platforms of both the Conservative and the Reform parties. As soon as the deficit is eliminated (and in the Conservative platform, even before), Ottawa should begin to implement a program of general tax cuts. These cuts, it is argued, would promote consumer spending, thereby stimulating economic growth. This position also reflects the view that government spending should continue to be restrained, and that an important element in permanently limiting the role of government is limiting government revenues.

The third option, a more liberal, interventionist one, is that resources should be put back into selected public services, particularly health care, labour market programs, and other social programs. The rationale behind this position is that these programs were seriously eroded in the struggle to eliminate the deficit, and now it is time to reinvest in them. Public opinion, according to an Angus Reid poll (November 2, 1996) and a study by Ekos Research Associates,[20] seems to be broadly in favour of this option. Increased spending on these programs were the most popular of several options, with a tax reduction at the bottom of the list. Indeed, some proponents of this course argue that this reinvestment is already overdue and that it should not wait for further deficit reduction.

These proponents, of course, see an important role for government in general, and for the federal government in particular. In their view, the original rationales for social spending have not lapsed during the years of deficit reduction and fiscal restraint. There may be justification for restructuring, but if anything, in a more competitive global economy these social needs are stronger than before.

The February 1997 Budget provided only very limited indications of the choice that a new Liberal government would make among these options. As already noted, maintaining the focus on the deficit remained at the forefront. Relatively small initiatives were announced in the fields of health care, child poverty, and research and development, suggesting that the government was sensitive to the traditional Liberal position in favour of more activist government. In interviews following the release of the budget, Mr. Martin also expressed a preference for tax cuts in the future, and suggested that there was need for public discussion on the appropriate size of the national debt. But in the short run it is clear that the government intends to try to keep public attention on the deficit. Beyond that, it has left its options open.

In some respects, the deficit reduction strategy of the Chrétien Liberal government over the past four years, and the much longer debate about deficit reduction,[21] have been a contest of values about the appropriate role of government in Canadian society. It would seem that this debate is entering a new stage. The proponents of small government, who for many years have fought under the banner of the deficit-busters, now must seek a new standard—debt reduction, tax cuts—under which to carry on their fight. The advocates of more active government, having lost many battles over the past decade (and more), may find their side strengthened as the success of the government's deficit reduction program leads to a shift of public attention toward the adequacy and quality of specific public services.

CONCLUSION

The federal government's deficits and debt have long served as a catalyst and a forum for contention between those holding rival ideas. Debate has tended to focus on such issues as the causes of deficits, their impact on the real economy, the burden of the public debt, intergenerational fairness, the sustainability of large public debts, and the appropriate role of government in the economy and society more generally.

These ethereal controversies have doubtless had a significant influence on governments' fiscal policies over the years. Most recently, reducing the deficit and putting the "fiscal house in order" has emerged as the first priority, at least rhetorically, of all Canadian federal governments elected since 1984. The Mulroney Tories, despite their ideological ardour for reduced deficits and small government, were largely unsuccessful in achieving meaningful and enduring deficit reduction. They also undermined the credibility of federal budgets by consistently failing to meet their deficit targets. The Chrétien Liberals, with a strong bent for an active federal government, have nevertheless cut program spending substantially, and have made tangible progress toward eliminating the deficit and reducing the relative size of the federal public debt, which has been steadily increasing for more than twenty years. Along the way, the Liberals have largely restored the fiscal credibility of the federal government by consistently meeting or surpassing their deficit reduction targets. The Liberals' much stronger determination to reduce the deficit, "come hell or high water," may be best explained by changes in the political environment, which allowed them, but not the Mulroney Tories, to remain politically popular while making unprecedented cuts to program spending.

It may be worth re-emphasizing that there is no broad consensus that the Liberal government's attack on the deficit has been appropriate. Some, though relatively few, still suggest that reducing the deficit and stabilizing the debt is not important. Many others would argue that the route to deficit reduction that the Liberals have taken, namely large cuts in program spending, has been ill-advised. This chapter has raised one of the most prominent of these arguments, which focuses on the role of the Bank of Canada and argues that in the last decade high interest rates have undermined the fiscal position of Canadian governments, damaged the economy, and caused widespread social harm.

The Liberals have clearly met and exceeded their Red Book promise to reduce the deficit to 3 percent of GDP by the end of 1996-97. As noted, however, the Liberals have taken much more drastic action against the deficit than that envisaged in the Red Book. They have fundamentally reduced the role of the federal government by introducing significant cuts in program spending that should have the effect of eliminating the deficit altogether over the next three fiscal years (some observers say two years). Some might suggest that the Liberals have broken an implicit promise by taking such strong action against the deficit. The Liberals packaged themselves as the moderate alternative in the 1993 election, and characterized the Conservatives' promise to eliminate the deficit in five years as "unrealistic."[22] The electorate certainly did not give them an explicit mandate to undertake such radical change.

The route the Liberals have taken to addressing the deficit is clearly a departure from their campaign promises. They have relied almost exclusively on reducing program spending, rather than simultaneously pursuing economic growth—the more balanced approach laid out in the Red Book. The latter asserted that the government's goal "must be to reduce the deficit in a manner that is compatible with putting Canadians back to work."[23] Most of Canada's unemployed are still waiting.

Beyond the extent to which it represents fulfilled or broken Red Book promises, the Liberal's fiscal policy record must be judged on its own merits. Arguments concerning the best means of deficit reduction aside, many would argue that balancing the budget by the turn of the century, and thereby stabilizing the size of the federal public debt and putting it on a downward track, was necessary and even moderate fiscal policy. Indeed, the majority of Canadians now seem to support the notion that public budgets should be balanced. Overseeing this sea change in public opinion and budgetary politics may be the Liberal's most important fiscal policy legacy.

NOTES

1 Liberal Party of Canada, *Creating Opportunity* (Ottawa, 1993).

2 While it did not contain an explicit commitment to eliminate the Goods and Services Tax, the Red Book also argued that the GST contributed to the recession and slowed the recovery because of its costly administration and its compliance requirements. Despite that, the simple abolition of the GST was never seriously contemplated, either in the Red Book or subsequently, in large part because of the concern with the deficit. The Red Book is fairly unambiguous on this point. It was the overblown rhetoric during the campaign, rather than the "official" Red Book promise itself, that was the source of so much grief for the Liberals once they were in office.

3 While final financial data are not available at the time of writing, the 1996-97 deficit is likely to be significantly lower than $19 billion, even after the inclusion of about $1 billion in new spending announced in the Budget of February 18, 1997, and charged to the 1996-97 budget. The Minister of Finance, in his budget speech, was careful to say that the deficit "will be no higher than $19 billion."

4 Given the record of the government, one can have some confidence that the deficit targets projected for the next two years are more than attainable.

5 This is the melodic accompaniment to the usual chorus of a new government that the "books are worse than we were led to believe."

6 At one time, budget observers distinguished between statutory and discretionary programs, and the relative inflexibility of the former compared to the latter. The pattern of spending cuts suggests there is no longer much, if any, explanatory power in this distinction.

7 National Angus Reid Poll, October 7, 1995, and National Angus Reid/Southam News Poll, October 7, 1996.

8 Edward Greenspon and Anthony Wilson-Smith, *Double Vision: The Inside Story of the Liberals in Power* (Toronto: Doubleday, 1996), 163-64.

9 Moreover, in the 1995 Budget, when higher than expected interest rates threatened the fiscal framework, the Minister made it clear that he would implement deeper program spending cuts rather than rely on the contingency fund to pay for the higher than expected debt charges.

10 This is based on the "one-year forecast," that is, the forecast provided near the start of the fiscal year in the Budget Speech. Based on a "two-year forecast," provided in the Budget Speech for the fiscal year beginning approximately 12 months hence, the Tory government forecasts of the deficit were, with one exception (1986-87), always underestimates.

11 Using comparable measures (e.g. "Net Financial Requirements," the actual new borrowing undertaken on financial markets), Canada's performance as compared to other G-7 countries is equally remarkable. In 1993, the Canadian deficit relative to the economy (using this measure) was well above the G-7 average; in 1997 it will be the lowest. Table 2.4 loosely follows the approach in a 1994 Ernst & Young report to the Department of Finance entitled "Review of the Forecasting Accuracy and Methods of the Department of Finance."

12 For assessments of Program Review see Arthur Kroeger, "The Central Agencies and Program Review" (Ottawa: Canadian Centre for Management Development, forthcoming), and Gilles Paquet and Robert Shepherd, "The Program Review Process: A Deconstruction," in Gene Swimmer, ed., *How Ottawa Spends 1996-97: Life Under the Knife* (Ottawa: Carleton University Press, 1996), 39-72.

13 See "Fiscal Facts and Trends" at the end of this volume.

14 See, for example, Paul Martin, Minister of Finance, *Budget Plan* (Ottawa: Canada Communication Group, 1996), and *The Economic and Fiscal Update*, October 9, 1996.

15 An analysis of recent Bank policy is provided in Calum M. Carmichael, "Banking on Transparency: An Interpretation of Recent Changes at the Bank of Canada," in Gene Swimmer, ed., *How Ottawa Spends 1996-97: Life Under the Knife* (Ottawa: Carleton University Press, 1996), 379-408.
16 See, for example, Lars Osberg and Pierre Fortin, eds., *Unnecessary Debts* (Toronto: Lorimer, 1996).
17 Liberal Party of Canada, *Creating Opportunity*, 20.
18 In recent decades, recessions have had large impacts on the debt to GDP ratio.
19 Nominal GDP growth of 4 percent per annum.
20 Ekos Research Associates, *Rethinking Government 1995, Final Report* (July, 1996).
21 David Wolfe, "The Politics of the Deficit," in G. Bruce Doern, ed., *The Politics of Economic Policy* (Toronto: University of Toronto Press, 1985), 111-62.
22 Liberal Party of Canada, *Creating Opportunity*, 20.
23 Ibid.

3

Cruising at 30,000 Feet with a Missing Engine: The Chrétien Government in the Aftermath of the Quebec Referendum

REG WHITAKER

The Liberal government of Jean Chrétien is by most measures an extraordinary political success. Into the fourth year of its mandate, despite some marginal decline in support, it still sits atop the polls, far ahead of its distant rivals.[1] One would have to return to the St. Laurent Liberal governments of the late 1940s and early 1950s for a historical precedent.

It is as if the Chrétien government were a well-appointed private airliner: on course, it cruises at 30,000 feet, far above the clouds, where the sun always shines. The confidence and exhilaration of the people lounging in the spacious cabin as they chat or glance out of the windows is palpable. And yet there is an uneasy undertone, a secret that is rarely spoken of, but shared by all, a queasy feeling in the pit of everyone's stomach: *one of the plane's engines is missing.*

The engine fell off on October 30, 1995, the night of the Quebec referendum on sovereignty. True, the sovereigntists failed to gain a majority, but only by the most paper-thin of margins. Mr. Chrétien tried to put the best face on things by offering a homely analogy to the post-referendum Liberal caucus: "In a hockey game and a tight one, nobody says it was a tie. We won, God damn it."[2] Despite the Prime Minister's bravado, most Liberals knew very well that the result objectively did amount to a "tie," an impasse between federalism and sovereignty that would continue to poison the atmosphere of the Chrétien government for the remainder of its mandate, and beyond. If the 1980 referendum had demonstrated that Quebecers had a "right" to national self-determination, even as they chose not to exercise that right, the 1995 referendum demonstrated something far more troubling to federalists—everyone now knows that Quebecers *could* opt for sovereignty, and may very well do so in the near future.

The first casualty of October 30, 1995 was the Liberal's pre-referendum strategy. This was one of serene insouciance, which I characterized in an article in an earlier volume of *How Ottawa Spends* as "What, me worry?"[3] No positive constitutional or economic benefits to Quebec were politically possible, but negative inducements in the form of warnings and threats were generally eschewed. This was a not indefensible strategy, so long as the polls showed a No majority. In the event of a clear No victory, it would have minimized antagonism in Quebec, in that there would have been no history of so-called "Plan B" threats and intimidation, and thus there would have been no credible basis for a post-referendum sovereigntist myth of a stolen No victory.

A funny thing happened on the way to referendum day. In the last weeks of the campaign, after Lucien Bouchard took over effective leadership of the Yes side, the polls swung sharply against federalism. In the despair and panic that settled upon the No campaign, the "What, me worry?" strategy deflated like a punctured balloon. Finance Minister Paul Martin hysterically—and counter-productively—warned of the loss of a million Quebec jobs in the event of independence. And then, against all previous wisdom but in the face of demands from the Quebec Liberals that put Ottawa publicly on the spot, Mr. Chrétien began hinting about constitutional offerings—a distinct society clause, a Quebec veto, transfer of manpower training to the provinces—that could follow a No vote.

The crack-up of the federal Liberals' referendum game plan represented, in a sense, the worst of all worlds: the near-victory of the Yes was matched by a splintering of federal resolve that predated the actual vote. In the aftermath of the vote, a new federal position would have to be constructed. Now there were promises to keep, and promises that were actually more specific than the vague aspirations toward renewal that Pierre Trudeau had thrown into the ring in 1980. Yet these promises might well alienate many Canadians outside of Quebec. Moreover, there was also post-referendum anger in the rest of Canada and a sense of stiffening resolve to be tougher with Quebec the next time. The failure of Mr. Chrétien's sunny optimism seemed, in the immediate aftermath, to have left him a diminished figure in the eyes of many English Canadians. The political damage has been largely repaired. The failure of a fragmented opposition to provide any credible national alternative makes the re-election of the Liberals very likely. They have been given breathing space to develop a policy riposte to the referendum result.

The post-referendum Liberal strategy differs sharply from the previous strategy in the frank recognition that *two tracks* must be pursued simultaneously. The first track is positive, echoing the Prime Minister's promises of changes in federalism and the Constitution in the late days of the referendum campaign; the second is more negative, at least from the point of view of Quebec sovereigntists, although not perhaps from the point of view of Canadians outside Quebec, nor of the non-Francophone minorities within Quebec: a promise of a tougher federal stance next time that would insist upon stricter conditions for triggering negotiations for separation, and a rejection of unilateral secession. These two tracks have been universally designated Plan A and Plan B. We will consider each in turn.

PLAN A

The referendum campaign promises made by the prime minister were in direct response to demands from Daniel Johnson, leader of the Quebec Liberals and head of the No campaign. As such, they were supposed to answer to the anxieties of the "soft nationalists" and the undecided that a No vote would only confirm the federalist *status quo*.

The *status quo* was decidedly unpopular in Quebec, even among those reluctant to support separation, and attempts by the federal Liberals to insist that federalism was "flexible" had made little impression, in the absence of firm commitment to constitutional change. Even so, Chrétien was careful in his referendum speech in Verdun to do no more than imply a constitutionalization of the distinct society or Quebec veto promises.[4] The third commitment, to transfer authority for manpower training to the provinces, did not require constitutional change, but it was unclear just how the first two promises could have any real substance without crossing over into constitutional entrenchment.

The constitutional route was indeed Mr. Chrétien's immediately preferred route in the glum days following the Quebec vote. He appears to have looked for at least six provinces to back a constitutional amendment recognizing Quebec's distinctive nature, thus putting the intransigent PQ on the spot as blocking a longstanding demand from Quebec nationalists (seven provinces representing at least 50 percent of the population of Canada would be required). The key to this strategy was Ontario, and it was the reluctance of the Ontario premier, Mike Harris, to line up behind Ottawa that put a quick end to a fast track on distinct society.[5] The window of opportunity opened by the scare of October 30 closed, and with this closing Ottawa's attention turned to alternative strategies.

VIRTUAL CONSTITUTIONAL REALITY?

On November 27, 1995 the government introduced resolutions to the House of Commons that amounted to "virtual" constitutional change. The first was a promise that the federal government would "lend" its constitutional veto to Quebec. The formula was that of the long-dead Victoria Charter of 1971, which saw four equal regions—the West, Ontario, Quebec, and Atlantic Canada—with vetoes, as opposed to the seven of ten with 50 percent plus formula of the Constitution Act of 1982. The second was a resolution that

whereas the People of Quebec have expressed the desire for recognition of Quebec's distinct society:
1. the House recognize that Quebec is a distinct society within Canada;
2. the House recognize that Quebec's distinct society includes its French-speaking majority, unique culture and civil law tradition;

3. the House undertake to be guided by this reality;
4. the House encourage all components of the legislative and executive branches of government to take note of this recognition and be guided in their conduct accordingly.[6]

Finally, there was a formal promise to transfer authority for manpower training to the provinces. The Liberals would for the moment confine themselves to what they could control, i.e., their parliamentary majority, while leaving the premiers on the back burner. The prime minister made it clear that "the recognition of Quebec as a distinct society should eventually be enshrined in the Canadian Constitution," but this was for another day.[7]

The response to these initiatives was not encouraging. No one took critical notice of the manpower training transfer, which was largely uncontroversial, but the same could hardly be said for the other two components. The distinct society resolution was, perhaps predictably, dismissed as too little and old-hat by Quebec sovereigntists, while the enemies of the concept in the rest of Canada—many of the premiers and the Reform party in the House—quickly denounced it as too much and contrary to the alleged principle of the equality of the provinces. Editorials and open-line comments, especially from the West, offered a sharp, bracing antidote to any naive notion that the rest of Canada had suddenly been converted to more conciliatory attitudes than evidenced during the Meech and Charlottetown fiascos, or that the emotional pro-Canada rally in Montreal in the last days of the referendum had changed any minds among those English Canadians who had not travelled to Montreal.

The real firestorm of criticism was reserved for the "virtual" Quebec veto proposal. British Columbians were loud in their denunciation of being lumped together with the three prairie provinces as one Western region. Having revealed insensitivity to the Pacific coast, Mr. Chrétien then backed down and revised the regional formula to include British Columbia as holding a fifth regional veto. Even though this revision in effect left Alberta with a veto as well (Alberta would represent 50 percent of the population of the three prairie provinces), the change did little to mollify Western criticism. In fact, the real basis of Western scepticism seemed to be a dislike of *any* provincial veto, and most specifically an anxiety that a Quebec veto would be wielded to prevent any future constitutional change attractive to the West, such as a Triple-E Senate. In short, in its attempt to address Quebec's legitimate concerns about protecting its distinctiveness from the potential threat of the English-speaking majority of provinces, Mr. Chrétien awakened old regional animosities out of slumber. Nor were the voices of concern only those of populist reaction. Respected academics from the West added their considered outrage at unilateral imposition on the West by a central-Canada dominated federal government of a quasi-constitutional change by extra-constitutional means.[8] All things considered, it was not an auspicious start for a post-referendum revival of federalist fortunes.

The long-term impact of the November 1995 essay into "virtual reality" seems rather limited. No visible impression appears to have been made on the "soft nationalists" in Quebec by these rather symbolic gestures. On the other hand, short-term Western anger has not translated into longer-term political damage to the Liberals, whose standing in the polls at the end of 1996 in the Western provinces is as strong as or stronger than in the 1993 election. In some ways, it is almost as if nothing at all had happened: virtual reality is not a substitute for reality.

"REBALANCING" THE FEDERATION?

The one uncontroversial element of the November initiatives, the manpower training transfer, did set in motion concrete steps—guided by a new minister brought in from Quebec to strengthen national unity, Pierre Pettigrew—which by December 1995 had resulted in the first federal-provincial agreement, with Alberta. Others will no doubt follow. This puts the PQ on the spot, given that they have primed their electorate to believe that control over manpower training is a key element in directing economic development. On this point at least, Mr. Chrétien has visibly abandoned his former centralism and permitted concrete steps toward devolution that could benefit Quebec as well as other provinces. Moreover, in the Speech from the Throne in February 1996 the federal government renounced any use of its spending power to create new shared-cost programs in areas of exclusive provincial jurisdiction without the consent of a majority of the provinces, thus reversing the decades-old pattern by which the federal government had undermined *de facto* provincial jurisdiction through its spending power. Cynics might suggest that this was no more than making a virtue of necessity in a government dominated by Finance Minister Paul Martin's powerful deficit-reduction imperative and the Canada Health and Social Transfer. Nevertheless, the signal to the provinces, including Quebec, was clear, and constitutes a not unimportant indication to moderate Quebec nationalists of a genuinely more flexible federalism. Above all, these things can be done without opening up the Constitution.

There is a potential route toward placating the moderate nationalists in Quebec without automatically setting off alarm bells among conservatives in the rest of Canada. The Reform opposition in Parliament has repeatedly pointed to a more "balanced" federalism, by which they mean a radically more decentralized federalism, and they have argued that such proposals "involve matters entirely within the capacity of a willing federal government to initiate," while "none of these proposals require that special status be created, either formally or informally, for Quebec or any other province."[9] The Conservative premiers of Alberta and Ontario have been increasingly vocal about what they call "rebalancing" the federation, and have indeed broadly hinted that this will be the price they might exact for supporting a constitutional initiative on the distinct society clause. The Quebec Liberal party has produced a set of proposals that seek constitutional entrenchment of a series of transfers of jurisdiction from Ottawa to the provinces,[10] although some of these might be accomplished without any constitutional adjustments.

Given the federal Liberals' fiscal drive toward disengagement from areas where the spending power has been used in the past to build a federal presence, and given their own voluntary renunciation of future use of the spending power, decentralization toward all might seem an attractive alternative. It is however unlikely that "rebalancing" will be a general answer, even though some aspects of it (such as manpower training) may be incorporated into the overall strategy. The reasons for Liberal reluctance are not hard to find. "Rebalancing" is less an agenda for rationalized federalism than an ideological agenda for the federal Reform and Alberta and Ontario Conservative parties. Upon closer examination, "rebalancing" is a misnomer, since all the proposed movement is one way, from Ottawa to the (wealthier) provinces.[11] A truly rationalized redistribution of federal-provincial powers in the new globalized world might indeed see considerable devolution downward, on the European "subsidiarity principle," but it might also see some current provincial powers transferred upward (environmental protection, for instance). The "social Liberals," routed though they may have been on most policy issues by Paul Martin and the Finance Department, will not agree to fall on the sacrificial sword, as is implied by the rebalancing agenda. Liberal insistence on the continued use of the Canada Health Act to enforce provincial compliance with national standards in health care delivery[12] indicates that the maintenance of Ottawa's federal leadership continues to animate the energies of the Chrétien government. Besides, there is little evidence to suggest that radical decentralization generates widespread popular support in Canada outside Quebec.[13] There is much evidence, however, to suggest that certain sectors of opinion on the centre-left for which the Liberals compete electorally, and the smaller and poorer provinces, some of which are represented by influential Liberal premiers like Brian Tobin and Frank McKenna, are suspicious of the decentralization agenda.

If decentralization is a doubtful Liberal political currency in English Canada, the utility of relying upon "rebalancing" to bring Quebec firmly into the federalist fold is even more suspect. No amount of raw meat thrown at the sovereigntists will satisfy their appetite for a separate national state. Yet, seeking to appease the soft nationalists, mainly grouped in or around the Quebec Liberal party, by wholesale transfer of powers, either *de facto* or *de jure*, runs the risk of denuding the federal government of any remaining attributes of positive connotation to Quebec voters, thus undermining the continued attractiveness of federalism. Already the federal government's cost-cutting priorities and the downsizing of the federal public sector have had the effect of diminishing the signs of any positive federal presence, thus enhancing the comparative attractiveness of the PQ's assertive and purposeful grand national project. The voluntary amputation of most of its remaining limbs will scarcely assist the federal government in recovering the esteem of Francophone Quebecers. There is a clear difference in outlook here between provincial and federal Liberals; the Ottawa Liberals are unlikely to proceed too far down the road their Quebec counterparts are pointing toward.

In summary, elements of a "rebalanced" federalism will be deployed, but the Liberals will not embrace the Reform-Conservative-Quebec

Liberal agenda as a general or overall strategy. They would be foolish to do so.

DIPPING LIBERAL TOES IN
THE CONSTITUTIONAL WHIRLPOOL

With regard to the other two elements of Chrétien's "Plan A" initiatives, the prospect of turning virtual reality into constitutional reality is no closer. The Quebec veto roused such a hornets' nest of opposition that its formal constitutionalization seems to have receded in urgency. The importance of recognizing Quebec's distinctiveness has been kept alive, not least by the addition to the cabinet early in 1996 of a new Minister of Intergovernmental Affairs, Stéphane Dion. Dion, a Quebec political scientist exceptionally attached to federalism, is a tireless advocate of the recognition of Quebec's distinctiveness as an antidote to separatism, a point he made clear in an unusual personal manifesto he insisted on delivering while being sworn into office.[14] Since that time, he has carried the same message across the country in a series of speeches and articles, not flinching from confronting anti-distinct society sentiments head-on,[15] and in a series of meetings with his provincial counterparts to line up support for a distinct society amendment.

While Dion's sincerity cannot be questioned, nor that of certain premiers, such as Roy Romanow of Saskatchewan or Frank McKenna of New Brunswick, the commitment of the Chrétien government as a whole and of the Prime Minister himself to actually press the constitutional process to resolution, before the next federal election and perhaps even after, is suspect. The issue has been forced to a head by Quebec Liberal leader Daniel Johnson. A Quebec Liberal party proposal put forward in December 1996 would seek support from six provinces for a distinct society clause, which Mr. Johnson would then place before the voters in the next Quebec election with the promise that if elected, he would add Quebec's support as the decisive seventh province to ratify the amendment. Once again, just as he did during the last weeks of the referendum campaign, Mr. Johnson has put Mr. Chrétien on the spot, where the Prime Minister is sure to feel uncomfortable. The last thing the Liberals need before the next federal election is a spotlight trained on a distinct society amendment.

It is not merely that the distinct society concept remains an object of aversion for many Canadians outside Quebec,[16] and thus not a popular cause for cautious premiers or MPs seeking re-election. The real problem is that the methods required to meet the Quebec Liberals' expectations will place a heavy strain on the credibility of the federal government. First, the assumption is that the 1982 amendment process (seven provinces with at least 50 percent of the population) will in effect supersede the virtual amendment process with its five regional vetoes in the November 1995 resolutions. Even if Ontario could be persuaded to come onside, under the virtual procedure either Alberta or British Columbia could veto any change: one or both of these provinces is likely to do so.[17] In this event, Ottawa could ignore its own resolution and attempt to proceed on the 1982 basis. To call this course politically risky would be an understatement.

Even if we assume against all probability that the support of the premiers of Ontario, Alberta, and British Columbia, as well as the majority of Atlantic premiers, could somehow be lined up (perhaps as a trade-off for across-the-board decentralization reluctantly and perhaps unwisely conceded by Ottawa), the difficulties do not stop there. The ghosts of Meech (the spectre of eleven men behind closed doors sealing the fate of the country) still haunt all constitutional change in English Canada. The populist outcry about "them" imposing a distinct society clause on "us" would be deafening. In any event, both the British Columbia and Alberta governments have bound themselves to submit any future constitutional change to their electorates in referendums, before their premiers give assent. Although the Prime Minister has expressed reluctance to consider any Charlottetown-like national vote, despite vague commitments from his government that Canadians would have a "say" in their constitutional future,[18] it is difficult to imagine Ontarians and Manitobans standing by quietly without a vote while their compatriots in British Columbia and Alberta exercise their democratic franchise on the question. With a binding national vote, the spectre of another Charlottetown fiasco would loom large, this time with disastrous consequences in Quebec. Yet one can readily imagine the parallel consequences if a distinct society clause were imposed on a strict 1982 formula against a clear "no" from the people of Alberta and/or British Columbia.

These are not pleasant scenarios. It is hardly surprising that the Prime Minister, cautious and unadventurous as he is by nature, will try to avoid bringing these matters to a head—certainly before his government is re-elected—despite pressures for a dramatic gesture from the Quebec Liberals and from some of his Quebec ministers. This is not a courageous stance, and he has been warned by columnist Richard Gwyn that he runs the risk of looking like a reincarnated Mackenzie King, "canny and adroit, but shapeless and, behind the charms and smiles, hollow."[19] Heroic gestures like challenging Canadians to approve a distinct society clause to save the country might appeal to journalists and academics, but not to politicians who face re-election. If such a gesture does occur, it will only come under great pressure, after the federal election, and then it will look very much like another "roll of the dice," to quote the former prime minister at the time of Meech Lake. The cannier, Mackenzie King-like approach (if circumstances permit) will be to keep the *prospect* of a distinct society clause on the agenda, but not at the top for immediate action. Stéphane Dion represents the promise, but the Prime Minister's own low profile on the issue proves what little priority his government is actually giving it.

In early 1997 one new constitutional development of considerable interest appeared. Quebec has requested that the federal government agree bilaterally to allow Quebec to establish linguistic rather than denominational school boards. Ottawa had earlier supported a bilateral constitutional change relating to Newfoundland's denominational school structure, so approval of Quebec's plan would seem appropriate. From the Liberals' point of view, this course would have two additional advantages. It would demonstrate to Quebecers that change is possible within federalism, and it would have the effect of making the PQ rely upon the hated 1982 Constitution Act, the legitimacy of which has always been denied on the basis of Quebec's refusal to sign. While it is s. 93 of the 1867 BNA Act that Quebec is seeking to change, amendments applying to one province alone by joint action of the federal and provincial government are enabled by s. 43 of the 1982 Act. This may not loom large on the wider field of constitutional confrontation, but it seems to offer the federal government one small win-win scenario, if agreement can be reached.[20]

ADMINISTERING PLAN A

One of the most obvious weaknesses of the Chrétien government in the face of the 1995 referendum was the rather startling weakness of the party's leadership in Quebec—starting with the Prime Minister himself. The paradox widely noted in the pre-referendum period, that a Quebec prime minister should enjoy high approval ratings in English Canada but be generally disparaged in his home province, remains just as true more than a year after the referendum. Nothing that Mr. Chrétien did during or following the referendum appears to have redeemed him in the eyes of his fellow Francophone Quebecers. Neither has he as yet fallen in the eyes of Canadians outside Quebec, 70 percent of whom in an Angus Reid survey reported in December 1996 approved of his performance; 53 percent of Quebecers in the same survey disapproved.[21] From the point of view of the national unity dossier, these figures seem to indicate that the public elements of the Plan A strategy have not got Mr. Chrétien into any serious difficulties in English Canada, but by the same token have made little headway in winning over Francophone Quebecers to federalism and the federal Liberal government. Despite well-publicized leadership problems in the post-Bouchard Bloc Québécois, that group's grip over a plurality of Quebec voters seems unshaken.[22] A re-elected Chrétien will still have considerable difficulty selling federalism in Quebec in another referendum, whatever the specific mix of positive alternatives that is finally put together. The product may be quite different than in 1995, but the salesman remains unpopular and distrusted in the targeted market. Lucien Bouchard, in marked contrast, and despite the inevitable strains involved in governing his province with a policy priority of fiscal austerity, has remained the most formidable figure on the Francophone political landscape, with a great deal of political capital to expend in another crusade for sovereignty. This is a real problem for the Liberals.

One of the solutions to weak leadership at the top is to seek strong lieutenants. The introduction of Stéphane Dion and Pierre Pettigrew, each with very specific tasks in the Plan A strategy, is an important but limited step. Yet, on the wider battlefield with the sovereigntists, neither is a name to conjure with on the scale of Lucien Bouchard. There has been some effort as well to co-ordinate national unity policy within the Cabinet. The Chrétien government has cut back drastically on formal cabinet committees, but there is an informal "national unity" committee that apparently includes, along with Dion, Treasury Board President Marcel Massé, Justice Minister Allan Rock (mainly for the Plan B side of the strategy, discussed below), Foreign Affairs Minister Lloyd Axworthy, and Deputy Prime Minister Sheila Copps.[23]

Weight has also been given to strengthening the administrative side. The Privy Council Office, Mr. Dion's portfolio, was given a new deputy minister for intergovernmental affairs in the summer of 1996. He is George Anderson, a veteran bureaucrat who is reported to have Liberal ties, and who had responsibility for the infrastructure program in the early days of the Chrétien government. Other changes at the PCO suggest a new focus on the national unity issue. There is for instance an intelligence unit within the PCO that closely monitors statements and events in Quebec, commissions polls, and advises the government on how to counter sovereigntist moves.[24] Certain influential advisers in the Prime Minister's Office such as Eddie Goldenberg have also been key players behind the scenes, although they emerged somewhat tarnished by the clumsiness of the Prime Minister's November 1995 resolutions.

The one institutional innovation the Liberals have brought to the Plan A campaign has also proved highly controversial. In early September 1996, the Canadian Information Office (CIO) went into operation under the direction of Sheila Copps in her capacity as Heritage Minister, but in co-ordination with the PCO's Quebec operation, with an initial budget of $20 million per year. The CIO is very reminiscent of some of the more controversial moves by the Trudeau Liberals to counter the first PQ challenge in the late 1970s and early 1980s. There is a fine line between "information" and "propaganda"; it is not at all clear that the CIO makes that distinction. At the press conference to launch the new agency, Ms. Copps was unspecific but suggestive about its mandate. The agency's task, she suggested, was to make information about "Canada's accomplishments" accessible to Canadians; this information was "necessary to keep this country together." She added, in more offensive mode, "We also want to make sure we counter the lies that are being propagated by the separatists."[25] There is no mention of this latter activity, as such, in the official mandate for the agency, which is couched in vague but positive terms.[26]

The CIO maintains a website on the Internet[27] and produces information sheets ("Focus on Canada") that extol the virtues of Canadian citizenship and the value of Canadian accomplishments. It quickly became the target of attacks by cost-conscious Reformers and BQ MPs, and reached a peak of public notoriety when Sheila Copps's promise of free flags to anyone who called turned into a mini-gold rush as thousands bombarded the office with requests. Pointedly, it was noted that most requests were coming from English Canada. The CIO may indeed be little more than a waste of money, if its object is to bring a pro-Canada message to Quebec. On the other hand, if "countering the separatists" in another referendum campaign is the hidden agenda, the federal government might consider very carefully the legitimacy question. The 1995 campaign showed that Francophone Quebecers tended to believe those spokespersons who had credibility in their eyes, and that these were more likely to be the sovereigntists than the federalists. The problem may thus be more the messenger than the message.

PLAN B

The genesis of Plan B does not rest with the Liberal government, but has been forced upon them from the outside by the repercussions of the referendum result. Some federalists had steadfastly refused to contemplate the possibility of separation, or had argued that the discussion of terms of separation would amount to a self-fulfilling prophecy. On the night of October 30, the chilling realization set in that separation could happen, and that refusing to discuss the terms and conditions of negotiation in advance had left the field uncontested to the sovereigntists to paint a rosy scenario of what Quebecers could gain from a Yes vote. Worse was the revelation that the PQ had a well thought-out plan in hand to move decisively toward sovereignty starting the morning after the vote—and to neutralize any federal counteroffensive.[28] The rest of Canada would, by contrast, be utterly unprepared, and likely in a state of disarray. There would be the possibility of chaos turning into violence, especially over such hot-button issues as the rejection of sovereignty by Quebec's Aboriginal peoples, and potential economic disaster arising out of acute uncertainty. Voices were soon raised in the rest of Canada that one glimpse into this abyss should be enough, that next time the rest of Canada had an obligation to clarify in advance its response to a Yes vote. Quebecers, former Ontario premier Bob Rae specified, "must go into the voting booth with a clear sense of what the consequences of their vote would be."[29] While premier, Rae had always adamantly refused to discuss possible separation scenarios. This was a signal that serious rethinking of previous positions was called for.

In the months following the referendum, proposals for a Plan B process were directed at the already disoriented Chrétien government.[30] These tended to focus on three main issue areas:

1)   what kind of question and what kind of majority should trigger negotiations?
2)   how should the transition between a Yes vote and accession to sovereignty be handled? and,
3)   what kind of negotiating mechanism and bottom-line conditions would Canada bring to the table?

Some of these issues had already been discussed and debated in independent studies prior to the referendum.[31] Plan B advocates now argued persuasively that the absence of an authoritative response from the rest of Canada had actually smoothed the path toward a Yes vote. Perhaps an authoritative response from the rest of Canada might even deter Quebecers from embarking on an adventure the costs and risks of which would now be made clearer. In any event, if Plan B failed to deter, the transition to sovereignty would at least be less chaotic and dangerous than in the absence of any prior planning.

Of all the Plan B suggestions, perhaps the most influential was from a one-time insider, the "mandarin's mandarin," former Clerk of the Privy Council Gordon Robertson. Mr. Robertson, now retired but still keeping an active hand in constitutional debates, circulated a paper among key players that called for Ottawa to pass "contingency legislation" that would only be activated in the event of a Yes vote. Crucial elements in this legislation would declare any unilateral declaration of independence by Quebec to be illegal until the federal government, in consultation with the nine other provinces and with Aboriginal leaders, agreed to constitutional amendments for lawful secession. Until that point the federal government and federal laws would retain their jurisdiction over Quebec territory. Certain conditions would have to be met in any agreement on separation: Quebec would have to accept responsibility for a share of the national debt proportional to its share of the population, and the Cree, Inuit, and other Aboriginal peoples in northern Quebec would be allowed to remain in Canada, with their lands. Robertson argued that one advantage of his proposal would be that a parliamentary debate on the contingency legislation would be an "extremely sobering" exercise: "every nasty, difficult argument would come out" before Quebecers decided whether they wanted to go down that road. Robertson, a supporter of Meech Lake, was quick to add that he preferred to see more positive methods of reconciliation tried first to avert another referendum; his contingency plan would only come into effect once a third referendum was already set.

The decisive point in Robertson's argument is that the threat to withhold agreement with and recognition of a secessionist Quebec is the "fundamental bargaining counter the government of Canada holds."[32] Without this, a post-Yes Quebec might feel free to declare independence unilaterally (as Parizeau was certainly prepared to do in 1995 if the outcome had been in his favour). In a legal and political vacuum, a discredited federal government, panicky but obstreperous provinces, and Aboriginal leaders adrift in uncharted seas, might have little capacity to set a firm agenda together, while the sovereigntists would hold the initiative. This points to the core of the Plan B approach. It is not, as some critics have argued, that Plan B is an effort to deny Quebec's "right to national self-determination" or to forcibly retain Quebec in Confederation against the will of a democratic majority in that province.[33] On the contrary, Plan B is really about *how* Quebec's secession can be peacefully and lawfully negotiated, but on terms acceptable to Canadians and Aboriginal peoples and not simply on terms unilaterally imposed by the secessionists. It is above all a demand for *clarity* in advance about terms and conditions, and an emphasis on the interest of all Canadians in the outcome. This latter point is one with considerable political clout outside Quebec, among Canadians fed up with passivity in the face of sovereigntist goading. Given the failure of the "What, me worry?" approach, the Liberals would certainly have felt compelled to institute some form of Plan B thinking for public relations reasons alone—but the case was compelling on its own merits as well.

Robertson's version of Plan B was received with the seriousness and respect befitting a statement from a bureaucratic elder statesman. As Jeffrey Simpson pointed out, however, Robertson's plan has one serious deficiency: it foresees an elite-driven response and one that is largely directed by the federal government:

> He underestimates the need for the rest of Canada to consult itself democratically. If the Yes side wins, people elsewhere in Canada will not stand for a federal government that lost the referendum negotiating anything substantial on its behalf.... The rest of Canada must debate options, consider different negotiating strategies, define its own self-interest and choose among various potential leaders. That's the same kind of debate Quebecers have been engaged in for years.[34]

Indeed, some Plan B advocates looked to an extraparliamentary mechanism, like Quebec's Bélanger-Campeau Commission, or a constituent assembly to set the rest of Canada's terms and conditions.[35] Meanwhile, the Reform party, the official opposition by default in English Canada, has been publicizing its own Plan B, which spells out hard bargaining positions in some considerable detail.[36]

The Liberals have responded cautiously and in a low-key manner to the demands for a Plan B track, but they have neither committed themselves publicly to as detailed a hard line in content as some critics would prefer, nor initiated any novel mechanisms for publicly arriving at a strategy. This circumspection is hardly surprising. The danger of a public Plan B debate has always been its potential for generating backlash and resentment in Quebec. While the Liberals have recognized the real concerns of Canadians that their interests be represented forthrightly, they are also acutely aware of the potential for any wider process to spin out of control, to be captured by those hard-liners who might wish to see Plan B thinking entirely displace more positive Plan A elements such as the distinct society and a Quebec veto. The government has played its Plan B cards very close to its vest, while strategically dropping hints from time to time about how powerful they are. Thus, the Prime Minister's tantalizing hints that a simple 50 percent plus one would be insufficient to trigger separation negotiations have been matched by coyness about just what level of support a Yes outcome would have to achieve as a negotiating threshold. Similarly, hints about the clarity required of a referendum question have been dropped, but without any precise specification of what would constitute clarity. Canadians were promised that in the event of another Quebec referendum, those outside Quebec would have a "say," but whether this implies a national referendum or some other device has been left unanswered. We may take it that this is studied ambiguity: the point is to raise the prospect, but leave the blanks unfilled.[37]

The one area where Plan B has taken on some definite shape is not on the field of political struggle, or even in the court of public opinion, but rather on the safer and more predictable terrain of the courts of law. In fact, leadership and direction of the Plan B track has largely fallen to the Minister of Justice, Allan Rock. It is appropriate that the Liberals should entrust Plan B to an Anglophone minister from outside Quebec: most of the national unity strategy has fallen into the hands of Quebecers, whether Francophone or Anglophone, many of whom, beginning with Mr. Chrétien himself, may not fully appreciate the feelings of non-Quebecers. Mr. Rock has been quite assertive in taking on this role, recognizing a leadership vacuum in the non-Quebec Liberal caucus.

THE SUPREME COURT REFERENCE

Rock's position as Minister of Justice is also a key to the Liberal Plan B strategy. His involvement began when the federal government felt required to respond officially to the Quebec government's brief for dismissal in the Guy Bertrand challenge to the legality of the sovereignty referendum. Mr. Bertrand, a renegade separatist, is a controversial figure much reviled by the sovereigntists and more widely among *bien-pensant* intellectuals in Quebec. Since his challenge seemed to question the right of the people of Quebec to determine their own future, any intervention by the federal government could appear antidemocratic and insulting to the people of Quebec. There was much huffing and puffing in PQ circles to the effect that any intervention would lead directly to a quick election or even a referendum call by Premier Bouchard. Rock specified quite clearly that the federal Justice

Department was intervening not on behalf of Mr. Bertrand or in support of his challenge, but simply to clarify questions that had been raised by the government of Quebec. Specifically, Quebec had argued that following a Yes vote, Canadian law and the Constitution would no longer be applicable to Quebec, but would be replaced by the international law of the self-determination of nations. This would of course allow a unilateral declaration of independence. The federal government could hardly let this assertion go unchallenged. Despite the earlier blustering from Quebec, no precipitous action was taken in response to the federal intervention, and when a Quebec court allowed Bertrand's challenge to proceed, Bouchard's government simply dropped out of any further representation in the case. For its part, the federal government did not take up Bertrand's appeal, but used the opportunity instead to launch what is for the moment the centrepiece of its public Plan B, a reference to the Supreme Court.

On September 26, 1996 the Minister of Justice rose in the House of Commons to announce that three questions were being submitted to the Supreme Court of Canada:

1. Under the constitution of Canada, can the National Assembly, legislature or government of Quebec effect the secession of Quebec from Canada unilaterally?
2. Does international law give the National Assembly, legislature or government of Quebec the right to effect the secession of Quebec from Canada unilaterally? In this regard, is there a right to self-determination under international law that would give the National Assembly, legislature or government of Quebec the right to effect the secession of Quebec from Canada unilaterally?
3. In the event of a conflict between domestic and international law on the right of the National Assembly, legislature or government of Quebec to effect the secession of Quebec from Canada unilaterally, which would take precedence in Canada?

He took pains to indicate that this reference was in no way directed at denying democratic rights, but rather at upholding the rule of law:

The issue is not whether a democracy such as Canada can keep a population against its will: of course, it cannot. The issue arises from the false claim of the government of Quebec that it alone, in a unilateral fashion that changes according to its short-term political interests, can decide the process that may lead to secession. Quebecers, as well as their fellow citizens from other provinces, would be dramatically affected by the breakup of our country. Everyone has the right to be certain that the process is clear, mutually acceptable and fair to all.... A unilateral declaration of independence would undermine political stability, interrupt the prevailing order and cast into doubt the interests and rights of Quebecers and all Canadians.[38]

The Supreme Court reference has several obvious advantages as a Plan B tactic. While judges can never be taken for granted, the government is no doubt justified in the confidence with which it awaits the rulings. It puts the Quebec government on the spot: Rock accompanied his speech to Parliament with a letter to the Attorney General of Quebec requesting his participation and pointedly suggesting that when there is serious disagreement in a democracy, "the fundamental issues must be clarified if we want to deal with any process related to the future of Canada and Quebec on a foundation that is stable, fair and respectful of the rule of law."[39] In short, if Quebec refuses to participate in a process that will almost certainly not be in its favour, it will appear in opposition to the rule of law and procedural fairness. The reference avoids the twin dangers of Plan B schemes by neatly slipping past any implications of denying the democratic legitimacy of a referendum consultation of the Quebec people, and by not straying into any specification of negotiating positions, which might alienate particular sectors of English Canadian opinion. Finally, any decision will very likely postdate the next federal election. By putting elements of Plan B before the court, the government appears to be doing something, while offering an ironclad excuse for avoiding detailed specification of the plan because it is awaiting authoritative clarification. If the eventual ruling does correspond to the government's expectations, it will then have a firm legal and constitutional footing on which to insist that any secession must be negotiated and approved by the rest of Canada—and to discourage any international recognition of a unilateral declaration of independence.

THE ABORIGINAL WILD CARD

In any discussion of Plan B, the wild card is the complex of questions surrounding the Aboriginal peoples of Quebec: the clash of nationalisms between Aboriginals and Québécois; the fiduciary responsibilities of the federal government toward Aboriginal peoples; Aboriginal rejection of the idea that they can be simply moved against their will from one jurisdiction to another like cattle. In the 1980 referendum, the idea of national self-determination was cast almost entirely in terms of Quebec aspirations, but in the 1990s rising political militancy among Aboriginal peoples and the growing acceptance of the inherent right to Aboriginal self-government (agreed upon in the text of the Charlottetown Accord and fleshed out in considerable detail in the 1996 Report of the Royal Commission on Aboriginal Affairs) has recast the issue in much more complex terms. Unfortunately for Quebec sovereigntists, this recasting has tended to place Quebec aspirations in direct collision with Aboriginal aspirations.[40] This was highlighted when some Native bands in Quebec held their own separate referendums on sovereignty just prior to the October 30 vote, and rejected the Yes option with near unanimity.

There is a profound philosophical dilemma here about national rights and self-determination that could also act as a kind of tripwire that might turn a secession process into the kind of violent confrontation that none of the parties wants, but that they might stumble into.[41] Any question of secessions within the secession immediately involves the volatile issue of redrawing borders, of partitioning of the territory of a secessionist Quebec. The issue is most acutely posed in the northern part of Quebec, where the Cree and Inuit peoples have been particularly adamant about refusing to recognize the jurisdiction of a secessionist Quebec over their ancestral lands.

There are at least two powerful arguments in favour of a partition, apart from the moral and legal standing of Aboriginal claims to self-determination. Northern Quebec was a post-Confederation addition to the province of Quebec, first in 1898, and second with the addition of the huge Ungava territory in 1912. Thus, these lands—about two-thirds of Quebec territory in area—are not part of any alleged original Confederation bargain that can be revoked by Quebec as an original partner.[42] There is also a strong democratic argument: Aboriginal peoples are a clear majority in the sparsely-populated north. Politically, the James Bay Cree have been a very effective lobby abroad—as witness their ability to force the PQ government to abandon the James Bay II hydroelectric megaproject.[43] Following a Yes vote in a future

Quebec referendum, it is quite clear that the Cree and other native groups in the north will resist inclusion and appeal to both the rest of Canada and the outside world to support this rejection.[44] Gordon Robertson's contingency plan is quite clear that partition of the north should be a bottom-line requirement of the federal position. Given the strength of the northern Aboriginal case, this may ultimately be a necessary part of any Plan B. However, the Liberals have been notably loath to talk about this or even to offer any real encouragement to the Aboriginal peoples of Quebec about federal support in the event of negotiations. It is not hard to see why: the partition issue is a political minefield.

The PQ have chosen to view partition as non-negotiable. Péquistes speak of Quebec's "sacred borders" and insist that their sovereignty is "indivisible." Notoriously, Lucien Bouchard asserted that Canada is divisible, but Quebec is not—because Canada is not a "real country," made up as it is of more than one nation, while Quebec is a "people" who require a separate state. Bouchard's words reveal utter conceptual muddle: claims to territorial sovereignty are different from claims to self-determination of peoples; if Quebec claims the right as a nation or people to split Canada, it cannot logically deny the equivalent right of native peoples to split Quebec, save by an outright denial of their status as peoples or nations.[45] They actually provide ammunition to the Aboriginal position, a point that the Cree were quick to pick up on.[46] The PQ, having redefined nationalism away from ethnic exclusiveness (despite Parizeau's infamous referendum night speech) toward a more liberal, civic version of territorial nationalism, finds itself impaled on the horns of a liberal dilemma: territories or provinces, as the Cree keep pointing out, do not have rights of national self-determination, only peoples.[47] On this criterion, Francophone Quebecers might have a right to self-determination, but not to take other peoples, like the Cree and Inuit, with them. Some sovereigntists (although never PQ officials) have admitted the validity of this point, despite the huge stake the Quebec economy has in James Bay power, but the real problem comes in moving beyond the territorially circumscribed area of northern Quebec.

Native peoples in southern Quebec do not necessarily have territory that can be readily detached from its surroundings. Yet their claims to self-government are just as strong, and their rejection of Quebec sovereignty just as forceful. There is already a history of violence between Quebec authorities and Mohawks at Oka, and continuing poor relations. Even more alarming from the sovereigntists' perspective is their manifest failure to enlist any significant support, or even benign indifference, from the Anglophone minority and from the Allophone communities (the "ethnics" that Mr. Parizeau blamed for defeat on referendum night). So intense was the fright and so deep the aversion to sovereignty on the part of Quebec's minority communities, that enthusiasm for post-separation partition has been high in a number of quarters. The prospect of the west island of Montreal, the Quebec side of the national capital region, Anglophone counties in West Quebec or the Eastern Townships, seceding from a secessionist Quebec might provoke gleeful anticipation in some parts of English Canada, but sober reflection suggests that this is a prescription for setting out down the grisly path of the former Yugoslavia.

It is hardly surprising that the sovereigntists should wish to draw the line at any discussion of partition, since it has the potential to gut the very possibility of a viable independent state. Nor should anyone underestimate the emotional reaction triggered among Francophone Quebecers by talk of dismemberment. From the federalist standpoint, to talk of partition is to play with fire, yet it remains, when confined to Aboriginal peoples, a powerful legal, moral, and political barrier to the fulfilment of the sovereigntist agenda. Thus Stéphane Dion has kept the idea on the table that Quebec separation would only open the field to further divisions,[48] while the government has remained cagey about specifying any particular partition scenarios. Used in moderation and with circumspection, partition is a useful caution and a reminder that the federal government does have a Plan B that will not be at all to sovereigntist liking. Used in excess, partition talk is definitely counterproductive. The Liberals are thus content to watch the James Bay Cree make their passionate and compelling case, without ever refuting or endorsing it directly. They are much less comfortable with some of the fiery Anglophone rights rhetoric of partition emanating from West Montreal, although they cannot, of course, control it. The same goes for the volatile issue of language law, used by both Anglophone and Francophone extremists to exacerbate tensions in

Montreal. The federal government has been notably cool toward controversial Anglophone rights activist Howard Galganov.

PLAN C?

Another possible federal strategy is to carefully use Ottawa's economic advantage over Quebec City to discourage sovereigntist support. Under the firm hand of Finance Minister Paul Martin, the federal government has taken charge of the deficit problem, earning the praise of the New York bond agencies in the process, while offloading much of the cost and the political blame onto the provinces. Quebec, meanwhile, fully accepting the same economic logic, is in the throes of launching major cutbacks in its public sector and social programs, which has damaged the prestige of the PQ among its core supporters. The Quebec economy suffers from higher levels of unemployment and a persistent lag in investment relative to Ontario and other provinces, some of which is no doubt attributable to foreign capital's unease about the political uncertainty associated with the sovereigntist agenda.

Montreal in particular tends to feel ignored by the PQ—and Montreal provided the lowest level of support to the Yes side in the referendum. The Prime Minister, addressing the Montreal Board of Trade, spelled out a positive message of how Ottawa, working with the Quebec and Montreal governments, would see Montreal "regain its dynamism and become a centre of technology and growth."[49] The sting in the tail of this argument was a warning that the threat of another referendum was dragging down Montreal's prospects. To give substance to its point, the federal government has reverted to throwing money at the Montreal economy, as with a $87 million loan to Bombardier. The political message was spelled out crudely and with uncharacteristic passion—and hyperbole—by Industry Minister John Manley at the 1996 Liberal Party Convention:

Speaking in French, Mr. Manley reminded Liberals that a year earlier they had rallied for Canada in Montreal. "Together we sang. Together we even cried. Together we hoped. And Montrealers one and all [*sic!*] chose Canada. Canada is not going to forget Montreal when they need our help." [50]

Emotive outbursts aside, the use of the so-called Plan C economic weapon is a decidedly double-edged strategy. In this era of negative redistribution, any federal largesse to Quebec has reverberations throughout the federation. The Bombardier loan fanned resentment elsewhere, and may have contributed to a deeper federal financial commitment to saving Western-based Canadian Airlines International than Ottawa would have liked. On the other side, the economic weapon can look very much like the economic intimidation that backfired so badly on the federalist side in the referendum, and against which Francophone Quebecers seem quite inoculated. Too heavy an emphasis on attributing the shortcomings of the Quebec economy to the separatist "threat" does look very much like federalist gloating, which will tend to arouse resentment against Ottawa, rather than Quebec. Premier Bouchard, unlike his predecessor, seems to have a good grasp of the "optics" of working on behalf of the Quebec economy. Thus he decided to join the Prime Minister's "Team Canada" trade delegations along with the other premiers, while Mr. Parizeau had boycotted them. Bouchard thus neatly undermines the anti-PQ thrust of the federal economic strategy.

There has been some wishful thinking in Ottawa that Bouchard's commitment to deficit elimination may eventually undermine support for the sovereignty option among the "social coalition" of unions, social movements, and feminists that was so important in 1995. While there is no doubt that hospital closings, cutbacks in social programs, and public sector wage rollbacks and layoffs have soured some PQ supporters and will no doubt do even more damage as the effects of the cutbacks really begin to bite in the course of 1997, there is little reason to anticipate defections to federalism from the social sector. Federalism in its current guise as the face of fiscal restraint, downsizing, and fiscal offloading, does not and will not in the near future present a positive alternative to the national project of sovereignty. Within Quebec, the Liberals under Daniel Johnson hardly present a left-wing alternative to the PQ. At most, disillusion with the PQ on the left may result in lessened enthusiasm and energy invested in the next Yes campaign, which could conceivably impede the ability of the PQ to mobilize a sufficient Francophone Yes vote to overcome the near-monolithic No of the non-Francophone electorate.

Plan C is too sketchy in conception and inconsistent in implementation to really rate as a third track. The economy may offer a kind of background accompaniment to the battle that probably works moderately against the sovereigntists—so long as the federal government does not push too many buttons too aggressively. If they do, they risk backlash both in Quebec and outside Quebec, for opposite reasons.

FINDING THE BALANCE, PLAYING FOR TIME

The Liberals are pursuing a two-track national unity strategy, but will avoid deciding the precise balance between the two tracks, at least past the next federal election. The Liberal Convention in October 1996 gives evidence of the public face the government wishes to put on its strategy. The follow-up to the Red Book (which never mentioned national unity at all) contains one relevant paragraph in its 119 pages. Under the heading "Fulfilling Commitments to Quebec," it reads,

Within weeks of the federalist victory in the 1995 Quebec referendum, the government delivered on specific commitments made by Prime Minister Chrétien during the referendum campaign. It passed a motion in the House of Commons recognizing Quebec as a distinct society, it passed legislation ensuring that no constitutional amendment could be passed without the consent of five regions (Atlantic Canada, Quebec, Ontario, the Prairies, and British Columbia), and it announced federal withdrawal from labour market training. [51]

In short: Plan A—no mention of Plan B. Similarly, a number of delegate resolutions on national unity that stressed tough-minded Plan B thinking were shunted aside. The resolution that was adopted lends support to the constitutional entrenchment of a distinct society clause and a Quebec veto, and goes on to promote "an innovative renewal of Canadian federalism to meet the requirements of the 21st century," emphasizing "flexibility" and the principle that "responsibility must be entrusted to the order of government in the best position to act in the interest of the people." It also contains a commitment to closer economic integration, intergovernmental co-operation, and the maintenance of equalization, thus evading the full-scale decentralization argument. The resolution ends with a declaration that the government should "underline the values of Canadian federalism and the essential role of Quebec in Canada; and take steps to refute any myths which may be harmful to national unity."[52] Amid the rhetorical pap, it is evident that for the Liberals Plan B remains a sleeping dragon, albeit one that can be woken when circumstances demand. It is Plan A, with its more positive and upbeat tone, that the party prefers to put on parade: but even here, it is on a short leash and hardly front and centre.

CONCLUSION

What may we conclude about the Liberals' management of the crisis precipitated by the referendum result? There are two very different answers, depending upon the time frame. Taking the short run (which is to say, simply to the next election), the Liberals have shown considerable adroitness, if not political cunning. By approaching potentially divisive issues elliptically, by studied evasion and careful use of ambiguity, they have succeeded in defusing the separation issue so far as the federal electorate is concerned, while avoiding any confrontation with the PQ that might force the issue to a head before the federal votes are counted. When pressed on national unity, the Liberals will refer to the potential, but not immediately threatening, elements of Plan A, while the Supreme Court reference safely sets Plan B aside for the moment. If they have any potential vulnerability on this stance, it is only to the BQ in Quebec (where they have little to lose in any event) and to the Reform party west of Quebec with its unequivocal rejection of a distinct society clause or any "special status" for Quebec. Preston Manning's party has been losing electoral momentum in any event, and the postponement past the election of any serious effort at constitutional entrenchment rather takes the edge off Reform attacks. The Conservative party under Jean Charest's leadership has endorsed the "distinct society," and thus represents no challenge on this score.

Yet even if the Liberals do sail unscathed past the electorate, the crunch is thereby only postponed. Plan A will be exceedingly difficult to pilot through to a constitutional resolution without hitting Meech- and Charlottetown-like shoals. Plan B becomes more controversial and contentious the more it is spelled out in detail, yet it cannot be left indefinitely at the level of sketchy generality. Thus, taking a longer time frame into account, the Liberal strategy looks less impressive and rather more like avoidance behaviour. Between the next election and the next referendum, there will be a point beyond which evasion and postponement will no longer be possible. It will be here that Jean Chrétien (or a successor, if Chrétien is unable or unwilling to assume the burden) will have to give up Mackenzie King as role model and turn to Pierre Trudeau—not to Trudeau's policies, as such, but to Trudeau's resolution and decisiveness in the face of crisis.

To return to my opening metaphor, the Liberal plane may continue to soar past the next election, but soon thereafter the missing engine will begin to be noticed. However electorally successful the Liberals may be, if Quebec leaves, the Liberal plane will crash. So may Canada as we know it.

NOTES

I would like to thank Gene Swimmer and Sandra Bach for helpful editorial comments, Ken McRoberts for valued advice, and Salvatore Pisani for research assistance.

1 A January 1997 Environics survey showed a slight decline in overall support to 47 percent. However, not only is this 6 percent above the Liberal popular vote in 1993, but the same survey tentatively worked this out as resulting in over 200 Liberal seats, a crushing majority. Hugh Winsor and Edward Greenspon, "Chrétien, Liberals Take Dip in Poll," *The Globe and Mail* [Toronto], January 22, 1997, A1.

2 Quoted in Edward Greenspon and Anthony Wilson-Smith, *Double Vision: The Inside Story of the Liberals in Power* (Toronto: Doubleday, 1996), 336.

3 Reg Whitaker, "The National Unity Portfolio," in Susan Phillips, ed., *How Ottawa Spends 1995-96: Mid-Life Crises* (Ottawa: Carleton University Press, 1995), 72.

4 Greenspon and Wilson-Smith, *Double Vision*, 323.

5 There is some dispute about the precise degree of Harris's opposition. According to Greenspon and Wilson-Smith, Chrétien's blunt request, "Can I have your support?" was met with an equally blunt "no" (Ibid., 338). Harris is reportedly "seriously annoyed" by this account, which he believes is being spread by "Chrétien's people" to deflect blame for the stalling of the constitutional initiative. Rosemary Spears, "Harris' 'No' to Quebec Was Really a 'Not Yet,'" *The*

Toronto Star, December 3, 1996. However, at best Harris was telling the prime minister that it was too soon for precipitous action. "Not yet" had the same objective effect as "no," since it left the prime minister short of the number of consenting premiers required to put the Quebec government on the spot.

6 House of Commons, *Order Paper,* November 29, 1995, No. 26.

7 House of Commons, *Debates,* November 28, 1995.

8 See, for instance, F.L. Morton, "Why Chrétien's Proposal Won't Wash in the West," *The Globe and Mail* [Toronto], November 30, 1995, A1. The usually moderate Roger Gibbon was quoted to the effect that "for the first time in my life, if there was some sort of Western separatist movement, I'd be interested in looking at it. This is little short of a constitutional coup d'état by the Prime Minister." Miro Cernetig, "Chrétien's Veto Proposal Backfires Badly in West," *The Globe and Mail* [Toronto], November 29, 1995, A7.

9 Reform Party of Canada, "New Confederation: Building the New Canada with a New Federalism," News Release, January 25, 1996.

10 Don Macpherson, "Uh-oh, Here We Go Again," *The Gazette* [Montreal], December 11, 1996; Edison Stewart, "Why 'Distinct Society' May Run Again," *The Toronto Star,* December 14, 1996.

11 This position has been given intellectual substance by economist Thomas Courchene, by Gordon Gibson, and by the Fraser Institute, among other voices.

12 Of course, the gradual reduction of federal transfers to the provinces for health care will eventually make the Canada Health Act a toothless tiger that wealthier provinces may finally choose to ignore, but that prospect lies beyond the immediate political time frame.

13 This was the message of a national survey by Ekos Research that showed "little appetite in English Canada for major devolution or decentralization.... A large plurality (48%) worry that as the federal government withdraws traditional programs and services our Canadian identity will be weakened." Ekos Research Associates, *Rethinking Government 1995, Final Report* (Ottawa, July 1966), 98, xv.

14 Dion cited the "two strengths" of the Canadian federation as "linguistic duality and decentralization," and expressed urgency about entrenching a guarantee of Quebec's "special distinction," which he saw as tied to its "French-language culture." Stéphane Dion, "The Constitution Must Recognize Quebec's 'Special Distinction,'" *The Globe and Mail* [Toronto], January 26, 1996, A15. Dion thus presents a sharp philosophical contrast to his predecessor as Quebec academic turned politician, Pierre Trudeau.

15 For instance, in an Alberta newspaper he argued that a distinct society clause would not only offer legal protection to Quebec's

language and culture, but "more importantly ... and from a human point of view, it would be a way for all Canadians to express solidarity with Quebecers in their effort to preserve a vibrant and dynamic Francophone society in North America. It would show that all Canadians embrace their majority Francophone province as a fundamental characteristic of Canada." Dion, "Fears About 'Distinct Society' Status Are Unfounded," *The Calgary Herald*, July 18, 1996, A11. Such arguments from federal spokespersons are unusual, to say the least, in the West, and drew a stern rebuke from Reform MP Stephen Harper ("'Myth-breaker' Dion Peddles Own Propaganda," *The Calgary Herald*, July 27, 1996, A12).

16 In an Environics poll taken nationally in October 1996, 52 percent of respondents indicated disapproval of a distinct society clause, even "if it would keep Quebec in Canada"; only 34 percent approved. In the West, opposition reached 59 percent. Environics Research Group, *The Focus Canada Report 1996-3*.

17 Premier Klein of Alberta is expected to go to the polls as soon as or earlier than the federal Liberals, making any constitutional commitment on his part very unlikely in the short term.

18 Susan Delacourt and Edward Greenspon, "PM Cool to Vote on Distinct Society," *The Globe and Mail* [Toronto], December 10, 1996, A1. The Prime Minister reiterated this reluctance in a private meeting with the editorial board of *The Toronto Star*. Richard Gwyn, "PM Dodging the Defining Issue of His Rule," *The Toronto Star,* December 13, 1996.

19 Richard Gwyn, "PM Dodging."

20 Even if opposition developed to such an amendment in the Senate, as was the case with the Newfoundland proposal, under s. 47 the House of Commons can override a Senate veto.

21 Angus Reid Group, "Federal Political Trends and the Public Agenda: The National Angus Reid/Southam News Poll," December 9, 1996.

22 A Léger & Léger poll taken in early December 1996, after the resignation of the party leader, Michel Gauthier, showed the BQ still leading the federal field in Quebec with 44.3 percent support. Richard Mackie, "Bouchard Losing Voter Support," *The Globe and Mail* [Toronto], December 19, 1996, A1.

23 Paul Wells, "Axworthy Denies Ambassadors Pushing Plan B Abroad," *The Gazette* [Montreal], December 17, 1996.

24 Hugh Winsor, "Information Agency Lauds Liberals," *The Globe and Mail* [Toronto], September 17, 1996, A4.

25 Ibid.

26 Canada, "Canada Information Office: Its Mission, Its Mandate, Its Activities," Press Release, no date.

27 http://www.infocan.gc.ca

28 "The Speech Jacques Parizeau Never Got to Give," *The Globe and Mail* [Toronto], February 23, 1996, A17; Philip Authier, "Here's What Would Have Happened if the Yes Vote Had Won the Oct. 30 Referendum," *The Gazette* [Montreal], March 2, 1996.

29 Bob Rae, "The Unfinished Business of the Quebec Referendum," *The Globe and Mail* [Toronto], December 12, 1995, A17. Rae's former deputy minister of intergovernmental affairs provided a carefully argued blueprint for how and why a response should be clarified before rather than after a future Yes vote. Jeff Rose, "Beginning to Think About the Next Referendum," Faculty of Law, University of Toronto, *Occasional Paper*, November 21, 1995. A shorter version of this paper was published in *Canada Watch* 4, 2 (Nov./Dec. 1995), 17-19.

30 Jeffrey Simpson, "Federalists Need a Plan B to Show to Secessionists in the Future," *The Globe and Mail* [Toronto], December 15, 1995, A20.

31 Of these the most impressive are Robert Young's exhaustive and relatively optimistic *The Secession of Quebec and the Future of Canada* (Montreal: McGill-Queen's University Press, 1995) and Patrick Monahan's more pessimistic *Cooler Heads Shall Prevail: Assessing the Costs and Consequences of Quebec Separation* (Toronto: C.D. Howe Institute, 1995).

32 Paul Wells, "Ex-bureaucrat Drafts Action Plan for Ottawa After Yes Vote," *The Gazette* [Montreal] March 5, 1996.

33 Quebec's self-proclaimed "right to national self-determination" has been tacitly or explicitly accepted by virtually all serious players, including the Prime Minister (who stated at his December 1996 CBC "Town Hall" appearance, "If ... a real majority of Quebecers, on a clear question, want to go, I'm a democrat." "Here's What the PM Said About Anglo Quebecers' Rights After a Yes Vote," *The Gazette* [Montreal] December 14, 1996). The Reform party has insisted that a simple 50 percent plus one vote would be enough to trigger negotiations. The James Bay Cree do not challenge Quebec's right to secede, only their right to take Aboriginal lands with them. The only voices suggesting coercion are those of journalists Diane Francis and Andrew Coyne.

34 Jeffrey Simpson, "A Strategy of Tough Love Would Prepare Canada in a Secession Bid," *The Globe and Mail* [Toronto] January 25,1996, A18.

35 I have argued this myself. Reg Whitaker, "Thinking About the Unthinkable: Planning for a Possible Secession," *Constitutional Forum*, 7, 2 and 3 (Winter/Spring 1996), 58-64.

36 Reform Party of Canada, "Reform responses to the twenty questions posed on June 8, 1994 to the Prime Minister of Canada," News

Release, December 5, 1995; "A fresh start for Canadians," News
Release, October 18, 1996, 21.

37 Other elements of Plan B may be in the bureaucratic works. A leaked
cabinet memorandum suggests a plan to limit Canadian citizenship
retention to post-separation Quebecers. See Alexander Norris,
"Citizenship Limits Okayed: Cabinet Approved Changes in Secret
Plan," *The Gazette* [Montreal], June 15, 1996.

38 House of Commons, *Debates*, September 26, 1996.

39 Allan Rock to Paul Bégin, September 26, 1996, copy released by the
Department of Justice.

40 An excellent overview of the issues can be found in Daniel Salée,
"Identities in Conflict: the Aboriginal Question and the Politics of
Recognition in Quebec," *Ethnic and Racial Studies*, 18, 2 (April
1995), 277-314.

41 Reg Whitaker, "Quebec's Self-Determination and Aboriginal Self-
Government: Conflict and Reconciliation?" in Joseph Carens, ed., *Is
Quebec Nationalism Just? Perspectives from Anglophone Canada*
(Montreal: McGill-Queen's University Press, 1995), 193-220. In this
article, I emphasized methods for reconciling conflicting claims
without recourse to partition, but today I would be much more
doubtful that partition can be avoided—although the idea of a formal
Quebec-Canada condominium in the north, with a high degree of
Aboriginal autonomy and self-government, might be worth consideration.

42 An even more pointed argument has been made that neither Quebec
nor Canada has strong legal claims over Ungava. Kent McNeil,
"Aboriginal Nations and Quebec's Boundaries: Canada Couldn't
Give What It Didn't Have," in Daniel Drache and Roberto Perin,
eds., *Negotiating with a Sovereign Quebec* (Toronto: James Lorimer,
1992), 107-23.

43 See the impressive case compiled by the Grand Council of the Crees,
*Sovereign Injustice: Forcible Inclusion of the James Bay Crees and
Cree Territory into a Sovereign Quebec* (Nemaska, Quebec: Grand
Council of the Crees, 1995).

44 A recent Supreme Court decision, *R. v. Côté* (23707, October 3,
1996), rejected a Quebec government argument that Aboriginal
rights had been extinguished within the former territories of New
France and ruled that Quebec Aborigines have the same rights as
those in other provinces and territories.

45 PQ Intergovernmental Affairs Minister Jacques Brassard has gone so
far as to deny flatly any Aboriginal right to secede, a right he
reserves to "peoples" like the Québécois, and has broadly hinted that
force would be used to prevent any secession. Elizabeth Thompson,

"Partition Forbidden: Brassard," *The Gazette* [Montreal], January 30, 1997.

46 Susan Delacourt, "Crees Turn Bouchard's Remarks to Own Benefit," *The Globe and Mail* [Toronto], January 30, 1996, A7.

47 See for instance, Mary Ellen Turpel, "Does the Road to Quebec Sovereignty Run Through Aboriginal Territory?" in Drache and Perin, *Negotiating with a Sovereign Quebec,* 93-106.

48 Paul Wells, "Quebec Separation Would Lead to Debate on Partition, Dion Says," *The Gazette* [Montreal], December 12, 1996.

49 "Threat of Referendum Hurts Investment, Chrétien Warns," *The Gazette* [Montreal], October 23, 1996.

50 Edward Greenspon, "Subtlety Order of the Day for Aspiring Successors to Chrétien," *The Globe and Mail* [Toronto], October 28, 1996, A8.

51 Liberal Party of Canada, *A Record of Achievement: A Report on the Liberal Government's 36 Months in Office* (Ottawa, 1996), 55.

52 Liberal Party of Canada, 1996 Biennial Convention, Ottawa, October 23-27, 1996, *Delegate Handbook,* 81-4.

4

Creating Opportunity or Creative Opportunism?: Liberal Labour Market Policy

PETER STOYKO

Orchestrated in the wake of a recession, the 1993 Liberal election campaign featured a highly publicized agenda of labour market reform. The Red Book's keynote—*"creating opportunity"*—emphasized the role of government in facilitating job creation and appealed to those disenchanted with the Conservative party's laissez-faire approach. "Liberals, unlike Conservatives, fundamentally believe that government can be a force of good in society," it was stressed within the Red Book; "[e]conomic growth is not a matter for market forces alone."[1] As the next election draws near, however, signs of a robust recovery have yet to materialize. The unemployment rate hovers around 9.5 percent, and employment growth has been lackluster. Attempts at labour market reform began on a promising note, but were quickly supplanted by deficit reduction and regional imperatives. Robbed of their flagship policies, the Reform party and the Bloc Québécois announced their intentions to campaign on job creation platforms during the next election.[2] The tables have turned, with one important exception. Unlike the previous Conservative government, the Liberals remain popular despite their lack of progress in creating tangible employment opportunities.

This situation cannot be explained by waning interest in job creation. Opinion polls continue to show public concern over the official unemployment rate, as well as heightened anxiety over a host of other labour market developments. In addition to chronically high levels of unemployment, Canadian labour markets have become subject to greater earnings inequality and reduced demand for low-skilled workers. This trend toward polarization became complicated by a growth in atypical forms of work, an aging workforce, reduced employment stability, and increased female labour force participation. Labour market policy has been slow to adapt to these secular changes. Gordon Betcherman characterizes the problem succinctly: "Although major differences clearly exist regarding the nature of appropriate reform, there is now widespread agreement that Canada's web of social and labor policies, largely designed in the 1960s, are not up to the challenges posed by the labor market of the 1990s and beyond."[3]

While the Liberals were adept at capitalizing on demands for policy reform during their 1993 election campaign, upon forming the government they soon found themselves confronted by a long list of new policy constraints. Businesses demand less government interference in labour markets, the politics of federalism have intensified, and deficit reduction has imposed additional constraints. The room in which policy makers are able to manoeuvre has diminished considerably. Under these circumstances, there would seem to be few policy options that do not either betray the expectations of Red Book reform or directly combat the contentious forces that limit federal government involvement in labour markets. Ultimately, the Chrétien government contented itself with putting a brave face on a significantly diminished role. The result is breathtaking in its irony. While the Red Book promised an alternative to the laissez-faire policies of the Conservative party, the Liberals' political technique has helped make less interventionist government more politically palatable. The technique itself is an inventive mixture of political calculation, cutback management tactics, cosmetic marketing, and high-tech fetishism—a policy recipe that some suggest is the defining feature of a "new politics" of welfare state retrenchment.[4]

THE RED BOOK AGENDA

Historically, labour market policy has served several functions. As part of the welfare state, labour market programs help ameliorate various social cleavages by redistributing income among regions and income classes. By insuring against the risk of unemployment, labour market programs provide individual workers with a measure of income security. By providing income security for a significant portion of workers, these programs provide economic stabilization during fluctuations in the business cycle. All three functions have been prominent features of "passive" income support measures, such as Unemployment Insurance (UI), since the beginning of the postwar era.[5] In addition, labour market policies such as make-work schemes and employment protection legislation have operated proactively to directly stimulate or stabilize demand for workers, and have provided a regulatory framework to deal with various workplace exigencies, such as labour law. In recent decades, however, a set of priorities related to labour supply has captured the attention of policy makers. Labour market policy may be viewed as a means by which businesses are made more competitive through the cultivation of a more flexible and skilled workforce. In the process, unemployed workers are said to become better equipped to find suitable employment. The Mulroney government emphasized this supply-side role over the more traditional welfare state approach, first with the development of the Canadian Jobs Strategy (1985) and then with the Labour Force Development Strategy (1990). These "active" labour market policies were the core of the UI system's "developmental uses," and included training, work experience, wage subsidies to encourage training within the workplace, and employment counselling. Given the variety of labour market policy functions, a systematic analysis of the Red Book is required to determine whether a coherent labour market agenda exists and, if so, whether it represents a departure from the Conservatives' treatment.

The Red Book pays homage both to the traditional welfare state ("social support network") functions of labour market policy and to the mobilization of labour supply, although its emphasis clearly lies with the latter, vis-à-vis the creation of a market environment conducive to private investment and the promotion of the "job readiness" of workers.[6] Table 4.1 provides a detailed overview of the Red Book's labour market commitments. A shift from passive support programs to active measures is emphasized, with an entire chapter devoted to "investment in people." The labour market pillars of this investment[i] are further development of apprenticeship and training, the creation of a Canadian Youth Service Corps to foster career development among young workers, and the creation of new child care spaces to ease the burden on working parents (discussed further in chapter 10 of this volume). The Youth Service Corps is the only proposal to include a specific funding target, $100 million per annum. While the Liberals stressed the need to reduce dependence on government transfers, the Red Book implies more of an integration of active measures and income support than a wholesale cutback of the latter: "Liberals believe that people experiencing economic difficulty must have income support available to them through social assistance."[7] This stance is understandable, given the political popularity of the historically rooted and regionally sensitive UI program. All told, this set of proposals does not represent a large-scale departure from the Conservatives' stated philosophy, although the Red Book correctly notes that the Mulroney government exacted substantial cuts in both active and passive measures during most of its term in office.[8]

The second touchstone of the Red Book agenda is, after enhanced career development, the creation of robust job growth. This is accomplished through two additional initiatives. The first initiative is new public works programs. The technologically inclined Infrastructure Works Program is a two-year project designed to upgrade Canada's infrastructure, create immediate jobs, and develop worker skills. Its $6 billion funding target is to be shared equally by federal, provincial, and municipal governments. The Residential Rehabilitation Assistance Program is a housing renovation program designed to add $50 million of new housing renovations to run-down neighbourhoods. The second job growth initiative is a general reduction of the regulatory and paper burden on businesses, particularly small and medium-sized ones, and the cultivation of co-operation between the major labour market stakeholders, notably business, labour, and educational institutions.

Table 4.1

The Red Book's Labour Market Commitments

Active labour market programs

General commitment: Increase "investment in people," with emphasis on high-tech skill development and co-operation with the provinces, educational institutions, and the private sector.

Specific commitments:

- Apprenticeship:
  i. increase funding for apprenticeship programs,
  ii. increase apprenticeship opportunities for women, minorities, and people with disabilities, and
  iii. establish common training certification standards for occupations without apprenticeship programs.
- Canadian Youth Service Corps: create an agency to support youth-oriented career development initiatives with funding of $100 million per year.
- Training: provide "significant increases" in workplace training, via both the unemployment insurance system and co-operation with the provinces and the private sector.
- Child care: create up to 150,000 new child care spaces, contingent upon provincial co-operation and a 3 percent economic growth rate.

Passive labour market programs

General commitment: Provide better integration of active measures within the UI system.

Specific commitment:

- Unemployment Insurance: "maintain" the UI system and redirect a portion of benefit spending to help the unemployed acquire skills.

Direct employment creation measures

General commitment: Invest in "state-of-the-art" infrastructure to create jobs quickly, develop worker skills, and bolster long-term economic growth.

Specific commitments:

- Infrastructure Program: create a two-year, $6 billion public works program to be funded equally by federal, provincial, and municipal governments.
- Residential Rehabilitation Assistance Program: create a two-year, $50 million housing renovation program for older, modest-income communities.

Regulatory measures

General commitment: Reduce the regulatory burden on business and foster co-operation between business, labour, and government.

Specific commitment:

- Regulatory and Paper Burdens: reduce the regulatory burden on business, particularly for small and medium-sized businesses.

Source: Created by author from the Liberal Party, *Creating Opportunity*.

No particular regulatory or partnership proposals are made. No specific employment goals are mentioned. One may infer from the 1993 election campaign that double-digit unemployment is considered unacceptable. On the first day of the election campaign, Kim Campbell was confronted with Liberal criticism of her suggestion that a single-digit unemployment rate was not a realistic goal for the next four years, but may come to fruition by the turn of the century.[9] It is a round of heckling that has come to haunt the Liberals, because their labour market agenda proved insufficient to address the problems and withstand the constraints imposed by the new policy environment.

THE NEW POLICY ENVIRONMENT

The steady growth in unemployment in industrialized nations has spawned a great deal of speculation on the causes and consequences of labour market change. Growth in the official unemployment rate in Canada, from a decade average of 6.7 percent in the 1970s to 10.1 percent so far in the 1990s, is now old news.[10] Alternative measures of unemployment, particularly those showing increased unemployment among poorly educated youth and the long-term unemployed, are revealing and suggest the need for more targeted policies. As disconcerting as these trends may be, it is widely recognized that unemployment rates provide an incomplete picture of changing labour market activity. It is therefore useful to look at what the empirical literature suggests is taking place within other facets of Canadian labour markets and to reflect upon how the possible causes of change also undermine government attempts to intervene.

Employment growth is showing an alarming trend in recent years. Whereas the Canadian employment rate grew astride the U.S. rate during most of the post-war era, the early 1990s have seen Canada's employment rate drop markedly toward stagnant European rates.[11] Moreover, a large portion of the new jobs created over the last two decades are part-time in form, such jobs growing from 14 percent of all jobs in 1975 to 23 percent by 1993.[12] Employment instability has increased by some measures, and there has been a polarization between long-term and short-term jobs across demographic and industrial groups.[13] For example, a recent OECD survey suggests that job turnover rates have not changed in industrialized countries since the late 1970s. Canada is the only major exception to this finding, with job turnover rates climbing steadily between 1977 and 1991.[14] Canada has thus moved from average levels of job instability to levels that are among the highest in the OECD. The growth in instability is most pronounced in the small business sector. This complicates the policy picture considerably, since small to medium-sized businesses are the overwhelming focus of the Red Book agenda. This emphasis is understandable, given the populist flavour of small business support and the increasingly difficult task of compelling large companies (particularly multinational ones) to hire new employees. Although small businesses have been a predominant source of employment growth in the 1980s, recent statistical evidence suggests that the relative size of small business employment growth tends to be exaggerated if the intense concentration of both job gains (42-48 percent between 1978 and 1992) *and* job losses in this sector (37-40 percent) is not taken into account.[15] Such figures highlight the dangers of an undivided focus on cultivating small business employment, especially when one considers the lower pay and benefit levels small businesses tend to offer.[16]

Trends in remuneration point to further employment challenges. Several studies suggest that the distribution of income from market sources has become increasingly unequal and polarized over the last few decades.[17] For example, Statistics Canada's official gini coefficient measure, an index between 0 (all incomes are equal) and 1 (one individual has all income within a population), shows that the distribution of family income from market sources has clearly become more unequal (from 0.386 in 1971 to 0.425 by 1994).[18] Most of this trend is explained by a polarization in the distribution of hours worked. A growing portion of the labour force is employed in "non-standard" work patterns, such as part-time work, self-employment, and short-term schedules, while a comparable share is becoming "over-employed" by taking on more overtime work. Indeed, there has been a boom in part-time, self-employed, and temporary work.[19] This growth in non-standard forms of work arrangement is fortuitous for many, particularly for workers with parental responsibilities. However, a large portion of this work is clearly involuntary. For example, the percentage of part-time workers seeking full-time employment has steadily increased since the mid-1970s, growing from roughly 11 percent of part-time employment in 1975 to just over 30 percent during the recession of the early

1980s and to 35.5 percent by 1993.[20] In many areas of the economy, particularly in the growing service sector, the increase in non-standard work arrangements has reduced job security, benefits, and the intrinsic rewards gleaned from work.[21] All told, these developments suggest that Canadian labour markets are experiencing not simply an immobility of labour supply, but a difficulty in prompting firms to create stable, long-term, and well-paying jobs for labour force participants of all education and skill levels.

While these developments pose a challenge to a government intent on creating jobs and career opportunities, confronting some of the causes poses a larger challenge still. One school of thought suggests that the competitive pressure created by globalized trade and investment compels business to minimize labour costs while adopting more flexible work arrangements.[22] In the process, businesses lobby government to provide more flexible labour markets and weakened labour market regulation. With various jurisdictions competing for business investment, there is pressure to lower the tax rates imposed upon companies and to reduce the intrusiveness of labour law.

A second school of thought suggests that new information and production technologies are causing large increases in unemployment by allowing organizations to do more with fewer workers.[23] These technologies also reduce the wages and the employment opportunities available to unskilled workers by placing a premium on both technological acumen and general problem-solving abilities.[24] With Canadian business's relatively poor record of investment in training, and information technology's bias toward "lifelong learning," the onus for a large portion of labour market training is being foisted upon the individual in the absence of government intervention.[25] Constrained by debt and deficit reduction, federal governments have limited ability to substantially increase training and other remedies. Government's inability to rein in the negative side-effects of computer technology is further compounded by a poor understanding of the nature of the problem and by the sheer scale of private investment in these new technologies.

Regional and federal politics have always been a key force in shaping labour market policy and have recently fostered an ideological shift from the post-Great Depression era view of the federal government as custodian of labour markets to the 1992 Charlottetown Accord's overwhelmingly provincialist vision. While Alberta and Quebec governments have long aspired to take over complete control of training, even historically less decentralist provinces, such as Manitoba, have demanded greater discretion over labour market program design (but perhaps not financing) to prevent fiscal off-loading and minimize the emigration of skilled labour. As deficit reduction gains momentum, pressure builds within the federal government to push users off more generous transfers (such as UI) and onto provincial schemes (such as welfare). The response has been the unyielding resistance to UI cutbacks within economically depressed regions, notably Atlantic Canada and Quebec, and provincial demands for greater control over labour market responsibilities. This was best illustrated in March 1996, when the provincial premiers demonstrated unprecedented consensus with their endorsement of the Report on the Ministerial Council on Social Policy Reform and Renewal.[26] This report called for provincial administration over income security, including that clearly within federal jurisdiction, such as UI, and some centralization to be handled by a national (but not necessarily federal government) authority.[27]

The combination of globalization, technological change, and deficit reduction has fuelled the spread of a public management philosophy espousing the virtues of service delivery through markets, reduced regulation of business, and reluctance to increase the tax burden.[28] This "new public management" approach to governance poses a challenge to traditional labour market instruments, such as income transfers, public works projects, and labour standards. Many public service reformers have embraced the notion of what Robert Haveman refers to as the "iron law of income support": "No single policy is capable of both assuring adequate income support to those without sufficient earnings (i.e. poverty reduction) and stimulating an increase in the employment of low-skilled workers."[29] Although empirical evidence indicates that the trade-off between social security levels and job creation is somewhat exaggerated,[30] it has become the starting point of policy reform proposals. Some go so far as to suggest that policy-making has adopted a "new paradigm," a new ideological predisposition that makes government policy-makers reluctant to interfere in labour markets regardless of larger transformations within the economy.[31]

It has yet to be determined whether these new challenges and constraints pose an intractable barrier to meaningful government action.

What does seem clear, however, is that the room to manoeuvre has diminished, and damage control strategies present a politically alluring alternative to direct confrontation of constraints. These strategies come in several forms. Budgetary tactics, perceived by the electorate as distributing the burden of cutbacks evenly among all major stakeholders, have a superficial ethical appeal and may be augmented by covert compensation to crucial political groups.[32] Much of this can be accomplished by altering the more technically complex facets of a program, either by "making the effects of policies more difficult to detect or by making it hard for voters to trace responsibility for these effects back to particular policy makers."[33] When the federal opposition parties and provincial premiers vehemently press for provincial divestiture or deficit reduction, the electorate tends to spread the blame for federal submission across the much broader group of politicians.[34] This provides the governing Liberals with the opportunity to capture favourable press by implementing cosmetic initiatives, particularly if they possess high-technology content. Some suggest that this leads to a "high-tech fetishism," whereby more substantive and suitable "low-tech" projects become quickly dismissed as passé.[35] In his 1994 budget speech, Paul Martin promised an end to such "stealthy" cutback management techniques and scolded the former Conservative government for its indulgences. The rest of this chapter provides a case study of the extent to which this promise was kept as the Liberals implemented the Red Book's labour market reforms.

PASSIVE LABOUR MARKET PROGRAMS

The far-reaching UI reform package announced in December 1995 was the culmination of a long process of brainstorming and negotiations that began in the spring of 1993, well before Human Resources Minister Lloyd Axworthy launched his Social Security Review. Employment Insurance (EI) became the program's new name, a title that underscores the government's emphasis on bolstering the job search activities of beneficiaries and provides a logo for the marketing of the program's reduced generosity. The intention to create an "employment insurance," a coinage made at the behest of Chrétien, was announced in Axworthy's 1994 Green Paper. Although subsequent consultation led many to expect a more earnest and transparent process, the process quickly became unwieldy. Once the Social Security Review's recommendations were released, the reform process was decidedly less public and more subject to the constraints lurking within government. Budget considerations, lobbying by the Liberals' Atlantic and Quebec caucuses, and the Finance Department's preference for a more user-pay approach, all conspired to provide EI with characteristics very different from the guiding principles outlined in the Final Report.

Total UI benefit payments having almost doubled between the late 1970s and the early 1990s,[36] the program became a conspicuous budget item and an obvious target of the deficit reduction process. The cuts arrived in two waves. The first round, $5.5 billion implemented over three years, was announced early in the Liberal mandate and came into force with the 1994 budget. [37] The political strategy by which these cuts were implemented has been described as Paul Martin's "blitzkrieg" approach to overcoming political opposition. "Each action would provide political cover for another action," suggest Edward Greenspon and Anthony Wilson-Smith, adding that Martin made it "difficult to isolate a single measure politically."[38] Benefit rates, previously reduced from 60 percent to 57 percent of previous earnings by the Conservatives (Bill C-21), were further reduced to 55 percent. Low-earning recipients with dependents were targeted to receive 60 percent of previous earnings, an increase in generosity for only about 10 percent of recipients.[39] This increase in generosity was offset by an increase in the number of weeks required for eligibility (from 10 to 12 weeks) and a reduction in the duration of benefit receipt (from an average of 35 weeks to an expected average of 32 weeks), both estimated to be disproportionate in their impact on low-income families, younger workers, and workers in the Atlantic provinces.[40]

The second round of cuts, $2 billion, or approximately 10 percent of benefit expenditures, was contained within the EI legislation (Bill C-12), which came into effect in July 1996. Unlike the cuts announced during the Chrétien government's honeymoon period, EI benefit reductions were faced with sensitized opposition within the Liberals' Atlantic and Quebec caucuses, as well as late mandate re-election plans. With the prospect of the Finance Ministry confiscating the resultant savings, Axworthy negotiated heatedly with Martin in order to reserve $800 million for active labour market programming. To secure broad acceptance for such programs, it was not enough simply to fold them into an integrated EI scheme: two additional measures were added. The first is a "transition period," whereby cuts are phased in over six years, which spreads the impact thinly over an extended (mostly post-election) period. The second measure, created with Atlantic Canada in mind, is a $300 million Jobs Fund designed to create jobs over a three-year (mostly pre-election) transitional period. The federal development agencies operating the Fund have a history of allocating money on the basis of political priorities, and in this case a large share went initially to the riding of the chief opponent of the EI budget cuts in cabinet, Brian Tobin.[41] The government signalled further sensitivity to Atlantic concerns in the cabinet shuffle of January 1996, in which northern New Brunswick MP Doug Young was given the Human Resources portfolio.

The EI cuts became operationalized in a complicated mixture of income targeting and insurance-oriented changes, making the assessment of winners, losers, and positive-sum gains a difficult undertaking. High-income earners become subject to a "clawback," whereby annual incomes greater than $48,750 (down from $63,570) are taxed back at a rate of 30 percent. The tax-back rate increases to between 50 percent and 100 percent depending on previous benefits received, with incomes over $39,000 taxed back at the higher rates if the recipient has claimed more than 21 weeks of benefits in the last five years.[42] A Family Supplement was added to provide more precise targeting than the former program's low-income dependent rate. By January 1997, a more select group of low-income recipients received up to 65 percent (80 percent by January 2000) of previous earnings. EI qualification also became based on hours worked instead of weeks, allowing the growing number of part time-workers access to benefits. This helps minimize the disincentives hindering full-time job creation, since the previous UI system provided a loophole whereby employers could avoid UI premiums by creating jobs with fewer than 15 hours of work a week.[43] Recipients are further encouraged to take on more part-time work to supplement benefits, a policy that provides incentives and assistance for those making the transition from unemployment to work.

EI compels frequent users to contribute a greater share of the financing burden in the hope of minimizing work disincentives, a reform that reverses most of the progressivity gained from new income-targeting reforms. The maximum duration of benefits for all users has been further reduced from 50 to 45 weeks. Experience rating is created by the program's modest "intensity" provision, whereby, according to one critic, beneficiaries are sorted into "the sheep and goats of frequent and occasional users."[44] Frequent users have their benefit rates reduced by as much as 5 percentage points, from 55 percent of previous income to 50 percent. The more generous rates provided to low-income recipients with dependents are also subject to this intensity rule. The same treatment is not afforded to employers who frequently lay off workers, a group that Axworthy derided as highly profitable big businesses with layoff practices subsidized by UI contributions.[45] Actually, the culprits represent 12 percent of firms (accounting for 38 percent of UI benefits paid) and are concentrated in the construction and primary resource industries of Quebec and the Atlantic provinces.[46] By not extending the experience rating principle to employers, the government avoided further opposition from politically sensitive regions. In the process, a source of job instability has been permitted to continue.

A less discussed, but nonetheless important, reform involves changes to the rate structure of EI premiums. Maximum Insurable Earnings (MIE) were reduced from $815 to $750 of weekly earnings and frozen at this level for four years, reducing high-income recipient coverage and premiums paid.[47] High-income recipients were net contributors to the UI scheme, because they were less likely to draw benefits.[48] This narrowing of the insurable earnings base reduces cross-subsidization and undermines progressivity, a user-pay reform hailed as more "market efficient" by intervening Finance Department officials. The Liberals have stated their preference for a reduction in EI premiums, which are borne by both employees and employers, based on the rationale that EI premiums tax away jobs.[49] These changes to MIE make this more difficult, according to Axworthy's own Social Security Review Final Report, because premiums are now paid by a smaller pool of employers and employees.

Despite the narrowing of the EI tax base, some modest premium reductions did take place. Employer premiums were reduced from $4.30 (for every $100 of insurable earnings) to $4.20 in the 1994 Budget, and then further reduced to $4.13 with the EI legislation. In November 1996, the employer premium was again reduced to $4.06 and a portion of the premiums are waived for some new hirings in 1997 and 1998.[50]

This New Hires Program, a tax holiday arguably designed to provide short-term employment stimulation in the period leading up to the next election, provides smaller firms with up to a total of $10,000 in relief. Another 10 cent reduction in premiums was included in the 1997 Budget. Although marketed as job creation measures, most changes were designed to free up tax room for Canada Pension Plan contributions. CPP contributions increased from 5.6 to 5.85 percent in January 1997 as a prelude to a much larger overhaul of the pension system, which includes a 69 percent increase in rates. All told, combined changes to EI premiums and CPP contributions amount to a significant increase in the payroll tax burden, and illustrate how deficit reduction and the aging of the Canadian workforce confound job creation initiatives predicated on payroll tax deductions.

ACTIVE LABOUR MARKET PROGRAMS

Active labour market programs have become the *cause célèbre* of public figures, politicians, and policy analysts, because of the political saliency of, to use the Red Book's phraseology, "investing in people." The bad news for the Liberals is that active measures, particularly high-skill training and continuing education initiatives, are very expensive. For this reason, the federal government has yet to devote more than 10 percent of UI expenditures to "developmental uses" since first introducing them in the late 1970s. Despite the political hype, federal active labour market expenditures (as a percentage of GDP) have declined slightly between fiscal years 1985-86 (0.65 percent) and 1995-96 (0.56 percent). The OECD average, in contrast, increased from 0.72 percent in 1985 to 0.99 percent by 1995.[51] The Canadian commitment does not increase appreciably if one adds the $800 million diverted from the EI account, scheduled to be spent on active measures by the year 2000.

Two political techniques have allowed the Liberals to obscure the magnitude of new investment in active measures. The first is the Human Resource Investment Fund (HRIF), a financing scheme created by the 1995 Budget to consolidate UI developmental measures into a global budget. This provides governments with a covert way of funding withdrawal: "Because there will be no new money for any of the government's stated [HRIF] objectives, it is difficult to imagine that the fund will serve any purpose other than creative financing."[52] The second technique involves increasing the number of distinct programs (or "tools"), which provides the impression of increased program spending and targeting in the absence of details of actual financial allotments. The EI program eventually provided $800 million in new funds for active measures, but spread these funds over a much broader array of active measures and over an extended period of time. The new package includes an array of programs falling under five categories: wage subsidies, earnings supplements, self-employment assistance, job-creation partnerships, and training funds. Since UI expenditures have declined, there are concerns that increasing pressure from Atlantic Canada will cause short-term job creation schemes (the $300 million Jobs Fund) to eat up a larger share of the active expenditures, effectively making EI a creative way of defunding the training and apprenticeships promised in the Red Book.[53]

For the most part, the specific active measures announced, HRIF and EI, have become moot in the aftermath of the Quebec referendum. Chrétien promised devolution of active programs, with attendant funding, to Quebec in November 1995. To reinforce the point, Quebec MP Pierre Pettigrew was made Minister of Human Resources and a formal devolution offer was put forth at the end of May 1996. Because the government did not wish to be shown pandering to Quebec, the first Federal-Provincial Labour Market Development Agreements were struck with Alberta and New Brunswick in December 1996. In exchange for stable funding over three years, all programs dealing with work experience, employment services (counselling, screening, and job placement), self-employment assistance, and training become the province's domain.[54] Without a framework in place to ensure that federal transfers are not used to finance existing provincial initiatives, however, there is little assurance that the Red Book's promise of training and apprenticeship increases will be fulfilled. Considering reductions in other federal transfers to the provinces and provincial deficit reduction efforts, the Red Book's promised increases will not likely come to pass.

The Labour Market Development Agreements have also prevented fulfilment of the Red Book's youth-oriented initiatives. Youth Services Canada (referred to as Canadian Youth Service Corps in the Red Book) was created in April 1994 to help out-of-school youth obtain work experience. Only 50 percent of the promised allocation of $100 million was devoted to the project by the 1996-97 budget year, a development the Liberals ruefully admit to be a partial fulfilment of a Red Book promise.[55] Frustrated by beleaguered youth employment growth in 1995, Chrétien resorted to goading business leaders into setting aside 1 percent of payroll costs to the hiring of young people. This act of moral suasion, stoking an ongoing negotiation between the government and business groups, became known as the "one percent solution."[56] The money eventually came from the 1996 budget, which set aside $315 million for new youth measures over three years. $60 million was spent on summer jobs before a new youth jobs plan was announced in February 1997. The plan focused solely on creating 30,000 summer jobs and 6,500 internships in areas that are closely tied to federal government ministries. Only 18- to 25-year-olds with some post-secondary education are accepted. This design ensured that the new youth initiatives do not conflict with plans to devolve active measures to the provinces. As Edward Greenspon points out, however, the new plan neglects young people without high school education (22.9 percent unemployment rate) and favours those with unemployment rates below the national average (9 percent), a contravention of both the 1996 Budget announcement's emphasis on targeting youth with low education levels and the Red Book's promise of a more comprehensive youth package that includes training and apprenticeships.[57]

The scaled-down youth initiative and moderate increases in student loan funding aside, the federal government is now left with a three-year active measure financing commitment and a role as custodian of vaguely defined active program standards. The only other policy area left is the dissemination of labour market information. In August 1995, the federal government announced a technologically endowed one-stop-shopping Service Delivery Vision. Up to 400 electronic kiosks and a telecommunications Service Delivery Network complemented a consolidation of Canada Employment Centres into a more streamlined set of parent and satellite Human Resource Centres. The Labour Market Development Agreements have replaced these centres with Federal-Provincial Service Centres and maintain the electronic kiosks. At any one time, however, the electronic kiosks typically offer fewer than 1,000 job placements across the country. The political benefit is far greater, on the other hand, allowing the Liberals to be seen investing simultaneously in high technology and employment enhancement.

The Liberals' primary foray into direct job creation involves the fulfilment of the Red Book commitment to create the Canada Infrastructure Works program. Federal offers were made to the provinces in November 1993 and shared cost agreements amounting to $6 billion were in place by February of the following year. The 1994 Budget fulfilled the much smaller infrastructure gesture, the $50 million Residential Rehabilitation Assistance Program. Although the Red Book's funding targets were achieved, other facets of the public works initiatives were not. Technologically oriented mass transit, telecommunications, and pollution control were to be the core infrastructure targets, particularly as envisaged by Red Book architect Martin.[58] This was an important selling point during the 1993 campaign, as Liberals attempted to convince voters that the initiative represented something other than an old-fashioned pork-barrelling exercise. Although the federal government was not in charge of selecting proposals, it did retain influence over selection and final approval. After 80 percent of expenditures were allocated, however, Liberal ridings granted funding were reported to have received an average of $5.38 million, while Reform and Bloc Québécois ridings averaged $2.18 million and $2.7 million respectively.[59] According to the Auditor General's review of Infrastructure Works, the selection criteria were broad enough to allow approval of numerous projects with little or no *prima facie* "infrastructure" content, never mind ventures oriented around high technology.[60]

Estimates of the total number of jobs created are also suspect, because the federal government did not take proper precautions to prevent a financing substitution effect. According to the Auditor General's estimates, around 35 percent of federal expenditures went not to new infrastructure initiatives, but to those already scheduled for implementation by the provinces.[61] Thus, Liberal estimates of 80,000 (eventually 100,000) new short-term jobs, and Treasury Board estimates of an additional 9,200 new long-term jobs, exaggerate the case somewhat.[62] When one considers this overestimation, in conjunction with the 45,000 jobs eliminated in the public service by the 1995 Budget, one is provided with an (admittedly crude) indicator of the net impact of the Chrétien government's direct job creation measures.

A second infrastructure program, a $1.8 billion version better tailored toward high-tech initiatives, was proposed by Chrétien in January 1997. With some provincial premiers expressing scepticism toward job stimulation ventures timed to coincide with the upcoming federal election (particularly in British Columbia and Quebec), the Liberals proceeded unilaterally by topping up 1997 infrastructure spending by $425 million (for a total of $600 million) in the 1997 Budget.[63] Given the absence of changes to the infrastructure project selection process, and a more frantic timeline for new project selection, many of the problems that plagued previous Infrastructure Works spending will likely persist. In order to bolster the high-tech cachet of direct job creation schemes, the Liberals resorted to marketing increases in research equipment grants—the $800 million Canada Foundation for Innovation announced in the 1997 Budget—as a "research infrastructure" reform.

LABOUR MARKET REGULATION

The Chrétien government's reform of labour market regulation has not been front page news, despite Liberal changes to federal legislation touted as the most dramatic since the early 1970s. This is somewhat understandable, given that the federal government's primary vehicle of labour market regulation—the Canadian Labour Code (CLC)—relates to only about 700,000 employees. This figure understates the strategic importance of the industries under CLC jurisdiction for the purpose of international trade.[64] Moreover, a number of recent government initiatives have placed these sectors on the front line of international competition. Examples include the "Open Skies" agreement on airline deregulation, the removal of the Crow Rate transportation subsidy, and privatization ventures (CN, airports, and marine authorities). Since these sectors are also highly unionized and contain some of the country's most centralized bargaining structures, the potential for new labour conflict is high.[65] This became clear when a series of labour disputes at CP Rail Systems, the Port of Vancouver, and the Port of Montreal brought much of Canada's transportation infrastructure to a halt in early 1995. The regionally sensitive shipment of resources and agricultural products stopped, prompting the federal government to enact back-to-work legislation aimed at Vancouver port employees. With the Red Book emphasizing labour market co-operation and the development of an internationally competitive infrastructure, high-profile interventions would not be politically sustainable.

In June 1995, Labour Minister Alfonso Gagliano created a Task Force, chaired by Alberta lawyer Andrew Sims, to discuss ways of making the CLC's collective bargaining provisions (Part I) consistent with the new labour market environment. After a hurried process of consultation with labour relations experts and stakeholder representatives, the Sims Task Force submitted its report, *Seeking a Balance*, in February 1996. A central theme of the report was, consistent with the Red Book priorities, the creation of a more balanced and investment-friendly environment by streamlining and depoliticizing labour relations within federal jurisdiction.[66] The Report's primary recommendations were submitted to the House of Commons in November 1996. The most newsworthy change made to the CLC involved a ban on replacement workers in a limited set of circumstances, a limitation to be interpreted by a new Canada Industrial Relations Board (CIRB). The CIRB is given greater powers than the former Canadian Labour Relations Board in administering the CLC, a shift in responsibilities designed to move the more contentious labour relations issues out of the political arena. Not long after the legislation was introduced, however, Gagliano voiced concerns over the security of 16,000 jobs when Canadian Airlines threatened bankruptcy if the Canadian Auto Workers did not accept a series of wage cuts. Gagliano proceeded to take a highly expansive interpretation of the CLC and ordered the union to allow its members to vote on management's offer. Although the crisis was short-lived, it illustrates a reluctance to withdraw from political intervention when the Liberals' credibility on job creation is at risk.

CONCLUSION

If the Red Book's economic framework is conceived of as having two key tracks, job creation and deficit reduction, the first track is clearly the Chrétien government's weakness. On the issue of implementation of Red Book specifics, the lion's share of commitments remain unfulfilled or fulfilled in a nominal sense. Despite an attempt to better target UI benefits to a small segment of those with low incomes and with parental responsibilities, most increases in targeting have been offset by overall reductions in benefit coverage, generosity, and progressivity. The reinvestment of UI funds toward active measures now remains contingent on provincial inclinations. All training and apprenticeship programs are being devolved to the provinces, with few assurances that modest increases in spending are maintained. Youth career development initiatives were afforded less funding than promised, and have been reduced to a very narrow set of internship programs for a select cadre of youth, most of whom have above average employment prospects. It is estimated that about a third of Infrastructure Works Program expenditures simply went to finance existing initiatives. A large share of the new infrastructure initiatives were politically inspired low-tech projects. A streamlining of labour regulations took place, but a depoliticization of labour relations has not been demonstrated. Cunning political techniques seem to have played a large role in shaping Red Book implementation. A satisfactory report card grade would not seem warranted.

Specific Red Book promises aside, the criterion by which the Chrétien government will likely be graded during the next election is the creation of tangible employment opportunities. By January 1997, however, Statistics Canada recorded 76 consecutive months in which the unemployment rate was above 9 percent, the longest such sequence since the Great Depression.[67] The best spin that could be placed on aggregate employment statistics can be found in the Liberals' Red Book report card, *A Record of Achievement*, which cited 670,000 jobs created between the election and August 1996.[68] Of these new jobs, it remains to be said, only about two-thirds are full time. Frustration with these summary indicators led to a marketing strategy designed to downplay the importance of official unemployment statistics. The first signs of this strategy can be found in the 1996 Budget, which suspiciously left the government's unemployment rate estimates unreported—an unprecedented manoeuvre. Next came a $150,000 investment in a media package, released to Liberal MPs in August 1996 under the title *An Agenda for Growth ... A Jobs Strategy*. The kit furnished "selected economic success stories from each province, sample reports to mail to their constituents, a ready-made article for community newspapers with blank spaces for MPs to insert regional data, and a video that captured the highlights of Ottawa's economic record."[69]

With the federal government unable or unwilling to confront the constraints of the new policy environment, few new proposals seem likely as the Liberals prepare for the next election. The 1997 Budget's "Job Strategy" placed most of its emphasis on the job creation potential of the low interest rates, expenditure allotments from previous budgets, and some modest increases in post-secondary education support. These education initiatives, mostly loan and tax support for students and new research grants, only partially offset previous cuts in transfers to the provinces. With both Martin and Chrétien downplaying expectations by publicly suggesting that governments cannot create jobs but can merely create an environment conducive to job creation,[70] any election promises will likely amount to a diet version of the Red Book strategy. The tables have turned indeed, with very little to distinguish the Liberals' current platform from that of the previous Conservative government.

NOTES

The author would like to thank Sandra Bach, John Godard, John McLean, Leslie Pal, Gene Swimmer, and several federal officials for their helpful comments on earlier drafts of this chapter.

1 Liberal Party of Canada, *Creating Opportunity: The Liberal Plan for Canada* (Ottawa, 1993), 10-11.
2 Reform Party of Canada, *A Fresh Start for Canadians* (Calgary, 1996); Canadian Press, "Jobs, Economy Priorities for Bloc in Next Session," *Canadian Press Newswire*, September 12, 1996.
3 Gordon Betcherman, "Inside the Black Box: Human Resource Management and the Labor Market," in John Richards and William G. Watson, eds., *Good Jobs, Bad Jobs, No Jobs: Tough Choices for Canadian Labor Law* (Toronto: C.D. Howe Institute, 1995), 70.
4 Paul Pierson, "The New Politics of the Welfare State," *World Politics*, 48 (1995), 145.
5 See Leonard Marsh, *Report on Social Security for Canada, 1943* (Toronto: University of Toronto Press, 1975).
6 Charlotte Yates, "'Job Ready, I Ready': Job Creation and Labour Market Reform in Canada," in Susan Phillips, ed., *How Ottawa*

Spends 1995-96: Mid-Life Crises (Ottawa: Carleton University Press, 1995), 84.

7 Liberal Party, *Creating Opportunity*, 21.

8 For example, spending on UI developmental uses declined by 39 percent (in real terms) between the 1984-85 and 1989-90 budgets. Grattan Gray, "Social Policy by Stealth," *Policy Options*, 11, 2 (1990), 28.

9 Edison Stewart, "Jobs: Battle Lines Drawn," *Toronto Star*, September 8, 1993, A3.

10 Statistics Canada, *Historical Labour Force Statistics* (Ottawa: Minister of Industry, 1996), 162.

11 Craig Riddell, "Employment and Unemployment in Canada: Assessing Recent Experience," *Policy Options*, 17, 6 (July 1996), 11.

12 Henry Pold, "Jobs, Jobs, Jobs," *Perspectives on Labour and Income*, 6, 3 (Autumn 1994), 15.

13 Andrew Heisz, "Changes in Job Tenure," *Perspectives on Labour and Income*, 8, 4 (Winter 1996), 34-35.

14 OECD, *Employment Outlook* (Paris, 1996), 161.

15 Figures are for annual gross job gains and losses among employers with fewer than 20 employees. Garnett Picot and Richard Dupuy, "Job Creation by Company Size Class: Concentration and Persistence of Job Gains and Losses in Canadian Companies," Analytical Studies Branch, Research Paper 93 (Ottawa: Statistics Canada, 1996), 8.

16 René Morissette, "Canadian Jobs and Firm Size: Small Firms Pay Less?" *Canadian Journal of Economics*, 26, 1 (February 1993), 171.

17 René Morissette, John Myles, and Garnett Picot, "Earnings Polarization in Canada, 1969-1991," in Keith G. Banting and Charles M. Beach, eds., *Labour Market Polarization and Social Policy Reform* (Kingston: Queen's University School of Policy Studies, 1995); Charles M. Beach and George A. Slotsve, *Are We Becoming Two Societies?* (Toronto: C.D. Howe Institute, 1996).

18 Statistics Canada, *Income After Tax, Distributions by Size in Canada* (Ottawa: Minister of Industry, 1996), 35.

19 Grant Schellenberg and Christopher Clark, *Temporary Employment in Canada: Profiles, Patterns, and Policy Considerations* (Ottawa: Canadian Council on Social Development, 1996).

20 Betcherman, "Inside the Black Box," 91-93.

21 Harvey Krahn, "Quality of Work in the Service Sector," General Social Survey, Analysis Series No. 6 (Ottawa: Statistics Canada, 1992).

22 Prominent contributions include Ethan Kapstein, "Workers and the World Economy," *Foreign Affairs*, 75, 3 (1996).

23 Prominent contributions include Lars Osberg, Fred Wien, and Jan
    Grude, *Vanishing Jobs: Canada's Changing Workplaces* (Toronto:
    James Lorimer & Company, 1995); Jeremy Rifkin, *The End of Work*
    (New York: Tarcher/Putnam,1995); Chris Freeman and Luc Soete,
    Work for All or Mass Unemployment (London: Pinter Publishers,
    1994).
24 Kathryn McMullen, "Skill and Employment Effects of Computer-
    Based Technology: The Results of the Working with Technology
    Survey III," CPRN Study No. W-01 (Ottawa: Canadian Policy
    Research Network, 1996), 52-56.
25 Graham S. Lowe, "The Future of Work: Implications for Unions,"
    The Fourteenth Sefton Memorial Lecture, University of Toronto,
    March 27, 1996, 14.
26 Ministerial Council on Social Policy Reform and Renewal, *Report To
    Premiers* (St. John's: Newfoundland Information Service, 1995).
27 Michael Mendelson, *The Provinces' Position: A Second Chance for
    the Social Security Reform?* (Ottawa: The Caledon Institute of Social
    Policy, 1996), 6.
28 Sandford Borins, "The New Public Management Is Here to Stay,"
    Canadian Public Administration, 38, 1 (Spring 1995), 123.
29 Robert Haveman, "Reducing Poverty While Increasing Employment:
    A Primer on Alternative Strategies, and a Blueprint," *OECD
    Economic Studies*, 26, 1 (1996), 29.
30 Miles Corak, "Unemployment Insurance, Work Disincentives, and
    the Canadian Labour Market: An Overview," Analytical Studies
    Branch, Research Paper 62 (Ottawa: Statistics Canada, 1994), 46.
    See also Anthony B. Atkinson and Gunnar Viby Mogensen, eds.,
    Welfare and Work Incentives: A North European Perspective
    (Oxford: Clarendon Press, 1993); Rebecca M. Blank, ed., *Social
    Protection Versus Economic Flexibility: Is There a Trade-Off?*
    (Chicago: University of Chicago Press, 1994).
31 John Godard, "Managerial Strategies, Labour and Employment
    Relations, and the State: The Canadian Case and Beyond," 1995
    Labour Process Conference (Blackpool, England), 28.
32 Robert Behn, "Cutback Budgeting," *Journal of Policy Analysis and
    Management*, 4, 2 (1985), 158; Robert Behn, "How To Terminate a
    Public Policy: A Dozen Hints for the Would-be Terminator," *Policy
    Analysis*, 4, 3 (Summer 1977), 407.
33 Pierson, "The New Politics," 147.
34 For an account of this dynamic, see R. Kent Weaver, "The Politics of
    Blame Avoidance," *Journal of Public Policy*, 6 (October–December,
    1986).

35 Sylvia Ostry and Richard R. Nelson, *Techno-Nationalism and Techno-Globalism* (Washington: The Brookings Institution, 1995), 60-61.

36 From $10.6 billion in 1978 to $19.7 billion by 1992. Human Resources Development Canada, *From Unemployment Insurance to Employment Insurance: Improving Social Security in Canada, A Supplementary Paper* (Ottawa: Minister of Supply and Services Canada, 1994), 11.

37 Lloyd Axworthy, Minister of Human Resources Development, *Proposed Changes to the Unemployment Insurance Program* (Ottawa: HRDC, 1994).

38 Edward Greenspon and Anthony Wilson-Smith, *Double Vision: The Inside Story of the Liberals in Power* (Toronto: Doubleday Canada, 1996), 243-44.

39 Michael Kidd and Michael Shannon, "An Empirical Analysis of Recent Legislative Changes to Unemployment Insurance: The Effects of Bill C-21 and the 1994 Budget," *Canadian Journal of Economics*, 29, Special Issue (1996), S16.

40 Ibid., S15.

41 Herman Bakvis, "Shrinking the House of 'HRIF': Program Review and the Department of Human Resources Development," in Gene Swimmer, ed., *How Ottawa Spends 1996-97: Life Under the Knife* (Ottawa: Carleton University Press, 1996), 152.

42 HRDC, *A 21st Century Employment System for Canada: Guide to the Employment Insurance Legislation* (Ottawa, 1995), 13.

43 Alice Nakamura, "Employment Insurance: A Framework for Real Reform," *C.D. Howe Institute Commentary*, 85 (October 1996), 8.

44 Tom Kent, "Ideas in the Wrong Order," in Ken Battle, ed., *Critical Commentaries on the Social Security Review* (Ottawa: Caledon Institute of Social Policy, 1995), 73.

45 Larry Welsh, "Big Business Abusing UI—Axworthy," *The Montreal Gazette*, October 18, 1994, B1.

46 Miles Corak and Wendy Pyper, "Firms, Industries, and Cross-subsidies: Patterns in the Distribution of UI Benefits and Taxes," Human Resources Development UI Evaluation Brief, 16 (March 1995), 10-12.

47 HRDC, *A 21st Century Employment System for Canada*, 17.

48 For example, workers earning over $50,000 per year constitute less than 3 percent of UI claimants, despite making up 12 percent of the labour force. HRDC, *From Unemployment Insurance to Employment Insurance: A Supplementary Paper, Improving Social Security In Canada* (Ottawa: Minister of Supply and Services Canada, 1994), 83.

49 It should be noted, however, that Canadian payroll taxes are among the lowest in the OECD, and roughly half the level (as a percentage of GDP) of U.S. payroll taxes. OECD, *Revenue Statistics of OECD Member Countries, 1965-1994* (Paris, 1996).

50 HRDC, "EI Premiums Reduced, Additional Premium Relief for Small Businesses in New Hires Program," News Release, November 19, 1996, 1.

51 OECD, *Employment Outlook* (Paris, 1996). Greece, Ireland, Italy, the Czech Republic, Mexico, and Turkey are excluded because of inadequate data. Western Germany data are only for the period prior to 1991. Canadian figures are for the federal government only.

52 Ken Battle and Sherri Torjman, *How Finance Re-Formed Social Policy* (Ottawa: The Caledon Institute of Social Policy, 1995), 11.

53 Bakvis, "Shrinking the House of HRIF," 155.

54 Alberta and New Brunswick were granted $317 million and $236 million respectively, to be paid out over three years. HRDC, "Canada and Alberta Sign Agreement on Labour Market Development," News Release, December 6, 1996; HRDC, "Canada and New Brunswick Sign Labour Market Development Agreement," News Release, December 13, 1996.

55 Liberal Party of Canada, *A Record of Achievement* (Ottawa, 1996), 32.

56 Canadian Press and Calgary Herald, "PM Issues Job Challenge," *Calgary Herald*, February 29, 1996, D9.

57 Edward Greenspon, "Youth Job Plan Sidesteps Training," *The Globe and Mail* [Toronto], February 6, 1997, A1.

58 Greenspon and Wilson-Smith, *Double Vision*, 381.

59 Canadian Press, "Infrastructure Money Flows to Repairs in Liberal Ridings," *The Globe and Mail* [Toronto], November 4, 1994, A9.

60 Auditor General of Canada, *Report of the Auditor General of Canada to the House of Commons* (Ottawa: Minister of Public Works and Government Services Canada, 1996), 26-13.

61 Ibid. 26-28.

62 Liberal Party, *A Record of Achievement*, 53; Treasury Board of Canada, Secretariat, *Performance Report for the Period Ending March 31, 1996* (Ottawa: Minister of Public Works and Government Services Canada, 1996), 28.

63 Department of Finance, *The Government's Jobs Strategy, Budget 1997* (Ottawa: Department of Finance, 1997), 16.

64 This covers the following sectors: broadcasting, chartered banks, postal service, airports and air transportation, shipping and navigation, interprovincial or international transportation, telecommunications, and a few industries "declared for the general advantage of

Canada" (most notably grain handling). Some crown corporations, Canada's two territories, and labour relations on First Nations reserves are also covered.

65 Almost 50 percent of workers under federal jurisdiction are covered by collective agreements.

66 HRDC, *Seeking a Balance* (Ottawa, 1996), 15.

67 Barrie McKenna, "Jobless Rate Stuck in High Gear," *The Globe and Mail* [Toronto], February 8, 1997, A1.

68 Liberal Party, *A Record of Achievement*, 12.

69 E. Kaye Fulton and Mary Janigan, "The Heat Is On," *Macleans*, 109, 41 (October 7, 1996), 17.

70 Edward Greenspon, "PM Challenged on Jobs, Quebec," *The Globe and Mail* [Toronto], December 11, 1996, A1.

5

International Trade as Foreign Policy: "Anything for a Buck"

CLAIRE TURENNE SJOLANDER

Jean Chrétien came to office in 1993 having made few explicit promises with respect to international trade. The Liberal party's most significant pledge concerned the need to renegotiate the North American
Free Trade Agreement (NAFTA), which was to come into effect on
January 1, 1994. Chrétien promised not to scrap the deal, as the NDP
would have done, nor to accept it wholeheartedly, as the Conservatives
had already done, but rather to modify it by negotiating a subsidies
code, changed rules on dumping, and new provisions on energy.[1] Apart
from this commitment to travel the partisan middle ground on North
American free trade, and despite the significance of the global marketplace for the Canadian economy, trade issues were not given much
space in the Liberal party's election platform, *Creating Opportunity:
The Liberal Plan for Canada* (the Red Book). In part, this illustrates
the paradox of trade policy for any capitalist state such as Canada:

firms are the key players in international trade, and governments have limited ability to influence the activities of those firms. Beyond NAFTA, therefore, Liberal commitments made during the 1993 campaign were limited to assisting Canadian firms to become more aggressive traders: "More Canadian businesses *must* become exporters, and government *must* help them develop the knowledge and skills to make that possible."[2] To that end, the Red Book commits the Liberal government to enhancing the ability of the Trade Commissioner Service (of the former Department of External Affairs and International Trade) to identify export and investment opportunities for Canadian firms.

While very little is said in the Red Book regarding trade, how it is said is particularly revealing. As Doern and Tomlin have suggested, while trade and industrial policy have often been treated as separate issues, over the past decade they have become increasingly linked, in part as a response to the realities of globalization.[3] In important ways, trade policy has become *de facto* industrial policy, in that the sweeping changes in the global economy have limited the scope for "domestic" industrial policy action, thus "internationalizing" industrial policy and necessarily intermingling it with international trade. The Red Book reflects this linkage, treating trade policy as *industrial* policy in a general discussion of the need to foster a more competitive and innovative Canadian economy, but not treating trade as a *foreign* policy issue. The (even thinner) discussion of foreign policy in the Red Book concentrates on the need to distinguish Canada's international presence from that of its American neighbour, reiterates Canadian commitments to peacekeeping, foreign aid, and multilateral forums, and pledges to democratize the process of foreign policy-making.[4] Liberal foreign policy as described in the Red Book contrasts the party's broad international orientation with characterizations of the Mulroney government's "obsession" with the United States,[5] and advocates a return to the "internationalist values" that were Lester B. Pearson's legacy to the Liberal party and to the country.

The conceptual separation of trade policy from foreign policy illustrates a recurring theme of the current Liberal government. Trade is money, and foreign policy, even within the context of an internationalist legacy, is a luxury that cannot always be afforded. As a result, trade policy is compartmentalized and isolated from the general context of Canadian foreign policy, and the impact of trade policy upon the conduct of foreign policy is discounted. This separation of trade from foreign policy is particularly ironic, given that it is precisely trade—in the image of "Team Canada" on the international hustings—that has become the hallmark of the Prime Minister's foreign policy initiatives.

Following from this observation of the separation of trade and foreign policies, this chapter presents two interrelated arguments. First, while trade policy is in important respects an "add-on" to foreign policy in the organization of the Department of Foreign Affairs and International Trade,[6] trade policy is now the "tail" that has begun to wag the foreign policy "dog." Broad foreign policy objectives are in large part secondary to the requirements of international trade promotion, with attendant consequences for the "internationalist values" applauded in the Red Book. Second, the attempt to distinguish Canada from the United States on the international stage has contributed to the tendency to give priority to international trade initiatives. In this respect, the "Team Canada" forays of the Chrétien government, while rooted in different understandings of the nature of the Canadian and international economies, harken back to policies of previous Liberal administrations, notably the trade diversification initiatives of the Trudeau government in the 1970s. Ironically, the Chrétien government finally appears to be putting into effect the policies that were promoted in 1970, when Trudeau's foreign policy papers, *Foreign Policy for Canadians*, were published. The Trudeau government rejected Canada's internationalist legacy, at least on paper, and argued that "Canada's 'traditional' middle-power role in the world seemed doomed to disappear."[7] While the Trudeau government in reality contributed to the maintenance of the internationalist legacy of Canadian foreign policy,[8] the Chrétien government appeared ready by default if not intent to uphold the original "anti-internationalist" intentions of his predecessor.

CANADA AND INTERNATIONAL TRADE: CONTINENTAL REALITIES

"We Canadians like to think of ourselves as international traders ... but in an important sense we really are not. At most we are North American traders."[9] In these two sentences, the paradox of Canada's international trade position is made clear. While trade exports have been growing at an impressive rate as a percentage of the Canadian Gross Domestic Product (GDP), representing 36 percent of the GDP by the first quarter of 1995, 81.8 percent of those exports are destined for the United States.[10] This heavy reliance on the U.S. market has characterized Canadian "international" trade since the late 1940s,[11] and this concentration has proved a relatively constant source of concern for Ottawa policy-makers. The height of this concern was expressed during the Trudeau administration, and led to such initiatives as the creation of Petro-Canada, the Canadian Development Corporation, and the Foreign Investment Review Agency, after the release of the "Third Option" discussion paper by Trudeau's Secretary of State for External Affairs, Mitchell Sharp.[12] This document outlined three options for the Canada-U.S. trade relationship, and argued the case for the "third option": the diversification of trade away from the United States in order to reduce Canada's perceived trade vulnerability. This was to be accomplished through the active promotion of alternative markets for Canadian exports, notably Western Europe and Japan. It also set the stage for the creation of a "contractual link" with the European Community in 1976, and an increased diplomatic focus on Canada as a country of the Pacific Rim. By 1983, however, the failure of these initiatives to diversify trade away from the United States led to the official abandonment of the Third Option policy.[13]

In 1993, the Liberals under Jean Chrétien found themselves confronted again with many of the troubling issues they faced during previous terms in office, although the world, and, indeed, Canadian trade policy frameworks, had changed considerably. The "second option" had become the centrepiece of Canadian trade policy with the conclusion of the Canada-U.S. free trade agreement, and the subsequent negotiation of the NAFTA. The Liberal campaign against the FTA had provided the focus and much of the passion for the 1988 "free trade" election, and the Liberal party in opposition had continued to speak out against the continental intensification of trade relations. "The Americans have laid down the rules and the Mulroney government is once again dancing to their tune.... In these circumstances, we must not enter into a trilateral free-trade deal with Mexico," Jean Chrétien vowed when NAFTA negotiations began in 1990.[14] By 1993, however, the Liberal party had become less sanguine about the prospect of rejecting continental trade agreements out of hand, and Chrétien chose instead to campaign on the need to make changes to the Agreement. Doern and Tomlin argue that this was in part possible because the intensity surrounding the issue of continental trade agreements had diminished since the 1988 campaign. "NAFTA was presented as the 'FTA plus Mexico', simply a fine-tuning of the FTA. As a result, NAFTA generated less emotion, though not less opposition, than did the FTA."[15]

While the decision to campaign on modifications to NAFTA rather than its wholesale abrogation appeared to be a watering-down of Liberal opposition to continentalism, the changes envisaged by the Liberal government were hardly minor. The idea of changes to the Agreement had arisen from the 1992 election of a new president in the United States. President Bill Clinton insisted on the negotiation of "side agreements" to the NAFTA, covering labour and the environment, as a precondition for the Democratic White House's support of the Republican-negotiated deal. Chrétien's changes were to be made much later in the NAFTA game (with only weeks between the October 25, 1993 election and the January 1, 1994 implementation date), and were much wider in scope, as they would alter the substance of the agreement itself rather than append parallel issues to it. As Peter Cook has argued, in requesting the addition of a subsidies code and changes to dumping rules in the NAFTA "[Jean Chrétien] is asking for big changes, and an overhaul of the US trade remedy laws to boot."[16]

The stridency of the Liberal opposition to continental trade agreements began to lessen, however, within weeks of the Liberal government's election. In part, this can be attributed to Chrétien's decision *not* to appoint Lloyd Axworthy as the first Canadian Minister of Foreign Affairs, giving the nod instead to long-time Quebec MP André Ouellet.[17] Whereas Axworthy often openly displayed his anti-Americanism and his opposition to continental free trade,[18] Ouellet had little experience and few convictions with respect to foreign policy. Chrétien, however, anticipating a Quebec referendum, ensured through Ouellet's nomination a Cabinet with a senior Quebec Francophone in a senior portfolio.[19] In addition to Ouellet, another senior Liberal, Roy MacLaren, was appointed Minister for International Trade. In contrast to Ouellet, however, MacLaren did have knowledge and experience related to his portfolio, given that he had previously served as a trade commissioner and had developed a strong commitment to free trade.[20]

Having made a commitment to renegotiate the NAFTA, however, the Liberal government could not simply accept its implementation without changes. MacLaren, working with U.S. Ambassador to Canada James Blanchard, was able to get the government "off the hook" by establishing, in December 1993, "NAFTA working groups," which would continue to discuss the issues the Liberals found most troublesome.[21] While the government, including Minister MacLaren, continued to stress the importance of these ongoing discussions,[22] it was clear that under the Chrétien government the "free trade" faction of the party had taken over the reins of Canada's foreign trade policy. More significantly, and contrary to the claims of the Red Book, Liberal foreign policy now had an international trade component, based upon the acceptance of the NAFTA as government policy. With Roy MacLaren as Minister for International Trade and André Ouellet increasingly sounding "a lot like a finance minister or a trade minister,"[23] foreign policy was becoming *foreign trade* policy.

Yet the ascendency of Liberal "free traders" was not a signal that concerns over the concentration of Canadian trade activity with the United States were a thing of the past. In part, the concerns were born of the changing U.S. position in the global economy, and, particularly, of one of the most concrete manifestations of this change: the waning U.S. commitment to multilateralism.[24] Since the late 1970s, the U.S. Congress had driven the Administration to an increasing use of unilateral "solutions" to international "problems," largely through the unilateral imposition of trade remedy penalties upon trading partners. In substantial part, this growing disdain for international trading rules exhibited by the Congress had provided the impetus for Canadian negotiators to seek a free trade agreement with the United States: if multilateral structures were not keeping U.S. legislators at bay, then perhaps a more narrowly regional arrangement would. MacLaren himself characterized this change in the U.S. attitude as "a corrosive mood of unilateralism and even economic isolationism," a trend that, for a heavily trade-dependent country like Canada, is, "to say the least, unsettling."[25] In terms of the Canada-U.S. relationship, this unilateralism is witnessed in the spate of repetitive trade disputes, over softwood lumber, cultural industries, or agricultural products, among others. As the Department of Foreign Affairs and International Trade (DFAIT) has argued, "continued vigilance is needed to defend Canadian interests whenever U.S. regulators or special interests attempt to bend the rules of either the North American Free Trade Agreement ... or the World Trade Organization."[26]

This perceived vulnerability, while a motivation for the FTA and the NAFTA,[27] also resonated with the Liberals' 1970s inclination to diversify trade relations away from an overwhelming reliance on the United States. Although the FTA has led to increased trade between Canada and the United States as a percentage of total trade, this has in itself exacerbated the residual unease in Liberal ranks over North American trade relations. For this reason, the Liberal government's newly-embraced free trade commitment was broadened to include not only the United States and Mexico, but virtually anyone who would listen. In an analysis strikingly reminiscent of that done by Secretary of State for External Affairs Mitchell Sharp 25 years earlier, MacLaren and other Liberals "worried that so much of Canada's trade is with a single country, the United States."[28] The Liberal solution to this vulnerability was trade diversification, where possible, within the context of negotiated free trade agreements. These agreements have taken the form of the negotiation of NAFTA-like provisions with Chile, without the United States,[29] as well as the expressed desire eventually to extend NAFTA "rules for free trade throughout the Western Hemisphere and even beyond."[30] The Chrétien government's endorsement of the Free Trade Area of the Americas, announced at the December 1994 Americas Miami Summit, reflects another element of the commitment to freer trade. The Free Trade Area, expected to be launched in 1998, is a process parallel and complementary to NAFTA and other regional free trade agreements throughout North and South America. Equally, the Liberal government has participated enthusiastically in the Asia-Pacific Economic Cooperation (APEC) forum, actively promoting the initiative of Pacific Rim Free Trade by 2015. Free trade between North America and the European Union, a plan derailed for a time by luke-warm support from Washington and a "fish war" with Spain, has been a favourite theme of Prime Minister Chrétien's.[31] Free trade with Israel came into effect on January 1, 1997, in part following upon an earlier deal negotiated between Israel and the United States,[32] and free trade between Canada and the Palestinian Authority appears a possibility by May 1997.[33]

Beyond the attempted negotiation and occasional conclusion of formal free trade agreements, the Liberal government has embraced trade diversification through a series of "Team Canada" initiatives. These travelling international road shows with the Prime Minister as the star, and a supporting cast including cabinet ministers, provincial premiers, municipal government officials, and business leaders, have targeted quickly-growing regions of the world economy in search of trade and investment opportunities for Canadian firms. These high-profile delegations are considered necessary to give political importance to what are essentially business trips. As a senior official at the DFAIT argued, "We open the doors, and our business people walk through them. We can act as a catalyst and, if it comes down to competition between Canada and another country, that's where the political overlay can make the difference."[34]

In essence, therefore, the Chrétien government has had to contend with the "inevitability" of continentalism in an era of greater integration and globalization. The concession to the NAFTA, given previous opposition and campaign reticence, is testament to this continental reality. Despite this, however, the Liberals have continued to manifest unease over the U.S. preponderance in Canadian foreign trade, and have pursued alternate trade agreements—to implicitly, and occasionally explicitly, counterbalance the weight of the United States. These attempts to search out counterweights are reminiscent of similar moves undertaken by the Trudeau Liberal government, of which Chrétien was a minister, in the 1970s. It is to the highest profile of these initiatives, the "Team Canada" voyages, and the context in which they have become the hallmark of the Chrétien government's foreign policy, that we now turn.

(TEAM) CANADA AND TRADE/INDUSTRIAL POLICY

As mentioned earlier, the Liberal party had pledged in the Red Book to democratize the process of foreign policy-making. This democratization, in its early phases, took the form of the March 1994 National Forum on Canada's International Relations, and was followed by

Special Joint Parliamentary hearings on a review of foreign policy.[35] All of this energy led up to the February 1995 publication of the Liberal government's reaction to the parliamentary hearings and its own statement on foreign policy.[36] Both documents, unsurprisingly, highlight the importance of trade and investment relations for Canadian foreign policy (which is quite distinct from the position presented in the Red Book). The government statement defines "the promotion of prosperity and employment" as the first of three key objectives for Canadian international activities,[37] and devotes an entire chapter to that theme. What is particularly notable is that both the government's Response to the parliamentary committee and the Foreign Policy Statement mention and pledge to continue the already privileged "Team Canada" tours.[38] In this sense, the government's response to the democratization of foreign policy-making was to celebrate the previously chosen foreign policy instruments, which is not surprising given the general nature of the parliamentary recommendations, which made it possible for the government to agree with virtually every one.[39]

Team Canada trade missions first began a year after the Liberal government came to office, and followed upon two smaller-scale trade promotion visits by the Prime Minister—to Seattle for a meeting with APEC leaders in mid-November 1993, and to Mexico in March 1994.[40] These initiatives marked the first time in twenty years that a Canadian prime minister led a trade promotion mission, the previous occasion being Pierre Trudeau's visit to China. The first Team Canada tour, in November 1994, grouping together the Prime Minister, nine provincial premiers (Quebec's Jacques Parizeau refused to participate), Trade Minister Roy MacLaren, Secretary of State for Asia Pacific Raymond Chan, and roughly 400 business leaders, went to the Far East to visit China, Hong Kong, Indonesia, and Vietnam. In January 1995, a somewhat scaled-down version of Team Canada (roughly 200 business leaders) headed for Latin America, visiting Trinidad, Uruguay, Argentina, Chile, Brazil, and Costa Rica. In January 1996, the third Team Canada mission targeted South and Southeast Asia, touching down in India, Pakistan, Indonesia, and Malaysia. Finally, in January 1997, the now apparently annual winter Team Canada pilgrimage took politicians and business leaders (including, for the first time, the Premier of Quebec) on a whirlwind tour of the Republic of Korea, Thailand, and the Philippines. Each of these trade promotion tours has been greeted with

great fanfare, and out of each has come reports of millions if not billions of dollars in contracts, commercial agreements, and letters of
understanding between Canadian businesses and international partners.[41]

Of the Team Canada missions, there is no doubt that the first trip to
China was the most successful and attracted the greatest attention,
both from the Canadian public and from Canadian business. That trade
trip was characterized as a "$9-billion orgy of [contract] signings"
and involved the participation of more premiers than subsequent trade
missions and twice as many firms.[42] In some respects, the Canadian
government has been trying to recapture the public enthusiasm for
Team Canada trade missions ever since, despite the fact that the huge
economic payoffs reaped in China were obviously the result of months
and years of work by individual firms. In many cases, "[t]he actual
deals ... [were] worked out and often signed well in advance of the
trade mission, only to be signed again before the cameras."[43] There
remains a significant commitment to the principle of Team Canada,
however, with the government insisting that companies would not be
as willing to participate, given that firms pay their own way, if the
missions did not generate concrete results, and, further, that many business people expressed enthusiasm about the Team Canada format and
prime ministerial participation.[44] The relative success of Team Canada
missions is equally demonstrated by the willingness of provinces to
copy the lead of the federal government in planning their own international travels. An example of this was the "Team Quebec" voyage to
South America featuring Deputy Premier and Finance Minister Ber-
nard Landry and business officials representing 32 Quebec companies.[45]

The trade missions and the foreign policy agenda they represent were
clearly set in motion by International Trade Minister Roy MacLaren
and Finance Minister Paul Martin. Martin's concern with budget trimming and economic growth led officials in his department to argue that
"Canada's foreign policy in the rapidly growing Asian and Latin American regions must have 'a more explicitly commercial orientation.'"[46]
MacLaren, for his part, supported and encouraged the growing trade
promotion focus of DFAIT, believing that the department could do
even more to provide a competitive edge for Canadian firms.[47] By the
first Team Canada mission, conducted before the completion of the

foreign policy review, it became clear that trade had come to dominate foreign policy priorities, leading some to suggest that "the government does not have the political energy to deal with anything else on the foreign policy agenda except trade."[48] Even Chrétien, who as prime minister has demonstrated only limited interest in foreign policy, considered it worthwhile to promote trade through Team Canada diplomacy rather than showcase his internationalism in an address to the United Nations General Assembly, as has been customary for Canadian prime ministers in the past.[49] Given that trade does not even figure as a foreign policy issue in the Red Book, but peacekeeping and the United Nations do, this prime ministerial non-attendance was significant, and pointed to the re-ordering of Canadian foreign policy priorities.

The Team Canada trade missions, however, are not the last word on the Team Canada concept. Rather, these very public trips abroad are the "front line" of the Red Book pledge to assist Canadian small and medium-sized businesses to operate in the international marketplace. In the government's analysis, which estimates that every $1 billion in exports can create as many as 12,000 Canadian jobs, export promotion is explicitly linked to job creation.[50] Team Canada is very much the answer to the Liberal party's election pledge of "jobs, jobs, jobs." Beyond international travels, Team Canada has become the code word for an integrated, multi-department approach to international trade and business development, as announced by Roy MacLaren (also speaking on behalf of Industry Minister John Manley). This greater co-ordination between federal departments is in part driven by the period of budget cuts, which have been the hallmark of the Chrétien government, and which have forced departments to work together to gain the best advantage from limited resources.

Led by DFAIT and involving sixteen federal departments and agencies, Canada's International Business Strategy (CIBS) "co-ordinates the efforts of all federal departments and provincial governments involved in supporting the international business development pursuits of the private sector."[51] Through direct consultation with the private sector, the CIBS defines strategies for a variety of sectors (22 in 1996-97), which involve government and industry assisting Canadian firms to "capture emerging global trade, technology and investment opportunities."[52] National Sector Teams direct the development and implementation of sectoral strategies within the CIBS, and Regional Trade

Networks co-ordinate the delivery of federal and provincial International Business Development programs at the local level, particularly with respect to export preparation for small and medium enterprises (SMEs).[53] In addition, the International Business Opportunities Centre, jointly operated by DFAIT and Industry Canada, matches business leads provided by trade commissioners abroad with export-capable Canadian firms, particularly SMEs.[54]

These changes related to the implementation of the CIBS have meant that federal bureaucracies, particularly DFAIT, which bears the burden of export promotion, have had to become more service-oriented. This, as mentioned earlier, has happened at a time of unprecedented budget cuts. Since 1988-89 DFAIT's budget has been cut ten times, so that by 1998-99 cumulative cuts will amount to $292 million.[55] The annual budget for trade missions and trade fairs sponsored by DFAIT has declined to $20 million in 1996-97, from $34 million in 1994-95. The annual budget of the Program for Export Market Development has also declined sharply, from $19.5 million in 1994-95 to $11.5 million in 1996-97.[56] "Doing more with less," particularly in a Team Canada environment, has led to calls for a number of other cuts and some restructuring. In particular, proposals have been made to drastically reduce the amount spent on trade promotions with the mature economies of the Organization for Economic Cooperation and Development (OECD), except in Japan.[57] These proposals have arisen because prospects for trade expansion seem limited, as in Europe, or markets are well known to prospective exporters, as in the United States. More radical proposals have involved the partial or wholesale privatization of DFAIT's Trade Commissioner Service, in keeping with models developed in countries such as Germany and Switzerland. Under this model, much of the responsibility for trade promotion would be turned over to industry associations and groups, which are felt to be "far better placed than trade officials to know the markets they're after and to target them effectively."[58]

These proposals have been met with fierce, and so far largely successful, resistance within DFAIT. The Department argues that a privatized Trade Commissioner Service will only want to serve in profitable, established markets where it has experience, making development of future markets (a big part of the goal of the Team Canada approach) more uncertain. This could potentially lead to the freezing of current trade patterns, as potential opportunities in more "marginal" areas of the world economy are ignored. Of course, effective trade promotion in emerging markets requires a considerable presence on the ground, and this in itself is harder to achieve in an era of budget cuts.

On the whole, however, the Liberal government can point to a trade promotion "record of achievement"[59] with respect to its explicit (and limited) Red Book promises. The Trade Commissioner Service has been provided with some of the tools necessary to assist SMEs in the identification of business opportunities abroad. As Doern and Tomlin point out, however, this new trade promotion "service to clients" orientation places a premium on the knowledge and information role of governments, and "almost all of this information will be given to firms. Whether firms, as opposed to interest groups, actually *want* to use this information remains to be seen."[60] Further, whether it is appropriate that governments collect market intelligence on behalf of firms (and which ones?) is an issue that may raise difficult questions. At any rate, industry pressures for the (partial) privatization of the Trade Commissioner Service suggest that industry groups, at least, may prefer their own information to that collected by a government service, although, as suggested, this might not in itself lead to the expansion or diversification of Canadian trade.

The "Team Canada" initiative has emphasized the way in which trade policy and industrial policy have become synonymous. DFAIT finds itself driven to develop ever tighter relationships with the private sector and "domestic" departments, a process that is not in itself a negative one, but that certainly changes departmental culture. When the role of government in industrial policy is defined as the facilitation of international market access for firms, foreign policy is of necessity going to become a key component of industrial policy.

INTERNATIONAL TRADE AS FOREIGN POLICY:
WHITHER INTERNATIONALISM?

While the Liberal government has been relatively successful in meeting its limited Red Book trade policy commitments, it is more difficult to argue that its foreign policy objectives have been met. This is a result of the priority given to international trade. In particular, as trade has driven the foreign policy agenda, some of the veneer of Canada's internationalist legacy has begun to wear off. What then are the implications for the predominance of trade policy over foreign policy? After all, we noted earlier that the Red Book did not treat trade policy as a foreign policy issue, raising it instead within the context of a discussion of industrial and domestic economic policy. International trade and industrial policy has become a substitute for much of Canadian foreign policy, and as a result international trade has begun to crowd out other international (and more traditionally "internationalist") concerns. Jeff Sallot, writing for *The Globe and Mail* after the first Team Canada trade mission, highlights the trade-offs most starkly:

> The best way to read Ottawa's foreign affairs agenda is to set aside those earnest policy speeches delivered when the Liberals were in opposition and look instead at Prime Minister Jean Chrétien's travel log.
>
> It is clear that the Liberals have adopted an agenda that places international trade and economic relations at the top. Issues such as the environment, human rights, arms control, conversion of defence plants to civilian production, foreign aid and United Nations reform—issues that used to animate the Liberals in opposition—slip toward the bottom.
>
> The United Nations is about an hour away from Ottawa by jet, and Canada, one of the major troop contributors to peacekeeping operations, conducts a lot of business there. The Prime Minister has received invitations to speak to the UN, but has not made the journey.
>
> In contrast, Mr. Chrétien is spending 12 days on a trade-promotion tour to three faraway Asian countries.[61]

Well before the first Team Canada mission to China, the suggestion that there might be trade-offs between trade and other foreign policy concerns was already being raised. Secretary of State for Asia Pacific Raymond Chan mused that "[l]inking human rights to better trade relations with China could be a serious mistake," a comment echoed by a foreign affairs official, who suggested that "human rights concerns have taken a back seat to fears about possible instability ahead" if China were isolated from the international community.[62] André Ouellet, speaking to the National Capital Chapter of the Canadian Institute of International Affairs, remarked that "Canadians believe in healthy, balanced trading relationships," and pointed out the opportunities to establish such a relationship with China, all the while seeking a "constructive dialogue" with its leaders to bring them along the path of sustainable development, peace and security, human rights, and the rule of law.[63] The Team Canada visit to China saw human rights concerns raised so briefly "that one of the Canadian participants in the private meeting, Nova Scotia Premier John Savage, missed the oblique reference," while Canadian firms agreed to participate in the massive Three Gorges Yangtze River dam project and the Prime Minister signed a nuclear co-operation agreement with China to help promote Candu reactor sales.[64]

By 1995, the Liberal government no longer pretended to balance human rights and trade concerns. André Ouellet argued forcefully that "[f]oreign trade, which creates progress in the economy, is the best way of spreading ... [democracy] to the population. Therefore, Canada has expressed, through this new government, our desire to vigorously pursue a series of [trading] initiatives in a number of countries irrespective of their human rights records."[65] The fact that no Red Book promise, or indeed any other election commitment, would have led Canadians to conclude that this was the Liberals' desire was conveniently set aside. While human rights issues might be raised, they would only be discussed in private. The Prime Minister would not "do anything that would publicly embarrass his hosts, such as meeting with local human rights activists."[66]

In January 1996, André Ouellet was replaced as Minister of International Affairs by Lloyd Axworthy. Art Eggleton joined Axworthy at the Department as Minister of International Trade, replacing Roy MacLaren, and Pierre Pettigrew was added as Minister for International Cooperation. At first glance, the changes in personnel appeared to signal a new, more traditionally "Liberal" outlook in foreign policy. Axworthy had a long history of interest in international relations and brought with him a considerable scepticism of free trade and the United States, while Pettigrew had had previous experience with issues of international assistance during the Trudeau administration.[67] Considering that Art Eggleton, the third member of the ministerial triumvirate, lacked the experience of the trade portfolio that MacLaren had brought, there appeared to be a possibility for a re-examination of foreign policy priorities.

While Axworthy has indeed sought to emphasize a social dimension to foreign policy, raising in particular issues relating to human rights, land mines, and the welfare of children,[68] the re-ordering of priorities has yet to be felt. In part, this would seem to be a result of the time and energy necessitated by the U.S. Helms-Burton sanctions on Cuba's trading partners. The Helms-Burton Act has subjected companies doing business in Cuba to sanctions, including denying such companies access to business in the United States and denying corporate directors and their families the right to travel to the United States. Together with Eggleton, Axworthy has had to repeatedly defend Canada's foreign policy autonomy in the face of a petulant American Congress and a recalcitrant White House. The Helms-Burton issue has generated a tremendous amount of attention by the Canadian Cabinet and DFAIT, in part because it is both a trade issue and a foreign policy issue in the traditional sense, focusing as it does upon U.S. respect (or lack thereof) for international law. Helms-Burton is equally an issue of interest to Axworthy, for it allows him the scope to express some of the reservations he continues to have about American policy more generally. By drowning out other issues, however, Helms-Burton, with its significant trade component, has not easily permitted the (slight) shift away from a trade policy focus that was anticipated with Axworthy's accession as Minister. As trade policy continues to drive the agenda, the internationalist legacy of Canadian foreign policy is diminished, and the narrower and more utilitarian vision of foreign policy defined in 1970 in Trudeau's *Foreign Policy for Canadians* is closer to being realized.

CONCLUSION

There are, of course, choices to be made in the conduct of foreign policy, and the human rights-international trade tightrope is a particularly troublesome one. If foreign trade substitutes for foreign policy, however, and foreign trade is not understood to *be* foreign policy, then the potential challenges posed by this tension are effectively nonexistent. As one Team Canada official pointed out, "I would consider jobs and economic growth to be the chief domestic priority.... Far from getting away from that priority ... I would suggest that this [Team Canada's trade mission to South and Southeast Asia] is really working on creating jobs and economic growth in Canada. So it's not getting away from domestic problems or priorities, it's actually helping solve problems and achieve our goals."[69] If international trade is understood conceptually as domestic industrial policy, as in the Red Book, then concerns over human rights in foreign lands appear quite marginal to trade. The problem arises, however, when at the same time foreign trade becomes a synonym for foreign policy. Compromises to the internationalist values heralded in the Red Book are inevitable, and while they may be necessary, the government has not been particularly self-aware in adopting them.

The final irony within the context of the Red Book commitments is that in basing, however inadvertently, a definition of foreign policy on an instrumental trade rationality, the Liberal government seems more and more to be adopting the foreign policy spelled out decades ago during the Trudeau government's early days in power. In part this might suggest that globalization has "forced" a more self-interested foreign policy upon the Canadian government, which no longer has the luxury of foregoing economic possibilities, even in the face of violations to Canada's internationalist posture. In that respect, the Trudeau pronouncements may just have been premature rather than wrong, and Chrétien, schooled in that earlier government, has carried them forward to their logical conclusion.

Are there alternatives to the trade policy "tail" wagging the foreign policy "dog"? Paradoxically, some of those alternatives were suggested during the Mulroney administration, when human rights concerns played a far more visible and substantial role in the definition of Canadian foreign policy than they do now. If globalization has so changed the landscape in the last four years that there is no longer the scope to exhibit sustained concern for "internationalist" values, then the world is a sorrier place for it. The frustration with trade and foreign policy under the Chrétien government, however, is that the trade-off between trade policy and internationalism has not been addressed or debated; it has simply happened, and the fact that the Red Book does not treat trade policy as foreign policy suggests the reasons why. Whereas the Chrétien government sought to establish a more "independent" foreign policy reflecting Canadian values of "tolerance, openness ..., and respect for human rights worldwide,"[70] the values unselfconsciously expressed since their electoral victory suggest the extent to which trade policy has subsumed those internationalist concerns.

NOTES

The author would like to thank David Black, Alan Bones, Gene Swimmer, Bruce Doern, and Sandra Bach for helpful comments on an earlier draft of this chapter.

1 Peter Cook, "Just What Does Canada Want?" *The Globe and Mail* [Toronto], November 19, 1993, B2.
2 Liberal Party of Canada, *Creating Opportunity: The Liberal Plan for Canada* (Ottawa, 1993), Chapter 3 (emphasis added).
3 G. Bruce Doern and Brian W. Tomlin, "Trade-Industrial Policy," in G. Bruce Doern, Leslie A. Pal, and Brian W. Tomlin, eds., *Border Crossings: The Internationalization of Canadian Public Policy* (Toronto: Oxford University Press, 1996), 167.
4 Liberal Party of Canada, *Creating Opportunity*, Chapter 8.
5 In this respect, the Red Book's claims are particularly stark, stating that Canadians "do not want Canadian foreign policy to be determined solely through special personal relationships between world leaders," a thinly veiled reference to the personal relationships between Ronald Reagan and Brian Mulroney, and then between George Bush and Brian Mulroney. Liberal Party of Canada, *Creating Opportunity,* Chapter 8.
6 See, for example, Kim Richard Nossal, *The Politics of Canadian Foreign Policy,* 3rd edition (Scarborough: Prentice Hall Canada, 1997), 234-64.
7 Canada, Secretary of State for External Affairs, *Foreign Policy for Canadians* (Ottawa: Information Canada, 1970), main booklet, 6.
8 See Kim Richard Nossal, *The Politics of Canadian Foreign Policy*, 59.
9 Drew Fagan, "Why Chrétien and Co. are Hitting the Road Again," *The Globe and Mail* [Toronto], January 19, 1995, A15.
10 Department of Foreign Affairs and International Trade, *Overview: Canada's International Business Strategy* (Ottawa: Supply and Services Canada, 1996), 3, 5. Exports of goods and services as a percentage of GDP have risen steadily over the past few years, up from 26.3 percent in 1992 through 29.4 percent in 1993, 33.2 percent in 1994, to 36 percent in the first quarter of 1995. This growth is reflective in part of new trade agreements (the Canada-United States free trade agreement [FTA], the North American free trade agreement [NAFTA], and the World Trade Organization [WTO]), as well as the deepening of globalization.
11 Claude Masson, "La politique commerciale," in Paul Painchaud, ed., *From Mackenzie King to Pierre Trudeau: Forty Years of Canadian*

Diplomacy, 1945-1985 (Québec: Les presses de l'Université Laval, 1989), 539.

12 Mitchell Sharp, "Canada-US Relations: Options for the Future," *International Perspectives* (Autumn 1972). The first two options were rejected as incapable of resolving Canada's trade vulnerability. The first option outlined was the maintenance of the status quo in Canada-U.S. trade, while the second option was the pursuit of a free trade arrangement with the United States.

13 See External Affairs Canada, *Canadian Trade Policy for the 1980s* (Ottawa: Supply and Services Canada, 1983). This document promoted a modified version of the "second option," calling for sectoral trade agreements with the United States following the model of the Auto Pact.

14 Terence Corcoran, "Liberal Platform Takes Another Pounding," *The Globe and Mail* [Toronto], December 13, 1994, B2.

15 G. Bruce Doern and Brian W. Tomlin, "Trade-Industrial Policy," 172. On the intensity of the 1988 opposition to the FTA, see G. Bruce Doern and Brian W. Tomlin, *Faith and Fear: The Free Trade Story* (Toronto: Stoddart, 1991).

16 Peter Cook, "Just What Does Canada Want?" B2.

17 Arguing that "External Affairs" was a holdover from Canada's colonial past, the Liberal government changed the name of the Department of External Affairs to the Department of Foreign Affairs and International Trade (DFAIT) and appointed a Minister at its helm, rather than a Secretary of State. As André Ouellet argued, this second change avoided confusion between the Minister and the two newly appointed Secretaries of State (Christine Stewart for Latin America and Africa and Raymond Chan for Asia Pacific), who would assist him. See André Ouellet, "The Commitments of a Liberal Foreign Policy Agenda," *Canadian Foreign Policy* 1, 3 (Fall 1993), 2.

18 On this point, see Kim Richard Nossal, *The Politics of Canadian Foreign Policy*, 188-89. As Nossal also mentions, a clear illustration of Axworthy's opposition to continentalism can be found in Lloyd Axworthy, "Canadian Foreign Policy: A Liberal Party Perspective," *Canadian Foreign Policy* 1, 1 (Winter 1992/93), 7-10.

19 Kim Richard Nossal, *The Politics of Canadian Foreign Policy*, 189.

20 The *Vancouver Sun* labelled MacLaren "one of the world's most enthusiastic proponents of free trade." Daphne Bramham, "New Kid on Block Quick to Catch On," *Vancouver Sun*, June 14, 1996, D7.

21 Jeff Sallot, "Emphasize Trade in Foreign Policy, Ottawa Urged," *The Globe and Mail* [Toronto], November 12, 1994, A4.

22 Roy MacLaren, "The Road from Marrakech: The Quest for Economic Internationalism in an Age of Ambivalence," *Canadian*

Foreign Policy, 2, 1 (Spring 1994), 4-5.

23 Jeff Sallot, "Emphasize Trade in Foreign Policy," A4.

24 On the changes to contemporary multilateralism, see David Black and Claire Turenne Sjolander, "Multilateralism Re-constituted and the Discourse of Canadian Foreign Policy," *Studies in Political Economy*, 49 (Spring 1996), 7-36.

25 Roy MacLaren, "The Road from Marrakech," 1, 2.

26 Department of Foreign Affairs and International Trade, *Overview: Canada's International Business Strategy*, 1.

27 See, for example, Laura Macdonald, "Going Global: The Politics of Canada's Foreign Economic Relations," in Wallace Clement, ed., *Understanding Canada: Building on the New Canadian Political Economy* (Montreal: McGill-Queen's University Press, 1997), 179. Macdonald makes the argument that both the FTA and the NAFTA were defensive arrangements, as Canada sought to preserve gains in continental markets in the face of U.S. protectionism. This argument with respect to the FTA is also made in G. Bruce Doern and Brian W. Tomlin, *Faith and Fear*.

28 Jeff Sallot, "Emphasize Trade in Foreign Policy," A4.

29 Scott Feschuk, "Canada Nears Deal with Chile," *The Globe and Mail* [Toronto], October 28, 1996, B1.

30 Jeff Sallot, "Emphasize Trade in Foreign Policy," A4.

31 See Larry Welsh, "PM Promotes N. American, European Pact," *Vancouver Sun,* December 3, 1994, B10, and Madelaine Drohan, "Deal with Europe a Top Priority," *The Globe and Mail* [Toronto], January 2, 1996, B4.

32 Norman Spector, "How Canada and Israel Signed Their Free-Trade Deal," *The Globe and Mail* [Toronto], August 16, 1996, A15.

33 "Canada, Palestinian Authority Expect to Sign Trade Deal in May," *The Ottawa Citizen*, February 27, 1997, D8.

34 Cited in Alan Freeman, "Why Our Political Leaders Have Gone into Sales," *The Globe and Mail* [Toronto], November 4, 1994, A13.

35 For an analysis of this process, see Denis Stairs, "The Public Politics of the Canadian Defence and Foreign Policy Reviews," *Canadian Foreign Policy*, 3, 1 (Spring 1995), 91-116.

36 Canada, *Government Response to the Recommendations of the Special Joint Parliamentary Committee Reviewing Canadian Foreign Policy*, Ottawa, 1995; Canada, *Canada in the World: Government Statement*, Ottawa, 1995; Internet address: http://www.dfait-maeci.gc.ca/english/foreignp/cnd-world/

37 The other two objectives are the protection of Canadian security, within a stable global framework, and the projection of Canadian values and culture abroad. See *Canada in the World*, Chapter 2.

38 *Government Response to the Recommendations*, 33-34, and *Canada in the World*, Chapter 3, which applauds the Team Canada initiative, speaking of the government's commitment to "build on the 'Team Canada' approach that it employed so effectively in Asia last year."

39 Denis Stairs, "The Public Politics ...," 113. Stairs argues that the range of issues before the parliamentary committee, and the relatively short time in which it had to produce a report, conspired to produce a report of such "breadth and generality" as to make a high degree of convergence between the committee and the government likely.

40 Interestingly, Nossal points out that Chrétien did not participate in an official visit to Washington in his first year in office, although he did meet with President Clinton at the Seattle APEC meeting. Kim Richard Nossal, *The Politics of Canadian Foreign Policy*, 184-85.

41 On the Team Canada trade missions, see the following: Alan Freeman, "Why Our Political Leaders Have Gone into Sales," *The Globe and Mail* [Toronto], November 4, 1994, A13; Drew Fagan, "Why Chrétien and Co. are Hitting the Road Again," *The Globe and Mail* [Toronto], January 19, 1995, A15; Barrie McKenna, "Team Canada Off Again," *The Globe and Mail* [Toronto], January 2, 1996, B4; and "Team Canada 1997: More than Meets the Eye," *CanadExport On-Line*, February 2, 1997 (Internet address: http://www.dfait-maeci.gc.ca/english/news/newsletr/canex/970204ae.html.)

42 Barrie McKenna, "Team Canada Off Again," B4.

43 Ibid.

44 Ibid.

45 Konrad Yakabuski, "Quebec Embarks on Trade Junket," *The Globe and Mail* [Toronto], August 29, 1996, B4.

46 Jeff Sallot, "Emphasize Trade in Foreign Policy," A4.

47 Ibid.

48 Ibid.

49 Ibid. Sallot points out that Chrétien passed up the opportunity to speak to the United Nations General Assembly in the fall of 1994 during a "showcase" of world leaders, which included speeches by Presidents Boris Yeltsin, Bill Clinton, and Nelson Mandela. More importantly, the theme of the speech, UN peacekeeping, harkened back to the internationalism of Lester Pearson and the 1980s Pierre Trudeau. Despite the fact that Kim Campbell had found the time during her short tenure in office to address the General Assembly, André Ouellet delivered the Canadian address for Chrétien.

50 Barrie McKenna, "Team Canada Off Again," B4.

51 Department of Finance, *Foreign Affairs and International Trade Canada Estimates 1995-96* (Ottawa: Supply and Services Canada,

1995), 2-25. The International Trade Business Plan was renamed Canada's International Business Strategy in 1995, and featured enhanced participation of the private sector. See Department of Finance, *Foreign Affairs and International Trade Canada Estimates 1996-97* (Ottawa: Supply and Services Canada, 1996), 22.

52 DFAIT, *Canada's International Business Strategy*, i.

53 Department of Finance, *1996-97 Estimates*, 22. See also Canada, *Government Response to the Standing Committee on Foreign Affairs and International Trade on Canadian SMEs in the World Economy: Developing Effective Business-Government Partnership for International Success* (November 1996). Internet address: http://www.dfait-maeci.gc.ca/english/trade/sme_e.html.

54 Ibid.

55 Evan H. Potter, "Niche Diplomacy as Canadian Foreign Policy," *International Journal* 52 (Winter 1996-97), 29. See also Evan H. Potter, "Redesigning Canadian Diplomacy in an Age of Fiscal Austerity," in Fen Osler Hampson and Maureen Appel Molot, eds., *Canada Among Nations 1996: Big Enough to Be Heard* (Ottawa: Carleton University Press, 1996). DFAIT's budgetary expenditures in 1994-95 were $106.7 million, which gives an idea of the magnitude of a $292 million cumulative cut over 10 years.

56 Barrie McKenna, "Team Canada Off Again," B4. Budgets under the Program for Export Market Development, which offers grants to companies that want to explore new markets, has been restricted so that only small and medium enterprises, with sales of less than $10 million, are eligible. Grants must also be repaid from any royalties earned on the resulting foreign sales.

57 Jeff Sallot, ""Money Must Be Found to Promote Trade," *The Globe and Mail* [Toronto], November 12, 1994, A4; Evan Potter, "Niche Diplomacy," 30. Japan is the exception, given language difficulties and the perception that the market is still relatively unknown to Canadian firms.

58 Barrie McKenna, "Team Canada Off Again," B4.

59 For the Liberal party's own evaluation of its achievements, see Liberal Party of Canada, *A Record of Achievement: A Report on the Liberal Government's 36 Months in Office* (Ottawa, 1996). For its evaluation of its own trade policy initiatives, see p. 44.

60 G. Bruce Doern and Brian W. Tomlin, "Trade-Industrial Policy," 184.

61 Jeff Sallot, "Emphasize Trade in Foreign Policy," A1, A4.

62 Dave Todd, "Liberals Depart from Human-Rights Link," *Vancouver Sun*, December 22, 1993, D2.

63 André Ouellet, "Squaring Our Trade Policy with Human Rights," *Canadian Speeches: Issues of the Day*, August/September 1994, 42.

64 Jeff Sallot, "Emphasize Trade in Foreign Policy," A4. In opposition, the Liberals had vigorously protested the Three Gorges project, which had the potential to force the relocation of more than a million Chinese, as "environmentally disastrous," and had strongly opposed Beijing's plans to upgrade its nuclear weapons arsenal.

65 Cited in Ross Howard, "Canada Puts Trade Before Rights," *The Globe and Mail* [Toronto], May 12, 1995, A1.

66 Barrie McKenna, "Team Canada Seeks Gold on Asia Trade Mission," *The Globe and Mail* [Toronto], January 5, 1996, B20.

67 The subsequent replacement of Pettigrew by Don Boudria, a new member of the Cabinet with little experience in foreign affairs, did not appear to signal a long-term commitment to international development issues.

68 Evan Potter, "Niche Diplomacy as Canadian Foreign Policy," 32.

69 Ibid.

70 Liberal Party of Canada, *Creating Opportunity,* ch. 8.

6

The Liberals' Internal Trade Agreement: The Beginning of a New Federal Assertiveness?

G. BRUCE DOERN

MARK MACDONALD

The Chrétien Liberal government included in its 1993 Red Book a commitment to negotiate an Agreement on Internal Trade with the goal of the "elimination of interprovincial trade barriers."[1] An "inherited" priority from the previous Mulroney Conservative government, the internal trade file was not, at first glance, a natural fit for a Liberal government that took power in the fall of 1993 with sceptical views of free trade in the then concluding NAFTA negotiations. However, given that the Canadian Manufacturers' Association has estimated annual interprovincial trade barrier costs to be in the order of $6 billion, and the fact that a preliminary bureaucratic machinery was already in place when the Liberals came to power,[2] the Liberals were unwilling to let the issue die.

By July 1994, the Liberals, under a new and inexperienced Minister of Industry, John Manley, had achieved a negotiated agreement to reduce the internal barriers to trade. As we will see, the overall reaction of commentators is that the Agreement, though a useful first step, is a weak and contradictory one. A recent assessment by Andrew Coyne stated that the Agreement was "collapsing under the weight of its own rickety, exception-riddled architecture."[3]

We will argue that the Agreement on Internal Trade (AIT) is in fact the "sleeper" in the Red Book, a deal with actual and potentially large long-term effects, including not only enhanced internal trade, but also changes in the federation and in policy formation. The analysis will show that in some respects it enhances federal power at the expense of the provinces by disciplining the use of provincial governing powers. Thus it runs counter to the conventional wisdom of the mid-1990s that decentralized federalism is the dominant governing trend in Canada and that a weakened federal government is both the cause and effect of such decentralization.

The chapter is organized into four parts. First, we look at how internal trade has appeared on the agenda in the last decade. Second, we briefly profile the structure and content of the Agreement. Third, we examine the key dynamics and aspects of the negotiations and the Agreement. In the fourth section we look at initial assessments of the Agreement. Conclusions then follow as to why these assessments are often incomplete and why we believe that the Agreement and its underlying politics both enhance internal trade and exhibit a new federal assertiveness.

GETTING INTERNAL TRADE ON THE AGENDA

On July 18, 1994, Prime Minister Jean Chrétien announced the signing of the Agreement on Internal Trade. The Prime Minister stressed that "for the first time, under this new Agreement, we will have: clear rules and an impartial dispute settlement mechanism to resolve trade differences between the provinces."[4] He further pointed out that there was now an "open procurement process—for all Canadian companies—for the $50 billion spent annually by governments across Canada; and a code of conduct to prevent provinces from luring away investment from each other."[5]

The simplicity of this statement of key achievements stood in contrast to the difficult journey involved both in getting internal trade on the political agenda and then in keeping it there. In effect, this longer run-up to the negotiations spans a 15-year period beginning in the late 1970s. Indeed, as early as 1940 problems relating to internal trade between the federal, provincial, and territorial governments of Canada had been identified.[6] In the late 1970s and early 1980s, academic analysis had suggested the value of reducing barriers.[7]

However, the push for *policies* to deal with the deleterious effects of internal trade barriers can be seen to have emerged from three main sources in the 1980s: the economic and policy arguments presented by the Macdonald Commission; the 1985 *Intergovernmental Position Paper on the Principles and Framework for Regional Economic Development*; and the emerging belief in the benefits at the political level of reducing barriers to internal trade.

It is useful to remember that there is an explicit Chrétien connection in the formation of the Macdonald Royal Commission. In the late 1970s, when aggressive provincial governments were challenging federal power, then Prime Minister Pierre Trudeau assigned Jean Chrétien to examine ways in which the "Canadian economic union" could be strengthened. This initiative was designed explicitly as a strategy to challenge provincial power and assert federal authority. When the Macdonald Commission was later appointed, half of its title (*The Royal Commission on the Economic Union and Development Prospects for Canada*) implied the strengthening of the economic union.

The 1985 *Report of the Royal Commission on the Economic Union and Development Prospects for Canada* presented a precise set of arguments about the harmful economic effects of barriers to internal trade.[8] While the *Report* offered no exact measure of the economic cost of barriers, the Commission argued that significant internal trade impediments did exist and that a conscientious effort should be made to reduce them. Perhaps equally important was the indication that a strong political rationale for barrier reduction also existed. As the Commission stated, "Above the economic rationale, the political rationale for the national right to free movement has a powerful attraction for most Canadians. For a producer to find it easier to sell in another country than in another province offends our sense of Canadianism."[9] By linking the economic and political rationales for barrier reduction, the Macdonald Commission was explicitly arguing for a policy on internal economic conduct. The Commission also proposed a specific process through which such a "Code of Economic Conduct" might be developed.

Mirroring the recommendations of the Macdonald Commission, a 1985 intergovernmental paper on the *Principles and Framework for Regional Economic Development* was released that focused on the principle of recognizing that Canadian economic efficiency and social equity is the responsibility of all political jurisdictions. In particular, the eighth principle of the paper suggested that "governments should explore opportunities for increasing interregional trade and eliminating barriers between provinces."[10]

The intergovernmental position paper represented the first time that all Canadian governments had given serious attention to internal trade as a significant policy issue. The product of work by the Committee of Regional Economic Development Ministers (CREDM), the position paper indicated that barriers to intergovernmental trade should be considered important in the context of both regional and national economic policy—a first in federal-provincial economic development initiatives. In addition, CREDM established a task force of officials, co-chaired by Saskatchewan and the federal government, to develop policy options for the implementation of the eighth principle, an important first step toward bureaucratically institutionalizing internal trade policy in federal-provincial collaborations.

In the early stages of this process, sector-specific issues were raised. For instance, in 1986 Statistics Canada was commissioned to present a report on government procurement and investment as an instrument of regional economic policy.[11] As time passed, however, a more comprehensive political understanding of interprovincial barriers as a whole emerged. At the 27th Annual Premiers' Conference, held in Edmonton on August 10-12, 1986, the premiers endorsed a set of four initiatives designed to steer efforts toward barrier reduction:

- a broad best-efforts moratorium on new barriers, subject to compelling considerations of provincial economic development,
- a permanent mechanism to reduce barriers,
- a process to validate an inventory of barriers, and
- a set of Guiding Principles for reducing barriers.[12]

While some momentum was gained through this endorsement, it could not be said that a driving political will was yet in evidence. Work was done on some sectors, but progress was sluggish, to say the least. The twin factors that produced a further impetus for negotiations were the successful negotiation of the FTA and then NAFTA as international trade agreements and the failure of the Meech Lake and Charlottetown constitutional reform initiatives. Crucially, at the federal ministerial level, Michael Wilson, as both Industry Minister and Trade Minister in 1993, supplied the early essential political muscle and influence in getting the negotiations going and especially in supplying a deadline. Wilson, a pivotal minister in both the FTA and NAFTA processes, had persuaded Prime Minister Brian Mulroney and other first ministers that an internal negotiation simply had to succeed. This argument for success was made more telling and imperative precisely because Meech Lake and Charlottetown had failed.

These failures were linked to the immediate prospect of a Quebec election late in 1994. This produced a need for success, but it also affected particular provisions in the Agreement, as each delegation reached its own judgment as to what it thought the Quebec Liberal government might need to defend itself against the Parti Québécois sovereigntist opposition. During the negotiations, as the fall 1994 election loomed with greater certainty, the Quebec situation also supplied a further reason why the June 30 deadline could not be allowed to slip.

In addition, some impetus for a new internal trade regime was supplied by the evolving debate across the country about trade-industrial policy, regional policy, and deficits. A full account is not possible here, but it is sufficient to say that these debates seriously questioned the provincial and federal governments' capacity to practise regional or industrial policy through grants and subsidies.[13]

THE AGREEMENT IN BRIEF

Space does not allow a detailed presentation of the full Agreement.[14] However, the basic architecture of the Agreement must be appreciated to make sense of the negotiations and of the key aspects examined below. Table 6.1 lays out the 18 chapters of the deal, which are divided into six parts. Each part is introduced briefly.

The bulk of the Agreement is in Part IV, the 11 chapters dealing with specific rules. These were handled mainly by the sectoral negotiating teams or "tables," although the procurement provisions were also kept very close to the main table of chief negotiators, who oversaw the entire package. It is worth noting that not all of the "sector" chapters and tables dealt with vertical industrial sectors such as autos or steel. Some fit this category, such as the chapters on alcoholic beverages and agriculture and food goods, but many other so-called sectors were in fact aspects of internal trade that cut across all or most sectors of the economy. This was certainly true of procurement, investment, labour mobility, consumer-related measures and standards, and environment. Other chapters, such as communications, transportation, natural resources processing, and energy were more hybrid. They were certainly seen as industrial sectors, but they were also horizontal and economy-wide in nature in that they were a crucial aspect of production in virtually every other sector of the economy.

The division between general and specific rules is crucial. Ideally, in any trade agreement the general rules ought to be paramount, with specific rules flowing from the generalities and not contradicting them. The Agreement on Internal Trade certainly violates this model. The essence of the negotiations in many respects concerned which chapters would take precedence over others.

The preamble and the overall provisions in Parts I, II, and III set out the basic objectives, operating principles, and general rules. At its core, the purpose of the Agreement was to promote "an open, efficient and stable domestic market for long-term job creation, economic growth and stability," and, accordingly, "to reduce and eliminate to the extent possible, barriers to the free movement of persons, goods, services and investments within Canada." The Agreement was also intended to "promote equal economic opportunity for Canadians" and several related objectives regarding competitiveness, sustainable environmental development, and better consultation on internal trade matters.[15]

The Agreement also reaffirms that nothing in the text alters the legislative or other authority of Parliament or the legislatures of the provinces under the Constitution of Canada. The Agreement, in short, although not an exercise in constitutional change, may be tantamount to a "side deal" on the constitution. This point is discussed further below.[16]

Table 6.1

The Agreement on Internal Trade at a Glance
(Six Parts and 18 Chapters)

Preamble

Part I	**General**
Chapter 1	Operating Principles
Chapter 2	General Definitions
Part II	**Constitutional Authorities**
Chapter 3	Reaffirmation of Constitutional Powers and Responsibilities
Part III	**General Rules**
Chapter 4	General Rules
Part IV	**Specific Rules**
Chapter 5	Procurement
Chapter 6	Investment
Chapter 7	Labour Mobility
Chapter 8	Consumer-Related Measures and Standards
Chapter 9	Agricultural and Food Goods
Chapter 10	Alcoholic Beverages
Chapter 11	Natural Resources Processing
Chapter 12	Energy
Chapter 13	Communications
Chapter 14	Transportation
Chapter 15	Environmental Protection
Part V	**Institutional Provisions and Dispute Resolution Procedures**
Chapter 16	Institutional Provisions
Chapter 17	Dispute Resolution Procedures
Part VI	**Final Provisions**
Chapter 18	Final Provisions
Annexes	

Source: Canada, *The Agreement on Internal Trade* (Ottawa: Government of Canada, 1994).

The general rules provisions in Part III of the Agreement include provisions regarding reciprocal non-discrimination, right of entry and exit, and transparency, but they also include provisions regarding "legitimate objectives." This latter provision was demanded by the provinces to enable them to practise certain policies that could be contrary to some or all of the general rules.[17] Such practices carried out in the name of legitimate objectives would still have to be put in place so as not to "impair unduly" the access of economic players, or to be "more trade restrictive than necessary."

Part IV contains the specific rules of the sectors and areas noted above. The chapter on procurement is by far the largest, reflecting its particular sensitivity in the negotiation. It deals with the government's own purchases of goods and services and the extent to which a province could discriminate in favour of its own citizens and firms in decisions to purchase items with taxpayers' money. The shortest "chapter" concerns energy, which is a one-line entry, since no agreement was reached. This impasse arose from disputes over wheeling electricity across provincial boundaries.

The other sectoral chapters all begin with statements regarding the extent to which their provisions are an exception from (in whole or part), or governed by, the general rules. With regard to both their content and their negotiating processes, these sectors should be seen in two important contexts. First, these chapters were typically negotiated by officials and experts from the line departments of the governments involved. Second, many of the issues and policy problems these officials and experts were dealing with had been in their sector's agenda for years. Accordingly, one of the issues is whether the internal trade arena of decision-making simply continued the process without much change or whether it altered the dynamics precisely because it was a different political-economic arena for such decisions.

Parts V and VI of the Agreement deal with institutional provisions and dispute settlement, and so-called "final provisions." These issues were very much in the hands of the main table of chief negotiators and ultimately the internal trade ministers as well. The final provisions included politically crucial issues that secured varying kinds of full or partial exemption from the Agreement, including regional economic development, Aboriginal peoples, culture, national security, taxation, and the financial sector. Many of these, situated as they are within federal, rather than just provincial, policy spheres, were included at the behest of the federal government.

The institutional provisions in Chapter 16 of the Agreement provide the foundation for implementing and building on the deal. A Committee on Internal Trade is established with cabinet-level representation. A jointly funded Internal Trade Secretariat is also established (now based in Winnipeg), as well as a working group on adjustment to assess the effects of the Agreement on each province in every fiscal year.

Even more crucial, however, are the agreed provisions regarding dispute resolution procedures, many of which are modelled on international trade dispute settlement practices.[18] These cover more than twenty pages of the Agreement and were the subject of intense bargaining. As Table 6.2 shows, there are procedures for both government-to-government and person-to-government dispute resolution. It was the Agreement's latter provisions for private access, and how extensive to make such private access, that created the greatest disagreement among negotiators. Under both types of dispute the process allows for a sequence of steps. The first ports of call are the chapter provisions, followed by the general dispute-resolution provisions. Within each, an aggrieved party or person goes through several steps, beginning with consultations, then proceeding to a possible request for assistance, and finally a request for a panel, and a panel stage. If a dispute goes to the ultimate panel stage, implementation of the independent panel report will first rely on compliance by the parties, or perhaps on the influence of adverse publicity. Under prescribed circumstances, retaliatory action can be taken.

The private access procedures contain a screening process to eliminate frivolous complaints, after which the same steps apply. An important exception is that a panel report may contain an award of costs of proceeding, but not damages. Dispute avoidance and settlement steps also vary across some of the sectoral chapters.

KEY NEGOTIATING DYNAMICS

The AIT must be seen in the context of three key negotiating dynamics: the different provincial governing political party views about the

Table 6.2

**The Two Main Internal Trade
Dispute Resolution Processes**

Government-to-Government	Person-to-Government
Consultations Assistance of Committee (including ADR processes) Request for Panel Establishment of Panel Panel Report Implementation of Report Non-Implementation • Publicity • Retaliatory Action	Initiation of proceedings Screening Consultations Assistance of Committee (including ADR processes) Request for Panel Establishment of Panel Panel Report (possible award of costs of proceedings) Implementation of Report Non-Implementation • Publicity

role of government; the meeting of two nominal policy communities in the negotiation process, namely a trade community and a federal-provincial policy community; and the debate about the federal trade and commerce power and the degree to which the AIT can be considered a side-deal on the Constitution.[19] It is also interesting to briefly review the political "drama" of the negotiations.

Provincial Governing Parties and the Role of the State
The core of the Agreement on Internal Trade negotiations was the battle over general rules versus exceptions and legitimate objectives. The political fault lines also involved dispute resolution provisions, the role of regional policy and Crown corporations, and procurement and investment issues. However, these issues were surrogates for a debate on the appropriate role of the provincial state in particular. The final pact was the product of negotiation and political (including personal)

interplay among the federal government, a neutral chair and secretariat, and twelve provincial/territorial governments and parties in power in 1993-1994. As in any complex multi-party negotiation over a 12-month period, the nature of the interplay had both stable alliances and shifting ones.[20]

The federal government, the Secretariat, Alberta, and Manitoba were the most supportive of an agreement that maximized the general rules and effective dispute settlement provisions and minimized the exceptions. They were the most inclined to see the AIT as a trade agreement rather than a governance issue. Although the three provincial NDP governments (Ontario, British Columbia, and Saskatchewan) did not agree with each other on every matter (far from it), they were united strategically and philosophically, by a scepticism about a free trade agenda in general, and about federal government intentions. The NDP-governed provinces led the forces that would have preferred a sectoral approach to internal trade, but in the resulting final agreement sought to maximize the exceptions and legitimate objectives and minimize general rules and dispute settlement.

Quebec in some respects fell into its own category. Its then Liberal government was supportive of an internal trade agreement, but its negotiating approach was inevitably couched in terms of an expected 1994 election. It had to show support for an economic union without giving up, or appearing to give up, provincial powers. Indeed, in the early 1990s the Liberals had openly debated the European Union (then European Community) as a model for Canada.[21] The impending 1994 Quebec election and the possibility of a Parti Québécois separatist victory was the unstated bottom line for those provinces that might otherwise have been tempted to walk away from the negotiations. Had they done so, federalism would have visibly failed for the third time in four years on a major negotiation.

The remaining players, the Atlantic Canada provinces and the two territorial governments, were cautiously supportive of more open internal markets, but they eventually signed on to an agreement from a negotiating position of recognized political weakness. They saw the AIT often as an exercise in damage control, where defensive postures were the only real option. Indeed, in many respects some Atlantic Canada provinces felt they were being abandoned by both the federal government and the larger provinces.

*The Trade Community and the Federal-Provincial Policy
Community in Collision*

The negotiations brought together, in one large multi-sector and multi-policy field process, ministers and officials from two different policy communities each with its own traditions, that of trade and that of federal-provincial relations. The basic nature of each of these two realms needs to be appreciated. Trade policy had previously been, by definition, an international activity.[22] Until the mid-1980s, the trade policy community had functioned in a small closed circle with the basic rhythm of activity governed by the periodic multi-year General Agreement on Tariffs and Trade (GATT) rounds. This relatively sequestered existence had changed markedly, beginning in the mid-1980s, when the FTA, NAFTA, and Uruguay GATT negotiations occurred. First, these negotiations as a whole were virtually continuous from 1985 to 1994. Second, they grew in scope (compared to earlier GATT rounds) to encompass areas of public policy that were previously seen as national, domestic, and, in essence, non-trade oriented. Third, they were accompanied by quite elaborate sectoral consultations with business through the Sectoral Advisory Groups on International Trade (SAGITs). Fourth, the trade negotiations also included federal-provincial consultation processes, which were quite combative in the FTA negotiations and somewhat smoother in the NAFTA and GATT negotiations. Fifth, within the federal government during these negotiations, the trade negotiation office and its team became, in a certain sense, a "mini-government," in that power and influence coalesced around it as it negotiated, within a Cabinet mandate, a multiple set of policies, all cast in the name of trade policy. By the end of this 10-year continuous trade negotiation process, and as the 1994 internal trade negotiations began, the trade policy community was flush with success, confident, and determined to extend trade concepts and thinking into wider realms.

It was a policy community that had some familiarity with federal-provincial relations. As mentioned, the more "domestic" trade had become, the more provincial jurisdictions were affected. However, at the same time, the trade policy community was not enmeshed in the traditions, memories, and lexicon of the federal-provincial policy community.

If the trade policy community is traditionally small and compact, the federal-provincial relations policy community is anything but that. Although it may seem to involve a smaller coterie of persons in federal-provincial relations ministries and offices in 11 governments, this core quickly expands when one thinks of the many areas of policy that were and are subject to federal-provincial policy processes of some kind. While this community was certainly aware of, and experienced in, processes that could include an actual negotiating format and dynamic, its policy and decision processes were typically more ambling and less driven by imposed deadlines. The processes, except for those related to fiscal federalism and constitutional change, were also typically not multi-policy field in nature.

One must be careful about excessively stereotyping either of these policy communities and their degrees of cohesion, but the players themselves agree that the internal trade negotiations confirmed that some of these ascribed tendencies and differences do exist.

The federal-provincial relations community entered the negotiations not with a sense of recent aggressive success, but rather with a sense of perceived failure, because of the demise of both the Meech Lake and Charlottetown constitutional accords in the 1990 to 1993 period. These failures also left a residue of considerable resentment among some of the players who were then involved in the internal trade file.

The problems associated with mixing and blending players from the two groupings arise not only from the players themselves and their sense of the process being a "negotiation" rather than "normal policy making." They also arise from the overriding ideas and agendas that were given prominence, such as the extent to which the outcome should be a trade deal rather than an agreement about governance.

The Debate on the Trade and Commerce Power

The Agreement on Internal Trade must be seen in the context of the debate about the use and extension of the federal trade and commerce power. Indeed, discussions about an internal trade agreement have always been couched in differing views about several related federal powers under the Canadian Constitution, including initially conferred powers such as the "peace, order and good government" and "trade and commerce" powers, but also the more recently conferred provisions under the Charter of Rights and Freedoms regarding mobility rights (Section 6). It is also germane that the Agreement on Internal Trade was not to involve the courts (it was a political agreement), nor was it supposed to change the Constitution.

The courts have generally interpreted the "peace, order and good government" and "trade and commerce" powers in a very narrow fashion. With respect to the trade and commerce power, this has meant that the federal government has had "very little scope to enact national legislation where divergent provincial regulatory approaches undermined the Canadian economic union."[23] The "peace, order and good government" powers were largely confined to national emergencies.

Recent legal analyses suggest that the courts are giving more scope to these federal powers. Historically, competition law had rested on federal powers over criminal law. Changes were made in 1986, though, when the Competition Act provided the federal government with new powers over anti-competitive behaviour in the areas of trade and commerce, powers that had the potential to collide with provincial jurisdiction over civil and property rights.[24] The constitutionality of this new federal competition law was challenged in the General Motors case,[25] but the court upheld the federal powers by activating the little-used "general regulation of trade" dimension of the trade and commerce power.[26] Thus, on matters related to securing the economic union, there is certainly some precedent for arguing that the trade and commerce power alone, or in combination with other powers, has resulted in more federal scope for action.

Howse's recent analysis suggests, however, some necessary points of caution. He advises that a national regulatory scheme is not likely to "simply pre-empt provincial laws but normally will operate concurrently with them."[27] Hence, co-operation with the provinces would be necessary in any event. Otherwise, such federal exercises may simply add another layer of barriers to internal trade in the form of added regulatory complexity.

Constitutional aspects of the Agreement on Internal Trade are also found in section 6 of the Charter of Rights and Freedoms. It provides for the right of Canadians to reside and gain a livelihood in any province subject to general "reasonable limits." A key limitation to this right is that it does not apply to corporations, and also there are some court decisions that suggest that it does not confer a right to "earn a livelihood independent of some element of mobility," (one may be forced to take up residence in another province in order to make a living).[28]

Prior to and during the internal trade negotiations the trade and commerce power debate inevitably raised its head, especially when strategies regarding dispute resolution (but also regarding the Agreement as a whole) were being considered. The trade and commerce power, as set out above, gave the federal government jurisdiction over interprovincial trade in *goods*, yet the extent of this jurisdiction over other issues, such as services and capital, and the degree to which the power could actually be exercised, had always been circumscribed by the legal uncertainties already mentioned, as well as by political realities. As a result, during the internal trade negotiations and the preparations for them, some voices within the federal government and within the lead department, Industry Canada, argued that the federal government should aggressively exercise such powers and test them to the limit, while other voices advocated extreme caution.

But politics usually dictated that the federal government could never fully play the trade and commerce card, because of the political conflicts with the provinces it would create. Some effort to play the card had been part of the Meech Lake and Charlottetown constitutional discussions, but these had ended in failure. Although the talks failed largely because of their collision with provincial desires to practise some form of regional (provincial) economic development policy, some provincial opposition was also expressed on more general political grounds, especially in the case of Quebec.

The trade and commerce strategy was therefore a kind of unspoken presence during the negotiations. It was known that the card could never be fully played, but it was also possible that if a successful internal trade agreement (and its dispute settlement provisions) was not obtained, then a future federal government might well conclude that it had to be even more aggressive, because it had tried all the alternatives.

The Politics of Negotiation
The debate over the content of the Agreement quite naturally took place in an arena of political end-game brinkmanship. Indeed, up until the eleventh hour of the negotiations, when federal and provincial trade

ministers were going over the final pieces of the Agreement, it was never entirely clear that a deal would be or could be struck.

Throughout the entire process, British Columbia was a bit of an enigma and proved to be the party most resistant to the Agreement. This resistance was due to its ideological reluctance to give up economic policy tools in the realm of regional development, coupled with its relatively small stake economically (most of British Columbia's trade is Pacific Rim, not internal). But for some intense pressure from Ontario and a strong brokering role played by the federal and Manitoba negotiating teams, British Columbia might well have scuttled the negotiations.

The Atlantic Provinces too were concerned about the loss of policy instruments, but were brought on side by their desire to obtain access to new markets in central and western Canada. Quebec's stance, on the other hand, was one of quiet wariness of the overall process at the outset, although in the final analysis it was an accepting party. Two issues were of particular importance: financial services (i.e. if financial services were to be included in the Agreement Quebec would not participate), and culture and cultural industries. In general, Quebec was concerned about maintaining as wide a range of policy instruments as possible for the daily governance of the province, and that the Agreement should not present undue impediments. Such a position stood in contrast to the one adopted by Alberta, which was the most "free-trade" oriented of the players.

Perhaps the most interesting role was played by Ontario, which started out with a negative stance, based, as in British Columbia's and Saskatchewan's case, on a desire for a sectoral approach and the preservation of policy tools for economic development. Along the way, however, this stance changed, mainly because of the strong presence of Frances Lankin, who was regarded as the most informed and skilled negotiator both in political and "technical" terms. In the final analysis, Ontario, in concert with the federal government, contributed the most resources, was able to plausibly influence Quebec and British Columbia to sign on, and was committed to the nationalist idea of forging a general agreement.

THE AGREEMENT: INITIAL ASSESSMENTS

Initial assessments of the AIT have come from three sources: business, scholars from the law and economics disciplines, and, emerging more slowly, scholars specializing in federal-provincial relations.

The most explicit business commentary has come from the Canadian Chamber of Commerce. The Chamber is "highly critical of the fundamental weaknesses, flaws and loopholes" in the Agreement.[29] It calls for a reduction in exceptions, an enforceable dispute resolution process, and opportunities for more effective private action. It uses not only normal economic arguments but the national unity issue as well. It concludes that "weak internal trade links mean less reason to stay united."[30] It also calls for direct business involvement in future negotiations.

The assessment of law and economics academics is best reflected in several C.D. Howe Institute publications. These assessments tend to start with the view that the AIT is a needed first step, but then to express a wide range of criticisms about the contradictions in the Agreement, its weak dispute resolution mechanisms, and, even by 1995, the slippage in its deadlines for implementing some provisions.[31]

Individual legal academics, such as Robert Howse, are also critical of the Agreement, but exhibit a greater edge of optimism by suggesting concretely how they think the federal government can build on the Agreement through the use of its constitutional powers.[32]

Mainstream scholars on federalism have been slower to comment, perhaps because they are less inclined to want to see federalism in trade-oriented terms. For example, Donald Lenihan focuses on the "legitimate objectives" features of the Agreement, and, though aware of the contradictions in the Agreement, he is much more tolerant of them as a needed democratic and governing compromise.[33]

One of the difficulties with these initial assessments is their focus on the Agreement itself without a complementary analysis of the politics of the negotiations or an attempt to situate them in the context of larger political forces or perspectives. Our conclusions try to take these forces more explicitly into account.

CONCLUSIONS

The Agreement on Internal Trade is an extremely important develop-ment in Canadian federal-provincial relations, largely because it not only advances the cause of internal trade, but also removes or lessens the capacities of governments, especially provincial governments, to act in ways that had been possible in the previous three decades. In a real sense, some specific tools have been taken out of the hands of policy-makers at both levels of government, or their use has been se-verely limited. As we suggest below, however, if the federal trade and commerce powers are taken into consideration, it seems reasonable to conclude that the loss of instrument choice has been levied more force-fully at the provincial level.

The Agreement also represents a considerable penetration into do-mestic policy agendas and institution building by the globalization-led liberalized international trade agenda. This is reflected in the very ar-chitecture of the Agreement, its language and terminology, and the trade-related backgrounds of many of the key negotiators.

Furthermore, the negotiations on the Agreement represent one of the first occasions where multiple policy field federal-provincial policy-making was conducted in the name of a negotiated trade agreement. In effect, the provinces were required to do in turn exactly what the fed-eral government had to do during the FTA, NAFTA, and GATT nego-tiations: determine what governing capacities they would give up, lessen, or discipline themselves in using, in the name of promoting liberalized trade and a more dynamic and competitive Canadian economy.

As we have seen, judgments vary about whether the Agreement en-hances or constrains the federal government's trade and commerce powers. Those who think that it has constrained the trade and com-merce power fear that it has set limits around the powers, and that the courts, using doctrines of "constitutional convention," may simply conclude that what is practised (namely the Agreement as a living document) is what the constitutional trade and commerce power in fact is. Since the trade and commerce power has never been fully de-fined, the Agreement will define it.

We side with the alternative line of argument, which is that the fed-eral trade and commerce powers are enhanced by the Agreement, be-cause it is the discriminatory powers of provincial governments that have been most reined in. There are many actions that are now simply more difficult for provinces to take. One result of this might be that there will be more room for federal discretion, especially in areas regarding the economic union. For this reason, the Agreement can be seen not only as a trade-specific document, but also implicitly as a "side-deal to the constitution." It remains to be seen what overall effect this will have on jurisdictional battles.

The 1994 negotiation process was also unlike recent trade agreements or federal-provincial dealings in that there was a decided absence of public and interest group involvement. Indeed, in terms of federal-provincial relations, the decision process was a throw-back to what has been called "executive federalism." The behind-the-scenes route was chosen for what seem to be sensible reasons. After all, the Meech Lake and Charlottetown constitutional processes, especially the latter, were broader, and involved public forums. And even though it can be argued that it was the problems of ratification, not of negotiation, that had led to the failures of the constitutional proposals, actors at both the federal and the provincial levels had negative memories about their most recent attempts at building national agreements. Furthermore, with the exception of stating its support for as liberalized an internal Canadian market as possible, the Canadian business community did not express any interest in the specifics of the internal trade negotiations. In addition, the lack of interest on the part of labour, social, and environmental groups may well have led, almost by default, to the somewhat closed negotiation process.

Given recent democratic trends, the 1994 process was remarkably contained. The question arises as to whether future rounds of internal trade reform will follow this route, as there are genuine and quite broad democratic concerns about the precise balances to be struck among the fundamental values involved as revealed in the debates and stances within the 1994 negotiations. In short, how much of the agenda should be determined by trade ideas and rationales? What basic aspects of governance in a federation need to be preserved and defended? What visions of national unity ought to prevail or be accommodated: a country of mobile citizens, workers, and investors with firm rights anywhere in the country, and/or a country of quasi-sovereign provinces sharing jurisdictions and real governing capacities with a national government?

As for future developments, perhaps the first and simplest question is whether there can or should be new "rounds" of negotiations as opposed to more limited processes for improving the Agreement. A formal second round is certainly a possibility. The various work programs and reporting requirements suggest that many items must be revisited. Ontario and other reluctant provinces did agree that any agreement should be organic and therefore would be built upon and improved. If the international trade analogy is continued, then one has the example of the GATT, where the original agreement in 1947 was followed by the Kennedy Round, the Tokyo Round, and the recent Uruguay Round. The internal trade agreement process could therefore now be looking for its "Kennedy" round.

The concept of rounds, or indeed the inherent notion of there being a multi-policy field, multi-party negotiation, involves the question of how big or how broad such a round should be. If it is too narrow, or confined to a small set of sectors, then it is more difficult to achieve trade-offs, mainly because interests can mobilize more easily against few, rather than many, sectors. At the international free trade level this has been borne out repeatedly wherever sectoral free trade approaches have been advocated (such as in the early 1980s between Canada and the United States).

But for the next internal trade round the question is how big is big enough to overcome these problems. It is also crucial that there be a muscular political deadline for negotiations. As emphasized, without a real deadline negotiations simply become endlessly incremental policy-making (which, of course, is what many players and interests prefer).

The federal government is still the main "demander" in this process, and thus it may push for as wide-ranging a set of issues as is possible. Many provinces are unwilling to enter a negotiation that is anywhere near as broad as the first. Some would prefer no further negotiations at all, though they agreed to launch work plans in many areas.

The political situation in Quebec, with a sovereigntist government in power, will also loom large. The Quebec government will want to show that it can make an internal market work, because the political salability of the sovereignty argument to Quebec voters is predicated on not losing access to the Canadian economic union. But a sovereigntist state, if that is what materializes, would also have strong instincts to preserve powers and capacities, because, after all, that is what sovereignty is all about.

If and when a new internal trade negotiating step or round occurs, there certainly are many areas/chapters that could be on the table. Some of these will also be propelled by obligations and pressures from the international trade realm, given that international trade is increasingly focusing on domestic policy measures rather than border measures. Thus the next steps could certainly deal with matters such as labour mobility, energy, agriculture and food, the environment, investment, and regional concerns. Federal policies may also be looked at more closely.

Dispute settlement is bound to become a key area again, but if the negotiations were held right away there would be extremely limited experience with the new processes and very few cases of dispute resolution. The federal government and Alberta will again press for stronger dispute settlement provisions, but the political issues around this are still quite complex and unpredictable. For example, in the 1993-94 round it is clear that dispute settlement with private action provisions was generally seen as a device through which businesses could get action against governments erecting barriers, with the emphasis on the "barriers." But the dispute settlement provisions apply to the whole Agreement, so it is possible in another round that other social interests will want the dispute settlement provisions strengthened to ensure that other provisions also enjoy full compliance, such as legitimate objectives, environmental standards, and various exemptions.

Some of the pressures in the next round, on dispute settlement and on other areas, thus depend upon whether it is designed again as executive federalism in operation or whether broader interest group and public input is invited as a systematic part of the process. It is doubtful that in the next steps interests will not be aware that internal trade is about much more than technical matters of trade.

The more that the Agreement on Internal Trade is seen both as an extension into Canada of international trade rules and as a crucial side deal on the constitution, the more likely it is that broader public input will be pushed for. These pressures may also alter the evolving balance regarding the degree to which the Agreement can be seen to be a political agreement as distinct from a legal agreement. The desire to keep the Agreement or dispute settlement out of the courts may follow the path that has partially transpired in areas such as environmental assessment. Federal approaches that were thought to be confinable to the status of guidelines were challenged in the courts and ruled to be law-like. It is hard not to see some provisions of the Agreement on Internal Trade moving out of the shadows of a political agreement and into a legal or quasi-legal or even quasi-constitutional realm.

A final feature of the next steps is that the provinces are likely to demand greater involvement in international trade processes than they have had in the past. The dynamic here is a simple one. If internal trade agreements move more and more into areas of provincial jurisdiction, then the provinces will want a stake in federal trade policy making. In short, if trade is everything then everyone wants to be involved.

In the final analysis, then, one must grant the Liberals more than a "passing grade" for keeping their promise of establishing an agreement for the elimination of interprovincial trade barriers. One might even be inclined to suggest that given the federal-provincial experiences with Meech and Charlottetown, the Liberals deserve critical acclaim for having led the negotiation of a national agreement at all. However, as we have indicated above, much still needs to be revealed, especially as future rounds of negotiation take place.

NOTES

1 Liberal Party of Canada, *Creating Opportunity: The Liberal Plan for Canada* (Ottawa, 1993), 22.

2 "Governments Agree on Comprehensive Negotiations to Reduce Internal Trade Barriers," News Release, March 18, 1993.

3 Andrew Coyne, untitled column, *The Ottawa Citizen*, September 17, 1996, A11.

4 Prime Minister Jean Chrétien, "Statement on the Internal Trade Agreement," July 18, 1994, 1.

5 Ibid.

6 See Canada, *Report of the Royal Commission on Dominion-Provincial Relations* (Rowell-Sirois Commission) (Ottawa: King's Printer, 1940).

7 See A.E. Safarian, *Ten Markets or One?* (Toronto: Ontario Economic Council, 1980).

8 Canada, Royal Commission on the Economic Union and Development Prospects for Canada, *Report*, Volume III (Ottawa: Minister of Supply and Services, 1985), Chapter 22.

9 Ibid., 135.

10 Canada, *Intergovernmental Position Paper on the Principles and Framework for Regional Economic Development* (Ottawa: Minister of Supply and Services, 1985), 13.

11 "Federal and Provincial Regional Development Ministers Meet," News Release, February 21, 1986.

12 27th Annual Premiers' Conference, "Communiqué on Trade," News Release, August 12, 1986.

13 For discussion of this debate see Bruce Doern, "Looking for the Core: Industry Canada and Program Review," in Gene Swimmer, ed., *How Ottawa Spends 1996-97: Life Under the Knife* (Ottawa: Carleton University Press, 1996), 73-97.

14 See Canada, *Agreement on Internal Trade* (Ottawa: Government of Canada, 1994), 1.

15 Ibid.

16 See Katherine Swinton, "Courting Our Way to Economic Integration: Judicial Review and the Canadian Economic Union," *Canadian Business Law Journal*, 25, 2 (July 1995), 280-304, and "Law, Politics and the Enforcement of the Agreement on Internal Trade," in Michael Trebilcock and Daniel Schwanen, eds., *Getting There* (Toronto: C.D. Howe Institute, 1995), 196-210.

17 See Donald G. Lenihan, "When a Legitimate Object Hits an Unnecessary Obstacle: Harmonizing Regulations and Standards in the Agreement on Internal Trade," in Michael Trebilcock and Daniel Schwanen, eds., *Getting There* (Toronto: C.D. Howe Institute, 1995), 98-118.

18 See Robert Howse, "Between Anarchy and the Rule of Law: Dispute Settlement and Related Implementation Issues in the Agreement on Internal Trade," in Michael Trebilcock and Daniel Schwanen, eds., *Getting There* (Toronto: C.D. Howe Institute, 1995), 177-95.

19 For a more detailed analysis of these and other issues about the negotiations, see Bruce Doern and Mark MacDonald, *Free Trade Federalism* (Toronto: University of Toronto Press, forthcoming).

20 This account of the alliances is based on the authors' interviews with federal and provincial officials involved in the 1994 negotiations.

21 See Quebec Liberal Party, Constitutional Committee, *A Quebec Free to Choose* (Quebec City, 1991); Quebec, *Commission on the Political and Constitutional Future of Quebec* (The Allaire Report) (Quebec City: Government of Quebec, 1991); and Bruce Doern, *Europe Uniting: The EC Model and Canada's Constitutional Debate* (Toronto: C.D. Howe Institute, 1991).

22 See Bruce Doern and Brian Tomlin, *Faith and Fear: The Free Trade Story* (Toronto: Stoddart, 1991), Chapter 3; and Michael Hart, "The End of Trade Policy?" in Fen Hampson and Christopher Maule, eds., *Canada Among Nations: 1993-94* (Ottawa: Carleton University Press, 1993), 85-105.

23 See Robert Howse, "Securing the Canadian Economic Union: Legal and Constitutional Options for the Federal Government," *C.D. Howe Institute Commentary*, No. 81, June 1996, 10.

24 See Bruce Doern, *Fairer Play: Canadian Competition Policy Institutions in a Global Market* (Toronto: C.D. Howe Institute, 1995), Chapters 1 and 2.

25 Ibid., 12.

26 See Howse, "Securing the Canadian Economic Union," 12.

27 Ibid., 12.

28 Ibid., 8.

29 Canadian Chamber of Commerce, *The Agreement on Internal Trade and Interprovincial Trade Flows: Building a Strong and United Canada* (Toronto: September 1996), 1.

30 Ibid., 21.

31 See Howse, "Between Anarchy and the Rule of Law," 177-95.

32 Howse, "Securing The Canadian Economic Union," 8-14.

33 Lenihan, "When a Legitimate Objective Hits an Unnecessary Objective."

7

Marketable Commodity or Public Good: The Conflict Between Domestic and Foreign Communications Policy

VINCENT MOSCO

This has been a historic period in the Canadian communication and cultural industries. In the last year alone we have seen the most significant cuts in the history of the Canadian Broadcasting Corporation, the largest newspaper takeover in Canadian history, and the first round of increases that will amount to the most substantial basic rate hike in the history of Canadian telephony. Following in the wake of earlier eruptions, such as the Rogers, Inc. takeover of the Maclean Hunter chain, these developments make communication and culture a continuing source of political debate and policy attention.

Technological convergence, information highways, media concentration, Canadian content, and national identity are terms that fill the popular press and occupy policy analysts. Yet, the Liberal record on communication and culture is not easy to assess, because the Red Book provides little guidance for judging the performance. The most explicit promise committed the Liberals to stable, multi-year financing for the CBC and other national cultural institutions, such as the Canada Council. This guarantee has attracted the most attention, because, as the government itself admits, promise fell far short of performance. What makes this failure all the more striking and critics less than forgiving is that the Red Book sharply contrasts its philosophy of support for national cultural institutions with the policy of the previous government:

At a time when globalization and the information and communications revolution are erasing national borders, Canada needs more than ever to commit itself to cultural development. Instead, the Conservative regime has deliberately undermined our national cultural institutions.

Funding cuts to the Canadian Broadcasting Corporation, the Canada Council, the National Film Board, Telefilm Canada, and other institutions illustrate the Tories' failure to appreciate the importance of cultural and industrial development.[1]

A Record of Achievement briefly acknowledges that "given the severe fiscal restraints facing the government" it was not able to live up to its commitments. Nevertheless, it maintains that the CBC will be able to participate in a $200 million production fund earmarked for the television and cable industry. Additionally, it notes that pending revisions of the Copyright Act will benefit the cultural sector by providing royalties to producers and performers of sound recordings, payments to creators for private copying through a tax on blank cassettes and tapes, and protection for Canadian book distributors.[2] Aside from a handful of minor points, there is nothing else in the Red Book or in *A Record of Achievement* that would convey the sense that we are in the midst of a significant period in Canadian communication policy history. Remarkably, there is no mention of this sector in the four pages of the Red Book's section on "A Trade Policy That Works for Canada," or in the three pages of *A Record of Achievement* that take up accomplishments in this area. Yet, trade in culture and communication played an important role in Canada-U.S. relations as well as in the early activities of the new World Trade Organization.

In order to provide a more comprehensive assessment of government communication and cultural policy than can be achieved by weighing Red Book promises against performance, it is useful to concentrate on the tension between the government's domestic and international strategies. Domestically, the Chrétien government has followed its immediate predecessors by pursuing a strategy that treats communication and information as marketable products not unlike any other commodities. This has moved Canadian policy further away from the position that communication and information are public resources that are vital to citizenship and nationhood, and therefore fundamentally different from marketable products.

Canada's international communication policy, particularly vis-à-vis the United States, is increasingly at odds with the domestic vision of communication "as just another industry." This chapter will address several cases in which the federal government argues that communication is fundamentally different from other products because it is a vital instrument for building national cultural identity. Accordingly, it maintains that communication merits special consideration in international relations, particularly in trade.

The chapter will conclude by assessing the significance of these developments. First, notwithstanding the discourse of expanding domestic competition, it appears that the federal government is pursuing an old policy, pioneered in the development of the national rail network, of identifying and advancing national champions who are protected from competition in order to promote Canadian interests—in this case, in the global economy. Second, it also appears that this strategy is increasingly unsustainable. With little evidence that there is anything more to its cultural protection policies than an interest in sheltering domestic economic interests, Canada is under growing pressure from the United States, the European Community, and the World Trade Organization to open domestic communication markets to foreign investment.

DOMESTIC POLICY: JUST ANOTHER INDUSTRY?

The CBC: From Stable Funding to "Like Everyone Else"
The Liberal party announced in *Creating Opportunity: The Liberal Plan for Canada* (the Red Book), that it "will be committed to stable multi-year financing for national cultural institutions such as the Canada Council and the CBC."[3] The Liberal government itself acknowledges that it has not been able to live up to this promise. In its Red Book report card, the government's CBC commitments receive a "not met"

grade. The CBC cuts are significant for their magnitude and for how they were justified.

By any measure, the CBC is experiencing cuts of historic proportions. According to its 1995-96 report, "as of April 1, 1998, the corporation's funding will be reduced by $414 million over 1994/95 levels." These reductions are a result of budget cuts ($294 million), discontinuation of Radio Canada International (RCI) funding ($15 million),[4] structural shortfall ($40 million), unfunded inflation and other increased costs ($30 million), and potential commercial revenue losses ($35 million).[5] The Corporation's budget stood at about $1.4 billion in 1994-1995, a reduction of almost 30 percent in real resources.

In its Red Book report card the government admits that "given the severe fiscal constraints facing the government, which necessitated cuts in many programs important to Canadians, cuts to the CBC and other major cultural agencies were reluctantly imposed."[6] Putting it more explicitly, Heritage Minister Sheila Copps concluded that "the reality is the CBC, like everyone else, has to cut."[7] These statements justify the imposition of severe cuts on the grounds that the CBC and other cultural agencies are no different from any other institutions significant to Canadians. Indeed, a comparison of the Budget Main Estimates 1995-96 with those of 1994-95 indicates that among thirteen budgetary categories, Heritage and Cultural Programs ranked fourth behind Transportation Programs, Natural Resource-based Programs, and Social Programs in the severity of its budgetary reduction. Programs in Defence, Foreign Affairs, Justice, and Industrial Support, among others, experienced less substantial reductions.[8] These developments signify more than just a reduction in appropriations. They are the explicit acknowledgment that the CBC and other cultural institutions are increasingly treated like any other agency or program in Canada, no more, and perhaps less, special. Furthermore, the addition of a Television and Cable Production Fund does more than temper cuts to the CBC, it suggests a shift in government priorities from supporting its public broadcaster to making production money available to all, including private broadcasters.

Rogers and Hollinger: Content Is Not a Factor
In 1996, Hollinger Inc. purchased the Southam Inc. newspaper chain, giving it control of over half the daily newspapers in Canada, repre-

senting just over 40 percent of daily circulation.[9] The takeover was the largest in Canadian newspaper history. It followed by two years this country's largest cross-media merger, the purchase by Rogers Communications Inc. of Maclean Hunter Ltd., which gave Rogers control over half of Canada's cable television market and Canada's only weekly news magazine, in addition to a national cellular telephone company and a variety of broadcasting and newspaper properties.[10] Although notable for the sheer magnitude of these mergers, the Hollinger and Rogers cases are also significant for what they reveal about the government's view of the communication and cultural industries in Canada.

In 1970, responding to concerns about media concentration, the government established a Special Senate Committee on the Mass Media (the Davey Committee), which carried out extensive studies and hearings and made recommendations to address the problem. In 1981, the government set up the Royal Commission on Newspapers in response to growing newspaper concentration, particularly to the folding on the same day of a Thomson newspaper in Ottawa and a Southam newspaper in Winnipeg, leaving each company with a monopoly in its market. Chaired by Tom Kent, the commission thoroughly reviewed the problem and made a series of recommendations, including the establishment of press councils, which continue to address complaints about media practices today.

The response of the government to the Rogers and Hollinger takeovers departed from previous practice. The government supported the former and took no action, leaving it to the Canadian Radio-television and Telecommunications Commission (CRTC) to review the case, because it involved the transfer of broadcast licences. The CRTC approved the merger, subject to the selling off of two television stations and the imposition of some structural barriers between editorial producers in its print and broadcast properties.[11] In the Hollinger case, the government made no comment about the implications for media concentration and editorial diversity. Instead, it sought the advice of the Director of Investigation and Research (DIR) of Industry Canada's Competition Bureau. The DIR issued an advanced ruling certificate approving the deal, after concluding that it would not give Hollinger an unfair advantage in local print advertising markets. In providing this approval, the DIR chose against recommending that the case be heard by a judicial body, the Competition Tribunal. Since the Bureau's mandate is limited to assessing the economic implications of proposed mergers, it did not consider content issues.[12] Indeed, in response to a question posed by an opposition member in the House, Minister of Industry John Manley made explicit the government's decision to steer clear of content questions:

Mrs. Suzanne Tremblay: Given that one corporation could take over almost 70 percent of all newspapers in Canada, what is the Minister of Industry planning to do to ensure some balance between financial interests and the right to public information?

Hon. John Manley: The balance she suggests, which indeed may be one in favour of which she can argue, is not a balance which is found within the Competition Act itself. If she reads the law itself she will find that the Competition Act, based on the decisions of the courts, deals with the economic interests and the concentration of ownership as it would impact on competition, within the framework of the business of newspaper publishing in this case. Content is not a factor which the Director of Investigation and Research in the Competition Bureau is capable of considering.[13]

In contrast to Tom Kent, who commented, "It's just appalling that it could be allowed to happen," and Senator Keith Davey, who referred to it as "awful," Industry Minister Manley answered a reporter's question about the deal by saying, "My opinion is irrelevant." The Minister of Heritage said simply that she had "no concern at the moment."[14]

It would be reasonable to argue that the consequences of government actions in past cases of media mergers, despite the studies and recommendations, did not amount to much more than what we observe today. Nevertheless, they did establish the principle that media mergers were, by virtue of their impact on the flow of ideas, information, and culture, fundamentally different from those in other industries and should be addressed differently.[15] There is no evidence in the current government's statements or policies to suggest that it concurs with this view. In the same way that it believes that the CBC should be treated just like any other agency, it maintains that media mergers should be viewed like just any other form of corporate acquisition.

Telecommunications: "Cost-Based" Pricing/Higher Local Rates
Telecommunications can be added to the list of areas in which historic rulings were reached over the past year or so. Following on a series of decisions that began with policy changes announced by the Mulroney government, the CRTC made explicit its commitment to remove subsidies that kept local telephone rates low, and in September of 1994 it implemented the largest local rate increase in Canadian telephone history.[16] The commission's initial decision, calling for cost-based pricing and "rate-rebalancing," imposed a $2 per month increase on local rates for each of three years, for a total of $6 per month by the final year.[17] Although it agreed with the commission's position that "meaningful regulatory reform, increased reliance on market forces and the competitive development of all markets require action to reduce this subsidy by a program of rate rebalancing,"[18] the government responded to a public uproar by referring the rate increase and its method of introduction to Cabinet. Upon reconsideration, the CRTC limited the rate increase to the first two years, left open a decision about the third year (the companies want a $3 monthly increase in the third year), and directed company revenue to the reduction of long distance rates.[19] Cabinet again reviewed the decision and this time accepted the rate increase and, in a step that pleased long distance carriers, removed the requirement that would, in effect, have ordered a compensating reduction in long distance rates.[20]

The outcome of this process was a substantial increase in local telephone rates and, on the assumption that the market would address the problem, no requirement that there be compensation for long distance reductions. After the first year of the rate increase, Bell Canada Enterprises (BCE), parent of the national consortium of telephone companies, announced profits of $1.15 billion, a 47 percent jump for the 1996 fiscal year. Moreover, the government and its regulator for the first time made explicit their commitment to treat the telecommunications industry like any other. With respect to the domestic marketplace, the historic tradition of maintaining rates sufficient to ensure universal access to the network (service is accessible to about 98.7 percent of Canadians compared to 94 percent of Americans) was replaced by market-determined cost-based pricing.

The Commercialization and Privatization of Information and Culture

The government has embarked on a series of commercialization and privatization initiatives that are consistent with a policy of increasingly treating this sector like any other. These include:

- the commercialization of CA*net Networking Inc., Canada's non-profit Internet transit service, by transferring it to a division of Bell Canada in 1997
- the privatization of 80 percent of the Canada Communication Group, the primary government printer
- the establishment of commercial fees for the purchase of Statistics Canada data[21]
- the National Research Council's Canada Institute for Scientific and Technical Information now recovers about 40 percent of its budget through the marketing of information
- the Canadian Heritage Information Network (CHIN) is a Special Operating Agency within the federal Department of Canadian Heritage, a status that permits the agency to retain revenues generated from brokering heritage information and providing management training, including the development of electronic resources, to Canadian and international heritage interests
- the government has endorsed the recommendations of its Information Highway Advisory Council, which, while calling for universal access to electronic information services, advocates private development of networks and market control over access[22]

There are certainly exceptions to this trend. For example, the government has tempered its cuts to CBC by approving a $200 million Canadian Television and Cable Production Fund. It has also supported inquiries on the impact on universal access to telecommunications and information services of its proposals to redistribute telephone rates and to price information along market principles. Nevertheless, the overriding thrust of recent policy-making is to treat communication, information, and culture like any other sectors of the domestic economy—private producers and distributors will treat content as a marketable commodity and price access according to commercial market principles.

The Liberals' domestic positions on communication and culture are increasingly at odds with those taken in the international arena. There the government continues to claim special status for communication and culture, arguing that those (particularly Americans) who maintain that communication and culture are like any other commodities do not understand their unique role in advancing citizenship and national identity.

Sports Illustrated *Go Home*
In 1993, Time Warner Inc. introduced a Canadian edition of *Sports Illustrated* magazine that included a small amount of material on Canadian sports but was mainly identical to issues sold in the United States. It then sold advertising in the regional, or "split-run" editions, to Canadian companies. Time Warner made use of new computer technology to circumvent "print in Canada" rules that were intended to encourage production of content in Canada, by electronically transmitting the main editorial content from the United States to a printer in Canada. As a result, in November 1995 the government passed Bill C-103, which imposed an excise tax of 80 percent on the total dollar value of the advertising in almost every split-run magazine sold in Canada, except for *Reader's Digest* and *Time*, which had for a long time produced Canadian editions. The bill also amended the Income Tax Act to ensure that newspapers and periodicals claiming an advertising cost deduction conform to Canadian ownership and control requirements. Speaking for the Minister of Finance, MP Michel Dupuy summarized the government's position as one that would "achieve a balance between the sometimes competing interests of our foreign trade, on the one hand, and the preservation of our cultural identity, on the other."[23]

Opponents, including the U.S. government, which has taken the case to the World Trade Organization, argue that it unfairly discriminates against non-Canadian cultural products. As the economic affairs editor of the *Montreal Gazette* put it, "the playing field for bananas and oranges is uneven too: tropical countries produce them much more cheaply than we do, but we do not insist Canadian fruit lovers buy Canadian-made oranges and bananas." He goes on to note that the Canadian publishing industry chided the government for introducing the Goods and Services Tax, claiming that while some countries burn books, Canada taxes them. By supporting an 80 percent tax on non-Canadian forms of reading, he concludes, "Burning books is OK, I guess, so long as the books are American."[24]

Hyperbole aside, most would agree that this decision advances the view that economic considerations can be modified to advance a cultural goal, here the support of Canadian-produced magazines. Questioning this position, the World Trade Organization issued a preliminary ruling in January 1997, upheld in its February final decision, that Canada could not try to ban Canadian editions of non-Canadian magazines by imposing excise taxes or other economic trade restraints, including favourable postal rates for domestic magazines. Commentators agree that this ruling would reduce Canada's ability to restrict foreign cultural imports in a variety of media.[25]

Of Books and Borders
In 1994, the large U.S. bookstore chain Borders Group Inc. proposed to establish a network of large bookstores in Canada. Borders Canada was to be headed by a Canadian chair and a majority of Canadian directors and promised to set aside 10 percent of its space for Canadian books. Another large U.S. chain, Barnes and Noble, also looked into the prospect of moving into the Canadian market. The government blocked these moves by means of a ruling by Industry Canada's Investment Review Division, which claimed that the minority of non-Canadian board members would exercise "control in fact." That control, the government claimed, would allow Borders to by-pass Canadian book distributors and use its integrated inventory control system to overrun Canadian booksellers. Once again, it determined that the protection of national culture should be upheld over open markets and free trade. The government dealt a further blow to foreign, especially American, booksellers by introducing amendments to its copyright legislation in April 1996 that would permit only Canadian companies to

distribute foreign books. As in the case of *Sports Illustrated*, the U.S. government vigorously opposed these actions and threatened to take the issue to a NAFTA panel as a violation of the "national treatment" provisions of the free trade treaty.[26]

Direct Satellite Broadcasting: None Is Better than Theirs
The United States has enjoyed a thriving alternative to cable television for the past several years, direct-to-home (DTH) satellite broadcasting, which delivers programming to a small (as small as 18 inches in diameter) dish receiver attached to a roof or outside wall of a home. Subscribers pay for the receiver, a monthly fee, and pay-per-view charges for certain programming. In return, they receive sharper video and clearer audio, and avoid the cable company. Local signals are not broadcast, so subscribers use old-fashioned set-top antennae for them. It is estimated that there are about 200,000 Canadian subscribers, but these are part of a "grey" market of people who use a U.S. billing address (which can be provided by Canadian dish receiver outlets) to purchase one of the U.S. services. After nine years of deliberation (the CRTC published its first public notice on DTH in 1987[27]), Canada does not yet have its own service, and non-Canadian firms are barred from operating openly in Canada.

There has been no shortage of potential DTH providers, including a consortium that includes Bell Canada (ExpressVu) and another that joins the Canadian Power Corp. with the leading U.S. DTH company Direct TV (Power DirecTv). Each has been licensed to provide service, but is reluctant to enter the market under existing regulatory conditions, including the use of Canadian satellites (which was made more difficult by the March 1996 failure of Telesat Canada's Anik E-1 satellite) and the provision of Canadian content.[28] In November 1996, Industry Canada issued a pamphlet that warned grey market users against purchasing services "from anyone but the lawful distributor— a person who has the lawful right in Canada to transmit an encoded signal and to authorize its decoding."[29] This can be viewed as an effort to limit the number of people who might be tempted by Christmas mark-downs to join the grey market. The concern here is that the grey market might swell to the point that no Canadian alternative would be economically viable. The government has also taken another stab at what it calls a "Made-in-Canada" solution. Responding to a July 1996

Federal Communications Commission (FCC) decision dismissing the request of a U.S. consortium to use discounted Telesat facilities for U.S. services, the Industry Minister began consultations with industry stakeholders to explore Canadian alternatives.[30]

The DTH case is admittedly complex and saturated with the fullest range of personal and institutional politics. But despite the complexities, the case reveals a consistent application of the Liberal communication policy. In domestic markets, treat culture and communication like any other industry, but when it comes to the international, and particularly the cross-border environment, treat them as exceptional arenas outside the seemingly inexorable logic of market and trade relations.

Telecommunications and Foreign Ownership

One of the major tests of how exceptional an industry is viewed can be found in the extent of foreign ownership permitted. Although in Investment Canada this country retains a review board for foreign takeovers, most Canadian industries are fully open to foreign investment. This is not the case in telecommunications. While the introduction of "cost-based" pricing and rate "rebalancing" has signalled the position that telecommunications would no longer be treated exceptionally in the domestic market, movement in this direction is not nearly as substantial or as clear in the international arena. It is true that the government has raised the maximum permitted foreign ownership from 20 percent to one-third. The government also accepted a February 1997 World Trade Organization agreement to raise the floor to 46.7 percent.[31] However, this was done primarily to permit the infusion of foreign investment, particularly from AT&T, to stave off the collapse of Unitel, a company that the government hoped would stimulate competition in the long-distance market.

Canada's lack of substantial action to liberalize foreign ownership of telecommunications companies has not gone unnoticed in the international arena. The United States and some European countries have been calling for the global lowering of foreign ownership limits, along with the elimination of Canadian monopolies and of rules that encourage the use of Canadian facilities for domestic and international traffic.[32] The United States is particularly concerned about the foreign ownership issue, because its liberal ownership rules permitted British

Telecommunications to take complete control of its second largest tele-communications carrier, MCI, in what amounted to the largest foreign purchase of a U.S. corporation.[33]

NATIONAL CHAMPIONS

One of the consequences of pursuing a policy that promotes a tradi-tional business approach to communication, culture, and information domestically, while treating them as exceptional and in need of protec-tion internationally, is the growth of dominant Canadian companies holding significant market power across these industries. The result is a set of national champions, the information-age descendants of na-tional giants that once ruled over the transportation and utility sectors. In the newspaper business, Hollinger enjoys market dominance in part because provisions of the Income Tax Act in effect prohibit foreign ownership. Banning Borders and Barnes and Noble enabled an inte-grated national chain combining SmithBooks and Coles Book Stores Limited (which were permitted to merge in 1995) to form a national network of department-store-sized Chapters bookstores that dwarf the competition. Rogers Communications Inc. has established local fran-chised cable monopolies across the country in part because the gov-ernment fears foreign control over the satellite-to-home alternative. Protection for the magazine industry also guarantees *Maclean's* a monopoly in the English language newsweekly market. Bell Canada Enterprises (BCE) has also been a major beneficiary. It continues to dominate basic telephony with nearly complete control of the local markets it serves, and it retains about 70 percent of the national long distance market.[34] BCE also holds majority control of Canada's major satellite company, Telesat Canada, and its only international telecom-munications carrier, Teleglobe Canada Inc. In addition, it controls the majority ownership in Northern Telecom (Nortel) and in BCE Mobile Communications Inc., one of two national mobile telephone compa-nies.

In effect, the Canadian communication arena is dominated by a hand-ful of large firms that set the pattern for development in their respec-tive industries and are increasingly integrated across this converging industry. This is not to conclude that such an outcome was planned or that it was an unanticipated consequence, nor to suggest that it is without exceptions. Rather, it is one consequence of a divided policy whose most important characteristic may be that it is increasingly unsustainable.

FOREIGN PRESSURES AND NEW THINKING

The gap between the domestic and the international components of Canada's communication policy has become increasingly obvious to trading partners. The vigorous pursuit of a domestic strategy that imposes historic cuts to its public broadcaster, eliminates the traditional practice of subsidizing access to telecommunications, and judges historic mergers in print and electronic media solely in terms of their impact on advertising markets, makes it more difficult to make the case internationally that Canada's communication and cultural industries need to be protected to advance a national purpose beyond mere market considerations. Canadian domestic policy lends credence to the view that keeping out foreign media is nothing more than economic protectionism.

The Liberal dual strategy has become more difficult to sustain, because barriers to foreign entry into communication markets have diminished in the rest of the world. This is especially the case in electronic media and telecommunications, where privatizations and regional and international treaty commitments have opened markets. As a result, companies like BCE have entered foreign telecommunications and cable television markets whose companies are barred from similar entry into Canada. Moreover, in markets like newspapers and book publishing, where foreign ownership has been barred or limited in Canada, though wide open in the places like the United States, firms have grown increasingly interested in using new electronic technologies to ease entry into foreign, including Canadian, markets.[35]

Admittedly, Canada has always been pressed to back off from protecting its communication and cultural industries, but the pressures are now more potent, because they are global. It is not just the United States that is demanding open Canadian markets, but the full complement of European telecommunications firms, with new mandates to compete globally. Moreover, the introduction of global institutions like the World Trade Organization, where the United States won its dispute over the split-run edition of *Sports Illustrated*, increases the pressure to harmonize policies and eliminate such exceptional cases as the policies to protect Canada's cultural industries.[36] Finally, some of the same companies protected by Canadian government policies are themselves worried about the consequences. Justifying his call for the liberalization of foreign ownership of Canadian telecommunications firms, the chairman and chief executive officer of Teleglobe Inc., Charles Sirois, said, "I don't want our small pond protected if it means we can't access the whole ocean."[37]

Developments such as these have prompted some to begin to address the inevitable collapse of Canada's dual communication policy. Ideas run the gamut from yielding to the inevitable elimination of special status for the communication industries and accepting their full absorption into a global market economy[38] to supporting the development of civic alternatives to a state-run public sphere and providing support for Canadian cultural production, if not for the institutions that traditionally housed it.[39] This debate is only beginning to filter through the government policy apparatus. The only assurance one can derive from this assessment is that we have not seen the last of historic decisions in Canadian communication policy.[40]

As for the Red Book promises, it is hard to find much that speaks positively of Liberal accomplishments. To its credit, the government committed $200 million to a new Canadian Television and Cable Production Fund. It also moved forward copyright legislation to assist Canadian producers and enhanced the profile of Canadian cultural products in its wider Team Canada strategy to promote Canadian exports. On the other hand, it failed to keep its promise to provide stable funding to national cultural institutions. Its cuts to the budget of the CBC do not simply continue the policy of its predecessor, which the Liberals attacked and committed to reverse, they impose the most severe cuts in the history of the Corporation, cuts that are substantially greater than those imposed on other government departments, such as the Department of National Defence. Moreover, the government's policy to protect Canadian culture against American imports does not appear to be succeeding. The decision of the World Trade Organization in support of the U.S. protest against the imposition of a tax on split-run magazines places in jeopardy the government's effort to keep restrictions on foreign entry in other media, such as books and newspapers.

With its policy of protecting culture by limiting imports in danger, the government is again considering what appears to be its only short-run alternative, direct subsidies to producers, an option that most agree is permissible under the NAFTA and GATT agreements.[41] The problem with this strategy is that it is inconsistent with the government's recent approach to the domestic marketplace. It is no small irony that in the same week that the WTO announced its preliminary decision in the *Sports Illustrated* case, Atlantic Canada's best known alternative magazine *New Maritimes* went out of business primarily because it had lost its Canada Council grant. Citing budget cuts and the consequent need to narrow its grant mandate, the Council has also warned the magazine *Canadian Forum* that its funding will be lost unless it shifts its focus from politics to the arts.[42]

The government has little room to manoeuvre within a policy strategy that, by and large, treats domestic culture and communication as a matter for the market to decide at the same time as it promotes cultural exceptionalism in the international arena. It is no wonder that our trading partners and international trade organizations are increasingly sceptical. The primary challenge facing the government is whether it is capable of fundamentally rethinking cultural and communication policy, even as it attempts to ameliorate the short-run political damage of its policy failures.

NOTES

I would like to thank Shawn Yerxa for his advice and assistance, as well as Leanne Yohemas-Hayes for her research assistance, and the Social Sciences and Humanities Research Council for a research grant.

1 Liberal Party of Canada, *Creating Opportunity: The Liberal Plan for Canada* (Ottawa, 1993), 88.
2 Liberal Party of Canada, *A Record of Achievement* (Ottawa, 1996), 88-89. Copyright Act revisions stalled in the winter of 1997 and commentators doubt whether new legislation will be enacted prior to the 1997 federal election.
3 Liberal Party of Canada, *Creating Opportunity*, 89.
4 On December 7, 1996, CBC President Perrin Beatty announced that Radio Canada International, the national short-wave radio service, would be shut down on March 31, 1997, because the CBC would not be able to share the cost of RCI's $16 million annual budget. Subse-

quent to this announcement, it appears that funding will be found in other agencies to keep it afloat for at least one more year.

5 Canadian Broadcasting Corporation, *CBC SRC Annual Report, 1995-1996*, (Ottawa), 51. "Structural shortfall" refers to the cumulative result of government funding cuts and new cost increases prior to 1995-96, which were managed through temporary measures that, according to the CBC, are no longer available.

6 Liberal Party of Canada, *A Record of Achievement*, 89.

7 As quoted in Canadian Press, "Copps Broke Pledge on CBC," *Hamilton Spectator*, September 20, 1996, A3. Responding to critics, the Heritage Minister agreed to add $10 million to the budget of CBC radio in February 1997.

8 Canada, *1995-1996 Estimates Part I, The Government Expenditure Plan* (Ottawa: Canada Communication Group), 22.

9 By December 1996 Hollinger Inc. controlled 58 of Canada's 105 daily newspapers, representing 41.4 percent of total daily circulation.

10 In order to pare down a debt load of $4.7 billion, Rogers Communications has sold some of these holdings, including its stake in Toronto Sun Publishing Corp. and $350 million worth of Ontario cable assets. Although its cable market share has dipped to just under 40 percent, Rogers remains the dominant cable company and a major force in publishing (*Maclean's* magazine), broadcasting, and telecommunications.

11 Canadian Radio-television and Telecommunications Commission (CRTC), *Rogers Communications Inc.*, Decision CRTC 94-923, Ottawa, December 19, 1994.

12 For an assessment of government competition policy that addresses the increasingly narrow grounds for finding excessive concentration see G. Bruce Doern, *Fairer Play: Canadian Competition Policy Institutions in a Global Market* (Toronto: C.D. Howe Institute, 1995).

13 Canada, *House of Commons Debates: Official Report (Hansard)*, 134 (June 3, 1996), 055, 2d Sess., 35th Parliament, 3317.

14 The Kent and Davey comments are contained in "Critics Attack Southam Deal; Public Approval Not Required, Says Federal Competition Official," *The Edmonton Journal*, May 26, 1996, A8. The statements of the Ministers of Industry and of Heritage are from Chris Cobb, "Concerns Over Competition: Watchdog Okayed Deal; Heritage Remains Mum," *The Montreal Gazette*, May 28, 1996, D4.

15 Consider these conclusions from the 1981 Royal Commission on Newspapers: "Just as it was necessary at first to keep the press out of the clutches of the State, so was it necessary in the age of mass communications to protect it from the abuse of the industrial plutocracy," and "The ownership and control of most newspapers is today highly concentrated under interests whose business concerns extend

far beyond the particular newspaper.... Extraneous interests, operating internally, are the chains that today limit the freedom of the press." Canada, *Royal Commission on Newspapers* (Ottawa: Supply and Services Canada, 1981), 21, 237.

16 For a review of earlier decisions see Kevin G. Wilson, "Competition in Long-Distance Telephony: A Critical Analysis of Telecom Decision CRTC 92-12," *Canadian Journal of Communication*, 20, 2 (1995), 167-90, and Dwayne Winseck, "Power Shift?: Toward a Political Economy of Canadian Telecommunications and Regulation," *Canadian Journal of Communication*, 20, 1 (1995), 81-106.

17 CRTC, *Telecom Decision CRTC 94-19: Review of Regulatory Framework*, Hull, September 16, 1994. Some question the direction of the subsidy and others see the determination of what constitutes a local or long distance call to be a political decision. For a review of these debates see Vincent Mosco, "The Mythology of Telecommunications Deregulation," *Journal of Communication*, 40, 1 (Winter 1990), 36-49.

18 CRTC, *Telecom Decision CRTC 94-19*, 17.

19 CRTC, *Telecom Decision CRTC 95-21: Implementation of Regulatory Framework—Splitting of the Rate Base and Related Issues*, Hull, 1995.

20 Canada, "Order Varying Telecom Decision CRTC 95-21, P.C. 1995-2196 19 December," *Canada Gazette*, Part II, 130 (1), 96-98.

21 This policy marks an acceleration of Mulroney government policies. For a review of the impact on data access and how StatsCan aims to address criticism, particularly with its "data liberation initiative," see April Lindgren, "Statistics Canada User Fees 'Discourage Use of Data,'" *The Ottawa Citizen*, July 4, 1996, A4.

22 Canada, Information Highway Advisory Council, *Connection, Community, Content: The Challenge of the Information Highway: Final Report* (Ottawa: Supply and Services Canada), 1995. Although it supports private sector development of computer communication networks, the government has committed public funding to assist private companies, mainly technology and infrastructure providers, in building them. See Canada, Industry Canada, *Building the Information Society: Moving Canada into the 21st Century* (Ottawa: Supply and Services Canada), 1996, 7-10.

23 Canada, *House of Commons Debates: Official Report (Hansard)*, 133, (November 2, 1995), 253, 1st Sess., 35th Parliament, 16122.

24 Ibid., 16125.

25 Laura Eggertson, "Cultural 'Assault' by U.S. Feared: WTO Ruling on Magazines 'Thin Edge of the Wedge,'" *The Globe and Mail* [Toronto], January 18, 1997, B1, and Anthony DePalma, "World Trade Body Opposes Canadian Magazine Tariffs," *New York Times*, January 20, 1997, D8.

26 Canada, *House of Commons Debates: Official Report (Hansard)*, 133 (November 24, 1995), 253, 1st Sess., 35th Parliament, 16781-82, and Peter Morton, "Canada: Ottawa's Protection of Publishing Angers U.S.," *The Financial Post* (Reuter Textline edition), April 26, 1996. Although NAFTA exempts the cultural industries, it permits retaliation against cultural protectionism in other sectors. The national treatment provision aims to subject all companies doing business in a country to the same national policies and regulations, irrespective of national origin.

27 CRTC, *Public Notice CRTC 1987-254: Regulatory Policy for Direct-to-Home (DTH) Satellite Broadcasting Systems, Multipoint Distribution Systems (MDS), and Subscription Television (STV) Systems,* Hull, 1987.

28 CRTC, *Public Notice CRTC 1995-217: Introductory Statement—Licensing of New Direct-to-Home (DTH) Satellite Distribution Undertakings and New DTH Pay-Per-View (PPV) Television Programming Undertakings,* Hull, 1995.

29 Canada, Industry Canada, "Direct-To-Home Satellite TV—Facts You Should Know," cited in Terence Corcoran, "Switch Off Your Set; The Feds Are Coming," *The Globe and Mail* [Toronto], November 20, 1996, B2.

30 Canada, Industry Canada, "Manley Calls for a 'Made-in-Canada' DBS Solution," News Release, Ottawa, July 18, 1996.

31 U.S. and European negotiators hoped to increase the floor to well over 50 percent and singled out Canada for intransigence on this and related issues. See Edmund L. Andrews, "68 Nations Agree to Widen Market in Communications," *The New York Times*, February 16, 1997, A1.

32 Canada, Industry Canada, "Notice No. DGTP-008-96,—Review of Canadian Telecommunications Policy in the Context of Global Trade Developments," *Canada Gazette Part I*, August 24, 1996, 2451.

33 Mark Landler, "MCI Deal Reverberates on Both Sides of the Atlantic," *The New York Times*, November 4, 1996, D1.

34 Competition has eroded the Bell monopoly in long distance, but a November 1996 report suggests a levelling off. Bell's market share slipped less than 1 percent between June and September 1996, the smallest quarterly drop since long distance competition was introduced. See Allan Swift, "Bell Finds Pain of Long-Distance Deregulation Eases with Time," *The Ottawa Citizen,* November 12, 1996, F3.

35 Foreign ownership of Canadian newspapers is opposed by all of the major Canadian chains, whose newspapers universally editorialize in support of free trade in almost every other industry. For an interesting analysis of this contradiction, see Terence Corcoran, "Restore Press Freedom in Canada," *The Globe and Mail* [Toronto], May 28, 1996, B2.

36 According to Dennis Brown, Canada's former consul general in Los Angeles and now Director of the Ottawa-based Centre for Trade Policy and Law, "What we *are* going to see after the (U.S.) election is a more vigorous attack on our cultural policies. If the Americans win at the World Trade Organization on the split-run magazine case, they'll be encouraged to take us on." Cited in Juliet O'Neil, "Cross-Border Politics a Question of Influence," *The Ottawa Citizen*, November 2, 1996, B5.

37 Lawrence Surtees, "Scrap Ownership Limits on Phone Firms: Sirois," *The Globe and Mail* [Toronto], November 29, 1996, B18.

38 See Steven Globerman, Hudson N. Janisch, and W.T. Stanbury, "Moving Toward Local-Distribution Network Competition in Canada," *Telecommunications Policy*, 20, 2 (1996), 141-57, and Steven Globerman, "Foreign Ownership in Telecommunications: A Policy Perspective," *Telecommunications Policy*, 19, 1 (1995), 21-28.

39 See Marc Raboy, "Public Television," and Michael Dorland, "Cultural Industries and the Canadian Experience: Reflections on the Emergence of a Field," in Michael Dorland, ed., *The Canadian Cultural Industries* (Toronto: Lorimer, 1996), 178-202 and 347-65.

40 As a result of the WTO decision in the split-run magazine case, the Liberals have begun to raise fundamental questions about cultural policy. Although he agrees with the need to "preserve Canadian culture," International Trade Minister Art Eggleton concludes, "Everything else is open for discussion. We may keep the combination of subsidies, regulation and foreign ownership rules but they may be weighted differently. Let's look at all the mechanisms. Some of them may still be appropriate. Some may need throwing out altogether." Cited in Juliet O'Neill, "Protection of Arts Open to Negotiation," *The Ottawa Citizen*, January 29, 1997, A2.

41 Susan Riley, "Experts Win Voice in Arts Policy: Trade Ruling Leads Copps to Call Private Meeting," *The Ottawa Citizen*, January 22, 1997, B5.

42 Susan Riley, "Magazines Told to Shift Focus to Arts from Politics or Risk Losing Funding," *The Ottawa Citizen*, January 15, 1997, C9.

8

From Great Leaps to Baby Steps: Environment and Sustainable Development Policy Under the Liberals

LUC JUILLET
GLEN TONER

Reading the Liberal party's Red Book back in the autumn of 1993, sympathetic observers of federal environmental policies could have found reason for sincere optimism. The electoral manifesto suggested that environmental concerns would be high on a Liberal government's agenda. The Red Book raised expectations by speaking of the need for "a fundamental shift in values and public policy" to reconcile economic growth with the preservation of a healthy natural environment.[1] An entire chapter, out of eight, was devoted to describing a progressive vision of the federal government's role in protecting the environment and achieving a more sustainable form of economic development. Economic and environmental policies would now reinforce each other, and strict environmental standards would help foster industrial innovation, employment, and sustainable growth. Political institutions would be reformed to assure that environmental concerns would now be addressed by all departments and better integrated into governmental decision-making processes. Pollution prevention would replace pollution management and clean-up as the central philosophy underpinning public intervention. Canada's international contribution to environmental efforts, such as curtailing global warming and protecting the ozone layer, would be strengthened.

Three years after the Liberals' ascendance to power, their record finds many critics. The Sierra Club of Canada has gone so far as to state that "the Liberal government record, thus far in their mandate, is significantly worse than that of their Conservative predecessors. In fact, in terms of environmental performance, this Government is arguably the worst since the creation of Environment Canada twenty-five years ago."[2] While not going to the same length, several other environmental organizations and national newspaper columnists have also condemned the Chrétien government for falling short on electoral commitments or for dragging its feet in introducing promised changes.

This chapter analyzes the Liberal government's environmental policies during the first three years of its mandate, and finds that in the transition from the campaign trail to the cabinet room the Liberals' environmental and sustainable development vision of aggressive activism was tamed by contact with the hard realities of Canadian politics in the 1990s. In explaining this shift, we emphasize the interplay among three factors: 1) the lack of political will within Cabinet and the opposition of economic departments with a traditional vision of economic development; 2) the overarching primacy given to an old-style economic agenda, in the face of deficit problems and high unemployment; and 3) the government's desire to avoid additional federal-provincial conflicts at a crucial period for national unity. The first section provides a critical assessment of the Liberals' performance in five important areas of environmental policy-making: control of toxic substances, environmental assessment of industrial projects, establishment of a framework for the protection of biodiversity and endangered species, the fight against global warming, and institutionalization of sustainable development in public administration. The second section explains the difficulties the Liberals faced in implementing their agenda.

ENVIRONMENTAL POLICIES AND THE
LIBERALS' EXPERIENCE IN POWER

*Pollution Prevention and the Canadian Environmental
Protection Act*
The Red Book made it clear that the control of toxic substances would
be a major part of the Liberal environmental policy agenda. A Liberal
government would focus on reducing pollution at the source, by rethinking production processes and by technological innovation, rather
than at the point of discharge. Pollution prevention would become a
national goal, and the use of the most persistent toxic substances would
be phased out. The concept of pollution prevention itself, understood
as a policy approach distinct from end-of-pipe regulations, is not new
in environmental policy. Pollution prevention legislation has been in
place in the United States since 1990.[3] In Canada, the automotive manufacturing industry has been co-operating with Environment Canada
(DOE)[4] on a pollution prevention project since 1992.[5] But the approach
is increasingly advocated by business gurus as a progressive way to
reconcile tough environmental protection measures with an economic
agenda based on competitiveness and innovation.[6] The Red Book and
its principal architect, Paul Martin, endorsed this new approach to
"green economics" and promised to move pollution prevention to the
centre of Canadian environmental policy.[7]

In the first year of the government, Environment Minister Sheila
Copps set out to keep the Red Book's promises on toxic substances.
After holding consultations in the fall of 1994, the government released two policy documents in the summer of 1995. The *Toxic Substances Management Policy* announced the government's position that
toxic substances found to be persistent and bioaccumulative would
have to be "virtually eliminated" from the environment, while all other
toxics would have to be properly managed throughout their life cycle
in order to minimize their release into the environment.[8] *Pollution Prevention: A Federal Strategy for Action* outlined a strategy almost entirely based on public education, information dissemination, and
voluntary measures, for the promotion of pollution prevention. While
promising to incorporate the principle of pollution prevention in the

work of all relevant departments and legislation in the future, the policy contained no immediate and tangible measures. Finally, in 1996, DOE announced that, starting with the 1997 reporting year, businesses would have to report pollution prevention measures through the National Pollutant Release Inventory.

While positioning the government with respect to philosophy and approach, these measures mostly laid the ground for the heart of its toxic substances agenda: the reform of the Canadian Environmental Protection Act (CEPA). In the context of a required statutory review of the Act, the Parliamentary Committee on the Environment and Sustainable Development released a report in June 1995 calling for faster toxicity assessments, regulation of more substances, greater enforcement powers, and a more prominent federal role in pollution management across the country.[9] It endorsed the government's shift toward pollution prevention and proposed two mechanisms to integrate pollution prevention into CEPA: companies should be required by law to submit pollution prevention plans for the virtual elimination of substances designated as toxic under the Act, and DOE should encourage the voluntary adoption of pollution prevention practices through the diffusion of information and the creation of an award program.

The parliamentary committee's report set off alarm bells in the business community and sharpened the terms of the debate on pollution prevention. While pollution prevention was supported in principle, industry groups denounced the proposed implementation approach as too bureaucratic and heavy-handed, and certain to lead to unprecedented intrusions into corporate operations. While traditional environmental standards dealt with emissions coming out of the production process, the use of mandatory pollution prevention plans would mean the federal government would now request detailed and confidential information about the design of a company's operations. In an attempt to shape the government's response, business groups, assisted by Natural Resources Canada (NRCan) and Industry Canada, lobbied DOE. Senior industry representatives even offered to help draft the government's response. It was proposed that a few industry people, sworn to respect departmental secrecy, could assist the department's staff in a personal capacity. The offer was rejected by DOE.

After a preliminary response published in December 1995, Environment Minister Sergio Marchi introduced in the House of Commons a bill proposing a renewed CEPA on December 10, 1996. The new Act would integrate the objectives of the government's 1995 toxic substance management policy and require the virtual elimination of the toxic substances found to be persistent and bioaccumulative.[10] The government also proposed changes to the toxicity assessment process to accelerate the evaluation of priority substances by modifying assessment criteria and making greater use of the data developed by other Organization for Economic Cooperation and Development (OECD) countries. It would also grant DOE inspectors more powers and give citizens the right to sue for damage to the environment when the government fails to enforce the new law. While the government accepted the committee's recommendation to add mandatory pollution prevention planning as a means of enforcement, it proposed a more flexible approach, limiting this requirement to certain toxic substances to be designated by the minister. Moreover, guidelines will be established in consultation with stakeholders to stipulate when pollution prevention planning would be appropriate. These decisions could be based on cost-benefit considerations and the industry's previous experience with pollution prevention planning.

The CEPA bill appeared to disappoint everyone. The *Financial Post* headline stated, "Business Enraged by Pollution Bill," while *The Toronto Star*, referring to the reaction of environmental groups, offered "Environment Act Changes Disappoint."[11] Industry associations claimed that, in its haste to regulate more chemicals, the government was sidestepping science and consultation. Mandatory pollution prevention measures and expanded regulatory powers, over areas such as fuel efficiency and international pollution, implied that DOE was reverting back to an old-style command-and-control approach, not giving sufficient credit to voluntary measures. Environmentalists were also critical, arguing that the new criteria for virtual elimination were so restrictive that few substances would actually be targeted. The Minister admitted that probably no more than 10 to 12 new chemicals would be designated for virtual elimination over the next 20 years.[12] This is a small number, considering that 23,000 substances are currently used in Canada, and that 1,000 new ones are invented every year around the world.[13]

In sum, the debate over pollution prevention, originally presented as a new way to reconcile economic competitiveness and environmental protection, had reverted to the old-style environmental politics of an earlier decade, with environmentalists demanding tougher regulations confronting industrial interests seeking less government involvement in their daily operations. The Liberals have taken the middle ground, pleasing neither camp.

Environmental Impact Assessment

The Red Book made two main promises about environmental impact assessment. First, decision-making powers would be shifted to an independent Canadian Environmental Assessment Agency, subject to appeal to Cabinet. No longer could ministers simply ignore the solid recommendations for environmental protection made by public review panels. Second, the Canadian Environmental Assessment Act (CEAA) would be amended to legally recognize intervener funding as an integral part of the assessment process.

While CEAA was amended to guarantee intervener funding, the independent status of the Canadian Environmental Assessment Agency never materialized. Instead, in a 1994 amendment to the Act, the Liberals shifted the final authorization, for those projects examined by review panels, from the responsible ministers alone to the Cabinet as a whole. Rather than simply consider appeals of decisions rendered by an independent agency, Cabinet would make the decisions in the first instance.

Given the history of environmental assessment within the bureaucracy, it is easy to understand the government's reluctance to grant more decision powers to an independent agency. The reform of the environmental impact assessment process was the result of a lengthy and difficult process started by the Conservatives in the late 1980s after a series of court cases forced the government to act, and it culminated in the adoption of CEAA in 1992. When the Liberals came to power in late 1993, CEAA was only awaiting the completion of its regulations to be proclaimed. At the time the legislation was drafted, resource departments and industrial associations had strongly opposed the centralization of the assessment process in the hands of an independent agency or DOE. Vocal criticism from some resource ministers about the bureaucratic delays created by the new assessment process made the allocation of more independence and decision powers to the Canadian Environmental Assessment Agency politically impossible.[14]

By the beginning of 1997, concerns about the dismissal of public review panel recommendations under the Conservatives had been replaced by concerns about the reluctance of the Liberal government to establish public review panels in the first place. Despite their disagreement with certain aspects of the legislation, environmental groups still had great expectations of CEAA. Eighteen months after its proclamation, they complained that the Act has been "nearly invisible."[15] Despite the assessment of more than a thousand projects under the provisions of the Act, only five public review panels had been announced. In at least one instance, environmental groups had to sue the government to force the establishment of a review panel.[16]

Meanwhile, resource departments, such as the Department of Fisheries and Oceans (DFO) and NRCan, and industry groups criticized CEAA for being too cumbersome, and lobbied for amendments to restrict its application. In a letter to Marchi early in 1996, Anne McLellan asked that time limits be imposed on environmental assessments, claiming that the bureaucratic delays they cause would limit the government's capacity to fulfil its jobs and growth agenda. NRCan was responding to industry criticism about delays in approving the Huckleberry gold and copper mine project in northern British Columbia. Earlier in the year, B.C. Premier Glen Clark, mining industry executives, and even the Canadian Ambassador to Japan had all called for limitations on the federal assessment process, claiming that the new Act would hurt Canada's reputation in the international investor community and jeopardize investments in the resource sector. Clark went so far as to suggest the federal government "get out of the assessment business" altogether.

To some, the Liberals seem to be responding favourably to provincial requests for less federal intervention in environmental assessments. In September 1996, environmental groups filed a citizen complaint against the Canadian government before the North American Commission for Environmental Cooperation, the international body created by the environmental side-deal of the North American Free Trade Agreement, for failing to enforce CEAA. Environmentalists have accused DFO of by-passing some regulatory provisions of the Fisheries Act to avoid triggering environmental assessments under CEAA.[17] They claim that the practice has resulted from DFO's reluctance to commit the necessary resources to conduct assessments and the Alberta government's dislike of federal assessments on provincial lands. Meanwhile, the number of DFO assessments for projects disturbing fish habitats under the Fisheries Act have reportedly declined from more than 12,000 in 1991-92 to a mere 233 in 1995-96.[18]

However, the legality of this informal delegation practice may soon become academic, because the Liberal government has introduced legislation in Parliament to formally delegate the responsibility for fish habitat management to the provinces. After the current legislative reform of the Fisheries Act, it will be possible for the federal government to conclude delegation agreements with the provinces regarding environmental protection. This would represent a major change for the environmental protection regime in Canada, as the habitat provisions of the Fisheries Act constitute some of the federal government's most important environmental regulatory measures. It could also confirm DFO's withdrawal from environmental assessment, because the authorization of projects requiring assessment would be delegated to the provinces, except for a list of projects that remains to be negotiated.

Endangered Species and the Protection of Biodiversity
The Liberals came to power a month before the United Nations Convention on Biological Diversity, signed at the 1992 Earth Summit in Rio de Janeiro, came into effect. An active participant in its negotiation, Canada was the first industrialized country to ratify the convention, in December 1992, and, even though the Red Book contained few commitments regarding the protection of biological diversity,[19] the issue quickly became an important item of the government's environmental agenda. After a lengthy and relatively low-profile consultation process, the government released a national biodiversity strategy in 1995, signed by all jurisdictions in Canada, that set a national framework for action in response to the international convention.

The government then announced its intention to introduce legislation to protect endangered species in the 1996 Throne Speech. The proposed Canadian Endangered Species Protection Act (CESPA) is the result of extensive stakeholder consultations. After public consultations across the country, DOE published a legislative proposal in August 1995. A multi-stakeholder task force was then established to advise the department on drafting the bill. In May 1996, the task force presented a consensus report, which was integrated to a great extent into the final legislative draft. CESPA would enshrine into law the existing administrative process used to list endangered species, with some modifications,[20] and would make it illegal to harm or capture a member of a listed species or to damage its residence. Subsequent to the listing of a species as endangered, the government would have one year to submit a plan stating how it intends to protect it and assist in its recovery.

Notwithstanding the consensus previously achieved by the multistakeholder task force, the government's bill quickly became the object of harsh criticism from virtually all corners. The main point of contention is the limited scope of the legislation. While over-harvesting remains a threat to some species, the vast majority of endangered species are threatened by the destruction or contamination of their natural habitat, through commercial activity (e.g. industrial pollution, forest clear-cutting, mining and farming practices) or urban sprawl. The protection of habitat involves the regulation of a wide array of activities on federal, provincial, and private lands, and is a daunting endeavour that requires extensive inter-jurisdictional co-operation.

While recognizing the requirement for such co-operation, many environmental groups have accused the federal government of refusing to fully occupy its jurisdiction regarding endangered species. They believe that the federal government possesses much more extensive jurisdiction than that exercised under CESPA, which only protects species found on federal lands (while they remain on federal lands) and only applies to "federally managed" species (i.e. those covered by the Migratory Birds Convention or the Fisheries Act). The legislation also contains provisions enabling, but not requiring, the Environment minister to make regulations for species crossing international borders. In total, CESPA would cover only about 40 percent of the species currently found on the national endangered species list. Environmental groups, the scientific community, and national newspapers have all condemned the Liberal government's refusal to assure more comprehensive coverage.[21]

The federal government is banking on provincial co-operation to assure adequate protection across the country. On October 2, 1996, the federal government and the provinces signed an agreement, the National Accord for the Protection of Species at Risk, committing the signatories to adopt complementary legislation. However, while four provinces already have legislation protecting endangered species, others are reluctant to pass the required legislation. In late 1996, British Columbia's Environment minister warned that he would not propose such legislation in the near future, in order to avoid alienating the provincial resource industries.[22]

Despite a national poll showing that 94 percent of Canadians support federal legislation for the protection of endangered species,[23] the Liberals have been unwilling to confront industry and landowners by establishing stringent habitat protection regulations. While CESPA will prohibit the destruction or damage of a listed species' "residence," it will not automatically prohibit the destruction of its habitat. Scientists have warned that the protection of nests or dens will not suffice to protect species if their breeding or feeding grounds are destroyed by commercial activities. Moreover, the proposed provisions seem so weak that an abundant fish species would get better habitat protection under existing provisions of the Fisheries Act than an endangered fish species under the proposed CESPA. Under the proposed act, habitat protection would be dealt with through recovery plans, which will have no legal force and will depend on co-operation and political will for their implementation.

Industrial associations and resource departments have opposed more stringent habitat provisions. Already unhappy with the current limited provisions, industrial associations have argued that the Act should not apply to private lands and that producers should participate directly in the drafting of recovery plans.[24] They maintain that the Act does not rely sufficiently on voluntary measures and that the regulations against the destruction of residences should clearly not apply to habitat. Federal departments such as Agriculture and Agri-Food, Transport, and Fisheries also argued strongly for limited regulatory measures, so that habitat protection would not hold up commercial activity. DFO was concerned, in particular, that listing species as endangered might hinder the commercial exploitation of fish stocks or erode its prerogative over the management of the fisheries.

Climate Change
At Rio, the Mulroney Conservatives committed Canada to stabilize carbon-dioxide (CO_2) emissions at 1990 levels by the year 2000 in accordance with the terms of the Framework Convention. In the Red

Book, the Liberals "outgreened" the Tories by stating that they would work with provincial and urban governments to improve energy efficiency and increase the use of renewable energies, with the goal of cutting CO_2 emissions by 20 percent from 1988 levels by the year 2005. The International Panel on Climate Change stated in 1995 that "[g]lobal mean surface temperature has increased by between about 0.3 and 0.6 degrees C since the late 19th century, a change that is unlikely to be entirely natural in origin. The balance of evidence, from changes in global mean surface air temperature and from changes in geographical, seasonal and vertical patterns of atmospheric temperature, suggests a discernible human influence on global climate."[25] Canada's average temperature has become about one degree warmer since 1895. Despite the increasing certainty of the science, the climate change debate in Canada became divisive along sectoral, regional, ideological, and policy lines.

Indeed, the climate change issue has bedeviled the Liberals. An extensive multi-stakeholder consultative process during 1993 and 1994 was unable to come to an agreement on a national strategy. As a result, Canada attended the first Conference of the Parties in Berlin in May 1995 noting that it was on course to be 13 percent above the target 1990 emissions level by 2000, but still committed to meeting the stabilization goal by 2000. By the Second Conference in Geneva in July 1996, Canadian ministers admitted that Canada's emissions had actually increased by over 9 percent since 1990 and that Canada would not meet the target.

Sheila Copps adopted a high-profile position on climate change that placed her in a state of confrontation with the oil and gas industry, the Conservative government of Alberta, and her cabinet colleague Anne McLellan, Minister of Natural Resources and the Alberta representative in Cabinet. McLellan's star rose in Cabinet as she forcefully defended the interests of the fossil fuel sector and the western resource economy. She rode her cabinet colleagues' anxiety about jobs and growth to gain acceptance for a cautious approach to the climate change question. As a result of these dynamics, open conflict between DOE and NRCan and between Copps and McClellan was a prominent feature of climate change politics. When Marchi took over as minister, he too became frustrated by the bureaucratic and cabinet politics that created the big gap between rhetoric and action, as indicated by the following November 1996 speech:

> It would be nice if I could stand before you at this symposium and tell you a long list of what Canada is doing to combat climate change and how we are succeeding. I have the list. It's the success that's somewhat lacking. Canada is not doing as well as it should. Period. No excuses. Full stop.... We ignore global warming at our peril. This is a *now* problem. It demands a *now* response ... current measures are inadequate to achieve stabilization of greenhouse gas emissions.... Climate change could ensure that the legendary four horseman of the apocalypse will have brothers. Flood, famine, fire, drought, and wars over depleting resources now moves from the realm of speculative fiction to realistic worry.[26]

The central dispute is over the policy instruments required to reduce emissions. McLellan, Alberta, and industry groups advocate voluntary emission reduction initiatives. Alberta is strongly opposed to the use of regulatory or fiscal instruments such as carbon taxes, which could reduce consumption of its oil, gas, and coal resources, while environmentalists have taken an increasingly strong position in favour of such charges. Internationally, the fossil fuel sector has led the industrial lobby against climate change actions by governments and has debated the International Panel's scientific evidence, asserting that there is an "open question" about climate change.[27] Domestically, representatives of Canadian industry continue to argue that "there is still a lot we don't know about how emissions of so-called greenhouse gases may affect the global climate."[28] The fossil fuel sector together with the government of Alberta and NRCan have formed a formidable juggernaut against regulating economic activities to achieve reductions in greenhouse gases and have been successful in promoting a National Action Plan that consists largely of a voluntary challenge and registry initiative and a joint implementation program.[29] DOE, the scientific community, and environmentalists share a much greater sense of urgency, and question the effectiveness of voluntary initiatives to fully meet the targets. The Climate Action Network in Canada, made up of more than 80 environmental and other non-governmental organizations, argues for a portfolio of measures that combine voluntary, regulatory, and economic instruments.[30]

When federal and provincial energy and environment ministers met in Toronto on December 12, 1996 they acknowledged that Canada would likely be between 8 and 13 percent above the 1990 emissions by 2000. Nonetheless, the federal and provincial governments reaffirmed their commitment to the existing action plan, while noting that the Voluntary Challenge and Registry had to be strengthened by "encouraging higher levels of action and encouraging participants to adopt more consistent and comprehensive reporting."[31] International pressures, however, may in time force more assertive action at home. At the third Conference of the Parties in Kyoto, Japan, in late 1997, signatory countries will consider post-2000 measures, with the United States and the European Community countries pushing for binding (not voluntary as the Rio pledge was) targets, possibly enforced through trade sanctions. This would certainly raise the stakes and the "discomfort level" for Canada:

In Kyoto, Canada could find itself uncomfortably on the wrong side of world opinion, lumped in with the OPEC oil producers and other hard-line Third World States. The meeting of federal provincial energy and environment ministers in Toronto this week reflected the deep industry-environment divide. The political result is activist rhetoric decorating cautious action—as in the decision to strengthen the federal government's lamentably weak voluntary program to encourage greenhouse gas conservation efforts by business.[32]

Canada will likely be pressured to join in a legally binding commitment that will cap emissions growth over the medium term. To date, there are no regional or sectoral targets, because federal and provincial ministers have been unwilling to deal with the difficult issue of accountability. Once a legally binding target is agreed upon, a clear understanding of who is responsible for what portion of the reductions will be required, one that makes the situation as equitable as possible to all regions and sectors. Only when these accountabilities have been negotated within Canada will companies and governments begin to take serious action on climate change. The litmus test for the Liberals will be the degree of success that can be achieved in allocating firm emission reduction quotas/targets to the different regions and economic sectors of the country.

Institutionalizing Sustainable Development

In June 1990, as part of its effort to institutionalize sustainable development practices, the Mulroney government introduced a non-statutory requirement to provide prior environmental assessment for all policies and programs coming before Cabinet. Thus, all departmental Memoranda to Cabinet now include an environmental analysis, though departments have been able to devise their own procedures for these, and they are not made public. While the Liberals retained this practice, they rejected pressure from environmentalists to make these policy assessments statutory. The Red Book promised to create an Environmental Auditor General, who would report directly to Parliament and hold individual departments and the government as a whole accountable for how successfully federal programs and spending are supporting the shift to sustainable development. In June 1996, the government named Brian Emmett the first Commissioner of the Environment and Sustainable Development. Each minister is required by statute to regularly table a departmental sustainable development strategy in Parliament. In developing their strategies, the departments will be required to assess their existing policies, programs, and operations in terms of their current impacts on the environment and society, and to consult with departmental stakeholders. The Commissioner will then use these strategies to evaluate each department's progress in implementing sustainable practices and policies.

To assist departments in developing their sustainable development strategies and to publicly signal support for this initiative, the federal government created a *Guide to Green Government*, which was signed by the Prime Minister and all members of Cabinet.[33] The Liberals introduced a complementary initiative, The Greening of Government Operations, to improve the federal government's environmental stewardship by requiring that all departments minimize water, fuel, and electricity use and waste production in the operations of their buildings, fleets, and lands. The initiative will also require that environmental impact be taken into account when purchasing goods and services. The intent is to use the government's procurement muscle to aid the development of environmentally progressive Canadian technologies and industrial practices, which will be competitive in export markets.[34]

Another Red Book promise was to conduct a baseline study of federal taxes, grants, and subsidies, in order to identify barriers and disincentives to sound environmental practices. The February 1994 Budget
announced that a multi-stakeholder task force would be created to find
effective ways to use economic instruments to protect the environment
and to identify barriers and disincentives to sound environmental practices. A multi-stakeholder task force was established in July 1994 and
reported in November, and some of its recommendations were implemented in the 1995 and 1996 budgets.[35] Given the brief time the task
force had to do its work, it could not perform the comprehensive baseline
review, but recommended that it be undertaken. The Standing Committee on Environment and Sustainable Development later recommended a process for completing the baseline study, but, in part because
of opposition from the Department of Finance, this important Red Book
commitment will not likely be completed by the end of 1997.[36] Finance
believes that the most egregious barriers and disincentives have already been removed by the extensive program review cuts to business
subsidies, and that the approach to dealing with the remaining barriers
and disincentives is to require each department to address them
sectorally as part of their sustainable development strategies.

BOLD VISION AND HARD REALITY:
EXPLAINING THE LIBERALS' PERFORMANCE

[While] the supremely cautious Chrétien government likes to sound fash-
ionably progressive on the environment, politically it isn't keen to rock
any boats with important industry groups or ... with Alberta's highly
vocal political establishment. Quiet incrementalism would be the
favoured tack, not aggressive activism.[37]

As the analysis indicates, it cannot be argued that the Liberals have
done nothing on this policy front. But there is also no question but that
the aggressive activism of the Red Book has been replaced, as Gherson
notes, by a cautious incrementalism. What emerges from their first
three years in power is a mixed, and somewhat disappointing, record.
Like the Tories before them, the Liberals experienced a significant
"performance gap" between rhetoric and action. In order to achieve

high marks in their self-assessment, the Liberals had to put the most optimistic spin on the outcome of every environmentally-related activity.[38] Yet, very few of the environment and sustainable development policy commitments outlined in the Red Book have been explicitly abandoned or rejected by the Liberals during their term in office. Rather, it is more the case that environmental initiatives were "sideswiped" by the Liberals' growing fascination with fiscal issues, job creation, economic growth, and national unity.[39] These broader government-wide concerns resulted in major cuts to federal environmental science and regulatory capacity, a reluctance to challenge industry on environmental issues, and a desire to devolve as much activity to the provinces as possible.

Political Will and Cabinet Politics

A crucial ingredient for the "fundamental shift in values and public policy" called for in the Red Book is strong executive leadership.[40] Such leadership has not been forthcoming from the Prime Minister or the central agencies of government. With no institutional capacity at the centre to oversee and co-ordinate interdepartmental issues, departments have been left to fight it out on an issue-by-issue basis.

Chrétien's inclination to delegate authority to his cabinet ministers puts the responsibility in the hands of the Environment Minister to lead the value shift that the Red Book refers to. As one might expect given recent history,[41] both Sheila Copps and Sergio Marchi faced considerable difficulty in attempting to lead such a change. Indeed, on initiatives like toxic substances, endangered species, and climate change that have major implications for industry, they faced outright opposition from their Cabinet colleagues. Even with very different personal styles, both ministers have only been able to move their initiatives through Cabinet slowly. And even then, this meant putting water in their wine in the face of strong ministerial and bureaucratic opposition from the economic departments. Their leadership capacity in Cabinet has not been helped by the fact that DOE, after a number of years of growth in size and influence, has been reduced by Program Review cuts to the status of the smallest line department in government. This reduction in policy and operational capacity has weakened DOE's ability and stature in negotiations with other departments.

In addition to the divisions within Cabinet, the broader Liberal party remains divided on these issues.[42] The strongest environmental advocate has been the Liberal-dominated Parliamentary Standing Committee on Environment and Sustainable Development, led by Trudeau-era environment minister Charles Caccia. It has been a very active committee, producing reports and holding hearings in virtually all of the key areas analyzed above. While it has managed to expand the debate in several areas, it has seldom been able to convince Cabinet to adopt its recommendations. This was the case with respect to CEPA, CESPA, the Commissioner, and the baseline study of fiscal instruments.

One might reasonably have expected Paul Martin to take the lead in expediting the fundamental shift in values and practice, given his prominence as opposition environment critic and author of the Red Book chapter on sustainable development. However, as Greenspon and Wilson-Smith document, the fiscal pressures that Martin faced as Minister of Finance diminished his commitment to other interests, including environmental and sustainable development issues. Nevertheless, he made a key decision that saved the government from gutting its environmental policy capacity. In assigning Program Review expenditure reduction targets, Martin allowed DOE to take its cut from a base that included the Green Plan funds the department had accumulated over the previous five years. It was the only department that was allowed to calculate Green Plan money into its base. Had Martin not agreed to this, DOE would have seen its budget reduced by 50 percent rather than 32 percent, which would have been devastating. Needless to say, the decision was not appreciated by departments such as Industry, Natural Resources, and Fisheries and Oceans, which also had significant Green Plan funded programs.

Bureaucratic Politics and the Dominance of the Traditional Economic Agenda

Pursuing an active environmental agenda has always been easier in times of relative economic prosperity. Over the past three years, the general concern with unemployment and productivity has provided industry and resource departments with substantial political leverage to portray environmental protection as a job-killer.[43] Despite its rhetoric of converging environmental and economic agendas, the Liberal government seems to have been receptive to the "jobs versus environment" discourse. Dependent upon the private sector to create badly-needed jobs, it has been reluctant to force stringent environmental measures upon industry on several issues, ranging from environmental assessment of projects to climate change.

In this way, the Liberal government's experience illustrates some of the current limitations of sustainable development as a paradigm for public policy-making. The emergence of the concept in the mid-1980s helped soften the confrontational nature of environmental politics, partly by bringing together business and environmental groups in a number of forums, such as round tables.[44] But a generalized commitment to an emerging paradigm has not been a sufficient basis for bridging the gap between traditional adversaries when concrete environmental decisions must be made.

During the Liberals' tenure in power, this gap has been most evident over the choice of policy instruments required to move toward a more sustainable form of development.[45] On pollution prevention, the protection of endangered species on private land, or the reduction of greenhouse gas emissions, industry representatives have largely rejected the use of regulatory and economic instruments, arguing instead for voluntary measures that rely on the good will and the environmental ethics of producers. For example, the government's initiatives on pollution prevention, as a means of generating both environmental and economic benefits, quickly came under the criticism of industry as being too intrusive. Meanwhile, environmental groups were disappointed with the limited scope of the proposed changes, arguing that virtual elimination was not stringent enough, and that the government should impose a complete ban on a wider range of substances. In the end, despite a common adherence to the principle of reduction at source through process innovations, environmentalists and industrialists remained divided on the regulatory measures required for promoting this new approach to environmental protection. Complicating this discord is the government's diminishing capacity to develop effective regulations as a result of cuts to its policy analysis personnel and information collection capability.

A similar conflict arose over climate change. With the assistance of NRCan and the government of Alberta, the fossil fuel industry succeeded in fighting off a regulatory plan for achieving Canada's international commitment. With on-going concerns about international competitiveness, it is unlikely that demands for more voluntary programs will wither in the near future. However, the likely failure of the voluntary registry program in delivering the targeted reduction in greenhouse gases will cast doubt on the effectiveness of voluntary approaches. The business community has not embraced the concept of sustainable development to a degree that would warrant relegating regulation to a secondary policy instrument for environmental protection.

Indeed, the harsh criticism of the environmental assessment process suggests that the integration of economic and environmental considerations in making business decisions is only supported when it imposes minimal constraints and delays on business activities. Years after the hard-won battle of environmentalists over environmental assessment, industry and resource departments are still reluctant to submit completely to the terms of CEAA. The "jobs versus the environment" arguments put forward by economic interests, both inside and outside of government, to criticize the delays caused by the assessment of projects is reminiscent of the adversarial environmental politics of the 1970s.

Sheila Copps's tenure as minister also strained the relationship between DOE and industry groups. An advocate of a strong government role in environmental protection, she was sceptical about the potential effectiveness of voluntary measures. She did not trust industry, and became increasingly uncomfortable with the overarching importance of economic objectives for the government. In interviews, industry representatives argued that she broke the trend toward decision by consensus and multi-stakeholder consultations. They felt ignored by DOE, and felt that "talking to Environment Canada is not going to do you any good." Similar views were expressed about the Standing Committee, which they condemned as too "ideological" and too close to the environmentalists. They complained that the Committee often did not realistically consider the costs of its proposed measures. In a nutshell, many industry representatives felt that business-government relations regarding environmental issues had taken a turn for the worse under the Liberals. Copps, on the other hand, believed that the consensus approach led to the lowest common denominator and left a void in environmental leadership in the country.

Ironically, difficult relations with DOE and the Standing Committee strengthened existing alliances between industry groups and economic departments. The dominance of the traditional jobs and growth agenda buttressed the influence of resource departments within the bureaucracy and allowed them to undermine the implementation of the Liberals' environmental agenda by stressing the potentially negative economic consequences of additional regulations.[46] The public criticism of the environmental assessment process by McLellan and the reluctance of DFO to fully comply with the intent of CEAA reveal the extent to which resource departments were willing to resist a new vision of economic development that would require the full integration of both environmental and economic factors in decision-making. Environmentalists viewed these actions as an indication that the government has lost interest in the environment file.

Indeed, cross-cutting issues such as the implementation of sustainable development cause significant management difficulties for most governments.[47] The Clerk of the Privy Council acknowledged that horizontal policy issues, particularly those that are long-term in nature, provide a special challenge, and admitted that the government has not done a very good job of managing the interdepartmental collaboration that is required.[48] The Organization for Economic Cooperation and Development argues that "[c]ross-cutting issues increase the need to integrate, rather than merely coordinate the policies of different ministries. The design of integrative mechanisms needs to strike a balance between competing objectives: strengthening the horizontal capacity of the government apparatus; ensuring that ministerial responsibilities remain clear; and maintaining the centre's role in the strategic management of actions."[49] The challenge is to find institutional linkages that correspond to the interdependencies inherent in cross-cutting issues.

The key institutional innovation that the Liberals have introduced to address the problem of internal cohesion is the creation of the independent Commissioner of Environment and Sustainable Development in the Office of the Auditor General. Still, the departmental sustainable development strategies will be sectorally oriented, and no formal, central co-ordinating function has been created in any of the central agencies to address the significant management difficulties the Clerk associated with complex, cross-cutting issues. The requirement of being held to account by a parliamentary officer once every few years for their efforts at enhancing environment and sustainable development is the primary motivation that the government has created to encourage departments to be more collaborative and forward-looking. This may or may not prove to be an adequate and effective mechanism for overcoming historical divisions.

Federal-Provincial Relations
Because environmental problems are complex and holistic, they require an approach that recognizes the interdependence of biophysical and social processes. Both the political realities of the Canadian federation and the transboundary nature of environmental problems require that environmental issues be dealt with through the collaboration of the different levels of government. The internationalization of environmental policy through the growing number of bilateral and multilateral transboundary agreements and the increasing importance of trade and environment issues combine to increase the importance of federal responsibilities for trade and commerce, science, information development and sharing, international negotiations, and taxation. This emerging trend places increasing demands on the federal government at the same time that resources are being cut significantly.[50] Paradoxically, this ascendancy of the federal role is countered domestically by decentralist pressures in response to Quebec separatism and the aggressive provincialism of other provinces, such as Alberta and Ontario. Issues such as environmental assessment and climate change have been the source of major inter-governmental conflict in recent years. For example, the mere mention of using regulatory or economic instruments as part of the climate change action plan prompted quick and public reaction in the business press of the fossil fuel-reliant provinces of Alberta, Saskatchewan, and Nova Scotia. Both CESPA and CEPA have important dimensions that raise provincial hackles.

This history of "irritants" led the Canadian Council of Ministers of the Environment to work over the 1993-95 period to develop an Environmental Management Framework Agreement that would redefine the "roles" of governments to reduce "overlap and duplication" in this area. This "harmonization" initiative was prompted by industry's argument that there was too much regulatory duplication, provinces' desire to have less federal "interference" in provincial economic development, and federal non-environmental interest in reducing budgets and seeking provincial approval to "renew the federation." Environmentalists, on the other hand, deny that there is much duplication or overlap. After participating in this exercise for her first two years in office, Copps rejected it precisely because of her concern that it weakened the federal role. Her rejection of the Framework was strongly supported by environmentalists, who were extremely suspicious of both the process and the substance.

Given the diversity of provincial capacity, Copps's rejection of the multilateral approach was understandable. There remains considerable scepticism about the capacity and motivation of the provinces to deal with additional environmental responsibilities.[51] For example, some provinces are engaging in deep cuts to regulatory controls on polluting activities. In the summer of 1996 the Harris government proposed cutting the number of Ontario's environmental regulations from 80 to 50.[52] While some of this reduction will be achieved through the merging of related regulations, the province also proposes to replace several regulations with voluntary codes and at the same time to rely increasingly on industry to monitor its own environmental performance. Moreover, the province has announced that new regulations will not be adopted if they fail the government's cost-benefit evaluation.[53]

The cash-strapped Bouchard government has announced its objective of cutting 500,000 permit regulations over the next two years. Overall, about 40 percent of Quebec's current environmental authorizations will no longer be required.[54] Quebec's main environmental legislation will also be amended in scope. In the past, industrialists could not build projects, with some exceptions, without proving to the environmental ministry that they would not result in unacceptable damage to the environment. Under the new system, the situation will be reversed: all projects will be deemed acceptable, with the exception of a list of activities requiring authorization.[55] The separatist government has also created a deregulation secretariat that will have to approve new legislation and regulations before they are considered by the provincial cabinet. The secretariat's mandate stipulates that new regulations must be scrutinized for their economic impact and that they should be no more stringent than comparable regulations in competing jurisdictions elsewhere in Canada and in the United States.[56]

Environmentalists in both provinces have expressed serious concerns about the impact of these reforms on provincial environmental protection regimes. They fear that a significant reduction in the federal government's role in environmental protection might result in a lack of adequate environmental standards in some regions of the country. Thus, they argue that the federal government should make sure that it is not delegating in a vacuum, with provincial governments lacking either the capacity or the will to set and enforce adequate environmental standards.

Still, there are political pressures on Marchi to formally engage the provinces in a new arrangement.[57] After the collapse of the Framework Agreement, governments went back to the negotiating table in the spring of 1996, and in November they signed a new Canada-Wide Accord on Environmental Harmonization.[58] Ostensibly, the Accord is less about efficiency and devolution than about environmental goals. The Accord does not alter the legislative or other authority of any of the governments, but it attempts to address the capacity issue by arguing that the roles and responsibilities outlined in multi-lateral sub-agreements will be undertaken by the governments best suited to perform them. There are also clauses that allow governments to re-intervene in an area where an agreement has been made if the other government is unable to fulfil its obligations. Nevertheless, given the history, doubts remain whether the Accord is any more viable than the Framework Agreement.[59]

CONCLUSION

It is now ten years since the publication of the landmark Brundtland Commission report *Our Common Future* and five years since world leaders met at the Earth Summit in Rio to sign *Agenda 21*. Despite progress in various areas, the global environment continues to decline. As we fall behind the goals set at Rio, the independent U.S. Worldwatch Institute concludes that "[u]nfortunately, few governments have even begun the policy changes that will be needed to put the world on an environmentally sustainable path."[60]

The Chrétien government has followed the unfortunate pattern of the Tory government that preceded it. Just as the Tories raised great expectations with their Green Plan and then "eco-backtracked" throughout their mandate, the Liberals promised great leaps forward, but, at best, have taken only baby steps. Liberal documents such as *Creating Opportunity* and the *Guide to Green Government* show that at the level of principle the government understands what needs to be done. The record, however, reveals that the government has not moved as far as is necessary to reconcile economic development and environmental quality; quite clearly there is an implementation gap between rhetoric and action.[61] The cabinet signatures on the *Guide to Green Government* have not yet resulted in the internalization of the message, either around the cabinet table or within the government. Large parts of the government still view environmental policy initiatives as political problems to be overcome. Consequently, the government is often at war with itself about what to do.

NOTES

The authors would like to thank Gene Swimmer, Sandra Bach, Tom Conway, Doug Russell, and François Bregha for helpful comments.

1 In last year's *How Ottawa Spends*, one of us argued that the Red Book chapter represented the Liberals' effort to "outgreen the Tories." See Glen Toner, "Environment Canada's Continuing Roller Coaster Ride," in Gene Swimmer, ed., *How Ottawa Spends 1996-97: Life Under the Knife* (Ottawa: Carleton University Press, 1996), 99-132.

2 Sierra Club of Canada, *1996 Rio Report Card: Report on Commitments Made by Federal and Provincial Governments at the United Nations Conference on Environment and Development* (Ottawa: Sierra Club of Canada, 1996), 22.

3 The U.S. *Pollution Prevention Act* was enacted in 1990, and the American Environmental Protection Agency adopted a comprehensive *Pollution Prevention Strategy* in 1991, targeting the manufacturing, agriculture, municipal waste, transportation, and energy sectors. By 1991, over half of American states had adopted at least one pollution prevention law, although the contents of these laws vary significantly. See Daniel J. Fiorino, *Making Environmental Policy* (Berkeley: University of California Press, 1995), 211-13, and Commission for Environmental Cooperation, *Status of Pollution Prevention in North America* (Montreal: Commission for Environmental Cooperation Secretariat, 1996), 60-63.

4 In 1974 , the Department of Environment became Environment Canada, as part of the Trudeau government's effort to incorporate more bilingual terminology into the federal lexicon. However, the old acronym "DOE" continues to be used.

5 See Automotive Manufacturing Pollution Prevention Task Force, *Third Task Force Progress Report* (Ottawa: Environment Canada,

June 1995). See also the voluntary reduction program of the Acceler-
ated Reduction and Elimination of Toxics (ARET) process. *Environmental Leaders 2: ARET Voluntary Action on Toxic Substances*
(Ottawa: Public Works and Government Services, January 1997).

6   See, for example, Michael Porter and Claas van der Linde, "Toward
a New Conception of the Environment-Competitiveness Relationship," *Journal of Economic Perspective*, 9, 4 (1995), and Michael
Porter and Claas van der Linde, "Green and Competitive: Ending the
Stalemate," *Harvard Business Review* (September-October 1995),
120-34.

7   Martin's conception of environmental protection was first laid out in
a discussion paper that he wrote as environment critic in 1992, in
which he presented a strong environmental regulatory framework as
an effective tool to promote industrial competitiveness. See Paul
Martin, *L'environnement : L'optique du Parti Libéral—Document de
travail* (Ottawa: Liberal Party of Canada, February 1992). Sheila
Copps reportedly came to this conception of environmental regulation only late in her stay at Environment Canada, after reading
Michael Porter's work in the *Harvard Business Review*. See Edward
Greenspon and Anthony Wilson-Smith, *Double Vision: The Inside
Story of the Liberals in Power* (Toronto: Doubleday Canada Limited,
1996), 284.

8   Under the policy, a substance is considered "persistent" when it takes
a long time to break down in the environment, and "bioaccumulative" means that it accumulates in living organisms, often in fat
tissues. The objective of "virtual elimination" stipulates that these
toxic substances can be released in the environment, so long as they
remain below measurable concentrations at any point in their life
cycle. The onus will be placed on the user or producer of the substance to show that this will be the case.

9   House of Commons, Standing Committee on Environment and
Sustainable Development, *It's About Our Health: Towards Pollution
Prevention* (Ottawa: Supply and Services Canada, 1995).

10 In the consultation process leading to the formulation of the policy in
1995, several industry associations had argued against integrating
the policy into CEPA, claiming that existing powers and voluntary
measures would be sufficient.

11 See John Geddes, "Business Enraged by Pollution Bill," The *Financial Post*, December 11, 1996, 5, and "Environment Act Changes
Disappoint," *The Toronto Star*, December 11, 1996, A11.

12 Michael Grange, "Dry-cleaning Chemical Put on Federal Toxic
List," *The Globe and Mail* [Toronto], February 11, 1997, A6.

13 See Dennis Bueckert, "New Bill on Environment Called Step
Backward," *The Edmonton Journal*, December 11, 1996, A13, and

Tom Spears, "Marchi Says Toxic-Pollution Bill Gives Inspectors Greater Powers," *The Ottawa Citizen*, December 11, 1996, A4.

14 See, for example, NRCan Minister Anne McLellan's comments in Dennis Bueckert, "Business Interest: Japanese Investors Frustrated with Environmental Assessment," *The Edmonton Journal*, March 18, 1996, A9.

15 Sierra Club of Canada, *1996 Rio Report Card,* 11-12.

16 Jeff Adams, "Sunshine Faces Full Review," *The Calgary Herald*, September 4, 1996, A6. The complete registry of environmental assessments can be consulted through the Canadian Environmental Assessment Agency's web site at http:\\www.ceaa.gc.ca.

17 The case was brought forward by the environmental group Friends of the Oldman River Society and concerns the assessment of the environmental impact of the construction of a logging road crossing several streams in Alberta. In its submission, the group alleges that the Department of Fisheries is using "a decision making process which frustrates the intention of Parliament and usurps the role of CEAA as a planning and decision making tool." The North American Commission for Environmental Cooperation is not authorized to enforce or make a judgment about appropriate continental environmental standards, but it is empowered to determine if a member country is enforcing its own environmental laws. If Canada is found not to be enforcing its legislation, monetary penalties may be imposed.

18 Brian Laghi, "Environmentalists Suing Fisheries Department," *The Globe and Mail* [Toronto], November 8, 1996, N7.

19 Aside from a general commitment to the protection of biodiversity, the Red Book's only commitment was to maintain the objective of completing the national parks system by the year 2000 and to work with the provinces to protect, in its natural state, a representative sample of each of the country's natural regions, amounting to 12 percent of Canada. To this end, the Prime Minister announced the creation of four new national parks in October 1996.

20 One contentious modification is that the final decision about the listing of species will be made by Cabinet, on the advice of the scientific body created by the law. Environmentalists and scientists have strongly opposed this change, arguing that decisions will be based on politics instead of science when there are economic pressures against listing a species. Recognizing the legitimate need for accountability, they argued that political trade-offs balancing economic and environmental objectives should be made by ministers at the stage of the recovery plans.

21 Two hundred scientists from Canadian universities signed a letter in 1995 criticizing the limited scope of the proposed legislation. They

reiterated their criticisms after the government released its final version of the bill. *The Globe and Mail*, in two editorials, criticized the government for not using the full extent of its constitutional jurisdiction. Other newspapers, such as the *The Victoria Times Colonist,* have done the same. See *The Globe and Mail* [Toronto], "Species, Spaces and Spunk," November 2, 1996, D8; *The Globe and Mail* [Toronto], "Endangered and Spaced Out," November 5, 1996, A16; Paul Minvielle, "New Law Won't Do Much to Protect Threatened Wildlife," *The Victoria Times Colonist*, November 1, 1996, A14. By 1997 the number of scientists demanding a tougher CESPA had grown. See Terrance Wills, "Toughen Endangered-Wildlife Law, 300 Scientists Tell PM," *The Gazette* [Montreal], February 5, 1997, A11.

22 Larry Pynn, "Act to Protect Animals 'a Start': Conservationists Say New Federal Legislation Fulfills International Commitments, but Falls Short in Protecting Endangered Species," *The Vancouver Sun*, November 1, 1996, B1.

23 Angus Reid Poll, August 1995, cited in "Copps Releases Draft Law to Protect Endangered Species," *The Kitchener-Waterloo Record*, August 18, 1995, B6; Anne McIlroy, "Tougher Measures for Wildlife Favoured: Canadians Want Wildlife Protected," *The Globe and Mail*, [Toronto], January 28, 1997, A4.

24 See the comments made by the Mining Association of Canada and the Canadian Pulp and Paper Association in House of Commons, *Evidence of the Standing Committee on Environment and Sustainable Development, Meeting No. 50*, November 21, 1996, and those made by the National Agriculture Environment Committee, the Canadian Farmers' Association, and the Canadian Cattlemen's Association, in House of Commons, *Evidence of the Standing Committee on Environment and Sustainable Development, Meeting No. 49*, November 19, 1996. See also "Resource Groups Assail Wildlife Bill," *The Globe and Mail* [Toronto], March 13, 1997, A8.

25 International Panel on Climate Change, *IPCC Second Assessment Synthesis of Scientific-Technical Information Relevant to Interpreting Article 2 of the UN Framework Convention on Climate Change*, 1995, 4.

26 Notes for a speech by the Honourable Sergio Marchi to the Climate Change Symposium organized by the Canadian Global Change Program, Ottawa, November 6, 1996, 1-2.

27 See Paul Brown, "Muddling the Truth About Global Warming," *The Guardian*, reprinted in the *The Ottawa Citizen*, July 10, 1996, A15.

28 John Dillon, "The Climate Debate Heats Up: Canada Should Support a Strategy That Works for Our Economy and for the Global Environment," *Opinions* (Business Council on National Issues, December

1996), 1. Business argues that climate change is a long-term issue, that developing countries should shoulder their share of the burden along with developed countries, and that a voluntary, go-slow approach that focuses on initiatives that also have economic benefits is the most that should be done.

29 The voluntary challenge and registry (VCR) program is being managed by NRCan. It involves individual companies from the major greenhouse gas emitting industrial sectors (electrical utilities, manufacturing, energy, transportation, forestry, pulp and paper, agriculture, mining) submitting action plans detailing the measures that will be taken to limit or reduce greenhouse gas emissions. By the end of 1996, over 600 companies responsible for more than 50 percent of Canada's total greenhouse gas emissions had signed on to the Registry. On joint implementation strategies, see United Nations Conference on Trade and Development, *The Strategy of Joint Implementation in the Framework Convention on Climate Change* (New York: 1995).

30 Economic instruments would include higher excise taxes on gasoline and a carbon charge (called an atmospheric user charge), which would be compensated for in part by a reduction in the GST. Existing regulatory and incentive initiatives would be strengthened to enhance fuel economy standards for vehicles, encourage commercial and residential building retrofit measures, and increase industrial energy use efficiency. Recognizing the importance of the "jobs agenda," environmentalists emphasize the job creation potential of a major energy efficiency initiative. They argue that, ironically, climate change provides Canada with an employment-generating and technology-advancing opportunity. See Climate Action Network, *Rational Energy Program: Analysis of the Impact of National Measures to the Year 2010* (Ottawa, September 1996).

31 See Canada, "Government of Canada Announces New and Strength-ened Climate Change Initiatives," News Release, Toronto, December 12, 1996. They also announced a few new information programs for the transportation and residential sectors, pilot projects to have DOE and NRCan purchase "green power" (power from renewable energy sources) from utilities in Ontario and Alberta, educational programs to enhance participation by municipalities and the public, and strengthened regulations in the commercial sector aimed at electrical motors, air conditioners, heat pumps, and transformers. Further, a major research initiative was announced called the Canada Country Study. This study will carry out the first-ever national integrated assessment of the social, biological, and economic impacts of climate variability and change in Canada.

32 Giles Gherson, "Canada's Debit on the Greenhouse Gas Ledger is a U.S. Credit," *The Ottawa Citizen,* December 13, 1996, A15. See also the following articles by Gherson in the *The Ottawa Citizen,* "Canada Feels the Heat as Clinton Tackles Environment," November 8, 1996, A14; "Canada Is All Talk on Carbon Emissions," November 10, 1996, A10; "Greenhouse Gas Issue May Be Left Until It's Too Hot to Handle," December 11, 1996, A16.

33 Canada, *A Guide to Green Government* (Ottawa, 1995).

34 Environment Canada, *Directions on Greening Government Operations* (Ottawa, 1995).

35 See Toner, "Environment Canada's Continuing Roller Coaster Ride," 130-31, for more details on the budgetary changes.

36 House of Commons Standing Committee on Environment and Sustainable Development, *Keeping a Promise: Towards a Sustainable Budget* (Ottawa: December 1995).

37 Gherson, "Canada Feels the Heat."

38 Liberal Party of Canada, *A Record of Achievement: A Report on the Liberal Government's 36 Months in Office* (Ottawa, 1996), 56-67.

39 See Greenspon and Wilson-Smith, *Double Vision.*

40 On this issue of leadership see Glen Toner and Bruce Doern, "Five Political and Policy Imperatives in Green Plan Formation," *Environmental Politics,* 3, 3 (Autumn, 1994), 395-420.

41 For an analysis of the experience of environment ministers during the Tory years see Glen Toner, "The Green Plan: From Great Expectations to Eco-Backtracking ... to Revitalization?" in Susan Phillips, ed., *How Ottawa Spends 1994-95: Making Change* (Ottawa: Carleton University Press, 1994), 229-60.

42 The Liberal party policy convention in October 1996 continued to support activist resolutions calling for a strong federal environmental role, an aggressive energy efficiency program, the reaffirmation of the Red Book commitment to reduce carbon dioxide emissions to 20 percent below 1988 levels by the year 2005, and budgetary reform in support of sustainable development, among others. See Liberal Party of Canada, *Adopted Resolutions: 1996 Biennial Convention* (Ottawa, 1996).

43 For an analysis of how industry groups use the economic climate to resist environmental regulation, see Ted Schrecker, "Resisting Environmental Regulation: The Cryptic Pattern of Business-Government Relations," in Robert Paelhke and Douglas Torgeson, eds., *Managing Leviathan: Environmental Politics and the Administrative State* (Peterborough: Broadview Press, 1990), 165-99.

44 On this shift in relations between industry groups and environmentalists, see Bruce Doern and Thomas Conway, *The Greening of*

Canada: Federal Institutions and Decisions (Toronto: University of Toronto Press, 1994), 107-16. The extent to which round tables were successful in bridging the gap between these communities is questioned in Jim Bruton and Michael Howlett, "Differences of Opinion: Round Tables, Policy Networks, and the Failure of Canadian Environmental Strategy," *Alternatives*, 19, 1 (1992), 25-33.

45 Business has long made the claim that sustainable development should not be pursued through regulation. See Doug Macdonald, *The Politics of Pollution: Why Canadians Are Failing Their Environment* (Toronto: McClelland & Stewart, 1991), 126-27.

46 This thesis is reaffirmed by Greenspon and Wilson-Smith in *Double Vision*.

47 See, for example, Ton Buhrs and Robert V. Bartlett, *Environmental Policy in New Zealand: The Politics of Clean and Green?* (Auckland: Oxford University Press, 1993), and for Australia, Elim Papadakis, *Environmental Politics and Institutional Change* (Melbourne: Cambridge University Press, 1996).

48 Jocelyne Bourgon, Privy Council Office, *Third Annual Report on the Public Service of Canada* (1995), http://info.ic.gc.ca/pco

49 OECD, *Building Policy Coherence: Tools and Tensions*, Public Management Occasional Papers, No. 12 (Paris, 1996), 29.

50 For more analysis of the internationalization of domestic policy see Glen Toner and Tom Conway, "Environmental Policy," in G.B. Doern, L.A. Pal, and B.W. Tomlin, eds., *Border Crossings: The Internationalization of Canadian Public Policy* (Toronto: Oxford University Press, 1996), 108-44.

51 Kathryn Harrison, *Passing the Buck: Federalism and Canadian Environmental Policy* (Vancouver: UBC Press, 1996), 155-61.

52 Ontario, Ministry of Environment and Energy, *Responsive Environmental Protection* (Toronto: Queen's Printer for Ontario, 1996), and Tom Spears, "Proposal Refines Environmental Regulations in Ontario," *The Ottawa Citizen*, September 14, 1996, B5.

53 See the following articles by Tom Spears: "Ontario Gets Ready to Slash Environmental Red Tape," *The Ottawa Citizen,* September 14, 1996, B1; "Old Toxic Waste Rules Too Restrictive Today," *The Ottawa Citizen*, September 14, 1996, B4; "Communities to Help Clear the Air," *The Ottawa Citizen*, September 14, 1996, B5; "Pulp Mills Could Scrap Their Zero-Chlorine Plans," *The Ottawa Citizen*, September 14, 1996, B5. In addition see Martin Mittlestaedt, "Ontario Weakening Needed Pollution Rules, Critics Argue," *The Globe and Mail* [Toronto], March 12, 1997, A8, and "Ontario Scraps Environment Overview," *The Globe and Mail* [Toronto], March 15, 1997, A5.

54 Louis-Gilles Francoeur, "Cliché se porte à la défense de Bouchard," *Le Devoir,* October 11, 1996, A5.

55 Louis-Gilles Francoeur, "Désormais, tout sera permis, sauf...," *Le Devoir*, October 28, 1996, A1.

56 Louis-Gilles Francoeur, "L'Environnement passé au tamis du 'Grand Inquisiteur,'" *Le Devoir*, December 1, 1996, A3.

57 The February 1996 Throne Speech was dominated by national unity concerns, and environmental management was mentioned as one of the areas where the federal government will make an effort to work in partnership with the provinces. Canada, *Speech from the Throne to Open the Second Session Thirty Fifth Parliament of Canada*, 10.

58 Canadian Council of Ministers of the Environment, *A Canada-Wide Accord on Environmental Harmonization* (Toronto, November 20, 1996).

59 See, for example, Rosemary Speirs, "Harmonized Environmental Rules a Recipe for Disaster," *The Toronto Star*, September 26, 1996, and Martin Middlestaedt, "Ministers Reach Pollution Accord: Marchi Defends Harmonization Plan," *The Globe and Mail* [Toronto], November 21, 1996.

60 "Five Years After Rio, Treatment of Earth Remains Bleak," *The Ottawa Citizen*, January 12, 1997, D8, and Jack Epstein, "Rio Summit's Promises Still Unfulfilled," *The Globe and Mail* [Toronto], March 13, 1997, A12.

61 Laura Eggertson, "Environmental Bill Endangered: Spring Election Forecast Means Vaunted Liberal Promise Likely Will Expire, Critics Fear," *The Globe and Mail* [Toronto], March 24, 1997, A4.

9

Lowering the Boom on the Boomers: Replacing Old Age Security with the New Seniors Benefit and Reforming the Canada Pension Plan

MICHAEL J. PRINCE

Therefore my age is a lusty winter, Frosty, but kindly.

William Shakespeare[1]

For 70 years, Canadians have had national legislation in one form or another for the public provision of old age income assistance. The pension policy field itself is now a senior. At the federal level today, the system comprises Old Age Security (OAS), the Guaranteed Income Supplement (GIS), Spouse's Allowance (SPA), Age Credit, and Pension Income Credit. While the Liberals espoused no platform on social programs for the elderly in their 1993 election campaign Red Book, once in power they undertook several important changes to this foundational level of the retirement income system. This chapter examines the restructuring of these programs, which culminates in the latest policy innovation in old age pensions, the Seniors Benefit. The recently announced reforms to the Canada Pension Plan (CPP) are also briefly examined. Taking effect in 2001, the Seniors Benefit will be the first new Canadian social program of the third millennium. As a fully indexed and non-taxable benefit, the Seniors Benefit promises to be lusty in offering a secure source of income for eligible seniors; somewhat frosty in that it will be more targeted, thereby excluding some higher-income older households; and kindly in that the new program is progressive in its design—yet it offers only a pint-sized increase in benefits to low-income seniors.

FEDERAL ELDERLY BENEFITS: THE CONSERVATIVE LEGACY, 1984-1993

In public affairs, as with personal life and larger human history, legacy is context. Past governmental programs and reforms (both those failed and those implemented) help shape the policy agenda and the design choices for new programs. Reforms to elderly benefit programs made by the Mulroney Conservatives are worth briefly reviewing to appreciate both the program setting and the political background the Liberals inherited in 1993. The key events and reforms of the Conservative legacy are shown in Table 9.1. At the same time as these policy changes were being made, anxiety was growing among many middle-aged and younger Canadians that public pension programs would not be there for them.[2]

Even today the best known pension initiative by the Conservatives, and the one most damaging politically, was the modified indexation of OAS payments proposed in the 1985 Budget. As part of the Government's plan for reducing the federal debt, the Budget announced that from 1986 the indexation of OAS payments would be modified, with benefits increasing yearly by the annual change in the consumer price index (CPI) in excess of three percentage points. Therefore, old age pensions would no longer be fully adjusted for increases in the cost of living. The proposal incited a strong outcry by seniors' groups, social policy organizations, some provincial governments, and even business lobbies. Barely four weeks after the Budget had been delivered, the Finance Minister withdrew the OAS deindexation measure. This dramatic and rapid reversal of a budgetary measure, a rare event

Table 9.1

**Changes to the Elderly Benefits System
by the Conservatives: 1985-93**

Change (year introduced)	Impact
Partial De-indexation of Old Age Security Benefits (1985)	Proposal withdrawn after strong political protest by seniors' groups and other organizations. Loss of anticipated savings compensated for by increases to corporate and gasoline taxes.
Expansion of Spouse's Allowance (1985)	Coverage extended to all widows and widowers aged 60 to 64 and in need, about 85,000 people.
Conversion of Age Exemption (1988)	Regressive exemption of $2,760 changed to a fairer non-refundable flat-rate tax credit with unused credit transferable to spouse. Partially indexed to inflation above 3 percent each year.
Conversion of Pension Income Deduction to Pension Income Credit (1988)	Regressive deduction of $1,000 of pension income changed to a 17 percent tax credit. Not indexed to inflation.
Clawback of Old Age Security Benefits (1989-91)	Surtax on benefits at a rate of 15 percent of individual net income over $50,000, phased in over three years. This income threshold was only partially indexed to inflation. An initial estimate of 128,000 seniors receiving no benefit or less benefit than before. Savings to Ottawa of about $300 million in 1991.
Exemption of elderly benefits from Expenditure Control Plan (1990-93)	Old Age Security and other elderly benefits exempt from 3 percent cap on annual spending increases.

in Canadian parliamentary politics, was interpreted by many commentators as the emergence of "grey power," the strong potential influence of seniors' groups on public policy making.

In 1985 the Mulroney government expanded the clientele of the SPA. Previously the program was paid only to spouses and widowed spouses of low-income old age pensioners aged 60 to 64. The reform extended eligibility to all low-income widowed persons in this age group, whether their spouses had been receiving the OAS or not. For the first full fiscal year, the extra allowance was expected to be paid to 85,000 people, mainly women, at an estimated cost of $350 million. Even with this change, those still *ineligible* for SPA benefits include low-income people age 60 through 64 who never married, people 60 through 64 who are divorced or separated, and older couples where both spouses are under 65.

In 1988, as part of a general tax reform exercise, the Age Exemption and Pension Income Deduction were converted to tax credits, making the elderly benefit system more progressive, though less progressive than if they were refundable tax credits. Exemptions and deductions reduce the amount of income that is subject to tax, making their value greater for those with higher incomes, because higher-income people have higher marginal tax rates. Tax credits, on the other hand, reduce tax payable and are generally worth the same, regardless of income. The Age Exemption was converted to a non-refundable tax credit worth $850 (in 1988) for all seniors. The new Age Credit was only partially indexed to the CPI, and so has gradually declined in real value over the subsequent years. The Pension Income Deduction, allowing a private pension income deduction of up to $1,000 for income tax purposes, was also changed to a tax credit of 17 percent of eligible income to a maximum in 1988 of $170 in federal income tax savings. Unlike the Age Credit, the new Pension Income Credit was not indexed to inflation, thus declining even more in real value over the years.

The most profound decision taken by the Conservatives on elderly benefits was the introduction in 1989 of a surtax or clawback on OAS payments. Once it was fully phased in, by 1991, the clawback had the effect of ending the universal nature of OAS, since some seniors would no longer retain any portion of their benefit, altering a near 40 year-old pillar of public pension policy. The clawback entailed seniors repaying 15 percent of their OAS pension for net individual income above an initial threshold of $50,000. Since 1990, the threshold has been partially indexed to inflation, so that each year more pensioners lose part or all of their OAS benefits. The clawback created a new tax haven in that it applied only to those who file Canadian tax returns. The clawback also resulted in a new inequity, in that a $100,000 couple, each with an income of $50,000, was unaffected by the clawback, whereas a $100,000 couple in which one spouse has all or most of the income repaid all of the OAS of the higher-income spouse. These were issues the Liberals would address in their reforms.

One reason for the upward trend in federal spending on elderly benefits over the Mulroney years was the decision reflected in the 1990 Budget to exempt the OAS, GIS, and SPA programs from the expenditure control plan that capped annual increases in program spending for most areas of the federal government at 3 percent. Before giving the Conservatives too much credit for this move, however, we should note that these are all statutory programs guaranteeing a certain level of benefits to all who qualify. The only way spending controls could have been introduced by the Mulroney government would have been to tamper with benefit levels. That would have required legislation in Parliament, and would have reopened the bitter memories of the 1985 battle on indexation.

The Conservatives' main goals for the elderly benefit system were to reduce the amount of OAS available to higher-income seniors, increase fairness on the tax side, and reduce the financial burden on the federal purse. In the end, they achieved all three.

The Conservatives also left a legacy of precedents in social program design choices: the clawback on OAS and the death of universality; the stealthy mechanisms of partial indexing of the OAS clawback and the Age Credit; and the non-indexing of the Pension Income Credit. Finally, the Conservative's retreat on OAS deindexation created a widespread perception of the strong political clout of the seniors movement in Canada.[3]

LIBERAL POLICY: LITTLE IN THE RED BOOK,
LOTS IN THE BLUE BOOKS

When in opposition in the early 1990s, the Liberals made few authoritative statements on pension policy or the need for pension reform. At a policy conference sponsored by the Liberals in November 1991, the prime focus was on issues other than social policy, though some ideas were floated about the need to rethink universality in income support programs like the OAS.[4] In their campaign platform Red Book for the 1993 federal election, seniors and pensions were only peripherally mentioned. On pensions, the Red Book noted only that the Mulroney Conservatives took billions of dollars from programs for seniors, children, and the unemployed, and that the OAS, GIS, SPA, and CPP are part of the Liberal legacy along with Medicare and the Canada Assistance Plan.[5] The intended implication was that the Liberals would revive such embattled programs, yet there are no specifics on priorities or program expenditures for seniors in the Red Book. For those in their golden years, it seemed that silence was golden as far as Liberal strategists were concerned. The same can be said of the 1993 general federal election campaign, in which old age pensions policy was not a significant issue.

Major changes to elderly benefit programs have been announced in budgets, with both the Prime Minister and the Finance Minister playing pivotal roles in this policy field.[6] The Liberals' approach to reforming elderly benefits embraces three objectives: retrenchment, redistribution, and reassurance. Reforms involve imposing losses on some middle- and higher-income seniors and allocating modest additional benefits to lower-income seniors, while at the same time allaying the fears of many Canadians over the sustainability of the programs. Changes to the elderly benefits system made by the Liberals over the 1994-97 period are shown in Table 9.2.

The 1994 Budget established income testing of the Age Credit, with the result that this tax relief is restricted to low- or middle-income seniors. For seniors with net incomes of $25,921 or more, the Age Credit is reduced by an amount equal to 15 percent of an individual's net income above that amount. About one-quarter of all seniors are affected. Income testing the Age Credit has meant increased taxes for

Table 9.2

Changes to the Elderly Benefits System
by the Liberals: 1994-97

Change (year introduced)	Impact
Income testing of Age Credit (1994)	600,000 seniors with incomes between $25,921 and $49,134 lose part of the credit and 200,000 seniors with incomes over $49,134 lose the entire tax reduction. Annual federal savings of $300 million by 1996-97.
Service delivery reforms for Guaranteed Income Supplement (1994-97)	Income tax data from Revenue Canada will replace renewal application forms and be used to reduce mispayments. Estimated savings of $12 to $35 million in 1996-97 and subsequent years.
Income testing of Old Age Security (1996)	Benefits no longer paid out to all; only benefits net of the clawback are paid. One-time savings to Ottawa of about $200 million in 1996-97 and $100 million in 1997-98.
Non-resident tax on Old Age Security and other public pension benefits (1996)	Pensioners living outside Canada considered non-residents subject to a tax withhold of 25 percent of their Old Age Security, and Canada and Quebec Pension Plan benefits.
Residency rule for Old Age Security benefits (1996)	Immigrants entering Canada after March 1996 Budget will receive lower or no benefits for the first 10 years they are in Canada.
Seniors Benefit program announced (1997)	To replace Old Age Security, Guaranteed Income Supplement, Age Credit, and Pension Income Credit in 2001.

those seniors affected, raising federal revenue of $20 million in 1994-95, $170 million in 1995-96, and $300 million in 1996-97.

Four other changes to the OAS program, aimed directly at high-income seniors and low-income immigrants, also were unveiled in the 1995 and 1996 budgets. First, OAS benefits became income-tested at the front end as of July 1996: benefits are now reduced *before* they are sent out rather than being taxed *after* seniors have received their cheques. Benefits are paid out net of the clawback amount, and are based on the previous year's tax return, a change that affects seniors with net incomes above $53,215. From an accounting perspective, this measure yields a one-time saving to the federal treasury of about $200 million in 1996-97 and $100 million in 1997-98. From a social policy perspective, the measure symbolizes the formal end of the universality of OAS, since not all seniors will receive benefits; old age pensions are now—every dollar of them—a selective program.

Second, from 1996 OAS recipients who do not live in Canada have to file a statement of their world-wide income in order to continue receiving OAS benefits. Until this change, non-resident seniors with high incomes, including many "snowbirds," escaped the clawback and were therefore treated more favourably than seniors living in Canada. Older Canadians who live abroad will lose at least one-quarter of their monthly OAS cheques. Low-income non-resident seniors can apply each year to Revenue Canada for a reduction in the level of benefits withheld.

Third, as of the March 6, 1996 Budget, immigrants entering Canada will receive lower benefits for the first 10 years they are in Canada. The benefit level will depend on whether they came from a country that has a social security agreement with Canada. If they do, they will get one-tenth of the GIS or SPA for each year of residence. After a decade living in Canada, they will qualify for full regular benefits. Furthermore, sponsored immigrants will be ineligible for either the GIS or SPA during their sponsorship period, up to 10 years.

Fourth, and by far the most significant policy initiative on elderly benefits in the past 30 years by either the Liberals or the Conservatives, is the new Seniors Benefit, to take effect in 2001. The Seniors Benefit will replace and incorporate the OAS and GIS as well as the Age Credit and Pension Income Credit, and both the benefit and the income threshold for determining eligibility will be fully indexed to the rate of inflation. Benefits will be based on family income (that is, the combined incomes of senior spouses) to determine eligibility and payment amounts. In the case of couples, each spouse will receive a monthly cheque divided equally. Furthermore, the Seniors Benefit will be tax-free. Those seniors with low incomes who currently receive the GIS will receive up to $120 more a year per household and seniors will only have to apply once for the SB when they turn 65. The SPA program will remain in place, separate from the new program, and benefits for those people aged 60 to 64 covered by the SPA will also be increased by $120 for a household in 2001.

During the Quebec sovereignty referendum campaign, the Prime Minister made a promise that no current seniors would see their OAS and GIS payments reduced as a result of reforms to the elderly benefit system. The Seniors Benefit reflects that promise and extends it to what the government calls "near seniors," anyone 60 and over on December 31, 1995, and their spouses, regardless of their age. Both current seniors and these near seniors are to be given the choice of obtaining their benefits under the existing OAS/GIS programs for the rest of their lives or to opt for the Seniors Benefit, whichever is more valuable to them. Under both options, however, the two tax credits disappear. Those who decide in 2001 to maintain their OAS/GIS payments may choose the Seniors Benefit at a later date. Thus, everyone 60 and over as of 1996, except for new immigrants, presumably, are guaranteed a public pension of at least as much as the current elderly benefit payments.[7]

Past policies and politics condition new policies and politics. The Seniors Benefit payment and threshold will be fully indexed, in notable contrast to the partial indexation of other social programs, such as the Goods and Service Tax (GST) Credit, the Child Tax Benefit, and the personal income tax brackets. Why? Not only because of the Prime Minister's referendum pledge in 1995, but largely because in 1985 the Conservatives were politically humiliated over their attempt to partly deindex OAS benefits. With that signal event fixed in their memories, the Liberals dared not tamper with the full indexation of old age benefits. At the same time, the Conservatives' record on elderly benefits created opportunities for pension reform by the Liberals. The income threshold of $25,951 for claiming the maximum payment under the Seniors Benefit is the same as that used for the GST Credit and the Child Tax Benefit, and for income-testing the Age Credit.

The reform of child benefits also influenced the reform of elderly benefits. In 1993, the Conservatives replaced Family Allowances, a universal program that like the OAS had been subject to a clawback, and the refundable and non-refundable tax credits, with a single, family income-tested Child Tax Benefit. With this major revision, which did not face any great political opposition, the Conservatives set a reform model and trajectory for the Liberals in public pensions.[8]

ASSESSING THE NEW SENIORS BENEFIT

The 1996 Budget cast elderly benefit reforms in terms of putting to rest public concerns that these programs are at risk from rising costs. The Seniors Benefit is presented as necessary for safeguarding a decent level of income support for Canadians. Assuring citizens that an old age pension will be there for them requires, the Liberals argue, further targeting of benefits, which will slow the growth rate of program expenditures and save Ottawa considerable amounts in payments over the next decades. Spending on income security for seniors is the largest block of program expenditures in the federal budget. This is a longstanding trend in how Ottawa has spent for the last 20 years or more. The Seniors Benefit, the government claims, also addresses the danger that the elderly programs will crowd out funding for other essential federal programs.[9]

Elderly benefits, as a percentage of federal program spending, gradually grew from the 1960s through the 1980s. In the 1990s, as Table 9.3 reports, their share went from 15.7 percent of federal program spending in 1990-91 to an estimated 20.1 percent in 1996-97, and is projected to be 22.7 percent in 1998-99. This rising share is not the result of a dramatic rate of growth in spending on transfers to seniors, though there has been steady expansion. Rather it is due largely to the declining absolute size of overall program spending under the Liberals. In fact, federal expenditure levels on income support for seniors are growing at a much lower average annual rate in the 1990s (4.3 percent) than in the 1980s (21.8 percent), partly because of lower inflation in the 1990s. True, the number of recipients of OAS, GIS, and SPA has grown from 3.9 million in the mid-1980s to over 4.9 million 10 years later. Yet, concurrently, the number of beneficiaries drawing full benefits under these programs over this period or longer has been falling.

The "partialization" of elderly benefits refers to the growing proportion of beneficiaries who receive less than the maximum payment because they have a level of outside income above the ceiling at which

Table 9.3

Federal Spending on Elderly Benefits

Year	Elderly Benefits ($ billions)	Total Program Spending ($ billions)	Benefits as % of Spending
1985-86	12.5	86.1	14.5
1986-87	13.4	90.0	14.9
1987-88	14.3	96.4	14.8
1988-89	15.2	99.7	15.2
1989-90	16.1	103.8	15.5
1990-91	17.1	108.8	15.7
1991-92	18.4	115.2	16.0
1992-93	19.1	122.6	15.6
1993-94	19.9	120.0	16.6
1994-95	20.5	118.7	17.3
1995-96	21.0	112.0	18.8
1996-97	21.6	109.0	19.8
1997-98	22.3	105.8	21.1
1998-99	22.9	103.5	22.1

Note:
All years are actual figures except 1996-97, which is a forecast, 1997-98, which is an estimate, and 1998-99, which is a projection.

Sources: *Public Accounts of Canada*, Vol. 1, various years; Paul Martin, Minister of Finance, *Budget Plan,* February 18, 1997, 20 and 64.

---

full benefits are paid. On average, 85 percent of GIS recipients received a partial payment in 1995, up from 43 percent in 1970. For the SPA, where only a small share have ever received the maximum benefit, 96 percent of regular SPA recipients and 86 percent of the widow's SPA recipients obtained a partial benefit in 1995. Until 1989, as a universal program the OAS provided full benefits to virtually all seniors. Since then, with the clawback, the share of benefits that are partial has crept up, and with the income testing measures announced in the 1995 and 1996 budgets, the proportion of partial benefits will grow further.[10]

This partialization of elderly benefits is good news, reflecting improvements in seniors' incomes from the CPP or QPP, occupational pension plans, retirement savings, interest, and investment income. A related trend is that the proportion of seniors, women and men, receiving either the GIS or SPA has been on the decline since the early to mid-1980s.[11] This too can be seen as a welcome trend. It may also, however, be viewed as a result of setting the income cut-off line, above which benefits are not paid, too low. In any case, the evidence does not support the Liberals' intimation that the elderly benefit programs are crowding out other programs, nor their claim that these programs are at imminent risk of financial collapse. Rather, the federal government is taking action to limit the role of the social safety net for seniors in the twenty-first century; it is lowering the boom on the boomers.

The Seniors Benefit fits with the Liberals' own social policy legacy of program and value choices. That the OAS should give way to a more selective approach, in which resources are concentrated upon those with the lowest incomes, is an idea voiced in Liberal-sponsored documents since the early 1970s.[12] In the 1980s and 1990s, this critical questioning gave way to concrete action. Over the history of old age pension policy, Liberal administrations have embraced a range of instruments and ideas: means-testing in the 1920s, universality in the 1950s, income-testing in the 1960s, indexation in the 1970s, and the capping of indexed benefits in the 1980s. The Seniors Benefit is the latest in a series of reforms to elderly benefits, each endeavouring in its own time to address the needs and concerns of Canadians as well as the fiscal cost and social care considerations of different officials within the federal bureaucracy and the Liberal party.[13]

A common criticism of the Seniors Benefit, put forward by pensioner and other social interest groups, is that it marks a return to the bad old days of means testing, and old age pensions as welfare.[14] In Canadian old age pension policy, means testing was operative from the late 1920s to the late 1960s. The means test, John Diefenbaker said, was the meanest test around. Seniors' personal affairs were closely and repeatedly scrutinized by provincial welfare administrators. Eligibility was determined by identifying the senior's income, putting an imputed cash value on their household assets, and making an assessment of the support adult children could provide to them. Income testing for pensions, like the GIS and SPA, is a more recent approach and is distinct from means testing. The determination of eligibility is far less intrusive, in that it is based on reported income, and benefits are graduated and linked to family income. The Seniors Benefit will actually simplify the process of claiming and maintaining benefits. Seniors will only have to apply once for the new program, rather than reapplying every year, as has been the case for GIS, and the benefit level will be recalculated annually, based on the previous year's tax return. For the ordinary users of the elderly benefit system, the Seniors Benefit represents greater stability, in that the benefit is tax-free and fully indexed. What they get is what they keep; and what they get will keep its real value over time.

The Seniors Benefit will be a narrower form of citizenship-based entitlement to income support than the OAS. The elderly remain socially valued and politically salient as a distinctive status group for distributing services and transfers, and thus remain a significant constituency of social policies. The OAS, GIS, and soon the Seniors Benefit are entitlements to a basic cash benefit, income-tested, true, but without direct reference to work history, wealth, or previous earnings or contributions, and provided by the federal government to seniors in all regions of the country. The death of the OAS represents the disappearance of horizontal equity in an elderly benefit system premised on the value that all seniors regardless of their income have a right to income support as seniors.[15] Even the concept of citizenship embodied in the OAS, from 1952 to 1989, was qualified by a residency requirement and shifting age level (from 70 down to 65), and since 1989 by the clawback.

With a focus on vertical equity, the Seniors Benefit is altering the citizenship entitlement for pensioners by reducing the program's constituency. The Liberals are offering equal access to a choice of benefit packages (OAS/GIS or SB) to everyone 60 and over as of 1996 below a certain income; equal access to younger Canadians to the Seniors Benefit upon reaching age 65; and equal benefit levels to seniors with similar income circumstances across all provinces and territories. If an individual meets the eligibility rules for claiming the Seniors Benefit, then he or she receives a benefit. The Seniors Benefit signifies that older Canadians have a right to income security protection, a right outside of the marketplace, based on age and income, provided by the national political community. The principle of graduated benefits is now the main characteristic of the Canadian elderly benefit system.

A comparison of the design features of the Seniors Benefit with the Liberals' reform principles, listed in Table 9.4, highlights the choices made and the intended results of the new policy. Undiminished protection will mean that no present senior or near-senior (those aged 60 to 64 in 1996) will receive fewer benefits than they receive or would receive today, but it also means that benefits are not substantially enhanced. Indeed, the benefit level is not planned to be increased until 2001, 16 years since the last increase to the GIS, and then by a puny $10 a month. The "less well-off seniors" will include not just pensioners with below-average incomes for seniors, but pensioners with average incomes. The Seniors Benefit replaces the OAS and GIS as the *de facto* guaranteed basic income for the elderly. At present, the GIS and SPA are fully indexed, the clawback threshold on the OAS is partly indexed as is the Age Credit, and the Pension Income Credit is not at all indexed. The promised full indexing of the Seniors Benefit is a social policy first in the 1990s.

When the 1995 Budget announced that one of the reform principles would be income testing based on family income, some Liberal backbenchers and public interest groups rightly raised concerns about the potential detrimental impacts on women seniors who might lose access to an OAS, since their husbands usually earned a higher income. The Seniors Benefit responds to that concern by planning to pay each spouse a separate cheque of an equal amount. Upper-income recipients will be subject to the same method of income testing as lower-income recipients have been subject to under the GIS and SPA for many years. Because of family income testing and further targeting of benefits, including the elimination of the Pension Income Credit, the Seniors Benefit will generate a more progressive distribution of payments than the existing system. For determining full benefits, the new program will use the $25,921 family income threshold. Thus, for a single pensioner the Seniors Benefit will vanish at $51,721 and for a pensioner couple at $77,521. By contrast, for individual OAS recipients the benefit disappeared at $84,484 in the 1995 tax year. With an average income in 1995 of $20,005 for unattached seniors ($23,763 for males and $18,741 for females) and $38,861 for married couples

Table 9.4

**Comparing the New Seniors Benefit
to the Liberal Government's Principles
for Reforming Elderly Benefit Programs**

Principle[a]	Seniors Benefit
1. Undiminished protection for less well-off seniors.	Payable to seniors with average and low incomes. Benefit to be non-taxable and to be marginally increased, but not until 2001. Spouse's Allowance maintained and increased as well.
2. Continued full indexation of benefits to protect seniors from inflation.	Both the benefit and the income threshold will be fully indexed so that it retains its real value over time. This is a positive departure from recent social policy.
3. Provision of Old Age Security benefits on the basis of family income rather than individual income.	Income tested on a family basis as are the Guaranteed Income Supplement and Spouse's Allowance. All couples with the same total income to be treated alike, and each spouse to receive a separate and equal cheque.
4. Greater progressivity of benefits by income level.	Yields a more progressive distribution of benefits than the existing system, because of family income testing and folding in of the tax credits. Frugal redistribution, however, as the benefit for lowest-income seniors is not significantly enhanced.
5. Control of program costs.	Restricts spending obligations and program growth. Modest savings of $200 million in 2001, projected to grow to massive annual savings of $8.2 billion in 2030.

Note:
a   These principles were set out in the 1995 Budget, 58.

with the head of household aged 65 or older, only elderly individuals or couples with incomes significantly above the average will lose benefits in a substantial fashion.[16]

The politics of pension reform involves the allocation of benefits and losses, resulting in pension winners and losers. Winners from the Seniors Benefit reform process include everyone 60 or over, who will be guaranteed no less than the current OAS/GIS payments; senior women, most of whom will get an increased benefit, given that the incidence of low income is notably greater for older women than for older men, both for most of those living with partners and for those living by themselves; single seniors and senior couples with total incomes up to about $40,000, who will have their benefits maintained, if not increased; recipients of the SPA, who will receive increased payments of $120 a year starting in 2001; and last, but by no means least, the federal treasury. Of course, not all of today's or tomorrow's seniors will benefit from this reform. Losers include well-off Canadians under age 60, especially those late pre-boomers, born during the Second World War, who will have relatively few years to make any necessary changes to their retirement savings plans; many two-income baby boomer couples when they reach 65; single seniors with other annual income above $52,000 and couples with total outside incomes above $78,000, who will no longer receive old age benefits. Moreover, the provincial governments overall will lose about $200 million a year in revenue with the tax-free Seniors Benefit.

The main criticism of the Seniors Benefit, coming from the political right, is that the reduction rate for determining the benefit amount will impose high marginal tax rates on middle- and higher-income seniors, and thus discourage personal savings for retirement through Registered Retirement Savings Plans (RRSPs) and private investments. Like any income-tested program, the Seniors Benefit will use a reduction rate for decreasing benefits when other income exceeds the level at which maximum benefits are paid. The Seniors Benefit reduction will be based on family income from such other sources as employment income, occupational pensions, RRSPs, and the CPP or QPP. The Liberals have proposed that the Seniors Benefit contain two reduction rates: a 50 percent rate on the first $12,520 for single seniors or $16,240 for senior couples, and a 20 percent rate on family incomes between

$25,921 and $51,721 for single seniors and $77,521 for senior couples. The first rate of 50 percent is effectively the current arrangement with respect to the GIS and SPA programs. The second rate is higher than the current 15 percent clawback on OAS benefits, will be applied at a much lower level than the OAS clawback, and will be based on family income rather than individual income. Pension consultants and financial advisors, among others, have attacked the Seniors Benefit on the grounds that some seniors will face large and punitive tax rates because their retirement income will be taxed twice, once through personal income taxation and then via the reduction rate applied to the benefit. According to the pension consultancy firm of William M. Mercer Ltd.:

If the marginal clawback rate for the Seniors Benefit and the marginal tax rate are added, senior citizens will lose between 47 cents and 78 cents on every dollar of post-65 income from all sources other than the Seniors Benefit, with a small exception for income between $17,000 and $26,000. Although government has not raised income taxes, the effect is close to a 50% flat tax for senior citizens.

The Seniors Benefit, once understood, will have a significant impact on retirement savings. Most Canadians, finding their marginal tax rates are higher after age 65, will avoid taxes by cutting back on savings and taking savings out of RRSPs before 65, thereby increasing the burden on the system.[17]

It is ironic, in these socially conservative times, that various financial interests are treating the Seniors Benefit as an entitlement rather than as a safety net program in relation to income, and are bemoaning the inevitable effects of selectivity, a principle that these groups have long promoted. The reduction rates associated with income-tested programs have now become marginal clawback rates, and the targeting of benefits represents tax increases. Surely the goal of all Canadians, but one most realizable by people with fairly stable middle and upper incomes, is to accumulate assets for their retirement so that reliance on the Seniors Benefit is not necessary. Predictions of large perverse impacts on retirement income planning seem highly exaggerated, "since higher-income Canadians already are much more likely to contribute to RRSPs and to belong to employer-sponsored pension plans; would they really decide that the loss of what amounts to a minor part of their retirement income is worth decimating that income by no longer putting aside money for RRSPs, especially given the lucrative tax break for such contributions?"[18] Given further the crisis of confidence many Canadians have in the future of the CPP and public benefits, it seems far more probable that baby boomers and Generation Xers will try to save more, not less, for their retirement nest egg.

With this distribution of gains and losses, it is understandable why the Seniors Benefit proposal evoked little attention or concern among present seniors. The large majority of today's seniors have nothing to fear from the new program, with its promised protection and indexation. It will be seniors of the next generation who will experience the cuts, not as cuts actually but rather as what the program is and is not offering then. The new program is designed to slow down the growth in transfers to seniors in the early decades of the next century. The key cost control features of the Seniors Benefit are the family-based income testing, the reduction rate of 20 percent for net family income above $25,921, and the pint-sized increase to the basic benefit in 2001. In addition, the SPA is not to be included in the Seniors Benefit and thus extended to offer income support to all low-income people aged 60 to 64. To do so would cost about $2 billion a year more, something the current and previous federal governments have rejected. The Seniors Benefit is expected to reap savings of about $200 million in the first year and $2.1 billion in 2011, when the baby boomers start turning 65, increasing to major annual savings of $8.2 billion by 2030.[19] By introducing cutbacks with considerable time lags, this pattern of savings offers the federal government a political advantage—the minimizing of opposition—though not a financial one. "Indeed," as Pierson has noted of pension reform across many industrial countries, "most of the successful efforts to trim public sector pension obligations have taken the form of long-term revisions that phase in very gradually, often in ways that affect only future retirees."[20]

As an income-tested national program, the Seniors Benefit will be a positive instrument for redistributing income, not only between higher-income and lower-income senior citizens and between non-senior taxpayers and low-income seniors, but also across provinces and regions. In all provinces, most senior households will receive more benefits under the Seniors Benefit than from the present system. The highest proportion of elderly households with more benefits under the Seniors Benefit will be those in Quebec (over 80 percent), Saskatchewan, and the Atlantic provinces (from approximately 70 to 76 percent).[21] Quebec has the highest proportion of seniors who will obtain more under the Seniors Benefit, in part because seniors in that province have lower average incomes than the national average for senior couples and single seniors, and because Quebec has an above-average proportion of single seniors, who do better from the Seniors Benefit as a group than couples. Ontario, followed closely by British Columbia, will have the smallest majority of senior households (about 60 percent) getting more benefits. These two provinces have the highest median incomes for senior couples and individuals and only three in ten pensioners qualify for the GIS, whereas in Quebec and the Maritimes it is five or six in ten, while in Newfoundland seven of every ten pensioners receive the GIS.[22] Given that proportionately more of the revenues to finance the program will be raised from Ontario, British Columbia, and Alberta, the Seniors Benefit will have an equalizing effect, tending to redistribute income from the have provinces to the have-not provinces. It may also serve as a federalist argument and symbol in any future referendum in Quebec.

REFORMING THE CANADA PENSION PLAN

Just days before the 1997 federal budget was presented, the Finance Minister announced a federal-provincial consensus on reforms to the CPP.[23] In brief, the reforms involve raising the contribution rates for funding the plan, altering the investment policy to earn higher returns, and trimming some benefits for future pensioners in order to slow the growth of costs.

The reforms agreed to by Ottawa and eight provinces (the British Columbia and Saskatchewan NDP governments dissenting) seek to moderate the impact of costs that would fall on future generations of workers and employers in the form of high contribution rates, while also shielding present seniors from any cuts to their existing benefits. As with the Seniors Benefit, today's seniors have little to fear from these reforms to the CPP. All retired pensioners or anyone age 65 as of 1997, about 3.6 million people, will not be affected. CPP benefits will remain fully indexed to inflation, and retirement ages remain the same.

Beginning in 1998, working Canadians will pay more in CPP contributions, which will rise from the current rate of 5.85 percent of earnings up to $35,000 to 9.9 percent of contributory earnings in 2003, a 69 percent increase. In contrast, the existing schedule of CPP rates projected an increase to 7.35 percent of pensionable earnings in 2003, a 26 percent rise.[24] CPP contributions will climb to a maximum of $1,635 a year in 2003 from the present top rate of $945. The federal-provincial view is that with this acceleration of contributions now, generating a large reserve fund for investing, the rate can then remain at this level instead of rising to higher levels. Thus, near seniors (aged 60 to 64) will pay higher than previously expected contributions for a few years, while pre-boomers (in their 50s) and particularly baby boomers (in their late 30s and 40s) will pay steeper rates for significant periods of their working lives. Generation X in the labour force will pay higher CPP rates sooner than heretofore planned, but not as high as would have been necessary in the second and third decades of the twenty-first century.

For all of these non-senior groups, various benefits under the CPP will be reduced. Retirement pensions will be based on the average of maximum pensionable earnings over the last five working years rather than the last three, having the effect of lowering maximum benefits by $144 a year, a cut slightly more than the planned increase of the Seniors Benefit. The CPP's death benefit, a one-time payment to the estate of a deceased CPP contributor, is to be reduced from $3580 to $2500 and deindexed. The eligibility for, and administration of, disability benefits are also becoming more restrictive. Finally, the yearly basic exemption, which is $3,500 and indexed to wages, will be frozen at that amount. Currently, contributions are made only on pensionable earnings above the exemption. This move adversely affects low-income and many part-time workers who, over time, will pay disproportionately more of their salaries as contributions to the CPP. While freezing the basic exemption may sound like a minor technical change to the CPP, it is an example of social policy reform by stealth. No longer indexed to the average industrial wage, the exemption will decline gradually in real terms, even though in nominal terms (current dollars) it would appear to be the same. The result is a steady lowering of the real basic exemption each year, imposing what amounts to a hidden payroll tax increase on low-income earners.

CONCLUSIONS: GRADING THE GRITS

The Chrétien government has not been idle in restructuring income security programs for the elderly nor shy in praising its record. In an update on the government's actions in implementing the Red Book, the Seniors Benefit is depicted as an example of preserving social programs for the twenty-first century and of breaking new ground with "innovative approaches to improving the quality of life of Canadians."[25] Viewed against recent social policy trends, however, many features of the Seniors Benefit are more incremental than innovative. The driving role in social policy assumed by the Finance Department under the Conservatives has continued under the Liberals. Curiously, the brief passage describing the Seniors Benefit is introduced by a heading that says, "A Pension System That Works for Everyone." This surely is a laudable aim but so far is not a Liberal achievement.

Combining four programs into one, with full indexation and a five-year period to plan for the change, represents a noteworthy reform. The Liberals lose political points, however, for deferring an increase in benefits to low-income seniors until 2001, and, at that, it is to be a minimal raise. At first glimpse, the Liberals may seem like Robin Hood, taking benefits away from the richest seniors to help the poorest seniors. On second look, the Liberals seem more like Ebenezer Scrooge, cutting back and giving only a miserly increment of 17 cents a day to the "truly needy" while keeping the rest. The poverty rate among today's seniors stands at 18.7 percent, and it is much higher for single elderly women (50.6 percent) and men (28.7 percent)—overall, 690,000 older citizens. In comparison, the poverty rate in Canada is 21.0 percent among children and 16.5 percent for those in the 18 to 64 age group.

With the announcement of the Seniors Benefit, have old age pensions been eliminated as a significant political issue for the upcoming federal election? It is important to realize that draft legislation for implementing the Seniors Benefit has not yet been introduced in Parliament, and some details of the new policy remain unclear. With a federal election looming, it seems unlikely that legislation will be introduced that would cut benefits in the near future for at least some seniors. It is 12 years since the last general increase, and the Liberals are telling low-income seniors they must wait for another four years. This will be the longest period during which benefits have not been augmented since the federal government entered this policy field in 1927. Perhaps in the lead-up to the next election, or after, in 1999, the International Year of Older Persons, we will see a much needed increase to the GIS and SPA. In a second term, Liberals need to focus their attention on these matters of pensions if old age in Canada is to be a lusty winter.

NOTES

For constructive comments and suggestions on the first draft of this chapter I want to thank Sandra Bach, Ken Battle, Steve Kerstetter, Gene Swimmer, Kathy Teghtsoonian, and Sherri Torjman.

1 *As You Like It*, II, iii, 52.
2 The following discussion draws from Michael J. Prince, "Startling Facts, Sobering Truths and Sacred Trust: Pension Policy and the Tories," in Allan M. Maslove, ed., *How Ottawa Spends 1985: Sharing the Pie* (Toronto: Methuen, 1985), 114-61; "From Meech Lake to Golden Pond: The Elderly, Pension Reform and Federalism in the 1990s," in Frances Abele, ed., *How Ottawa Spends 1991-92: The Politics of Fragmentation* (Ottawa: Carleton University Press, 1991), 307-56; and "Public Apprehension over the CPP: How Real Is It?" *Perception* 20, 1 (Spring 1996), 3-4.
3 See Ann Finlayson, *Whose Money Is It Anyway? The Showdown on Pensions* (Markham: Penguin, 1988); C.G. Gifford, *Canada's Fighting Seniors* (Toronto: James Lorimer, 1990); and Edward Greenspon and Anthony Wilson-Smith, *Double Vision: The Inside Story of the Liberal Party* (Toronto: Doubleday, 1996), 258-59. For a more qualified view of "grey power" in Canada, see Prince, "From Meech Lake." While set back on deindexing the OAS in 1985, the Conservatives went on to end the universality of the OAS in 1988 with the clawback.
4 See Ken Battle, "Limits of Social Policy," in Jean Chrétien, ed., *Finding Common Ground* (Hull: Voyageur, 1992), 161.
5 Liberal Party of Canada, *Creating Opportunity: The Liberal Plan for Canada* (Ottawa, 1993), 73-74. The Red Book gave no hint that the Liberals would rival or outdo the Tories in taking money away from the unemployed and other groups in need.
6 See Greenspon and Wilson-Smith, *Double Vision*, Chapter 16, and Michael J. Prince, "From Expanding Coverage to Heading for Cover: Shifts in the Politics and Policies of Canadian Pension Reform," in A. Joshi and E. Berger, eds., *Aging Workforce, Income Security, and Retirement Policy* (Hamilton: McMaster University, 1996), 56-66.

7 Because the Age Credit and Pension Income Credit will be termi-
nated, well-to-do people 60 and over who stick with the OAS/GIS
option will actually be worse off in 2001 than under the current
system.

8 Indeed, a leading progressive social policy analyst, Ken Battle,
proposed transferring the essence of the child benefit reform to the
elderly benefit system. See his *Thinking the Unthinkable: A Targeted,
Not Universal, Old Age Pension* (Ottawa: Caledon Institute of Social
Policy, October 1993). At the time, Battle stood virtually alone in the
social policy community in calling for a non-universal elderly
program. Caledon's proposal foreshadowed and influenced the
design of the Seniors Benefit, and Battle served as an unofficial
adviser to the Minister of Finance and as policy architect on this
issue. See also Ken Battle, "Why Solange Denis Smiled: Public
Pension Reform in the 1990s," *Canadian Review of Social Policy*, 38
(1996), 125-38.

9 Paul Martin, Minister of Finance, *Budget Speech* (Ottawa: Canada
Communication Group, 1996), and *The Seniors Benefit: Securing
the Future* (Ottawa: Canada Communication Group, 1996), 5-6.

10 Canadian Council on Social Development, "Women and Pension
Fact Sheets" (Ottawa: Centre for International Statistics at the
CCSD, March 1996), Fact Sheets 3, 4, and 5. The figures cited above
have been extended and updated courtesy of the Caledon Institute of
Social Policy.

11 Ibid., Fact Sheets 4 and 5. Also see Statistics Canada, *Canada's
Retirement Income Programs: A Statistical Overview* (Ottawa:
Supply and Services Canada, 1996).

12 See, for example, John Munro, Minister of National Health and
Welfare, *Income Security for Canadians* (Ottawa: Queen's Printer,
1970); *Report*, Royal Commission on the Economic Union and
Development Prospects for Canada, (Ottawa: Supply and Services
Canada, 1985), Volume Two; and Battle, in Chrétien, *Finding
Common Ground*.

13 The classic work is Kenneth Bryden, *Old Age Pensions and Policy-
Making in Canada* (Montreal and London: McGill-Queen's
University Press, 1974). On the ideological dualism of the Liberal
Party, see Christina McCall and Stephen Clarkson, *Trudeau and Our
Times Volume 2: The Historic Delusion* (Toronto: McClelland and
Stewart, 1994), and Greenspon and Wilson-Smith, *Double Vision*.

14 One Voice, The Canadian Seniors Network, *Newsletter*, 10, 2 (Spring
1996), 9; The Council of Canadians, *Joint Statement, Public
Pensions For All Canadians* (Ottawa: 1996); and Canadian Grey
Panthers Advocacy Network, iw@io.org. Even veteran political

journalists such as Greenspon and Wilson-Smith, in *Double Vision*, 258, mistakenly call the GIS means-tested.

15 In the same way, the Child Tax Benefit, introduced in 1993, effectively ended the parental recognition/horizontal equity objective of the child benefits system, in that upper-income families no longer receive child benefits. The eclipse of horizontal equity from the Canadian income security system is a story worth fuller examination by policy analysts and social advocates.

16 See Ken Battle, "A New Old Age Pension," in Keith G. Banting and Robin Boadway, eds., *Reform of Retirement Income: International and Canadian Perspectives* (Kingston: School of Policy Studies, Queen's University, 1997), 155-56, and Statistics Canada, *A Portrait of Seniors in Canada: Second Edition* (Ottawa: Supply and Services, 1997).

17 *The Mercer Bulletin*, 46, 4, April 1996, 1-2. See also Garth Turner, "Why Bother Saving for Your Old Age?" *Canadian Business*, August 1996, 67, and John Geddes, "Ottawa Turns the Rule of Thrift Upside Down," *The Financial Post*, January 11, 1997, 6-7.

18 Ken Battle, "Talk Versus Action: Pension Reform in Canada," revised version of a paper presented at the annual conference of the Canadian Association of Gerontology, March 1996, 23.

19 Paul Martin, Minister of Finance, *Budget Plan* (Ottawa: Canada Communication Group, 1996).

20 Paul Pierson, "The Politics of Pension Reform," in Banting and Boadway, eds., *Reform of Retirement Income*, 279.

21 Unpublished data on senior households with more benefits, by province, supplied to the author by HRDC. On the geography of seniors, see Eric Moore and Mark Rosenberg, *Growing Old in Canada* (Ottawa: Statistics Canada, Supply and Services Canada, 1996).

22 National Council of Welfare, *A Pension Primer* (Ottawa: Supply and Services, 1996), 7. Also worth reading is the Council's *Guide to the Seniors Benefit* (Ottawa: Supply and Services Canada, 1996).

23 Department of Finance, *Securing the Canada Pension Plan* (Ottawa: Canada Communication Group, 1997). Amendments to the CPP require Ottawa getting the support of at least two-thirds of the provinces with two-thirds of the population.

24 See National Council of Welfare, *Improving the Canada Pension Plan* (Ottawa: Supply and Services Canada, Autumn 1996), and Newman Lam, Michael J. Prince, and James Outt, "Restoring the Canada Pension Plan," in John R. Burbidge et al., *When We're 65: Reforming Canada's Retirement Income System* (Toronto: C.D. Howe Institute, 1996), 129-70.

25 Liberal Party of Canada, *A Record of Achievement: A Report on the Liberal Government's 36 Months in Office* (Ottawa, 1996), 72.

10

Constructing a New Social Union: Child Care Beyond Infancy?

SANDRA BACH

SUSAN D. PHILLIPS

Child care was seen by the Liberals as a potentially winning issue with Canadian voters in the 1993 election. Their Red Book promised $720 million for a federal-provincial shared-cost program that would expand existing child care in Canada by as much as 150,000 new spaces over three years. The fulfilment of this commitment would have marked a significantly increased federal role in the shaping and development of regulated child care, amounting to a 41 percent increase in the number of regulated spaces.[1] The Liberal promise, however, was made contingent upon satisfying two conditions: a 3 percent annual economic growth rate, and agreement of the provinces.[2]

In its 1996 self-report card, *A Record of Achievement*, the Chrétien government acknowledged child care as an unfulfilled promise.[3] It gave two reasons for the failure to meet the commitment. First, an insufficient number of provinces had indicated interest in the federal government's December 1995 shared-cost proposal to allow it to proceed with a program in an area of provincial jurisdiction. Second, the minimum threshold of a 3-percent growth rate in GDP had been achieved in only one year of the Liberals' term. These reasons, however, are an inadequate explanation of why the Chrétien government failed to fulfil its child care promise.

This chapter examines the political context, evolution, and eventual abandonment of the Liberal child care plan. We argue that neither the provinces nor the state of the economy were responsible for the demise of the child care commitment, although both could be seen as accomplices. Rather, child care has been the first fatality of the construction by the federal and provincial governments of a New Social Union, which has shifted the balance from primarily public to greater private provision of social services, from direct state funding of services to reliance upon the tax system for redistributing income to individuals and families, and from a moderate degree of federal involvement in social services and welfare to emphasis upon the primacy of the provinces. This New Social Union has been shaped mainly by the Liberals' responses to fiscal considerations and decentralist political pressures, rather than by an electoral mandate or public consultation.

Both the federal and provincial governments have reoriented political priorities toward a focus on child poverty with the 1997 federal budget announcement of an enriched and restructured National Child Benefit System (NCBS). Although the NCBS will enhance income support through the tax system for children of working-poor families, it will do little to improve the accessibility, affordability, or quality of child care services.

CHILD CARE IN POLITICAL CONTEXT

Child care is linked to a number of broad policy objectives, including child development, poverty alleviation, parental employment support, and the promotion of women's equality. In Canada, the child care system has been less connected to these broader public policy goals than in many other countries,[4] and has been focused more narrowly on employment support.

At the heart of the child care debate lie differing interests and philosophies with regard to the question as to whether child care is mainly a private parental responsibility to be purchased through the market, or a societal responsibility requiring the investment of public finances. Child care in Canada has evolved as a two-tier system using a mixture of public and private service-providers. Most parents choose the type of care they want from the private "market," according to their ability to pay. Public financing is limited to a number of tax assistance measures and some narrowly targeted welfare-oriented subsidies.

Until 1996, welfare-based assistance was provided under the federal-provincial shared-cost Canada Assistance Plan (CAP). Provincial governments, however, remain responsible for deciding the amount and form of assistance to be provided to lower-income parents, and for regulating child care services. Provincial support is generally offered as subsidized spaces in licensed centres, or family day care arrangements. The degree of public funding and the supply and type of child care services differ dramatically from one province to another.

The federal government also provides support to families with children through the income tax system in the form of credits and deductions. The Child Care Expense Deduction (CCED), the major federal tax expenditure directly related to child care, allows the lower-income parent to deduct a portion of the cost of receipted care expenses.[5] The CCED favours middle- and upper-income parents, in that its value increases with income. On the other hand, the Child Tax Benefit (CTB) is the primary tax measure aimed at income assistance for poor families with children, although parents are not required to have children in care to receive the credit.

One of the fundamental problems with Canada's system is that demand for high quality, affordable care far exceeds supply. Long waiting lists exist for a very limited number of subsidized services, and the demand for high quality, non-parental child care continues to grow as more women enter the paid work force. The labour force participation rate of women with children under three years of age has increased from 31 percent in 1975 to 65 percent in 1996, and from 40 percent to 70 percent for women with children aged three to five.[6] While the majority of children are now in non-parental care, child care is largely unregulated. The percentage of children served by regulated child care is low: 11 percent for children aged zero to three years; 31 percent for children three to six years; and 6 percent for children six to thirteen years.[7]

The concern about unregulated care is that its quality can be highly variable. High quality care involves licensing, optimal child-staff ratios, and environments supportive of healthy child development.[8] It also requires trained child care workers who are receiving adequate wages, so as to improve job satisfaction and reduce staff turnover (increasing the trust and bonding of children with workers, an important consideration during the years of early development when children are particularly vulnerable). Without the aid of government regulation and licensing, parents may not be able to monitor adequately the specific conditions or quality of the service they are purchasing. Regulated care, while generally of high quality, is often costly and inaccessible.

Over the past 25 years, advocacy groups and a series of task forces, beginning with the 1970 Report of the Royal Commission on the Status of Women, have pressed governments to expand child care as a regulated, public system. Their underlying goal has been to make it more affordable and widely accessible, rather than predominantly welfare-oriented. The first attempt by a federal government to negotiate a shared-cost program for the creation of subsidized child care spaces outside the welfare-based CAP was the Mulroney government's Child Care Act (Bill C-144), introduced in 1987.[9] It proposed a federal block fund of $4 billion over seven years to assist the provinces in creating and operating 200,000 new child care spaces. The Act met with enormous resistance from child care advocates, because of its willingness to subsidize for-profit care and its absence of national objectives. Ultimately the bill died on the order paper when the 1988 election was called. Despite the Conservative campaign promise to re-introduce the Child Care Act, by February 1992 the Conservative Health Minister formally stated that a national child care strategy would not be pursued, because of fiscal restraint. The Mulroney government also announced it was initiating a new focus on child poverty, thereby diverting public attention from the child care issue.

During the run-up to the 1993 election, a number of well-organized child care, women's, and other groups directed their efforts at lobbying all parties to commit to a national child care program. The Liberal party, as vociferous critics of the Conservative government's child care record during their opposition years, responded to public and demographic pressures by including a potentially substantial—but carefully worded—commitment to child care space expansion in its 1993 Red Book.

LIBERAL CHILD CARE POLICY:
DEVELOPING A NATIONAL PROGRAM?

Was the Red Book promise concerning child care ever intended to lead to the development of a national child care program? The evolution of the proposed child care agreement and its eventual abandonment casts light upon the Liberals' real commitment to child care, and upon the development of a reorientation of federal and provincial roles.

The $720-million Liberal Red Book promise was based upon a cost-sharing arrangement of 40-40-20 (federal-provincial-parental, based upon ability to pay) for the creation of regulated spaces. Originally, it was designed as a "top up" to fit within the CAP system, rather than the development of a national program. Many federal officials felt that the federal proposal was insufficient to support a national program. [10] The child care community, on the other hand, viewed the promise as "laying the groundwork" for a broader national and more publicly-financed program, arguing that an increase of 150,000 regulated spaces was not a modest proposal, and, further, that the federal government had not previously been directly involved with child care space creation.

In the early part of the mandate, the Liberal government appeared intent on developing a national child care program. The February 1994 Budget allocated the first two years of child care federal funding: $120 million for the fiscal year 1995-96 and $240 million for 1996-97. Real dollars had begun to be attached to electoral rhetoric, although most of this would later be withdrawn.

A strong federal commitment to child care was also evident during the 1994-95 Social Security Review (SSR) process, the comprehensive public consultation process on social security reform. The SSR, led by the Parliamentary Committee on Human Resources Development, heard from approximately 100,000 Canadians. The federal government's 1994 SSR Child Care and Development Discussion Paper addressed many of the key issues in the child care debate, and, notably, emphasized the importance of developing a national framework of principles. Child care was viewed in a broad public policy context, supporting "optimal" child development, as well as employment and poverty alleviation objectives.[11] Yet, while there are many similarities between the Discussion Paper and the Committee's Final Report, released in February 1995, the latter made no reference to "national principles."[12] This is not surprising, however, given the pre-referendum and pre-budget timing of its release.

During the Social Security Review, federal negotiators engaged in preliminary consultations with all provinces except Quebec, which refused to participate formally in this process. Provincial governments at this point were naturally reluctant to engage in formal negotiations on child care before the conclusion of the SSR and the enactment of the 1995 Budget.

LIBERAL MID-TERM SHIFTS

A number of broad political, institutional, and fiscal policy developments occurring during the Liberal government's mid-term period worked against the fulfilment of a national child care program. Significantly, though, many of these fiscal and policy constraints on government action were *self-imposed*.

The Fiscal Shift: The Canada Health and Social Transfer
The February 1995 federal Budget, initiating the Canada Health and Social Transfer (CHST), represented a key turning point in the evolution of the federal child care plan and, more broadly, in the federal role in national social programs. The CHST combined two main policy objectives of the Liberal government: fiscal restraint and increased flexibility of provinces to allocate reduced transfers according to their own priorities. The pre-existing federal block fund for health and post-secondary education, Established Programs Financing (EPF), and the shared cost grant for welfare programs, CAP, were combined into the CHST super-block grant. CAP, which previously provided approximately $300 million of federal child care funds to the provinces, was abolished on April 1, 1996, producing a *de facto* redefinition of the federal funding role in child care. No additional child care funding was specifically designated in the 1995 Budget (nor in subsequent ones).

Cash transfers to the provinces have declined, by approximately 33 percent between 1995-96 and 1997-98, from $18.6 billion in 1995-96 to $12.5 billion in 1997-98.[13] Of significance to child care, the large CHST cuts reduce the fiscal capacity of provinces to match federal funds for a future shared-cost program. Transfer reductions are forcing provinces to make difficult expenditure choices between social program areas, with potentially negative consequences for the less established social program areas such as child care.

The response of the child care community to the CHST was swift and forthright. The Ontario Coalition for Better Child Care argued before the Commons Finance Committee prior to the passage of the CHST budget bill (C-76) in June 1995 that "the Tories may have killed their promise for a national child care program. This bill, if passed, will bury any future possibilities."[14]

While the Red Book commitment recognized provincial jurisdiction over child care, there was an emphasis upon the conditions of *high quality* child care (to be defined through negotiations) and an *enhancement* of the pre-existing system. Yet the unconditional nature of the CHST created a situation in which provinces would not be required to meet any conditions or to account for child care expenditures. It would be nearly impossible to hold the pre-existing provincial child care funding base constant in the face of the pressure to merely substitute the new federal funds for the CHST reductions in provincial budgets. In terms of fiscal transparency and accountability, unconditional block grant designs do not fit well with those of shared-cost grants in the same program area, such as child care.

It has been argued that the shared cost child care commitment was designed for a pre-CHST fiscal and political environment. The CHST was essentially a self-imposed *gestalt switch*, which, while not preventing the fulfilment of the child care commitment, made it much more difficult for the federal government and the provinces both to finance and to agree upon a new shared-cost program. It also represents a foundational pillar in the construction of the New Social Union— a redefinition of the rights, roles, and responsibilities between Canadian citizens and their governments, among governments of the federation, and between markets and society.

Decentralist Shifts: Unity and Provincialist Positions
The fall 1995 Quebec referendum had at least a temporary inhibitory effect upon the Liberal government's political will to push forward with the development of a national child care program. The federal cabinet and central agencies (particularly the Privy Council Office and the Prime Minister's Office) halted all federal initiatives that would potentially lend support to the sovereigntist movement in Quebec. From the federal perspective, a proposal for a shared-cost program that could be interpreted in Quebec as impinging upon provincial jurisdiction by a "centralist" federal government was simply too politically sensitive.

Provinces were also proceeding with a joint exercise to determine their own social program priorities, aided by the Ministerial Council on Social Policy Reform. This interprovincial institution was formed by the provincial premiers in 1995 to "improve coordination and take on a leadership role with respect to national matters that affect provincial jurisdiction."[15] In its December 1995 Report, the Council recommended that "services for children and families," such as child care, be managed and delivered exclusively by the provinces and territories.[16] While this statement does not necessarily preclude a federal child care funding role, the political priorities of the majority of the provinces had changed. The Council was placing a high priority upon reducing child poverty by the development of a national Child Tax Benefit, combining the existing federal Child Tax Benefit with provincial child welfare spending.

Rebuilding and Launching the Liberal Child Care Proposal
Despite the fiscal and political difficulties posed by the CHST and concerns over national unity, the child care plan was not immediately scuttled, for two reasons. First, a number of provincial governments signalled their interest, although "interest" varied in both degree and content. The second factor was the intense personal commitment to child care by HRDC Minister Lloyd Axworthy. Federal negotiators continued to consult with the provinces in the fall of 1995. Despite some internal political and institutional resistance, mainly from the Privy Council Office, the Finance Department, and ministers supporting decentralist and cost containment policy goals, Cabinet ultimately supported the official proposal to the provinces, which was offered by Minister Axworthy on December 13, 1995.[17] Contrary to explanations

given later that the 3 percent GDP growth rate required for fulfilling the child care plan had not been met, this federal proposal was launched despite the 1995 Budget estimate for 1996 real GDP growth of 2.5 percent, and the updated December 6, 1995 fiscal forecasts of 2.2 and 2.3 percent for 1995 and 1996, respectively.

The December 1995 proposal was based on a shared-cost offer of $630 million to the provinces over a five-year period (1996-2001), plus a $72 million First Nations/Inuit child care initiative and an $18 million research program called Child Care Visions.[18] It allowed for a greater degree of flexibility than the original Red Book commitment, in recognition of post-CHST political and fiscal circumstances. Minister Axworthy's proposal was a very loose framework that made no attempt to impose national standards on provincial child care systems and purposely left many potentially contentious details vague or unspecified. The Red Book reference to *regulated* care was replaced by the language of *high quality* child care arrangements, thereby implying more provincial discretion in defining quality. The notion of *space creation* was replaced with the offer to *expand and improve* child care systems. Clearly, the federal government's role was to stimulate and facilitate the creation and improvement of provincial child care systems, not to control the nature of the delivery system. While recognizing child care as within provincial jurisdiction, and entertaining, but rejecting, the possibility of bilateral arrangements, the federal government did require that there be *sufficient* provincial participation to establish a national program. The minimum number of provinces required was not laid out.

Swimming Against the Tide: The Demise of the Child Care Plan
Given an inhospitable political, institutional, and fiscal environment for a national shared-cost program, a strong commitment on the part of the HRDC Minister was required. In the January 1996 Cabinet shuffle, Minister Lloyd Axworthy moved to Foreign Affairs, to be replaced in HRDC by Doug Young. Minister Young's clear political priority was to focus upon Unemployment Insurance reform, and he had little interest in pursuing the politically divisive child care file.

While the provinces formally expressed interest in proceeding with discussions, some provincial responses to the federal offer involved even greater flexibility in the use of federal funds than Axworthy's proposal would have accommodated. Official provincial responses included British Columbia's fairly enthusiastic support for the federal proposal, the interest (with minor concerns) of New Brunswick and Nova Scotia, the conditional (tied to supporting an integrated Child Tax Benefit) of Saskatchewan, and Ontario's belated, somewhat non-committal response. Quebec expressed interest in pursuing discussions if the federal government agreed to recognize their position that child care was exclusively within their jurisdictional realm, and declared that they would not accept any national conditions or shared-cost funding, preferring instead a tax point transfer or unconditional block grant. This qualified interest by Quebec is not surprising, given that it has always had one of the most extensive and progressive public child care systems in the country. "Opting out" arrangements by Quebec in shared-cost national social programs (such as CAP, as well as post-secondary education before EPF) have been common historically and would have been anticipated. In addition, a number of provinces claimed that it would be difficult for them to enter into a shared-cost agreement, given the reduction of federal fiscal transfers.

In mid-February 1996, the Axworthy child care proposal was abandoned by the Liberal government, because of a "lack of provincial interest."[19] It is important to note that this decision was made *prior* to any formal federal-provincial bargaining. The hard negotiations had never been given a chance to succeed, or fail. As with the history of the initial development of shared-cost national social programs such as health and post-secondary education (before EPF), a strong political commitment by the federal government was necessary to pursue what would undoubtedly have been difficult negotiations. But the situation had changed since such programs were developed, in that the federal spending power had been curtailed through the creation of the CHST fiscal regime in 1995. This, combined with the presence of a new Minister focused upon Unemployment Insurance reform, and a mixed degree of support within Cabinet, collectively undermined the political will required to follow through with the government's own proposal.

It is quite likely that the Liberals expected to pay only a small political price for abandoning child care. After all, they had witnessed the precedent of the Conservatives reneging on their child care promises only a few years earlier with minimal public outcry. Moreover, child care was only one of many social programs that the Liberal government argued it could no longer afford to support. And, like the Tories before them, the Liberals promised to concentrate their efforts on fighting child poverty by using the tax system.

Quasi-Constitutional Changes: Sealing the End of the Promise?
Not only did the Liberal government abandon its immediate plans for enhancing Canada's child care system, but it imposed on itself longer-term restrictions that will make future possibilities for a shared-cost national child care plan difficult. The 1995 federal budget had stated that "it is now time to complete the gradual evolution away from cost-sharing to block funding of programs in areas of provincial responsibility."[20] This position was reinforced by the February 1996 Throne Speech, which claimed, in language reflective of the 1992 Charlottetown Accord, that "the Government will not use its spending power to create new shared cost programs in areas of exclusive provincial jurisdiction without the consent of a majority of the provinces."[21] Prime Minister Chrétien stated in the House of Commons on February 28, 1996, "This is the first time any Federal government has undertaken formally to restrict its use of the spending power outside a constitutional negotiation."[22]

The combined effects of the CHST and the Throne Speech are *de facto* and quasi-constitutional restrictions on the federal spending power. The possibility of pursuing any shared-cost child care program in a Liberal second term, should the Liberals be re-elected, has been significantly curtailed.

CHILD CARE SPENDING:
ASSESSING THE LIBERAL RECORD

An assessment of federal spending on child care reveals that the Chrétien government has significantly reconfigured its fiscal and political priorities, moving away from direct spending on child care services and toward the use of tax-based redistributive measures that are focused upon children. In addition, its overall spending on child care has been cut significantly.

Table 10.1

Federal Expenditures on Child Care Services (Estimates)
($ Millions)

	1993-94	1994-95	1995-96	1996-97	1997-98
FEDERAL CHILD CARE SERVICES FUNDING					
General					
Canada Assistance Plan/CHST (HRDC/Finance)[a]	300	300	300	240[a]	201[a]
Child Care Initiatives Fund/Child Care Visions (HRDC)[b]	12	5.5	6	6	6
Total	**312**	**305.5**	**306**	**246**	**207**
Overall Change: -33.5%					
Aboriginal Children					
Aboriginal Child Care (INAC)	12	15	17	18	18
First Nations and Inuit Child Care (HRDC)	n/a	n/a	6	26	40
Total	**12**	**15**	**23**	**44**	**58**
Overall Change: +483%					
TOTAL CHILD CARE FUNDING	**324**	**320.5**	**329**	**290**	**265**
Overall Change: -19%					
UNFULFILLED RED BOOK FUNDING[c]	**0**	**0**	**108**	**208**	**274**

NOTES TO TABLE 10.1

a   The Canada Assistance Plan was folded into the CHST in 1996-97. We have
    taken the previous federal CAP expenditures of $300 million, adjusted for
    proportional annual CHST cash reductions of 33% (20% in 1996-97 and a
    further cut of 13% in 1997-98), and assumed that the proportional spending
    will remain roughly equivalent to that under CAP. These are *very conservative*
    estimates of spending reductions (see text for fuller explanation).
b   The Child Care Initiatives Fund (Research) program expired on March 31,
    1995, and was replaced by a similar program, Child Care Visions. The latter
    does not directly fund child care spaces, but funds research linked to evaluat-
    ing and improving child care systems.
c   Those programs that were part of and funded by the December 1995 federal
    proposal, such as the expenditures on Child Care Visions and the First
    Nations and Inuit Initiative, have been deducted from the Red Book commit-
    ted funding of $720 million over three years.

Source: Canada, Department of Finance, Social Policy and Tax Policy Divisions,
1996-97; also, assistance from departmental officials from HRDC, INAC, and
Health Canada. All assumptions, comparisons, and calculations are the authors'.

Direct Spending on Child Care Services

When the Liberal government entered office in the fall of 1993, direct
program spending on child care services was made largely through
CAP and two small programs within HRDC and Indian and Northern
Affairs (INAC).[23] Table 10.1 compares federal allocations to child
care when the Liberals entered office with current amounts.

   In 1997 the federal government is spending approximately approximately one-third less ($105 million) on child care services for the gen-
eral population than it was in 1993; and roughly $274 million less than
it had promised in the Red Book. These enormous reductions in current spending are due to the CHST cuts, which abolished the $300
million portion of CAP directed annually to child care. Funding for
child care research has also decreased slightly. While $18 million has
been allocated over three years to the Child Care Visions research and
development program, this is largely an extension of the previously
funded Canadian Child Care Initiative Fund.

   Our estimates of spending reductions are very conservative, because
provinces are assumed to continue spending proportionately the same
on child care as they did under CAP, adjusting the previous federal
CAP expenditures (now incorporated into the CHST) for proportional

annual CHST reductions. In reality, the shared-cost CAP funding provided a greater incentive than the CHST for provinces to spend on child care, and, further, the CHST need not be spent on child care at all. Ongoing provincial social program cutbacks and pressures to maintain more established social programs suggest that many provinces will allocate proportionately fewer transfer dollars to child care than they did in 1993.

In addition, our estimates do not include child care spending related to labour market training that is currently being devolved to the provinces. The Dependent Care Allowance provided $20 per day for child care expenses for parents in training courses, at a federal cost in 1995-96 of $76 million. These allowances were essentially vouchers for purchasing regulated or unregulated care, but seldom covered its cost, and were not monitored to ensure that the money was actually spent on child care.

In contrast to services supported by the CHST, money for First Nations and Inuit child care has increased substantially since 1993, although this is a very small proportion of total child care spending. Direct funding for Aboriginal child care has been increased by $46 million between 1993 and 1997, nearly a five-fold increase. New federal funding includes the $72 million First Nations and Inuit child care fund (over three years), which creates 6,000 child care spaces.

Tax Transfers Related to Child Care
The two main types of tax measure for the support of families with children are the Child Care Expense Deduction and the Child Tax Benefit (and its supplements).

The CCED tax expenditure has remained roughly the same since 1993-94, although the age limit was raised to 16 in 1996, at an annual cost of $10 million.[24] The federal cost in terms of foregone revenues from the CCED was $305 million in 1993-94, and is estimated at between $310 and $330 million for the fiscal year 1997-98. The CCED has long been criticized as a regressive measure, because its value increases as an individual's marginal tax rate increases. Its actual value ranges from approximately $752 for families with incomes under $10,000, to $1,684 for incomes between $30,000 and $40,000, to $1,952 for those with incomes over $100,000.[25] The requirement of receipts for the CCED is problematic, in that many care-givers in the informal sector do not file tax returns and declare the income, and therefore are unwilling to provide receipts. This further contributes to its regressive nature, because low-income families are more likely than those with higher incomes to rely upon the informal sector.

In contrast, the CTB and its supplements provide general support for families, as opposed to tax assistance tied directly to the purchase of child care. Prior to 1997, it gave families with dependents under the age of 18 and a net family income under $25,921 a maximum benefit of $1,020 per child.[26] The $213 Young Child Supplement provides a form of direct child care tax assistance for parents with children under the age of seven who have not claimed child care expenses under the CCED.

The Liberal government has made a number of changes to the tax system to redistribute income to families and children. First, the Working Income Supplement (WIS) to the CTB for low-income working parents was slated for enrichment in the 1996 Budget from the previous maximum of $500 per family to $750 in 1997 and $1000 in 1998, at an annual cost upon full implementation of $250 million.[27] Second, child support payment tax rules were also changed in the 1996 Budget, so that the custodial parent is no longer required to pay tax on child support. This change is expected to increase federal revenues by an estimated $200 million over a three-year period.

The major change, announced in the 1997 Budget, is the restructuring and enrichment of the CTB, renamed the Canada Child Tax Benefit (CCTB). It will form the preliminary foundation for building a national child benefit system in Canada that will eventually integrate federal and provincial child benefits. Its primary goal is to encourage people to move from welfare to work by offering income supplements to working-poor families. As a first step toward implementing the CCTB, a $70 million additional enrichment to the federal contribution to the WIS will occur in 1997-98. It will be provided on a per child rather than a per family basis, at varying rates.[28] In August 1998, federal funding for the CCTB will increase by $600 million, for a total annual expenditure of $6 billion. Federal estimates are that the CCTB will enhance tax benefits to approximately 1.4 million families and 2.5 million children.

The CCTB and the $213 Young Child Supplement will be provided to all low-income parents, whether their income is derived from work

Table 10.2

Federal Expenditures on Tax Assistance to Families with Children (Estimates)

Child Care Tax Assistance and Funding ($ Millions)						
	1993-94[a]	1994-95	1995-96	1996-97	1997-98	
Child Care Expense Deduction[b]	305	305-330	305-330	310-330	310-330	

Tax Assistance for Families with Children ($ Billions)						
	1993-94	1994-95	1995-96	1996-97	1997-98	1998-99
(Canada) Child Tax Benefit	5.2	5.29	5.17	5.16	5.35	6.0

Notes:

a Note that the annual estimates for tax assistance are not based upon fiscal years, but upon Revenue Canada's July-July payment periods.

b The ranges for the CCED estimates from 1994-95 to 1996-97 are based upon *unofficial* Department of Finance estimates. It should also be noted that the Young Child Supplement to the CTB is considered to be direct funding for child care for those not claiming the CCED. The annual federal cost of $400 million for this supplement, however, is captured in the CTB estimates.

Sources: Department of Finance, Tax Policy Branch, Correspondence, 1997.

or from provincial welfare, with maximum benefits subject to an income threshold of $20,921 before benefits begin to be taxed back. Working parents with two or more children will receive enhanced benefits from the CCTB. Working-poor families with one child, however, will actually receive less money under the CCTB than they would have if the WIS was fully enriched by $1,000, based on the 1996 budget plans. As the National Child Benefit System evolves over the next few years, and provincial welfare funding is reallocated, overall benefits to the working poor are to be expanded further.

THE FEDERAL RETREAT FROM CHILD CARE

As part of its redefinition of its place in a New Social Union, the federal government has retreated from a leadership role in helping the provinces expand their child care systems. Instead, it is now using the tax system, particularly the enriched CCTB, as its main vehicle for involvement in social policy related to children. The development of a "national" child care program has been left to the "consent" of the provinces. This reconfigured role raises three questions. Will the CCTB be an effective alternative to the Red Book promise as a means of helping parents obtain child care? Is there still a need for a national child care system? Are the provinces likely to assume the leadership mantle in creating a "national" as opposed to a federally led child care system?

The National Child Benefit System
The CCTB is planned to be integrated with provincial child tax assistance and welfare benefits to form a National Child Benefit System (NCBS). Any loose framework of conditions for reallocating provincial child welfare benefits to tax assistance or increased services aimed at the working poor will be developed through further federal-provincial negotiations and public consultation.

The enriched federal CCTB as a way to fight child poverty may garner some public approval. As a pre-election strategy, it is aimed at refurbishing the image of the Chrétien government as liberals with a social conscience after years of social program cuts. The benefits of the federal CCTB have been argued on two main grounds. First, when more money is put in the hands of poor families, more income is available to be spent on the needs of children, including the purchase of child care.[29] Parents rather than governments, it is asserted, will make better choices about the type and mix of services children need. Second, injection of money through the CCTB is intended to free up provincial funding in the child welfare "envelope" that can be spent on additional supplements or other services for children of the working poor.

The notion that this tax measure is a substitute for direct federal spending on child care is mistaken in our view. It is not clear that the provinces will allocate the room created in their child welfare envelopes by an enriched CCTB toward increasing or improving child care. Although several provinces, such as Quebec and British Columbia, are actively expanding their child care systems, others have been withdrawing child care funding and regulatory supervision. Many provinces are likely to reallocate child welfare expenditures by increasing supplements to the working poor, currently a popular measure, rather than freeing up funds for child care services. Indeed, funding for child care services may be in direct competition with the CCTB and its provincial supplements.

Further, the additional income provided by the CCTB is not sufficient to purchase high quality care in the private market. Under the CCTB, a family with an annual net income of $20,000 and two children under the age of seven would receive an annual benefit of $3,050 (and an additional $426 if they did not claim the CCED). Even in the unlikely scenario that they would spend the entire benefit on receipted child care (increasing tax benefits to over $5,000 for their two children, combining the CCTB and CCED), it would be inadequate to meet the cost of roughly $11,000 per year (in Ontario) for two preschoolers in full-time regulated family day care.[30] But working-poor families still need child care, even if they cannot afford regulated facilities. The impact of the CCTB, therefore, may be simply to reinforce use of the lower-cost, unregulated market.

The merits of a future NCBS for reducing the incidence of child poverty are not the subject of this analysis. It is important to emphasize, however, that the system is not even a partial replacement of the unfulfilled Liberal Red Book promise on child care. Tax measures do not directly support comprehensive, affordable, or high quality non-parental child care. They are based on the implicit principle that child care is a private responsibility of parents, rather than a public policy issue.

Federal Tax Assistance Versus Direct Spending on Child Care
We have argued that the federal retreat from direct spending on child care services and the reorientation to enhancing tax benefits to working-poor families is likely to lead to the "defunding" of child care and increased provincial variation in levels of service provision. Increasingly, Canada's approach to child care will be provided in the market on a user-pay basis. As Friendly and Oloman note, "[P]arents able to pay for the best possible product for their children are most likely to be able to access quality while others, with less purchasing power, have to settle for an inferior product or no product at all."[31]

The rationale for direct federal financing of child care services is similar to the case made for public financing of other "national" social programs. Child care is a quasi-public good, with significant social and economic benefits for the country as a whole. *High quality* child care will be underprovided in a privately financed child care market that does not take into account the "public good," or long-term economic and social pay-offs.[32] A national child care system, stimulated and sustained by federal funds, recognizes these broader benefits at least to some degree and encourages the maintenance of direct public financing.

An Interprovincial "National" Child Care System?
The Ministerial Council has become the interprovincial forum for discussion of social policy for "clarifying the respective role and responsibilities" of both orders of government. While it has supported a nationally integrated child tax benefit system, it has also been exploring the feasibility of working toward a loose national framework of child care principles.

In our view, however, the Ministerial Council is unlikely to develop and enforce a national child care system without federal money. Existing provincial systems are extremely diverse in terms of the services provided, degree and types of regulation, for-profit or non-profit care arrangements, and funding levels. Provincial political and fiscal priorities toward child care differ widely. Not only can the Ministerial

Council offer no carrots of its own, it has no stick to wield to encourage provincial governments to establish "national" principles for, or spending on, expanding child care.

CONCLUSION

The Liberals have claimed that the provinces and the state of the economy prevented them from fulfilling their Red Book promise on child care. We have argued that this blame is misplaced. The federal government imposed quasi-constitutional constraints on its spending power through the design and implementation of the CHST and the 1996 Throne Speech. By doing so, it has limited its ability to participate in the development of a national child care program. There is little to suggest that significant political will existed after the departure of Minister Lloyd Axworthy from HRDC for the hard bargaining with the provinces necessary to reach an agreement. That some provinces were lukewarm or resistant to the shared-cost federal child care proposal of December 1995 was partially a fiscally induced political reaction to the large reductions in federal transfers.

During the Liberals' first term, the federal government and the provinces have engaged in extensive intergovernmental negotiations aimed at realigning roles and responsibilities in an emerging New Social Union. This has led to a more unified position on further restricting the federal role in child care and other social programs. Yet the Canadian public has been largely excluded from this process, as demonstrated by the child care case. The Liberal government received a public mandate to pursue its Red Book child care commitment in the 1993 election campaign and its comprehensive Social Security Review process. While an argument might be made that the Liberals had little choice but to respond to the need to reduce its deficit by the implementation of the CHST—and that deficit reduction was supported by public opinion polls—there was no public mandate for the Liberals to withdraw *permanently* from the federal role in child care services.

The contours of a New Social Union for child care and social services have solidified during the Liberal term. There has been a clear shift from a designated federal funding role in child care services to one of income redistribution to poor families with children through the tax system. The prevailing paradigm at the federal level is now un-equivocally provincial choice. Responsibility has been devolved not only from federal to provincial governments, but from governments to parents. While no one denies parental responsibility for the care of children, the broader question of the public benefits of high quality, affordable care, and therefore of societal and state responsibility for it, has been overlooked.

While the National Child Benefit system is intended to redistribute income to working-poor families, it will do little to help parents access affordable and high quality care for their children in a largely private and unregulated child care market. And given the shock to the under-developed provincial child care systems arising from the withdrawal of federal, and in many cases provincial, public financing, the already fragile existing child care systems will be in jeopardy.

The deleterious social and economic policy effects of this lack of access to affordable, accessible, and high quality non-parental child care are unlikely to subside. The public policy implications include impeded healthy child development, increased future demands upon the social welfare system, and adversely affected future labour mar-kets. The policy consequences for women and their equality in the labour force will be particularly onerous. Yet given how the New So-cial Union is being defined by both the federal and provincial govern-ments, it seems unlikely that child care will reappear on the federal policy agenda in the near future unless governments begin to connect child development, which is enhanced by high quality care, with hu-man infrastructure development.

NOTES

We would like to acknowledge and thank Martha Friendly and Diane Bascombe for providing valuable information for this chapter. Gene Swimmer, Rianne Mahon, Allan Maslove, Martha Friendly, and Katherine Teghtsoonian provided constructive and thoughtful comments and suggestions. We would also like to thank the numerous federal and provincial officials who generously gave their time to enhance our understanding of child care policy and the positions of governments. Officials within the Finance Department kindly assisted in obtaining expenditure and tax information. Interpretations of child care policy under the Liberal term, however, as well as any errors or omissions, are the responsibility of the authors.

1 The existing number of regulated child care spaces in 1993 (including day-care centres and family day care) was 362,818. Human Resources Development Canada (HRDC), *Status of Day Care in Canada, 1993* (Ottawa: Supply and Services Canada, 1994), Table 2.

2 Liberal Party of Canada, *Creating Opportunity: The Liberal Plan for Canada* (Ottawa, Sept. 1993), 40.

3 Liberal Party of Canada, *A Record of Achievement: A Report on the Liberal Government's 36 Months in Office* (Ottawa, 1996), 35.

4 Rianne Mahon, "Both Wage Earner and Mother: Women's Organizing and Childcare in Sweden and Canada," unpublished paper (Ottawa: Carleton University, 1997).

5 The maximum amount a family can claim is $5,000 per child under the age of 7 (or older children with severe disabilities), and $3,000 per child between the ages of 7 and 14 (or older children with moderate disabilities).

6 1975 estimates are based on data compiled by Martha Friendly in *Child Care Policy in Canada: Putting the Pieces Together* (Don Mills: Addison-Wesley, 1994), 32; recent estimates are obtained from Statistics Canada, *Labour Force Survey*, Cat # 71-001-XPB (Ottawa, October 1996).

7 HRDC, *Status of Day Care in Canada 1994* (Ottawa: Supply and Services Canada, 1995), Tables 7, 8, 9, and 11.

8 See Gillian Doherty-Derkowski, *Quality Matters: Excellence in Early Childhood Programs* (Don Mills: Addison-Wesley Publishers Ltd., 1995).

9 For a discussion of the Tory child care strategy, see Susan D. Phillips, "Rock-a-bye, Brian: The National Strategy on Child Care," in Katherine A. Graham, ed., *How Ottawa Spends 1989-90: The Buck Stops Where?* (Ottawa: Carleton University Press, 1989), 165-208, and Katherine Teghtsoonian, "Neo-Conservative Ideology and Opposition to Federal Regulation of Child Care Services in the United States and Canada," *Canadian Journal of Political Science*, 26, 1 (March 1993), 97-121.

10 Personal interviews, HRDC officials.

11 HRDC, *Child Care and Development: A Supplementary Paper* (Ottawa: Supply and Services Canada, 1994), 21.

12 Canada, House of Commons, Standing Committee on Human Resources Development, *Security, Opportunities and Fairness: Canadians Renewing Their Social Programs* (Ottawa: Supply and Services Canada, 1995).

13 Based upon Allan Maslove, "The Canada Health and Social Transfer: Forcing Issues," in Gene Swimmer, ed., *How Ottawa Spends
   1996-97: Life Under the Knife* (Ottawa: Carleton University Press,
   1996), 285, and Paul Martin, Minister of Finance, *Budget Plan*
   (Ottawa: Canada Communication Group, 1997), 64.
14 Ontario Coalition for Better Child Care, *Burying a National Child
   Care Program*, Brief to the House of Commons Standing Committee
   on Finance, May 9, 1995, 7.
15 Annual Premiers' Conference Provincial-Territorial Working Group
   on Social Policy Reform and Renewal, *Issues Paper on Social Policy
   Reform and Renewal: Next Steps* (Jasper, August 1996), 1.
16 Ministerial Council on Social Policy Reform and Renewal, *Report to
   Premiers*, December 15, 1995, 14.
17 There were inconsistencies between accounts of when the child care
   plan went to Cabinet.
18 HRDC, News Release, Ottawa, December 13, 1996, 2.
19 "Federal Child-Care Plan Report Doomed," *The Globe and Mail*
   [Toronto], Canadian Press, February 16, 1996, A1; Wendy Cox,
   "Provinces 'Used as an Excuse' to Kill Child Care Pledge,"
   Vancouver Sun, February 17, 1996, A5. Media accounts were
   confirmed through a number of interviews.
20 Paul Martin, Minister of Finance, *Budget Plan* (Ottawa: Canada
   Communication Group, 1995), 52.
21 Canada, House of Commons, *Debates*, Vol. 134, February 27, 1996,
   4.
22 House of Commons, *Debates*, February 28, 1996, 57.
23 Child development programs, such as the Community Action Plan
   for Children (CAP-C) and Aboriginal Head Start, have not been
   included in these comparisons. These programs, while they are
   targeted toward at-risk children and their families, do not directly
   fund child care spaces.
24 Department of Finance, Tax Division, Correspondence, November
   1996.
25 Ruth Rose, "Analysis of Revenue Canada 1993, Taxation Statistics:
   Analyzing the Returns of Individuals for the 1991 Taxation Year and
   Miscellaneous Statistics," Table 11, in Doherty et al., *Child Care:
   Canada Can't Work Without It* (Toronto: Childcare Resource and
   Research Unit, 1995), 17.
26 Canada, Department of Finance, *The New Child Support Package*,
   Budget 1996 (Ottawa, 1996), 25.
27 Department of Finance, Tax Division, Correspondence, November
   1996.
28 The rates will be $605 for the first child, $405 for the second, and
   $330 for each additional child.

29 This argument has been made by Minister Paul Martin, other Liberal members, and a number of social policy analysts. See Mark Kennedy, "Social Policy Challenge of the Generation," *The Ottawa Citizen,* January 10, 1997, A11.

30 Childcare Resource and Research Unit, *Childcare in Canada: Provinces and Territories, 1993* (Toronto: CRRU, 1994). This is an average Ontario cost.

31 Martha Friendly and Mab Oloman, "Childcare at the Centre: Child Care on the Social, Economic and Political Agenda in the 1990s," in J. Pulkingham and Gordon Ternowetsky, eds., *Remaking Canadian Social Policy: Social Security in the Late 1990s* (Halifax: Fernwood Publishing, 1996), 282.

32 For further elaboration of these arguments, see Michael Krashinsky and Gordon Cleveland, "Rethinking the Rationales for Public Funding of Child Care," *Policy Options,* 18, 1 (January/February 1997), 16-19, and Lisa Powell, "Family Behaviour and Child Care Costs: Policy Implications," *Policy Options,* 18,1 (1997), 11-15.

11

Renovation or Abandonment?: Canadian Social Housing at a Crossroads

FRAN KLODAWSKY

ARON SPECTOR

This chapter examines why 1997 is likely to mark the last year of direct federal involvement in social housing, and what the implications might be. We begin with a brief historical overview and then provide evidence for our central argument: that current federal policy echoes and continues the initiatives begun under the previous Conservative government to devolve to the provinces, as fully as possible, responsibility for producing and maintaining social housing. Given a long history of provincial reticence to encourage or produce social housing without strong federal urging, the most probable outcome is a slow and steady erosion in its quantity and quality, and a return to a reliance on the private market to produce housing for low- and moderate-income Canadians.

The context of the current federal policy directions is presented through an examination of two sets of housing policy debates. These concern the ability of the private market to provide affordable housing of reasonable quality to those with low and moderate incomes, and the role that social housing should assume as a component of social policy. We also examine the implications of the lack of attention to shelter-related considerations in recent discussions about the future directions of Canadian social policy.

THE CURRENT FEDERAL PARTICIPATION IN SOCIAL HOUSING PROVISION

Interpretations of the British North America Act have universally placed the lion's share of responsibility for social housing with the provinces. The federal government, though, has the capacity to unilaterally initiate social housing programs in the national interest, and, in these cases, to solicit provincial participation. Over the last half-century, the federal government has led rather than followed the provinces and frequently has acted with a range of other partners, including most of Canada's local governments and a myriad of community groups. For the most part, provincial legislation related to social housing has been directed toward enabling participation in federally initiated social housing programs.[1]

The current federally administered social housing stock (both rental and co-operative) of approximately 630,000 units was produced over the last 47 years under the aegis of numerous housing programs initiated under eight different sections of the current National Housing Act.[2] The federal government participated in the development and continues to have a role in administering the operations of well over nine-tenths of all social housing built in the country. In 1995, that stock made up just under 7 percent of all Canada's occupied dwellings and 20 percent of its rental stock. It provides housing for an estimated 1.5 million Canadians, or 5 percent of Canada's population. While it shelters only about 14 percent of households on social assistance, it provides housing for approximately one-third of low-income households, according to Statistics Canada's definitions.[3]

In 1995, expenditures to maintain existing social housing administered by the federal government were in the range of $1.9 billion, which was combined with an additional $.7 billion (approximately) of provincial funding.[4] In that year, 1,100 new social housing units were completed (all located on Indian reserves), augmenting the total by .2 percent. Currently, the federal government's intent is to divest itself of administrative responsibility for all but 2 percent of its total commitment (16,000 housing units, located on-reserve).[5]

The federal, provincial, or territorial governments rarely build or manage social housing. Instead, they have almost always depended upon partnerships with "active parties," including local governments, quasi-governmental local housing authorities, private property managers, non-profit co-operatives, and other third sector organizations of various types (for example, benevolent societies, church groups, social service delivery agents, or non-profit corporations).[6] While resources and broad program objectives have been provided by senior governments, project concepts and plans have come predominantly from these "active parties," who have overseen the construction of new stock and then moved on to operate the social housing under the provisions of long-term operating agreements.[7]

The operating agreement is a contract that stretches from the date at which the housing is ready for occupancy to that at which the housing cost is fully amortized (a period of between 30 and 50 years). It translates prevailing program objectives into a set of contractual obligations. In return, during the term of the agreement senior government partners generally provide subsidy dollars that allow the active party to operate housing at a "break even" level and to provide housing subsidies to eligible low-income households.[8]

While minor renegotiation of details of the operating agreement is possible, this contract has the effect of largely "casting in stone" the program objectives of the era in which the agreement was signed. Perspectives on how to operationalize program objectives also are "concretized" into the project's physical and architectural design. For example, pre-1972 public housing was fully targeted to certain low-income households, and designed to be modest and austere, and, emphatically, not to provide the same amenity level as housing provided in the private market.[9] In contrast, federally funded co-operative housing, which for the most part began in 1972, was built to provide modest, affordable housing appropriate for low- *and* moderate-income families and individuals, and to encourage the integration of families

and individuals of varying incomes.[10] Unlike public housing, co-op
housing was designed as a remedy for failures of the private rental
housing market and of public housing. During its early history it was
to "house mainly families whose incomes may be too high for public
housing, but who cannot compete in the open market for housing."[11]
While still modest, in comparison with public housing co-op units tended
to be larger, to have more attractive finishings, and to have multiple
bedrooms in order to house families. In its later years, co-op housing
became a component of the market housing programs of Canada Mortgage and Housing Corporation (CMHC). In line with growing tensions associated with the deep recession of the early 1980s, the last
co-op program initiated in 1986 incorporated a stipulation promoting
security of tenure for households unable to access homeownership.[12]

Overall, the federally funded social housing portfolio provides housing for both low- and moderate-income Canadians in projects that target anywhere from 30 percent to 100 percent of units to low-income
households.[13] Universally, the housing was designed to provide "modest" accommodations, although how this is defined has varied considerably. Given existing resources, the shelter provided is intended to
satisfy a number of minimum standards—it is to be adequate (in good
repair and with basic amenities such as hot and cold running water,
operating washing, bathing, and toilet facilities), suitable (not
crowded—satisfying the National Occupancy Standard), and affordable (requiring the dedication of approximately 30 percent of household income).[14]

Within the broad limitations of standard operating agreements, federally financed social housing has been quite flexible in adapting to a
range of needs. Partners have often written additional requirements
into the operating agreements of specific projects or groups of projects.
For example, some projects have been specifically targeted to Aboriginal
peoples, others required a minimum percentage of units to be occupied
by persons with disabilities, and still others have been limited to seniors, female lone-parents, or female victims of domestic violence.[15]
Social housing projects have often been specifically designed or rede-
signed to provide appropriate space for the delivery of social and health
services (for example, on-site attendant care for persons with severe
disabilities). In addition, federal participation has often been "piggy-

backed" and co-ordinated with a range of other programs and activities. For example, in Aboriginal programs, economic development and job training goals have often been taken into account when determining how and by whom the design, development, and operation of social housing projects have been undertaken.[16] As with the design and implementation of general elements of operating agreements, the degree, magnitude, nature, and direction of "piggy-backing" has varied over time and from one federal regime to another.

Since 1992, no significant amounts of new social housing have been built with federal government support. While modest additions to the social housing stock have been initiated by the provinces of Quebec, British Columbia, and New Brunswick, the only large unilateral program approximating the scale of federal initiatives occurred in Ontario, and this was abruptly halted with the election of the Progressive Conservative government in 1994. The trend of withdrawing from new production and slowly allowing existing commitments to lapse continues a process that began with the 1986 Regina Accord—the last federal-provincial agreement on social housing—which was supposed to establish a new, and stronger, provincial role in the area of social housing.[17]

There is little doubt that the current Liberal government policy of inaction and divestment in the absence of concerted provincial and territorial efforts is slowly leading to the emergence of a patchwork, both of programs and of levels of social housing availability.

THE LIBERAL GOVERNMENT, THE RED BOOK, AND THE STATUS QUO

No mention was made in the Red Book of future social housing plans, despite an acknowledgement, in relation to Aboriginal peoples, that "[a]dequate shelter is a fundamental need of any society and a basic prerequisite for community prosperity."[18] Liberal government actions and statements outside the Red Book seem to be a straightforward extension of policy initiated during the previous Conservative government. In particular, the 1996 Throne Speech clearly re-invented complete constitutional devolution of housing-related responsibilities to the provinces, as originally proposed in the Charlottetown Accord.

This time, however, the objective would be achieved through administrative fiat. The subsequent Budget indicated that the government would actively seek to devolve the administration of all existing social housing programs to provincial and territorial governments, including those unilaterally administered by the federal government, by offering a fixed amount of money to cover existing operating agreements. When these agreements expire, so, too, with the exception of housing on-reserve, will funding for social housing.[19] In the spring of 1997, two provinces, Saskatchewan and New Brunswick, agreed to take on the administration of their social housing stocks. The agreement with Saskatchewan suggests that the federal government would not stand in the way of redirecting to other housing-related programs social housing operating funds gained through the renegotiation of operating agreements or through administrative or system efficiencies.[20] Provincial reactions have varied substantially. For example, New Brunswick's strengthening of third sector social housing organizations is quite at odds with Nova Scotia's centralization of social housing administration in its newly enlarged municipalities.[21]

The previous Conservative government began the process of divestment by slowly reducing new commitments for social housing units. The current government has continued and extended this approach to include cutting funds and allowing existing commitments to lapse. Although expenditures for social housing originally were capped at $2 billion annually, the current minister, Diane Marleau, recently announced a funding reduction of approximately 12 percent by fiscal year 1998-99, in order to meet deficit reduction targets.[22]

The impression that divestment and devolution are the federal government's priorities, with little regard to the importance of social housing for low-income Canadians, has been reinforced in several ways:

- Operating agreements with private sector and municipal housing providers have lapsed without any move to ensure a continued commitment to using this stock for low- and moderate-income Canadians. Since 1992, this has led to a .5 percent annual reduction in the stock administered by the federal government.[23]

- The federal government has not reacted to Ontario's moves to severely curtail the use of the rent supplements, whereby federal and provincial funds are utilized to "top up" rents paid by low-income households to private sector landlords[24] or to sell off single-family detached housing in its public housing portfolio.[25] To this date, it has also been mute in response to the Ontario government announcement in February, 1997 of its intention to devolve the administration and funding of social housing, including that jointly funded with the federal government, to the municipalities.[26] One significant unknown is whether the federal government will permit the transfer to the municipalities of the approximately one-third of total social housing funding that it controls.

- Much social housing is financed through medium-term mortgages. With the current fall in interest rates and CMHC's shift to direct lending, there have been considerable savings over budgeted commitments. At first, the government committed itself to "reploughing" these and other savings into non-profit housing. Instead, these savings and others brought about through the introduction of "system efficiencies" have been lost to budget reductions, with only a small fraction being recommitted to social housing, primarily to particular special-needs initiatives.[27]

For the Liberals, as for their Conservative predecessors, social housing appears to be a convenient pawn, both in their deficit-cutting efforts and in their eagerness to promote flexible federalism. Outside the community of social housing providers, there has been very little notice of, or opposition to, devolution. For example, a recent large-scale opinion survey concerning government priorities indicated that housing issues are well below matters such as job creation, unemployment, or the debt.[28]

The efficiencies that would be derived from an incorporation of the knowledge base built over many years by the active third parties in non-profit housing are largely missing from the deliberations thus far. Yet, this involvement has been a significant factor in the relative success of housing programs for low- and moderate-income households in

Canada, as compared to the United States.[29] While the Canadian Housing and Renewal Association (CHRA) and the Co-operative Housing Federation of Canada (CHFC) have made numerous attempts to intervene on behalf of these "active parties," the federal government has shown very little interest. In May 1996, CHRA submitted a revised proposal for a sectoral management model for social housing administration to the Housing Minister.[30] Minister Marleau's only response, until very recently, was to indicate her preference that CHRA negotiate directly with the provinces and territories.[31] In December 1996, however, she did request that "CHRA forward conditions for entering into agreements with provinces and territories which would protect the stock."[32]

While reducing overall support to social housing providers, the federal government has indicated an interest in continuing to play a selective role in helping specific target groups deal with shelter problems. Mention of housing occurs in two sections of the Red Book, although without any focus on social housing. First, through the reinstatement of $50 million annually for a two-year period for the Residential Rehabilitation Assistance Program (RRAP),[33] limited incentives would be provided to owner-occupiers and private sector landlords for renovations designed to aid seniors with disabilities and low-income singles residing in rooming houses.[34] Second, recognizing the extreme housing crisis faced by many Aboriginal peoples, the Red Book indicated that a federal Liberal government would "work with Aboriginal peoples to develop an approach in line with existing social housing *objectives* to emphasize community control, local resources, and flexibility in design and labour requirements."[35]

In *A Record of Achievement*, the Liberals identified both commitments as areas where its promises had been met or surpassed.[36] The RRAP was reintroduced in the 1994 Budget and extended, in December 1995, for an additional two years at $50 million per year. The July 1996 announcement of the Aboriginal Housing Policy also was described. This policy involved an additional five-year, $140 million commitment over regular funding structures for new housing on-reserve and the Emergency Repair Program for off-reserve and northern housing.[37] A very small fraction of this funding has been used to rehabilitate or create social housing.

A single reference in *A Record of Achievement* to the promotion of "Safe Homes, Safe Streets," and services for battered women and their children, has translated into some additional social housing commitment.[38] CMHC's 1995 Annual Report indicated that:

the federal government approved additional funding for a one-year extension to March 31, 1996 of the Family Violence Initiative. The funding will be used to develop new shelter spaces, to rehabilitate and improve existing spaces, and to make these accessible to persons with disabilities.[39]

Overall, the government's action with regard to social housing is similar to a more general shift from universal social programs to narrowly targeted social supports. Quite particular to social housing is the degree to which public discussion is absent. For example, the public review and evaluation of CMHC's Non-Profit Housing Programs, begun in 1992 and slated for completion in 1994, have not yet been completed in early 1997. The largely invisible shift away from the direction of policy and toward a "hands-off" approach to existing social housing commitments represents the passing of an era. An appreciation of the contemporary debates about "housing as social policy" adds insight into discussions that have encouraged this change in federal thinking.

EXAMINING THE "UNIVERSE OF POLITICAL DISCOURSE"[40] FOR SOCIAL HOUSING

Housing and shelter have been almost completely ignored in the small but significant body of scholarly materials that has been published in the wake of Axworthy's failed Social Security Review and the more recent federal proposals to restructure federal-provincial relations on social policy. Despite the incorporation of a wide range of issues in these studies, they have included no focused discussions on housing, beyond an acknowledgement of the extreme housing problems of Aboriginal peoples.[41] Considerable evidence exists that housing's near invisibility in current social policy debates is related to a situation in which housing need has become almost exclusively a problem of the poorest Canadian households.[42]

In addition, there is a public perception that social housing has "failed," both as decent housing for the poor who reside there, and as a targeted benefit for those most in need. Evidence in support of these perceptions is quite contentious, and is not accessible to those without a detailed knowledge of Canadian housing policy and practice. Examining this evidence involves looking more closely at two debates within which arguments about "success," "failure," and "what to do next" are posed:

- the extent to which low-income households have access to decent, affordable shelter when the private housing market is the key source of low-cost housing (with or without income support), as opposed to when the production of non-profit housing is an important component;
- the nature of the relationship between housing and social policy: should housing be viewed as a basic need, where assistance is provided if, and only for as long as, necessary, or as a means of preventing and ameliorating other social problems?

Although these various debates overlap in significant ways, the assumptions, similarities, and differences among them deserve examination. Below, the range of opinion within each of these debates is described briefly, together with the resulting prescriptions for federal government involvement. While it is clear from our previous work that we support strategies that include non-profit housing and a preventative approach to problem-solving, the aim here is to outline both sides of the debates and link them to current government practices.

The Private Market or Government Intervention
A central debate in the literature considers the costs and benefits of social housing in comparison to what private housing markets might provide to low-income households. For those favouring market solutions, the critique of social housing centres on a relatively narrow view of costs and benefits and on the extent of inequities between those households that do and those that do not have access to social housing. This argument is posed as a choice between the provision of "bricks

and mortar" and the provision of "income support."[43] Among those
who acknowledge a gap between the cost of constructing and maintaining housing and what low-income households can actually afford,
shelter allowances are often put forward as a more efficient and fair
solution. Most, though, favour a continuing, reduced, direct role for
government in providing social housing, targeted to the poorest households, which alone cannot be well served in the marketplace. Thus,
there is a call to halt new social housing production, with a few exceptions, such as housing for victims of family violence and for persons
with disabilities, and perhaps for Aboriginal people on-reserve and in
the far north. To assure that targeting is more focused, these authors
call for an end to the subsidies of units that house moderate-income
households. The particular example of co-operative housing is used to
illustrate a "bricks and mortar" housing program that has purportedly
gone awry because it is not sufficiently targeted, since substantial subsidy is seen to benefit middle-income households.[44] Although some
acknowledgement is made of the benefits of mixed-income communities, this is not seen as a reason for continuing such subsidies. Thus,
there is a call for a continuing, but curtailed, commitment of subsidies
to the existing social housing portfolio:

We have 640,000 social housing units to be used as an instrument of
social policy. What is the best use of these units? Perhaps some will prove
excess to our needs and should be sold to the occupants.[45]

Authors with these views often also call for administrative cost savings and the merging of housing and other social service objectives for
targeted groups. There is a belief that a major role for provincial and
local administrators exists to reduce costs by removing planning and
land use control impediments, which are seen as significant barriers to
allowing the private sector to develop more modest-priced housing.

The current Liberal government has acted in a manner congruent
with most of these arguments, by allowing a slow withdrawal from
existing commitments to social housing, and by very narrowly targeting meagre new social housing commitments to special needs groups.
As well, it has encouraged research and initiatives to examine the removal of land use and planning impediments.[46]

On the other side of this debate are those who call for continued government intervention with an orientation generally in support of "decent housing as a right for all citizens."[47] The fact that more than 1.2 million low-income households have core housing needs is put forth as evidence that more should be done. The strong correlations between reductions in the percentage of low-income households living in crowded conditions or in housing in poor repair and lacking basic amenities, and the growth in the social housing stock are noted.[48] Vertical inequities in access to "affordable housing" are emphasized. Horizontal inequities among low-income households are presented as a general failure of the private market to produce adequate housing at a price affordable to these households. Thus the need for universal provision of housing as a minimum standard merit good is advocated. In particular, the current practice of providing shelter subsidies to social assistance recipients for private rental housing (approximately $5.2 billion) is seen as largely inefficient.[49] Further, recent CMHC program evaluations and subsequent consultations indicate that both co-operative and public housing largely met their original objectives and exhibited considerable flexibility to adjust to changing priorities.[50]

There is consensus with market-oriented analysts about the importance of the existing social housing stock and the need to encourage a fuller integration of the income security and housing policy systems, but proposed solutions differ. Those favouring continued government support for non-profit housing emphasize the need for long-term solutions to ensure an on-going commitment to housing that is affordable, meets a series of minimum standards, and is integrated with other health and social service supports. They see the federal government's continuing involvement as valuable for two reasons: first, it has a unique ability to "establish a national housing strategy, set national objectives and standards, and work toward achieving access to safe, affordable and appropriate shelter in all regions of the country";[51] and second, it has a responsibility to maintain its ongoing obligations for existing social housing. In contrast, the current terms of devolution do not ensure sufficient funds for maintaining existing commitments or the same levels of access now available for low- and moderate-income households.

Housing as Social Service or Housing as Part of a Support Nexus
The social service perspective argues for housing being made available to provide for basic need, with assistance available only as long as necessary, and in a manner that discourages dependency and encourages self-sufficiency.[52] Social housing is thus narrowly targeted to those having very significant housing problems.

In contrast, there are those who argue that housing should be understood as part of a support nexus (or as a structure necessary for effective social policy implementation). Shelter policies are seen as potential means of problem prevention and amelioration that are integral to the effective operation of other elements of social policy implementation.[53] The support nexus view is akin to a wellness model, where housing is seen as having an important mediating role in supporting, or, conversely, undermining, health and well-being. This perspective favours an approach that is more sensitive to the multi-dimensional nature of low-income housing need. It takes into consideration the relations between household characteristics, home/community design, security of tenure, and involvement in housing management.

Both perspectives favour closer co-ordination of the income security and social housing systems, but again for somewhat different reasons. While the social service perspective's overriding concern is to limit benefits to those most in need and to encourage self-sufficiency, it does not necessarily imply support for the withdrawal of federal funding from social housing. Proponents do, however, emphasize greater provincial control over the distribution of social benefits. For example, Thomas identifies the federal-provincial public housing cost-sharing arrangements as key to the restructuring being promoted in New Brunswick to bring housing policy and social policy closer together.[54] This approach is highly reminiscent of the federal-provincial partnership in existing public housing programs.

Those who see housing as part of a support nexus consider more fully the socio-demographic characteristics of those in housing need. Research in the area has found the greatest and fastest-growing housing need to be among the primarily female lone-parent families and the persons living alone, who now make up the majority of the low-income population. Focus is placed upon the positive impact of stable, secure, and decent housing on overall well-being. Thus, "[i]t may be important to offer services ... [b]ut unless those services reverse the disempowerment experienced by many people—not least their helplessness with respect to obtaining decent housing—nothing will improve for them."[55] This perspective emphasizes the beneficial effects of stable housing on the ability to access and use social services effectively, and, conversely, the problems that occur when stable housing is not available. Two recent examples of such evidence are, first, the investigations of clients in shelters for battered women, who typically identified the lack of affordable housing as a key barrier for women seeking a life without violence,[56] and second, a longitudinal study (between 1987 and 1994) of low-income mother-led families in which the majority moved several times, either to reduce shelter-related expenses or to improve quality, and where this had a range of negative effects upon family well-being, especially for children.[57]

CHRA has incorporated this perspective of housing as nexus of support into its arguments for retaining an active federal government role:

> Housing issues will need to be considered at the same time as health and social services. Housing ... is a critical determinant of health so health ministries should be considering the benefits of investing in better housing. Leadership in garnering inter-departmental co-operation should come from the federal government. Without leadership, including the setting of standards, little will happen and disparities among provinces will increase.[58]

Unfortunately, as one moves away from debates among those specifically concerned with housing policy to more globally-oriented social policy discussions, a focus on shelter and its integral role in enhancing social welfare is lost.[59] The recent deliberations at the Ministerial Council on Social Policy Reform and Renewal suggest an interest in combining federally funded, targeted income supplements (for persons with disabilities and children), and a provincial commitment to match these funds with money to various support services. Housing has not been a focus in this context. According to Minister Responsible for Human Resources Development, Pierre Pettigrew, "[t]his base of 'national benefits' is the foundation upon which the provinces build additional supports that are more responsive to regional circumstances and individual needs."[60]

It would appear that underlying this statement is the assumption that such a change will somehow automatically promote local and regional partnerships that are more sensitive to specific circumstances. Yet half a century of experience indicates otherwise. Most immediately, in the Ontario context, the idea of downloading has been adopted to pass on the costs of social housing to an even more junior level of government.

Although many have commented on the potential of provincial governments to promote greater co-ordination, the outcomes are likely to vary, depending upon the ideological leanings and the fiscal capacity of the government in power. Moreover, past federal involvement has been compatible with innovative and proactive efforts on the part of numerous municipalities, non-profit organizations,[61] and some provinces. For example, British Columbia is promoting a variety of partnerships between housing and other social service providers, largely piggy-backing its efforts onto existing federally-initiated social housing that incorporates a determinants-of-health approach as a starting point.[62] It is finding fertile ground for innovation among co-operatives and other non-profit housing providers. New Brunswick, on the other hand, which sees its primary role as discouraging dependency and promoting autonomy, has also found a ready area of experimentation in the existing public housing stock.[63]

RENOVATION OR ABANDONMENT?

Three important trends are evident in current policy directions in the social housing arena. First, the federal government is moving to divest itself of the administration of all existing social housing programs in favour of provincial and territorial governments while slowly extricating itself from existing commitments. Second, and in line with this move, the federal government is tacitly increasing its reliance on the private housing market to produce housing for all except those in extreme need. This is occurring despite an increasing dependence on the rental market among lower-income households and, in the 1990s, a sharp increase in the proportion of income they dedicate to shelter. Third, the present Liberal government has, for the most part, allowed housing issues to be decoupled from social policy debates.

Together, these directions bode ill for the future state of housing available to low- and moderate-income households in Canada. Until now, federal negotiations with the provinces seem to have been dominated by national unity and deficit reduction concerns, with social housing being used as a convenient pawn. There is no evidence that exclusive reliance on more junior levels of government, or on the private sector, has improved the housing situations of low- or moderate-income Canadians. The likelihood that a valuable national housing resource may be abandoned certainly has increased under the guise of federal/provincial renewal. The federal government's lack of reaction to the recent Ontario proposals to download the cost and administrative responsibility of social housing to the municipalities is simply the latest indication that abandonment is a realistic possibility. If successful, the Ontario initiatives will further threaten the fiscal base of existing social housing and close the door to uniform access across the province.

Similarly, the federal government appears to be abandoning the significant third sector housing management structure and expertise that it has fostered over the past 25 years. The approach of combining broad program goals and other objectives within operating agreements has encouraged the development of a sophisticated third sector in housing that is responsive to local conditions. The combination of strong ideological agendas and severe fiscal constraints in some provinces has led to more centralization and control, significantly reducing the possibility for effective input from this sector.

Thus far, the Liberal government has excluded active party involvement in discussions about devolution and in negotiation with the provinces and territories.[64] These moves have reversed past federal efforts to foster and strengthen the roles of communities and non-profit partners in creating supportive, empowering environments for low- and moderate-income Canadians. This shift of focus signals an abandonment of past federal governments' efforts to foster innovative approaches in dealing with shelter concerns, sharply reversing Canada's internationally acclaimed approach to social housing.

NOTES

1 See John Bacher, *Keeping to the Marketplace* (Montreal: McGill-Queen's University Press, 1993).

2 Estimated using Canada Mortgage and Housing Corporation (CMHC), *Canadian Housing Statistics, 1995* (Ottawa, 1996), Tables 67 and 68. Assisted homeownership, and subsidies and grants for the repair of private residences and privately managed rental property, are excluded.

3 Estimates for the proportion of households on social assistance in social housing come from Steve Pomeroy, "Housing as Social Policy," in *The Role of Housing in Social Policy*, Caledon Institute of Social Policy (Ottawa, 1996), 4-6. Pomeroy's figures exclude low-income seniors and Aboriginal peoples living on-reserve. Other estimates are calculated from the data available for about 46 percent of federal social housing stock in CMHC, *Evaluation of the Public Housing Program* (Ottawa, 1990); CMHC, *Evaluation of the Federal Co-operative Housing Program* (Ottawa, 1992a); CMHC, *Evaluation of the Rural and Native Housing Program, Main Report* (Ottawa, 1992b); and Ark Research Associates, *The Housing Conditions of Aboriginal Peoples* (Ottawa: CMHC, 1996).

4 Federal and provincial expenditures are estimated using CMHC, *Annual Report, 1994* (Ottawa, 1995), 38, CMHC, *Canadian Housing Statistics, 1995*, Tables 58 and 61, and Ontario Ministry of Housing, *Canadian Encyclopedia of Housing Programs* (Toronto, 1992).

5 Judy Forrest, "The Impact of Devolution," *Canadian Housing*, 13, 2 (Spring 1996), 6.

6 See John Bacher, *Keeping to the Marketplace*, 273, and Peter Dreier and J. David Hulchanski, "The Role of Nonprofit Housing in Canada and the United States: Some Comparisons," *Housing Policy Debate*, 4, 1 (1993), 43.

7 Operating agreements for various social housing programs can be found in CMHC, *Guidelines and Procedures Manual* (Ottawa, various dates), Volume 6.

8 Private sector rental operators are allowed a return on their investments.

9 See Michael Dennis and Susan Fish, *Programs in Search of a Policy* (Ottawa: CMHC, 1972), 173-74.

10 CMHC, *Evaluation of the Federal Co-operative Housing Program*, 15-16.

11 Ibid., 15.

12 Ibid., 19.

13 Estimated from CMHC, *Evaluation of the Public Housing Program*; CMHC, *Evaluation of the Federal Co-operative Housing Program*; CMHC, *Evaluation of the Rural and Native Housing Programs* (Ottawa, 1992); and CMHC, *Assessment Report of Private Non-Profit Housing Programs* (Ottawa, 1993).

14 Over time, these standards have changed, and, particularly with regard to housing built on-reserve and in northern and remote locales, these objectives were not fully feasible. CMHC, *Rural and Native,* 444-46. In addition, "affordability" standards vary from program to program and have been modified in accord with provincial standards.

15 See, for example, Gerda Wekerle, *Women's Housing Projects in Eight Canadian Cities* (Ottawa: CMHC, 1988). Although most operating agreements now include wording that forbids discrimination as defined under the terms of the Canadian Human Rights Code, in the past, third parties were allowed to limit entry on the basis of a wide range of specific socio-demographic characteristics.

16 See, for example, CMHC, *The Rural and Native Housing Demonstration Program* (Ottawa, 1991).

17 See Keith Banting, "Social Housing in a Divided State," in George Fallis and Alex Murray, eds., *Housing the Homeless and the Poor* (Toronto: University of Toronto Press, 1990), 136.

18 Liberal Party of Canada, *Creating Opportunity: The Liberal Plan for Canada* (Ottawa, 1993), 100.

19 Forrest, "The Impact of Devolution," 7.

20 *The Social Housing Agreement Between Canada Mortgage and Housing Corporation and the Saskatchewan Housing Corporation,* March 4, 1997, 4-6.

21 Personal communication with Grant Wanzel, current President of the Canadian Housing and Renewal Association (CHRA).

22 Forrest, "The Impact of Devolution," 7.

23 Derived using data from CMHC, *Canadian Housing Statistics* (Ottawa, 1992), Tables 67 and 68, and CMHC, *Canadian Housing Statistics* (Ottawa, 1993-95), Tables 68 and 69.

24 In total, there are approximately 14,000 units where federal-provincial rent supplements are applied in Ontario. This comprises 2 percent of the stock administered by the federal government, as calculated from CMHC, *Housing Statistics,* 1995, Table 67.

25 For example, in December 1996 housing owned by the Ottawa Carleton Housing Authority was listed for sale on the private market (Coalition to Protect Social Housing in Ottawa-Carleton, "Sale of publicly-owned home ignores desperate need for housing," Press Release, December 17, 1996). Under the existing federal-provincial agreement, such sales require CMHC agreement.

26 There is no evidence of either consultation or research about the implications of Ontario's intent to divest in favour of local governments. David Crombie, chair of the provincial task force responsible for making recommendations on government re-organization, stated, "We had no discussion on social housing. I don't know of any public discussion on social housing." In Bruce DeMara, "Crombie Blasts Tories on Welfare," *The Toronto Star*, January 28, 1997. It is likely that such a move will further accentuate differences in access to social housing across Ontario, and would substantially increase the financial burden for those local governments with large social housing stocks. Social housing costs include not only ongoing expenses but also outstanding mortgage payments.

27 CMHC, *Annual Report 1995* (Ottawa, 1996), 12.

28 Frank Graves, *Rethinking Government 95* (Ottawa: Ekos Research Associates, 1995).

29 See Peter Dreier and J. David Hulchanski, "The Role of Nonprofit Housing in Canada and the United States: Some Comparisons," *Housing Policy Debate*, 4, 1 (1993), 43-80.

30 CHRA, *Structure and Logic of a Sectoral Management Model for Social Housing Administration* (Ottawa: CHRA, Revised May 9, 1996).

31 See J. Grant Wanzel, "Indulging the Rich, Punishing the Poor: The Federal Government's Retreat from Housing," *Canadian Housing*, 13, 2 (Autumn 1996), 4.

32 CHRA, *Canadian Housing Update*, December 4, 1996, 1.

33 Liberal Party, *Creating Opportunity*, 61.

34 CMHC, *Annual Report 1995*, 12.

35 Liberal Party, *Creating Opportunity*, 100.

36 Liberal Party of Canada, *A Record of Achievement: A Report of the Liberals' 36 Months in Office* (Ottawa, 1996), 53.

37 Ibid., 105. The Emergency Repair Program is primarily directed toward providing one-time grants to owner-occupied housing in northern and remote areas.

38 Ibid., 77.

39 CMHC, *Annual Report 1995*, 13.

40 Jenson has coined this expression as a tool in the study of how meaning is constructed and debated. See, for example, Jane Jenson, "Gender and Reproduction: Or, Babies and the State," *Studies in Political Economy*, 20 (Summer 1986), 9-46.

41 This general absence stems, in part, from Axworthy's decision to exclude housing from the Social Security Review's terms of reference, despite a proposal that it be included. See CHRA, *Response to "Improving Social Security in Canada"* (Ottawa, 1994). The traditional separation of housing policy and other federal government

policy processes is also noteworthy. See Michael Prince, "The Canadian Housing Policy Context," *Housing Policy Debate*, 6, 3 (1995), 751.

42 "[The] two periods [late 1960s and late 1970s to early 1980s] in which housing has briefly been a national priority suggest that the federal government will play a role during hard economic times when the interests of middle class homeowners ... are at stake." Prince, "The Canadian Housing Policy Context," 748. Unlike other Canadian households, those with low incomes (defined here as those in the lowest income quintile) are increasingly renters—in 1995, 64 percent rented, in contrast to 58 percent a decade earlier and 53 percent in 1975. Poorer households are thus increasingly excluded from an important source of wealth accumulation. Further, during the period 1989-95, the proportion of household income dedicated to rent has increased among those low-income renter households that are unable to obtain subsidized shelter—from 47 percent to 56 percent. At the same time, among Canadian households with higher incomes the proportion of renters has declined during the same period, as has the proportion of household income dedicated to shelter. Derived from Statistics Canada, *Household Facilities by Income and Other Characteristics* (Ottawa: Industry Science and Technology, 1978 to 1995 inclusive), Tables 5 and 12, and corresponding microdata files.

43 A recent work published by the C.D. Howe Institute has provided an influential forum for those who favour income support. Some of the contributions in this volume illustrate the extremes in this debate—often flavoured by rhetorical vehemence and supported by the selective presentation of statistical and financial data. See, for example, Michael Poulton, "Affordable Homes at an Affordable (Social) Price," in John Richards and William G. Watson, eds., *Home Remedies: Rethinking Canadian Housing Policy* (Ottawa: C.D. Howe Institute, 1995), 50-122, and Lawrence B. Smith, "Ontario Housing Policy: The Unlearned Lessons," in *Home Remedies*, 123-89. For more moderate points of view, see George Fallis, "The Social Policy Challenge and Social Housing," in *Home Remedies*, 1-49, and Steve Pomeroy, "Housing as Social Policy," 2-14. These latter studies have been the basis of our discussion on the potential of the private market to provide housing for low-income households.

44 See Poulton, "Affordable Homes," 68-70.

45 Fallis, "The Social Policy Challenge and Social Housing," 42.

46 *Affordability and Choice Today (A.C.T.)*, a program with these aims, was initiated in 1993. See CMHC, *Annual Report 1995,* 20.

47 Sources used to capture this argument include CHRA, *Response to "Improving Social Security in Canada,"* 2-4; Veronica Doyle and Douglas Page, "Social Policy and Housing Strategy in British Columbia," in Caledon Institute of Social Policy, ed., *The Role of Housing in Social Policy* (Ottawa: Caledon Institute of Social Policy, April 1996), 27-33; and Sharon Chisholm, "Presentation by CHRA to Pre-Budget Hearings of the Standing Committee on Finance," October 24, 1996.

48 Although a causal link has been made for some groups, no study exists that unambiguously makes this connection for the population as a whole. See CMHC, *Rural and Native*, 105, and CMHC, *On-Reserve Housing Evaluation* (Ottawa, 1987), 64-70.

49 It is argued that the return on the cost of building new housing or converting existing housing to minimum standards for low-income households is well below the profit margins of most other investments. Thus, the supply of low-cost housing is inelastic, and shelter allowances produce high-return, low-quality housing. The recent downward adjustment of rents in Ontario in parallel with reductions to shelter allowances provides a case in point. See Maria Bohuslawsky, "Let's Make a Deal: With Welfare Benefits Cut by One-fifth, Some Landlords Find They Too Can Get By on Less," *The Ottawa Citizen*, October 24, 1995, B3.

50 See for example, CMHC, *Co-operative Housing Program*, 318-21; CMHC, *Public Housing Program*, 280-81 and 288; and CMHC, *What We Heard: Report on the Public Housing Program Consultation Process* (Ottawa, 1990).

51 CHRA, *Response to "Improving Social Security in Canada,"* 2-4.

52 See Pomeroy, "Housing as Social Policy," 10, and Janet Thomas, "Housing and Social Policy in New Brunswick," in Caledon Institute of Social Policy, *The Role of Housing in Social Policy*, 17.

53 Sources used to capture this argument are: Ark Research Associates, *The Housing Needs of Persons with Disabilities* (Ottawa: CMHC, forthcoming); CMHC, *Families, Children and Housing Need in Canada* (Ottawa, 1991); Tom Carter, Renate Bublick, Christine McKee, and Linda McFadyen, *Interaction of Social Housing and Safety Net Programs* (Ottawa: CMHC, 1993); Chisholm, "Pre-Budget"; V. Doyle, B. Burnside, and S. Scott, *Health and Housing for Single-Parent Families* (Ottawa: National Welfare Grants, Human Resources Development Canada, forthcoming); Doyle and Page, "Social Policy and Housing Strategy in British Columbia," 27-33; and CMHC, *Habitat II, Canadian National Report, United Nations Conference on Human Settlements*, Istanbul, Turkey, June 1996, 18.

54 Thomas, "Housing and Social Policy in New Brunswick," 24-26.

55 Doyle and Page, "Social Policy and Housing Strategy in British Columbia," 30.

56 Program Evaluation Division, CMHC, *Project Haven Evaluation* (Ottawa: CMHC, 1995) 7.

57 "90 percent of children said they moved residence (50 percent of whom moved 4 to 7 times), 79 percent changed schools (27 percent more than four times) and 65 percent said their friends changed." A. Gorlick, *Taking Chances: Single Mothers and Their Children Exiting Welfare*, unpublished paper, School of Social Work, King's College, University of Western Ontario, not dated, 33.

58 Chisholm, "Pre-Budget," 2.

59 See Keith Banting and Ken Battle, eds., *A New Social Vision for Canada? Perspectives on the Federal Discussion Paper on Social Policy Reform* (Kingston: School of Policy Studies, Queen's University and Caledon Institute of Social Policy, 1994); Janine Brodie, *Women and Canadian Public Policy* (Toronto: Harcourt Brace and Company, Canada, 1996); Alfred LeBlanc, "Making Cities Work," *Policy Options*, 17, 5 (June 1996); Alfred LeBlanc, "National Standards," *Policy Options*, 17, 7 (September 1996); and Jane Pulkingham and Gordon Ternowetsky, eds., *Remaking Canadian Social Policy: Social Security in the Late 1990s* (Halifax: Fernwood Publishing, 1996).

60 Havi Echenberg, *Social Policy Update*, III, 4 (September, 1996), 1, and III, 7 (November, 1996), 1.

61 Doyle and Page, "Social Policy," 31-33; Tom Carter and Ann McAfee, "The Municipal Role in Housing the Homeless and the Poor," in George Fallis and Alex Murray, eds., *Housing the Homeless and the Poor: New Partnerships Among the Private, Public and Third Sectors* (Toronto: University of Toronto Press, 1990); and J. David Hulchanski, Margaret Eberle, Michael Lytton, and Kris Olds, *The Municipal Role in the Supply and Maintenance of Low Cost Housing: A Review of Canadian Initiatives* (Ottawa: CMHC, 1990).

62 Doyle and Page, "Social Policy," 31-33.

63 See Thomas, "Housing and Social Policy in New Brunswick," and Doyle and Page, "Social Policy."

64 J. Grant Wanzel, "Indulging the Rich, Punishing the Poor," 4.

12

Principle Versus Partisanship: The Chrétien Government's Record on Integrity Issues

IAN GREENE

One of the key promises in the Red Book was to tackle the image of corruption and dishonesty in government established during the Mulroney years, by assuring voters that a Liberal government would govern with integrity. Chapter six, entitled *Governing with Integrity*, identified "cynicism about public institutions" as a critical issue, and promised that "honesty and integrity in our political institutions" would be restored.[1] In the introduction to the Liberal party's 1996 self-evaluation of its three-year performance, *A Record of Achievement*, Chrétien wrote that "of all the Red Book commitments we have kept, none gives me greater pride than our living up to our pledge to govern with integrity.... We have been honest with Canadians."[2]

This chapter provides a follow-up to Michael Atkinson's mid-term analysis of the Liberal government's integrity record in *How Ottawa*

Spends 1995-96. Atkinson's approach was based on the idea that "the core of integrity in government is respect for the purposes of public office ... [which] entails fiduciary responsibilities, the most critical of which is the responsibility to place public duties ahead of private interests."[3] Atkinson shows that the Chrétien government relied primarily on the promotion by the party leadership of the selection of candidates with integrity rather than on the creation of clearer rules that proscribe unethical behaviour, except with regard to the regulation of lobbyists. He claims that the government's approach to integrity issues stems from the fact that the Liberal party is a traditional Canadian party, where partisan considerations such as winning elections regardless of principle and rewarding the party faithful are paramount, and these sometimes run contrary to an integrity agenda. He argues that while the Chrétien government's integrity record is far better than that of the Mulroney government, its overall performance on integrity has been mediocre.

Atkinson rejects John Langford and Allan Tupper's argument that "[d]emocratic politics is inherently corrupt and corrupting of those involved in it."[4] However, he claims that there is a tendency for governments to become "so comfortable with the exercise of power" that they become "complacent about integrity,"[5] and that this tendency is almost inevitable because of the partisan nature of political parties. From this perspective, a certain level of corruption is inevitable in democratic politics, but the integrity agenda of a government should be never to let the level of corruption rise so high that the resultant erosion of public trust makes the country ungovernable.

My own expectations for ethical politics are more stringent than those of Langford and Tupper, because my starting point for ethical analysis is the principle of *mutual respect*—the acceptance of responsibility for treating others with the same concern and respect as that which we expect from them—an aspect of Canadian democracy that has slowly become more important since the time of Confederation. Just as there have been advances since 1867, based on the principle of mutual respect, about other expectations of Canadians, such as procedures that are less partisan for the selection of judges, judicial impartiality, and the protection of minority rights, expectations about the ethical behaviour of politicians have similarly increased.[6]

This analysis will evaluate the Liberal government's performance on ethics issues from the perspective of the mutual respect principle. The extent to which the Red Book integrity promises were implemented, as well as whether these promises addressed the key ethics issues facing the new government, will be considered. I argue that the government has missed a golden opportunity to implement major ethical reforms in the areas of patronage, conflict of interest, and party financing, because while old habits do die hard, the Liberals failed to give due consideration to the higher expectations for democratic government that accompany an increasingly well-educated and attentive public.

A FRAMEWORK FOR THE ANALYSIS
OF ETHICAL ISSUES IN POLITICS

An ethics analysis in politics concerns the extent to which the behaviour of political actors conforms to expectations derived from principle. The Rawlsian principle of mutual respect is a useful concept on which to base ethical expectations in a liberal democratic society. "Mutual respect means that we owe the same consideration to others, while making decisions that have an impact on these others, as we feel that we are owed by others when they make decisions that affect us."[7] The basic principles on which democratic government is founded can be deduced from mutual respect: social equality, deference to the majority, minority rights, freedom, and integrity. These principles generate three ethical duties for public officials: to be impartial when administering programs sanctioned by the law, to act in the public interest (fiduciary trust), and to be accountable for ethical behaviour.

The Chrétien government will be evaluated with respect to the major ethical issues present when it took office: conflicts of interest, patronage, party financing, undue influence by lobbyists, dishonest or "dirty-handed" political practices, and the constraints that traditional party discipline places on MPs in fulfilling their fiduciary responsibility. These are listed and discussed in an order of importance that seems most in accord with the ethical concerns of Canadians.[8]

THE REGULATION OF CONFLICTS OF INTEREST

A conflict of interest occurs when a public official can take advantage of public office for personal gain. Conflicts of interest are unacceptable both because they violate the expectation of impartiality in administering the law, and because they breach fiduciary responsibilities.

After becoming prime minister in 1984, Brian Mulroney revamped the conflict of interest guidelines for federal cabinet ministers adopted by Prime Minister Pierre Trudeau in 1980. During the next two years, the Mulroney government suffered through fourteen episodes of conflict of interest accusations affecting cabinet ministers or their senior advisors.[9] The most publicized of these was the Sinclair Stevens affair, which led to a public inquiry by Mr. Justice William Parker, former Chief Justice of the High Court of Ontario. Parker found that Stevens had been in a conflict of interest situation on at least fourteen occasions, and recommended that the guidelines be replaced by actual legislation that could be enforced by an independent ethics commission responsible to Parliament.

In response, the Conservative government introduced conflict of interest legislation in February 1988, but it died on the order paper. It was re-introduced during Mulroney's second term in office, but suffered a similar fate. Thus, in 1993 federal cabinet ministers, MPs, and senators were still not subjected to legislated conflict of interest rules, while four provinces (Ontario, British Columbia, Alberta, and Newfoundland) had conflict of interest legislation, together with independent ethics commissioners.[10] The combination of clear, legislated conflict of interest guidelines and the appointment of independent ethics commissioners has been extraordinarily successful in preventing major scandals in jurisdictions that have adopted these procedures.[11]

The Liberal party stopped short of promising conflict of interest legislation and an independent ethics commissioner in the 1993 Red Book, focusing instead on a Code of Conduct to guide public officials in their "dealings with lobbyists," and an "independent Ethics Counsellor" to advise on the application of the Code.[12]

From 1974 to 1993, successive prime ministers had issued to their cabinets conflict of interest guidelines that included the duty to disclose their assets and liabilities, a summary of which would be made available through a public registry. The official designated to handle these disclosures was the Assistant Deputy Registrar General (ADRG). In June 1994, the title was changed to "Ethics Counsellor," and the holder of the position was made to report directly to the prime minister. After consultation with the opposition parties, Chrétien appointed Howard Wilson, a career public servant, to the new post.[13]

Chrétien announced that Wilson would be asked to recommend changes to the Conflict of Interest Code to strengthen it, and that a joint Senate-House of Commons Committee would be established to "develop a Code of Conduct for MPs and Senators."[14] Later in 1994, Wilson invited several political scientists who specialized in political ethics to Ottawa for a one-day meeting with senior officials about the implementation of the Red Book ethics promises. He was advised that ethical rules need to be equally strong and consistent in all related areas: conflicts of interest, lobbyists, and general integrity. If a code of ethical conduct for MPs and senators applied only to relations with lobbyists and not conflicts of interest, a loophole would be created that might precipitate an ethics scandal.

In the fall of 1994, Parliament created a Special Joint Committee on a Code of Conduct, with sufficiently broad terms of reference to recommend a legislated code that would cover conflicts of interest as well as the regulation of lobbyists. Witnesses included the independent provincial ethics commissioners, all of whom recommended that the code of conduct should be legislated, should cover conflicts of interest, and should provide for an independent ethics commissioner.[15]

The nature and scope of a legislated code of conduct to cover conflicts of interest was clearly a controversial topic for committee members, including government members. There was vociferous opposition from both Liberal and Conservative members of the Senate when the Mulroney government had proposed conflict of interest legislation. It has been a tradition for both Liberal and Conservative governments to appoint some senators to represent the financial interests of Canadian entrepreneurs, most notably those from Bay Street. These senators have usually not regarded it as a conflict of interest to propose changes to legislation affecting banks and other large financial interests while continuing to hold positions on the boards of directors of these institutions.[16] As well, spouses of MPs objected to being included in legislated disclosure requirements. MPs from both sides were also worried that disclosure requirements might prevent well-qualified candidates with significant private investments from running for office.[17] These fears were still present in 1995. The tension between the Liberal government's desire to propose legislation to bolster their ethics agenda and the concerns of the senators and backbenchers may explain why the joint committee twice postponed the release of its final report, until March 1997. The report recommended that Parliament appoint an independent ethics commissioner, known as a "jurisconsult," for a seven-year term. The jurisconsult would be responsible for advising MPs and senators on complying with a comprehensive code of conduct to be adopted by both houses, making public the required declarations of assets, and investigating alleged breaches of the code. If the Chrétien government implements these recommendations prior to the election, its record on integrity issues will be considerably enhanced.

The Liberal government has taken two other initiatives to prevent conflicts of interest. First, the Prime Minister's conflict of interest code covering ministers, secretaries of state, parliamentary secretaries, and senior public servants was revised and strengthened in 1994 on the advice of the new Ethics Counsellor. The code's purpose was clearly set out in ten guiding principles, making it easier to comprehend, and the rules were broadened to include the activities of family members and to prohibit preferential treatment to individuals or firms represented by lobbyists.[18] Second, early in his term Chrétien appointed Mitchell Sharp as his personal advisor on ethics. According to the Liberal party's 1996 self-evaluation, "This approach has had positive results. In contrast to the scandals that plagued the previous administration, the current Liberal government has been untouched by scandal."[19]

The Red Book had promised an *independent* Ethics Counsellor. What has been delivered so far is an Ethics Counsellor accountable to the prime minister who is mandated to report annually to Parliament,[20] and a personal ethics advisor, Mitchell Sharp, in the Prime Minister's Office. Although neither of these officials is independent, insofar as they are accountable to the prime minister, the Liberal party considered in its self-evaluation report that the promise had been kept.[21] This claim is not entirely accurate, in that the term "independence" in the public sector has come to mean the ability to act independently from the Cabinet and the prime minister. The ethics counsellor does have more scope for providing autonomous advice than the ADRG did, but is nevertheless subject to direction from the prime minister. The self-evaluation report explains this situation in the following way: "As the Prime Minister has said, 'There can be no substitute for responsibility at the top.'"[22]

There is no doubt that these appointments, together with a commitment to take ethics seriously, partially explain the Chrétien government's good record in avoiding serious conflict of interest problems. But the record is not flawless: it was marred by two relatively minor incidents.

In October 1994, it was revealed that Heritage Canada Minister Michel Dupuy had sent a letter urging the Canadian Radio-television and Telecommunications Commission (CRTC) to give an application for a licence for a Greek-language radio outlet in his constituency "due consideration."[23] The CRTC is considered a quasi-judicial as well as a legislative tribunal, and cabinet ministers are not supposed to intervene in the proceedings of such tribunals in a way that might be perceived as an attempt to reduce their objectivity. This canon was particularly important for the Heritage Minister, who is responsible for the CRTC. This expectation, however, was not absolutely clear from Chrétien's conflict of interest guidelines, and apparently neither the Ethics Counsellor nor Mitchell Sharp discussed the matter in meetings with cabinet ministers. The problem was exacerbated by the revelation that three other ministers and a secretary of state had sent letters to the CRTC on behalf of constituents.[24]

Chrétien apologized for these errors, stating that the ministers had made an "honest mistake." He announced that "[t]here is no scandal here. No violation of integrity. No breach of the public trust."[25] He announced that henceforth ministers would have to abide by a supplemental set of stricter guidelines regulating their interface with quasi-judicial tribunals, but rejected calls from opposition parties for Dupuy's resignation (Dupuy remained in the Cabinet until the 1995 shuffle.).

The new supplemental guidelines stated that "[m]inisters shall not intervene, or appear to intervene, on behalf of any person or entity, with federal quasi-judicial tribunals on any matter before them that requires a decision in their quasi-judicial capacity, unless otherwise authorized by law."[26] The Ethics Counsellor was given the responsibility for briefing ministers about how to comply with this guideline, and cabinet ministers were required to clear communications with quasi-judicial tribunals through Wilson's office. Nevertheless, Defence Minister David Collenette resigned in October 1996, because he admitted to having breached the supplemental guidelines, after the media discovered that an assistant sent a letter with Mr. Collenette's signature to the Immigration and Refugee Board requesting that it speed up consideration of the case of a person related to one of Mr. Collenette's constituents. Collenette's breach of the rules was considered more serious than that of Dupuy's because the supplemental guidelines were in place.[27]

Though conflict of interest problems encountered by the Chrétien government have been minuscule compared to those of the Mulroney cabinet, Chrétien's preventative mechanisms are problematic. First, a semi-independent ethics counsellor does not have the same clout in enforcing ethics standards as does an independent ethics commissioner. For example, several opinions rendered by the Hon. Gregory Evans, Ontario's independent ethics commissioner, provide advice about how to avoid the type of situation that Dupuy and Collenette found themselves in.[28] Second, because the ethics counsellor is ultimately accountable to the prime minister, his impartiality may be open to question. When David Collenette resigned ostensibly because the Ethics Counsellor found that he had breached the supplemental guidelines, there were questions as to whether an independent ethics counsellor would have found this breach sufficiently serious to warrant resignation. On the one hand, it is commendable for the Prime Minister to take responsibility for the ethical standards of the Cabinet, but he cannot boast that ethical standards are always placed above partisan considerations unless there is a fully independent official whose judgments are free of potential coercion.

PATRONAGE

One of the theoretical justifications for responsible government, first developed in the United Kingdom in the mid-eighteenth century, is that selecting ministers from the party with the greatest support in the House of Commons would make ministers more accountable to the electorate. One of the less savory side-effects was that the party in power gained the ability to provide rewards to its supporters in the form of contracts and appointments to the public service. While patronage has been routed out of most of the public sector since the 1950s, it remains at upper-level appointments such as the approximately 3,000 order-in-council appointments available to the federal Cabinet.

During her short term in office, Prime Minister Kim Campbell set out to address the ethics concerns of Canadian voters about the Mulroney government. To distance herself from the organized patronage of the Mulroney government,[29] Campbell advertised in the *Canada Gazette* for qualified applicants for many order-in-council positions, such as appointments to the Immigration and Refugee Board. Campbell lost the 1993 general election prior to having the opportunity to make appointments under the new system, but the Chrétien government used her system to make its first series of appointments in 1993 and 1994. The government received wide praise for beginning the hard process of replacing patronage at upper levels with merit-based appointments. However, not much time passed before the Liberal government seemed to be dabbling in patronage nearly as much as its predecessor. Although there were a number of merit-based appointments, a parallel system of patronage appointments still operates. However, the Prime Minister's appointments secretary has tried to ensure that friends of the Liberal party who receive appointments are qualified for their jobs.[30]

The tradition of rewarding lawyers who are party loyalists by appointing them as federal "legal agents" has continued with minor adjustments. Whenever the party in power in Ottawa changes, nearly all of the legal agents appointed by the previous government are fired, and replaced by legal agents loyal to the governing party. During the 1994-95 fiscal year "Ottawa handed out nearly $45-million to 600 legal agents."[31]

In 1980, I interviewed a representative sample of 134 judges, lawyers, provincial crown attorneys, and court administrators in Ontario about sources of inefficiency in the court system, and the patronage system of appointing the federal legal agents figured high on the list. There were complaints from judges, crown attorneys, and court administrators that legal agents were underqualified and overpaid, and that this resulted in delays and botched prosecutions.[32]

Justice Minister Allan Rock tried to reform the system of appointing federal legal agents, but he was faced with a wall of resistance from Liberal lawyers who had been expecting their rewards, especially in small-town Canada.[33] The best he could do was to reduce the overall number of federal legal agents (replacing some with Department of Justice lawyers), and ensure that Liberal lawyers receiving plum appointments were at least minimally qualified. As well, some of the better-qualified Tory-appointed agents were kept on.

The Liberal government has also made some reforms to reduce patronage concerns in judicial appointments. The Mulroney government had been criticized because its system to recommend appointments to the nearly 2,000 federal judicial positions resulted in a disproportionate number of people with Conservative party connections receiving the jobs.[34] The revisions to the system announced by Justice Minister Allan Rock in 1995 broadened the membership of the judicial appointments advisory committees, established a much more comprehensive application form, and for the first time established a procedure to advertise positions to expand the pool of applicants.[35] It is too early to tell whether these reforms will reduce the impact of partisan considerations in judicial appointments, but it is at least a step in the right direction.

The Liberals promised to review boards and commissions subject to order-in-council appointments, and to eliminate unnecessary positions. Their self-evaluation claimed this a fulfilled promise: 868 positions, or 28 percent of the total, were eliminated, saving an estimated $10 million annually.[36] Yet, according to Ross Howard, there has been a great deal of tension in the current Liberal Cabinet between some of the more senior ministers, such as Lloyd Axworthy, David Dingwall, and André Ouellet, who are steeped in the patronage tradition, and "younger and first-time cabinet members," who want a "hands-off policy" for both order-in-council appointments and the federal government's advertising and polling contracts, which are worth about $100 million annually.[37] The newer ministers were not only concerned that maintaining patronage might damage the government's reputation on ethics issues, but also that the government is potentially vulnerable when it receives advice from pollsters too closely connected with the party to provide an objective analysis.

The principle of mutual respect cannot justify order-in-council appointments, or the basing of advertising and polling contracts on patronage considerations. The two common objections to this position are that a rewards structure is necessary to encourage people to work for political parties, and that the government has a right to implement its policy objectives by appointing or contracting its trusted allies to key posts.[38] However, it can be argued that party faithful motivated by the desire to do public service rather than by the hope of personal reward provide a more reliable base of support. Additionally, governments have the ability to pursue their policy agendas in part through specifying qualifications that they think should be held by those applying for order-in-council positions. A background in partisan politics could be listed as an asset for some applicants not because of political connections, but rather because of the policy savvy that results from such experience.

Thus, the Chrétien government's record on patronage, although disappointing, can be seen as at least a slow step in the right direction, and perhaps all that could be expected as long as traditional partisan attitudes hold sway in the Liberal party.

PARTY FINANCING

One of the most serious ethical issues facing the citizens of any democracy is the potential for money to corrupt the electoral process and the policy process. It takes a great deal of money for a party to elect a leader, hold policy conventions, and fight election campaigns. The ethical challenge is to find procedures for financing party activities that do not result in trading financial contributions for public office favours, explicitly or implicitly.

The Mulroney government's response to this problem was to create the Royal Commission on Electoral Reform and Party Financing. The Commission recommended that undue influence through party contributions be addressed by political parties developing codes of ethics rather than limiting annual contributions from single sources (the approach used in the provinces of Ontario, Quebec, and Alberta).

Media accounts indicate that the possible relation between political contributions and public office favours is an important ethical concern to Canadians.[39] The Red Book promised amendments to the Elections Act that would "limit the role of special-interest groups in election campaigns" by means of "tough spending rules." The amendments would also close "loopholes in election spending" and make the "costs of polling and direct mail" subject to election spending limits.[40]

As Atkinson has pointed out,[41] these Red Book promises were a weak response to an important issue. It is surprising that the promised reforms to the Elections Act were not even mentioned in the Liberal party's 1996 self-evaluation. Again, the Liberals' failure to tackle the issue of undue influence in party financing can be explained by the predominance of traditional ideas about how parties operate.

UNDUE INFLUENCE BY LOBBYISTS

The centrepiece of the Red Book promises on integrity was the promise to strengthen control over lobbyists, and here the fulfilment of commitments has been most impressive. The Liberals promised to implement the unanimous recommendations made by a House of Commons committee in June 1993, on strengthening the Lobbyists Registration Act. The most significant of these recommendations, which became law in June 1995, require consultant lobbyists (as opposed to in-house or corporate lobbyists) to provide more information about their lobbying techniques and the true beneficiaries of their efforts, prohibit government suppliers from paying lobbyists to obtain contracts, and stipulate stiffer penalties for breach of the Act. A Code of Conduct for government officials in dealing with lobbyists was also promised. This commitment was partially fulfilled by the creation of a Joint Parliamentary Committee to recommend a Code of Conduct (although the committee will not report until spring 1997), and a change in the conflict of interest guidelines that prohibits preferential treatment to those represented by lobbyists. The independent ethics counsellor promised by the Liberals to enforce the Code of Conduct for public officials became the semi-independent Ethics Counsellor. A Code of Conduct for lobbyists was also promised, and, after consultation with the lobbyist industry and the public, the Ethics Counsellor developed and published such a code. Amendments to the Lobbyists Registration Act gave the Ethics Counsellor the power to enforce the Code.

In spite of these reforms, the Chrétien government has not been free from allegations that lobbyists have exercised undue influence over government decisions. According to Ross Howard, the government's lobbying reforms were themselves delayed because of pressure from lobbying companies.[42] Amendments to the Lobbyists Registration Act do not require lobbyists to disclose their fees,[43] and a clause in an early draft of the Code of Conduct for Lobbyists requiring fees to be "fair and reasonable" was eventually deleted. However, the Code empowered the Ethics Counsellor to investigate allegations of its violation, and to disclose in his report the details of lobbyist payments.

The original Lobbyists Registration Act came about partly because of the potential impact of lobbyists in the decision of Air Canada, while it was still a Crown Corporation, to purchase a new fleet of airliners from Airbus Industrie.

Airbus

The controversy over Air Canada's purchase of a fleet of 34 passenger jets from the European consortium Airbus Industrie, the botched police investigation of the possible role of former Prime Minister Brian Mulroney in the sale, Mulroney's subsequent $50 million lawsuit against Justice Minister Allan Rock and the RCMP, and the government's out-of-court settlement may well become the most important story of political intrigue in Canadian history. As this chapter is being written, the story is still incomplete.

In the late 1980s Airbus Industrie's major competitor was the U.S. Boeing corporation, and a large contract with Air Canada would have given Airbus a major boost in its quest to break into the world market. Airbus acquired the services of lobbyist Frank Moores. Moores had nominated Brian Mulroney for the federal Conservative leadership in 1976. After Mulroney became prime minister in 1984, Moores started a lobby firm in Ottawa, Government Consultants International (GCI), that became "the biggest lobby firm in Ottawa, with billings of close to $5 million a year" by 1986.[44]

In 1985, Mulroney announced a consultation process to establish rules to register lobbyists. Some claim that he was forced into this position because the lobbying activities of Moores had raised so many concerns about undue influence.[45] After the Conservatives' massive defeat in the 1993 election, Moores sold his interest in GCI.

In March 1985, Brian Mulroney fired the Liberal-appointed board of Air Canada, and replaced it with Conservative patronage appointments, including Frank Moores. Shortly afterward, the Air Canada board considered replacing 34 of its older Boeing 727 aircraft. As it turned out, Moores was also a paid lobbyist for Airbus at the time, and for two of Air Canada's competitor airlines. Although Moores claimed that there was no conflict of interest, later in 1985 he was forced to resign his board seat by public pressure.[46] The Mulroney-appointed Air Canada board made two major decisions in 1988. First, Airbus Industrie was awarded the contract to replace Air Canada's fleet. Second, Air Canada was privatized shortly after the fleet purchase decision.

In 1994, journalist Paul Palango claimed that Brian Mulroney pressured Air Canada, prior to its privatization, to pay $5 million in consulting fees to Frank Moores's consulting company, a charge that was vociferously denied by both Moores and Mulroney. Then in March 1995, both CBC television and the German media suggested that Airbus may have paid bribes to Canadians to ensure the sale of their aircraft to Air Canada.[47] Possibly as a result of these reports, the RCMP revived an earlier investigation of the Airbus sale.

The federal Department of Justice, in September of 1995, requested that Swiss authorities assist in the RCMP investigation, and freeze a bank account they claimed may have been set up as a conduit for the receipt of bribes by Brian Mulroney. Mulroney learned that he was being investigated, and he obtained an unofficial translation of the Department of Justice letter to Swiss authorities. Somehow, this letter ended up in the hands of *The Financial Post*, which published its contents in November. Shortly afterward, Mulroney launched a lawsuit for $50 million against the federal government.

Government lawyers unsuccessfully attempted to delay proceedings under the suit, claiming that evidence presented in the course of the lawsuit might jeopardize its investigation of Mulroney. On the eve of the opening of the court hearing in January 1997, the government reached an out-of-court settlement with Mulroney. The government apologized for the wording of the letter to Swiss authorities, because the letter suggested—wrongly—that the Department of Justice already had evidence that Mulroney had committed a criminal offence. As well, the government agreed to pay Mulroney's legal bills, which had reached nearly $1 million. A less categorical apology was sent to Moores.

In a related development, in July of 1996 the Federal Court decided that the Charter of Rights and Freedoms applies to the actions of Canadian government officials abroad. According to Charter decisions, officials wanting to examine private records must obtain a search warrant signed by a judge, who would have to be convinced that an offence had probably been committed. Department of Justice officials had not obtained a search warrant for the Swiss bank accounts because they felt the duties created by the Charter did not apply outside of Canada.

The Liberal government's apology to Brian Mulroney raised concerns that the investigation had been politically motivated, but the settlement included a statement agreed to by Mulroney that Justice Minister Allan Rock had not known about the police investigation until shortly before the letter to the Swiss authorities became public. Concern was then directed to the issue of Rock's lack of knowledge of the investigation, with some claiming that he should have been informed about the investigation so that he could ensure its legitimacy.

My own view is that to protect the integrity of police investigations, cabinet ministers should not be informed of investigations about current or former politicians. However, the prime minister should know about whether a member of Cabinet is being investigated, yet keep this information confidential. Even though the justice minister ought not to be involved in an investigation of contemporary political figures, the minister has a duty to ensure the integrity of investigative procedures in general, and the procedures were clearly not up to standard concerning the process for obtaining evidence outside Canada. The problem was that from an ethical perspective, the standards of procedural fairness established by the Charter of Rights *ought* to apply in principle to Canadian government offices abroad, as well as to government operations within the country. Otherwise, the result is a double standard: police investigators are not allowed to go on "fishing expeditions" in Canada out of respect for individual privacy, but they are allowed to run roughshod over the rights of Canadians as soon as they leave the country. From an ethical perspective, the double standard cannot be maintained, and the government must be held accountable.

Pearson Airport
About three weeks prior to the October 25, 1993 election, Prime Minister Kim Campbell prepared to approve an agreement giving a private company, Pearson Development Corporation (PDC), a 57-year lease on Terminals 1 and 2 at Pearson International Airport in Toronto. There

were media reports that prominent Conservative party supporters and lobbyists could reap substantial financial benefits from this agreement, which committed PDC to up to $700 million in investments. The Liberals attacked the agreement as another extravagant example of Tory patronage, and Chrétien urged Campbell not to approve it so close to the election. He promised that if she did, he would review it once elected, and cancel it with legislation if necessary.

Campbell's subsequent approval of the contract was a factor in the humiliating defeat of the Conservatives. Three days after the October 25 election, Chrétien appointed Robert Nixon, a friend and the former Liberal Treasurer of Ontario, to review the Pearson Airport agreement. Nixon found that the contract was "inadequate," and that the process leading up to it was "under the shadow of possible political manipulation." He recommended cancellation, and on December 3 Chrétien accepted this advice, even though the cost might reach $700 million.

After failed negotiations with PDC over cancellation costs, the government introduced legislation in April 1994 to limit compensation to out-of-pocket expenses of about $30 to 40 million. In response, the Senate established a Special Committee on the Pearson deal in May 1995, and the Committee reported in December after hearing from 65 witnesses. The majority on the committee, reflecting the Conservative majority in the Senate, condemned the Chrétien government for scrapping a deal that was in the public interest. The Liberal minority issued a separate report, which not only confirmed the conclusions of the Nixon report, but provided additional ammunition for the Liberal government's position.[48] The Senate defeated the compensation bill on June 19, 1996. PDC launched a suit against the government for about $660 million, and the government handed over authority for administration of Terminals 1 and 2 to a not-for-profit Local Development Corporation.

In an attempt to minimize damages, government lawyers argued that PDC had erred in its calculations, and would actually have lost money had the Campbell contract been honoured. This contradiction of the government's claims in 1993 about the excessive profits that the Conservatives were allegedly handing over to PDC, together with the Senate majority report's condemnation of the cancellation of the contract, raised concerns about whether the decision to cancel the Pearson airport deal was based on petty partisanship rather than an ethical high ground.

I would argue that the Liberal and Conservative politicians involved in the Pearson Airport fiasco were all so immersed in partisan politics that no one behaved in an ethically scrupulous fashion. The Senate majority report showed that although senior public servants insisted on maintaining departmental standards during the negotiations leading to the contract with PDC, there was unprecedented political involvement from the Prime Minister's office, raising serious questions about whether partisan considerations played an unacceptable role. And Prime Minister Campbell's defence of signing the deal so close to the election is not convincing. Given the high stakes, however, Chrétien's decision to appoint a partisan ally—Robert Nixon—to review the Pearson deal was equally indefensible. Although some of Nixon's criticisms of the Pearson deal were valid, they would have been more convincing coming from a neutral source. In addition, if a neutral source had recommended legislation to limit compensation to PDC, it would have been more difficult for a Conservative-controlled Senate to have defeated such a bill while claiming to act with integrity.

Although the Liberal government has fulfilled most of its promises to curtail undue influence from lobbyists in the policy process, it has not always handled in a fair way the problems related to lobbying inherited from the Mulroney era. In particular, the government failed to meet its ethical responsibility to ensure that the same procedural safeguards that apply to police investigations in Canada will apply to Canadian offices abroad. And it failed to reverse the Pearson airport deal—which it had every right to do—in a fair and impartial manner. The former lapse can be attributed to a lack of deliberation about the implications of ethical standards in a democracy, while the latter is directly related to traditional partisan practice.

DISHONEST OR "DIRTY-HANDED"
POLITICAL PRACTICES

Since before the time of Machiavelli, philosophers and statesmen have debated whether politicians ought to be or even can be honest. Greene and Shugarman argue that dishonest and corrupt political practices can never be justified in a democratic regime where mutual respect is valued, at least during peacetime.[49] Statements about integrity in government in the Liberal Red Book and in the 1996 Liberal self-evaluation report and by Chrétien himself are consistent with this view. A litmus test for the Liberals' performance on honesty issues is the Red Book record on promises themselves—particularly the promise made about replacing the Goods and Services Tax (GST)—and the decision to require the Somalia inquiry to report before it could investigate all the issues related to the cover-up of the atrocities committed by Canadian soldiers.

Red Book Promises and the GST

The Liberals claimed that they "broke new ground" by publishing the Red Book in 1993, and by publishing their 1996 evaluation of the extent to which the promises in it were kept. Indeed they did, and the Liberal party should be given credit for spelling out its election platform in a fair amount of detail, and for insisting on being held accountable for promises made. The perceived tendency of politicians to make promises during election campaigns only to weasel out of them once elected has been one of the main reasons for the increasing cynicism of Canadian voters about their political system.[50] Approval ratings for the Prime Minister and other Canadian politicians began to climb after 1993, after reaching historic lows, providing an indication that the Liberals responded somewhat successfully to the ethical demands of voters.[51]

Nevertheless, there are two major problems with the Liberal approach to the keeping of election promises. First, the federal Liberals may not have left themselves with enough scope to re-evaluate promises that may have turned out, upon further research and reflection, not to be in the public interest. Of all the Red Book's high profile promises, the commitment to "replace" the GST turned out to be the most difficult to keep. In early 1996, Finance Minister Paul Martin admitted that the government would not be able to replace the GST with an entirely different kind of tax that would produce the same revenues. Taxation policy, he explained, was simply more complex than the Liberals had imagined, and the credible options were fewer than expected.

In early 1996, Sheila Copps resigned as Deputy Prime Minister and MP for Hamilton-Mountain because she had made a categorical promise during the 1993 federal election campaign to resign if the Liberal party did not abolish the GST. During the week before her resignation, Copps made light of her 1993 promise as simply being an example of her "big mouth." During the campaign for the subsequent by-election, she avoided the GST issue, and her failure to confront the issue squarely may account for the fact that although re-elected, she achieved a lower level of support than in 1993.

It seems likely that Copps sincerely believed that the Liberal party *would* abolish the GST once in office. From this perspective, Copps acted with integrity by resigning and contesting her seat again, although to make light of this promise during the week prior to her resignation and to avoid the GST issue during the campaign were certainly not acts of political integrity.

John Nunziata, a Liberal MP from the Toronto area, voted against Paul Martin's budget in 1995 because he believed that the broken GST promise reflected negatively on the government's integrity. For this stand he was expelled from the Liberal caucus, and has been unable to negotiate his way back in.[52]

Jean Chrétien's position, up to December 1996, was that the Liberals did not really break their promise on the GST. What they had promised to do was to replace the GST with a harmonized federal-provincial sales tax that "is fairer to consumers and to small business." Because the harmonization has been achieved in part, the Liberal self-evaluation indicated that the implementation of the GST promise was "in progress" rather than a promise broken.[53] When Chrétien took this position in a CBC television "town hall" broadcast in December 1996, his approval ratings took a steep dive, and he had the political sense to apologize and to admit that most Canadians had expected the Liberals to replace the GST with an entirely different tax. Chrétien's initial refusal to apologize for breaking the promise about the GST likely did more harm to the Liberals' reputation for integrity than the breaking of the promise itself.

The integrity of election promises is an important and difficult ethical problem. There are two approaches that might keep parties and candidates out of ethical hot water. First, political parties need better policy research units, and should avoid making specific promises unless they have solid evidence that fulfilment of the promise appears to be feasible. Second, it would be useful for parties to develop their own codes of ethics, which, among other things, would address the ethics of making and keeping election promises.

The other problem with the Liberals' ethical stance on election promises is that the 1996 self-evaluation clearly does not represent an impartial attempt to review the party's record. There are many examples of Red Book promises that are simply left out of the self-evaluation (such as the promise to reform the Elections Act) and claims that promises have been fully implemented when they have not, such as the promise to appoint an *independent* ethics counsellor. Although the self-evaluation was a good idea in principle, it would have been better for the Liberals to have hired an independent firm to evaluate the extent to which their election promises were kept, even if the results would not have indicated that 78 percent of the promises had been kept and another 12 percent are "in progress."[54]

Somalia Inquiry

Another issue that has hurt the Liberals' record on honesty is the decision of Defence Minister Doug Young to require the Somalia Inquiry to wind up its hearings by March 31, 1997, and report by June 30. The inquiry was created by the Liberal government early in 1995 to investigate "all aspects of the Canadian Airborne Regiment's 1992-93 mission to Somalia[, which was] marred by the March 16, 1993 torture and murder of a Somali teenager"[55] and other alleged abuses. The inquiry was originally supposed to report at the end of 1995, but was given two extensions into 1996 because its efforts to obtain information were hampered by alleged defence department cover-ups.

The question of whether the government acted ethically in ordering the inquiry to wind up earlier than the commissioners had hoped is contentious. There are questions about the impact of an extended inquiry on the already severely demoralized armed forces, the financial cost of a long extension, and the inability of the government to take decisive action to tackle ethical problems in the defence department in the meantime. On the other hand, it could be argued that, having opened a Pandora's box, the government now has the duty to ensure that no evidence relating to ethical lapses in the armed forces is left untouched.

It does not appear that the government's decision to limit the length of the Somalia inquiry is driven by partisan considerations, in that the main events that the inquiry is investigating occurred when Kim Campbell was Defence Minister. Nevertheless, the government needs to be held accountable for the ethical dimensions of the decision.

Although the Chrétien government boasts that it has been honest with Canadians, its standard for honesty may not be as high as that expected by most members of the public. It may be that years of experience in partisan politics distort one's perception of what constitutes truth.

FIDUCIARY TRUST VERSUS
TRADITIONAL PARTY DISCIPLINE

Voter cynicism about the constraints that party discipline places on the ability of MPs to represent their constituents effectively was addressed in the Red Book by promising to give House of Commons committees an enhanced role, to allow more free votes, and to give MPs more clout in the budget process and in the reviewing of senior order-in-council appointments. The Liberals promised to end "double-dipping" by MPs (collecting Parliamentary pensions as well as pay from other federal employment) and to reduce the budget for ministers' political staff by at least $10 million annually.

These promises have generally been kept. Some important policy items, such as the question of the proposed Code of Conduct, are now referred to legislative committees before the second reading stage or even before legislation is drafted. Private members' bills requiring public financing may now proceed, with the government's permission, and the Liberals allowed 49 free votes up to the time of publication of the self-evaluation. "These total up to more free votes in Parliament in just three years than over the previous 50 years combined."[56]

The House of Commons Finance Committee is now empowered to hold public hearings prior to the release of the budget as a means of providing more public input into the budget process. Bill C-85, which became law in July 1995, ends "double-dipping" by MPs, and the size of ministerial exempt staff has been reduced. However, the Liberal self-evaluation admitted that "no new mechanisms have been introduced" to allow MPs to review the qualifications of senior order-in-council appointments.[57]

Nevertheless, the Liberals only addressed the problem of partisanship to a very limited extent. The John Nunziatas of the Liberal party were not allowed to voice their real thoughts about the integrity agenda free of the constraints of party discipline, and although MPs now have a little more say about some government policies, there has not been a significant shift of power away from the Cabinet and to elected members.

CONCLUSION

Although the Chrétien government's record on integrity has been a great deal better than the Mulroney government's, its progress on promoting integrity in government has been disappointing. The government had a golden opportunity to make significant breakthroughs, such as promoting a lobbyists registration act that required real transparency, limiting financial contributions to political parties from single sources to prevent undue influence, eliminating patronage appointments to independent agencies, boards, and commissions, and copying the conflict of interest legislation in provinces such as Ontario and British Columbia. Yet no progress has been made on these fronts.

Still, the Liberals must be given credit for setting out their election promises in the Red Book and accepting the premise that they must be held accountable for these promises. This is a bold initiative that one hopes will not be derailed by the glitches in the experiment. In particular, the Liberals should give more careful consideration to ensuring that election promises are thoroughly researched, and to methods of extricating themselves honestly from promises that cannot be kept. As well, they should consider commissioning an independent evaluation of their record.

It is the Liberal party's traditional approach to partisan politics that stands between what appears to be an honest desire to achieve a higher measure of integrity in government and the practical ability to achieve that goal. If the Liberal party accepted the Royal Commission on Electoral Reform recommendation made to all political parties to develop their own codes of ethics, the party might be able to develop a creative approach to a problem that has plagued the Westminster system since the advent of responsible government two hundred years ago.

The dilemma is how to pursue a party's agenda while, at the same time, promoting the ethical requirements of democratic government that stem from the principle of mutual respect. It must be remembered that the Westminster system was intended to be flexible and to evolve to meet changing public expectations, and clearly the time has come for the patronage and party discipline habits of traditional partisan politics to give way to the demands of ethical politics based on mutual respect. The extent to which the Liberal government has the creative energy to contribute to that evolution may be an important factor in determining whether it can continue to command support from a plurality of Canadians.

NOTES

I would like to thank Gene Swimmer, Sandra Bach, and Michael Hicks for their helpful comments regarding an earlier draft of this chapter. Some of the ideas for this chapter were derived from Ian Greene and David P. Shugarman, *Honest Politics: Seeking Integrity in Canadian Public Life* (Toronto: Lorimer, 1997).

1 The Liberal Party of Canada, *Creating Opportunity* (Ottawa, 1993), 91-95.
2 The Liberal Party of Canada, *A Record of Achievement: A Report on the Liberal Government's 36 Months in Office* (Ottawa, 1996), 9.
3 Michael M. Atkinson, "The Integrity Agenda: Lead Us Not into Temptation," in Susan Philips, ed., *How Ottawa Spends 1995-96: Mid-Life Crises* (Ottawa: Carleton University Press, 1995), 237.
4 Ibid., 238, quoting from John Langford and Allan Tupper, "The Good, the Bad and the Ugly: Thinking About the Conduct of Public Officials," in John Langford and Allan Tupper, eds., *Corruption, Character and Conduct: Essays on Canadian Governmental Ethics* (Toronto: Oxford University Press, 1993), 15.
5 Ibid., 260.
6 An ethics analysis based on mutual respect subsumes rather than contradicts the approaches developed by Atkinson and by Langford and Tupper.
7 Ian Greene and David Shugarman, *Honest Politics: Seeking Integrity in Canadian Public Life* (Toronto: Lorimer, 1997), 4. See John

Rawls, *A Theory of Justice* (Cambridge: Harvard University Press, 1971).

8 This order was derived from two studies of media reports of ethics issues in Canadian politics since 1980. See Ian Greene, "Conflict of Interest and the Constitution," *Canadian Journal of Political Science*, 23 (1990), 233, and "Allegations of Undue Influence in Canadian Politics," in Janet Hiebert, ed., *Political Ethics: A Canadian Perspective*, Vol. 12 of Research Studies of the Royal Commission on Electoral Reform and Party Financing (Toronto: Dundurn Press, 1992), 101.

9 See Greene, "Conflict of Interest and the Constitution."

10 Since 1993, Saskatchewan, the Northwest Territories, and Yukon have joined this group.

11 The only exception to this achievement is Ralph Klein and the Multi-Corp scandal in Alberta. Klein and his wife did not initially reveal all the details of Mrs. Klein's investment in Multi-Corp to the ethics commissioner, and thus could not benefit from the advice that the commissioner would have given not to acquire shares in Multi-Corp without paying for them. Second, the Alberta ethics commissioner is a former politician and public official who once worked with Klein, and thus his ability to be objective when absolving Klein of blame for his predicament was in some doubt. See Greene and Shugarman, *Honest Politics*, Chapter 6, and Sean Gordon, "Grits Oppose New Term for Clark," *The Calgary Herald*, January 14, 1997, A4.

12 Liberal Party, *Creating Opportunity*, 95.

13 Office of the Prime Minister, "Prime Minister Appoints Canada's First Ethics Counsellor, Announces Integrity Measures," News Release, June 16, 1994.

14 Ibid., 1.

15 The testimony of the ethics commissioners in October 1995 is reproduced in *Canadian Parliamentary Review* (Winter 1995-96), 25-32.

16 Colin Campbell, *The Canadian Senate: A Lobby from Within* (Toronto: Macmillan, 1978).

17 Geoffrey York, "Conflict-of-interest Rules to Be Weakened," *The Globe and Mail* [Toronto], March 4, 1993, A4.

18 The Code states that "a public office holder shall ensure that no persons or groups are given preferential treatment based on the individuals hired to represent them." Office of the Ethics Counsellor, *Conflict of Interest Code and Post-Employment Code for Public Office Holders* (Ottawa, June 1994), s. 23(2).

19 Liberal Party, *A Record of Achievement*, 95.

20 The Ethics Counsellor delivered his First Annual Report to Parliament in June, 1996.

21 Liberal Party, *A Record of Achievement*, 95.
22 Ibid.
23 Hugh Winsor, "Accident-prone Minister Trips the PM," *The Globe and Mail* [Toronto], November 5, 1994, A1.
24 The fact that some or all of these letters may have been sent by ministerial assistants indicates that ministerial staff need to receive ethics counselling, in addition to the ministers themselves. Also, Atkinson's interpretation of the Code of Conduct was that it already clearly indicated that cabinet ministers ought not to intervene in cases before quasi-judicial tribunals. See Atkinson, "The Integrity Agenda," 258.
25 Susan Delacourt, "New Guidelines for Ministers Promised in Wake of Dupuy Affair," *The Globe and Mail* [Toronto], November 1, 1994, A1, A2.
26 Office of the Ethics Counsellor, "Dealings with Quasi-Judicial Tribunals," November, 1994.
27 Nevertheless, there was considerable speculation that the real reason for Collenette's resignation was his continued support for General Jean Boyle as Chief of Defence Staff in spite of Boyle's damaging testimony before the Létourneau inquiry into the killings committed by Canadian soldiers while on peacekeeping duty in Somalia. See Jeffrey Simpson, "What Are These Ethical Guidelines That Brought Down Collenette?" *The Globe and Mail* [Toronto], October 8, 1996, A18.
28 Ontario, Office of the Integrity Commissioner, *Annual Reports*, 1989-96. For a summary of some of these opinions, see Greene and Shugarman, *Honest Politics*, Appendix III.
29 Organized patronage in the Mulroney government has been thoroughly documented in Jeffrey Simpson, *The Spoils of Power: The Politics of Patronage* (Toronto: W. Collins, 1988), and Stevie Cameron, *On the Take: Crime, Corruption and Greed in the Mulroney Years* (Toronto: McFarlane Walter & Ross, 1994).
30 A well-publicized example of how patronage can trump the *Canada Gazette* system is the December, 1993 appointment of Marian Robson, a loyal Liberal worker in Vancouver, as the Pacific member of the National Transportation Agency. See Edward Greenspon, "Job Advertised, but Saved for Party's Friend," *The Globe and Mail* [Toronto], February 6, 1995, A1.
31 Tu Tranh Ha, "Liberals on Trial over System of Legal Agents," *The Globe and Mail* [Toronto], February 7, 1996, A6.
32 Ian Greene, *The Politics of Judicial Administration: The Ontario Case* (Ph.D. thesis, University of Toronto, 1983).
33 Tu Tranh Ha, "Liberals on Trial."

34 Peter H. Russell and Jacob S. Ziegel, "Federal Judicial Appointments: An Appraisal of the First Mulroney Government's Appointments and the New Judiciary Advisory Committees," *University of Toronto Law Journal*, 41 (1991).

35 Department of Justice, "Judicial Appointments Process Improved," News Release, April 28, 1994.

36 Liberal Party, *A Record of Achievement*, 93.

37 Ross Howard, "Ethics Package Stalled in Cabinet," *The Globe and Mail* [Toronto], March 18, 1994, A8.

38 In the United Kingdom, however, governments in recent decades have been able to muster plenty of loyal workers without relying nearly so heavily on patronage considerations. See Sharon Sutherland, "The Canadian Federal Government: Patronage, Unity, Security and Purity," in Langford and Tupper, *Corruption,* 123.

39 Ian Greene, "Allegations of Undue Influence."

40 Liberal Party, *Creating Opportunity*, 94.

41 Atkinson, "The Integrity Agenda," 247-48.

42 Howard, "Ethics Package."

43 House of Commons, Standing Committee on Industry, Sub-Committee on Bill C-43, An Act to Amend the Lobbyists Registration Act and to Make Related Amendments to Other Acts, March, 1995.

44 Peter Cheney and Dale Brazao, "Moores King of Movers, Shakers," *The Toronto Star*, December 3, 1995, A18.

45 Ibid.

46 Ibid.

47 Such dealings are not uncommon in the very competitive international aircraft industry; European community rules even permitted Airbus to claim bribe payments on their corporate income tax returns. But the allegation of the payment of bribes in a first-world country raised international eyebrows. See Carolyn Abraham, "Bribes Rampant in Aerospace Industry," Southam News Homepage, World Wide Web, December 22, 1995.

48 Senate of Canada, *Report of the Special Senate Committee on the Pearson Airport Agreements* (Ottawa, 1995).

49 Greene and Shugarman, *Honest Politics*, Chapter 6.

50 André Blais and Elisabeth Gidengil, *Making Representative Democracy Work: The Views of Canadians* (Toronto: Dundurn Press, Research Studies of the Royal Commission on Electoral Reform and Party Financing, v. 17, 1991).

51 See Reginald W. Bibby, *The Bibby Report: Social Trends Canadian Style* (Toronto: Stoddart, 1995), 111. The Liberals also acted quickly on some other promises not included in the Red Book, such as the September, 1993, promise to review the Pearson Airport agreement, and the promise made during the 1995 Quebec referendum to

recognize Quebec's distinct status in confederation. The latter
promise was kept in the form of a House of Commons resolution;
constitutional fulfilment will require the support of seven provinces,
including Ontario or Quebec.

52 Liberal MP Warren Allmand also voted against the 1995 budget,
because he felt that cuts to social programs broke Red Book promises. Although he was not expelled from the caucus, the Liberal whip
removed him as chair of the House justice committee. In February,
1997, Allmand resigned his seat and Chrétien appointed him
president of the International Centre for Human Rights and Democratic Development, thus resolving the question of how to handle an
MP who bucks party discipline yet is so respected for his integrity
that he cannot be expelled from caucus.

53 Liberal Party, *A Record of Achievement*, 17.

54 Ibid., 9.

55 Allan Thompson, "Somalia Probe Gets a March 31 Deadline," *The
Toronto Star*, January 11, 1997, A1.

56 Liberal Party, *A Record of Achievement*, 91.

57 Ibid., 92.

APPENDIX

This appendix presents an overview of the federal government's fiscal position and includes certain major economic policy indicators for 1987-1996, as well as some international comparisons.

Facts and trends are presented for federal revenue sources, federal expenditures by policy sector, the government's share of the economy, interest and inflation rates, Canadian balance of payments in total and with the United States in particular, and other national economic indicators. In addition, international comparisons on real growth, unemployment, inflation and productivity are reported for Canada, the U.S., Japan, Germany and the U.K.

The figures and time series are updated each year, providing readers with an ongoing current record of major budgetary and economic variables.

Table A.1

Federal Revenue by Source
1986-87 to 1995-96

As a Percentage of Total

Fiscal Year	Personal Tax (a)	Corporate Tax	Indirect Taxes (b)	Other Revenue (c)	Total Revenue	Annual Change
1986-87	65.2	11.5	24.5	8.7	100.0	11.7
1987-88	56.9	11.1	23.5	8.4	100.0	13.6
1988-89	55.1	11.3	24.8	8.9	100.0	6.6
1989-90	55.1	11.5	24.8	8.7	100.0	9.3
1990-91	58.9	9.8	21.9	9.4	100.0	5.0
1991-92	62.8	7.7	20.6	8.9	100.0	2.2
1992-93	63.0	6.0	21.7	9.4	100.0	-1.4
1993-94	60.1	8.1	23.0	8.8	100.0	-3.7
1994-95	61.0	9.4	22.0	7.6	100.0	6.3
1995-96	60.4	12.2	20.4	7.0	100.0	5.7

Revenue by Source is on a net basis.

(a) Unemployment insurance contributions are included in the total.
(b) Consists of sales taxes, energy taxes (except for petroleum and gas revenue tax and incremental oil revenue tax), excise duties, customs import duties, and the GST.
(c) Consists of non-resident income tax, petroleum and gas revenue tax, incremental oil revenue tax, miscellaneous other taxes and non-tax revenue.

Source: Department of Finance, *Fiscal Reference Tables,* October 1996, Table 3.

Figure A.1

**Sources of Federal Revenue as a
Percentage of Total
1996**

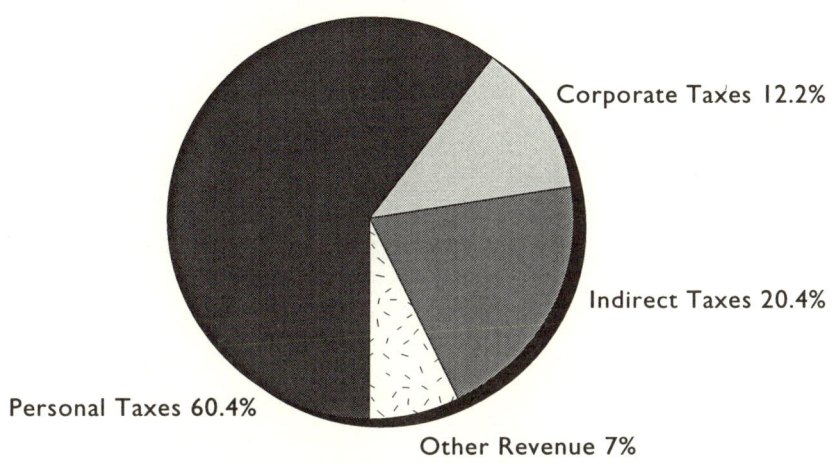

Corporate Taxes 12.2%

Indirect Taxes 20.4%

Personal Taxes 60.4%

Other Revenue 7%

Source: Department of Finance, *Fiscal Reference Tables*, October 1996, Table 3.

Figure A.2
Federal Expenditures by Sector
1997-98 Estimates

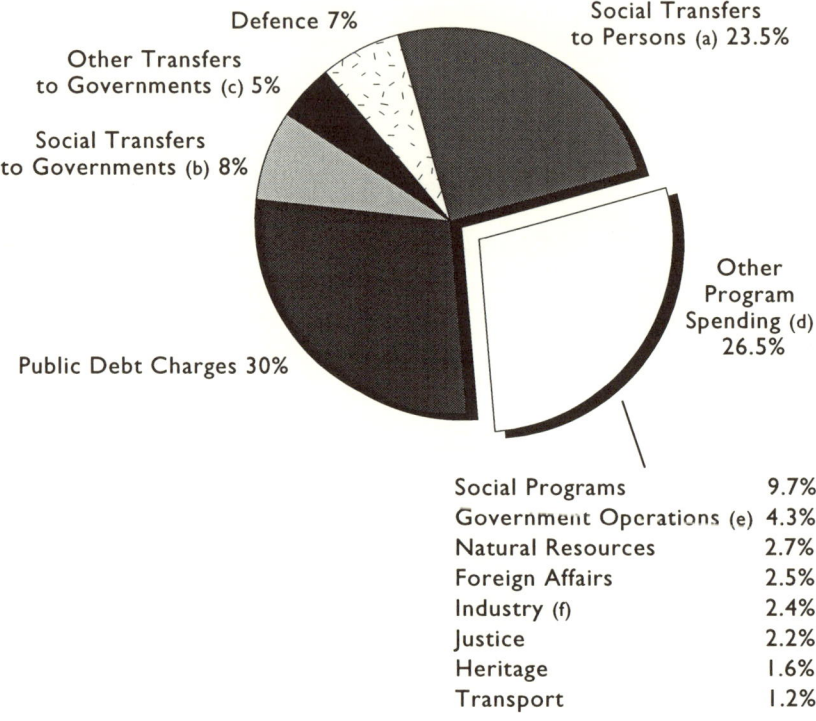

Social Programs	9.7%
Government Operations (e)	4.3%
Natural Resources	2.7%
Foreign Affairs	2.5%
Industry (f)	2.4%
Justice	2.2%
Heritage	1.6%
Transport	1.2%

(a) Consists of elderly benefits and employment insurance benefits
(b) Canada Health and Social Transfer
(c) Consists of primarily fiscal equalization and transfers to Territories
(d) Consists of all other federal non-defence operating and capital expenditures
(e) Includes general government services, Parliament and the Governor General
(f) Includes industrial, regional and scientific-technological support

All expenditures are calculated on a net basis.

Source: Treasury Board of Canada, *Program Expenditure Detail: A Profile of Departmental Spending*, February 20, 1997, 9-10, 13.

Figure A.3

Federal Expenditures by Sector
1992-93 to 1997-98

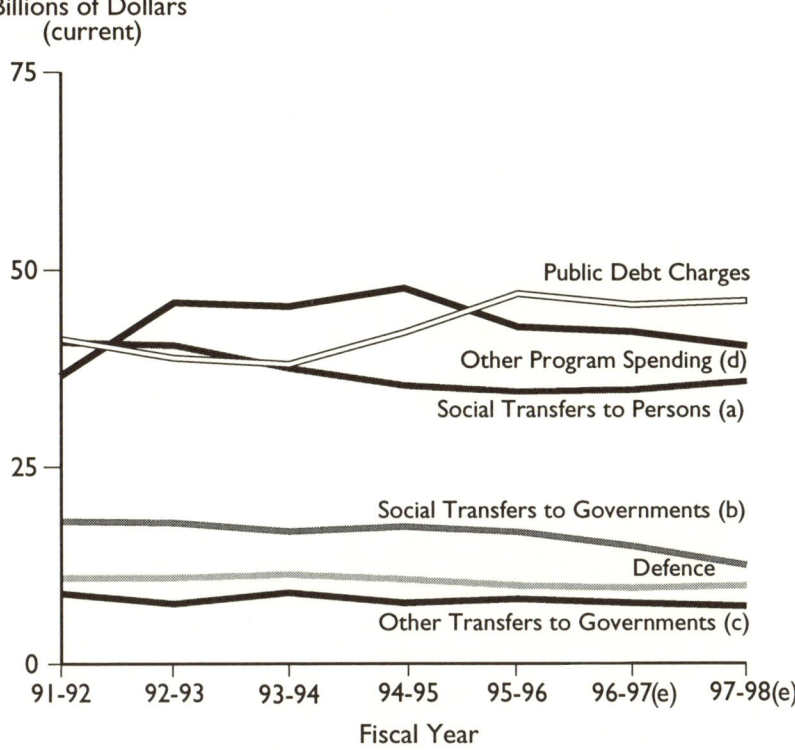

(a) Consists of elderly benefits and employment insurance benefits.

(b) Consists of the Canada Health and Social Transfer (CHST). Prior to the CHST, this component consisted of health and post-secondary education expenditures through Established Program Financing, and welfare funding through the Canada Assistance Plan.

(c) Consists of primarily fiscal equalization and transfers to Territories, net Alternative Payments for Standing Programs.

(d) Includes all other federal non-defence operating and capital expenditures.

(e) Figures for these years are estimates.

Federal Expenditures by component may differ for years prior to 1996-97 from the 1997-98 Budget figures, given changes to component categories and accounting practices of the Main Estimates, Budgetary Plan and the Public Accounts of Canada. All expenditures are calculated on a net basis.

Source: *Budget Plan*, February 18, 1997, 64; *Main Estimates*, Part I, 1997-98; *Public Accounts of Canada*, Vol. I, External Expenditures by Type, various years.

Figure A.4

Federal Revenue, Program Spending, and Deficit as Percentages of GDP 1988-89 to 1997-98

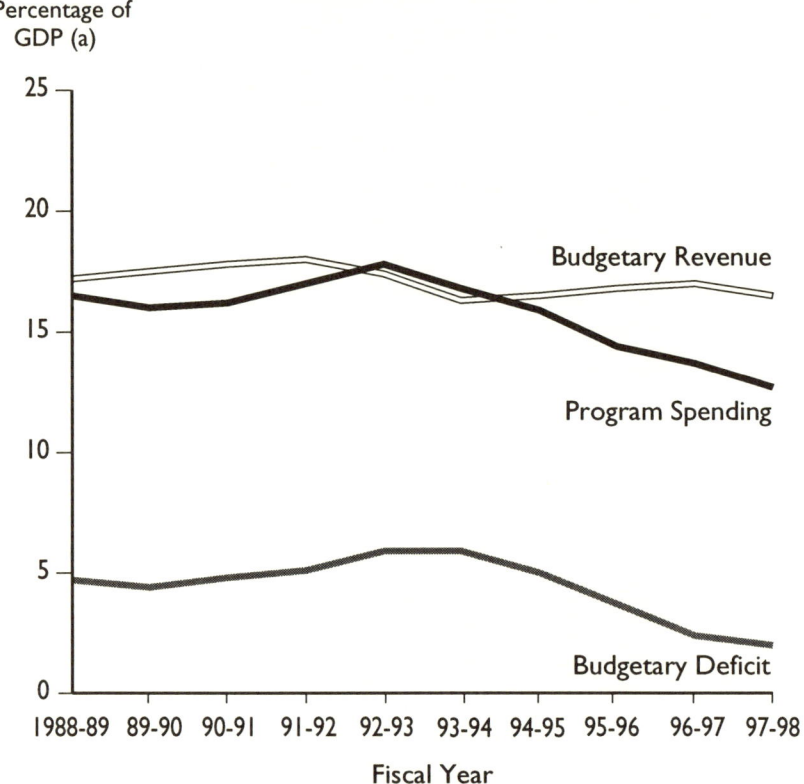

Budgetary revenue and program spending are based upon fiscal years, while GDP is based on the calendar year.

Revenue, program spending and the deficit are on a net basis. Program spending does not include public interest charges. GDP is nominal GDP.

Source: Department of Finance, *Fiscal Reference Tables*, October 1996, Table 2, *Budget Plan*, February 18, 1997, 44.

Table A.2

Federal Deficit

1988-89 to 1997-98

Billions of Dollars (current)

Fiscal Year	Budgetary Revenue	Total Expenditures	Budgetary Deficit	Annual % Change	As % of GDP
1988-89	104.1	132.8	28.8	3.6	4.7
1989-90	113.7	142.6	28.9	3.5	4.4
1990-91	119.4	151.4	32.0	10.7	4.8
1991-92	122.0	156.4	34.4	7.5	5.1
1992-93	120.4	161.4	41.0	19.2	5.9
1993-94	116.0	158.0	42.0	2.4	5.9
1994-95	123.3	160.8	37.5	-10.7	5.0
1995-96	130.3	158.9	28.6	-23.7	3.7
1996-97(a)	135.5	154.5	19.0	-33.6	2.4
1997-98(a)	137.8	151.8	17.0	-10.5	2.0

(a) Figures for these years are estimates.

While revenue, expenditures and deficit categories refer to fiscal years, nominal GDP is based upon a calendar year.

Source: Department of Finance, *Fiscal Reference Tables*, October 1996, Tables 1 and 2; Department of Finance, *Budget Plan*, February 18, 1997, Table 3.1.

Figure A.5

Federal Revenue, Expenditures and the Deficit
1988-89 to 1997-98

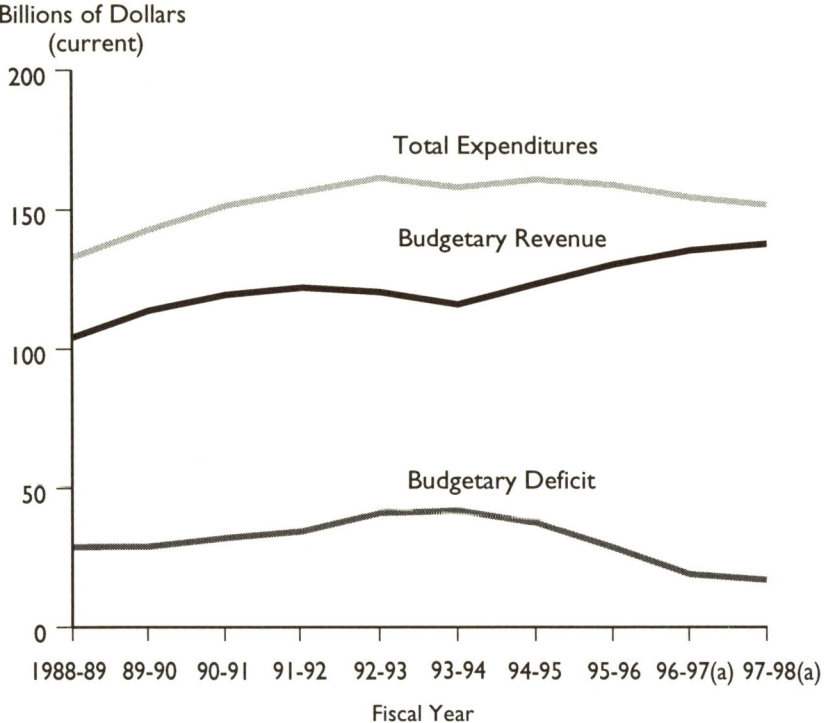

(a) Figures for these years are estimates.

Total expenditures include program spending and public interest charges on the debt.

Source: Department of Finance, *Fiscal Reference Tables*, October 1996, Table 1; Department of Finance, *Budget Plan*, February 18, 1997, Table 3.1; *Public Accounts of Canada*, Statement of Revenues and Expenditures, various years.

Figure A.6
Growth in Real GDP
1987-96

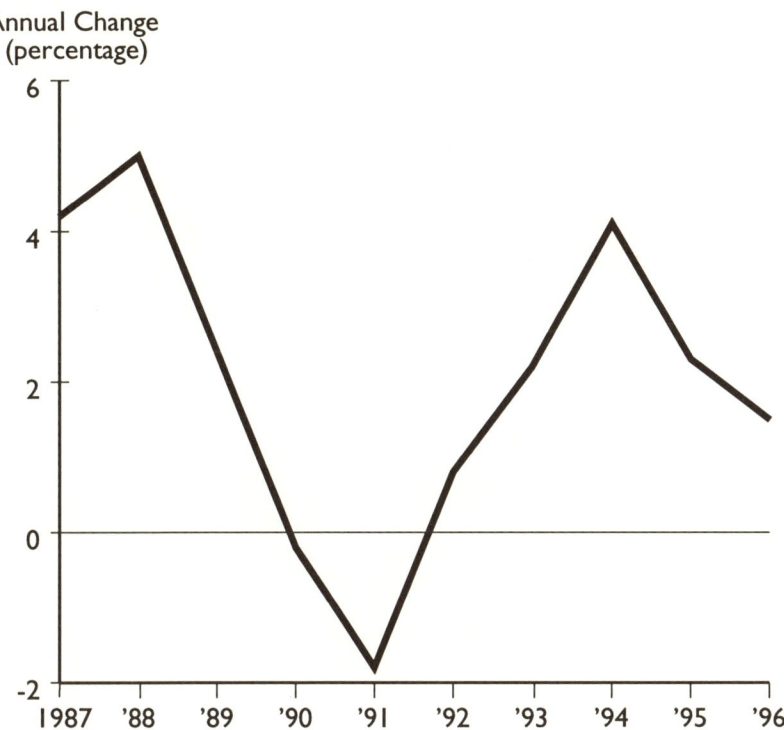

Source: Statistics Canada, *The Daily*, Cat # 13-001, various years, and based upon updated figures as at March 4, 1997.

Figure A.7
**Rates of Unemployment and
Employment Growth
1987-96**

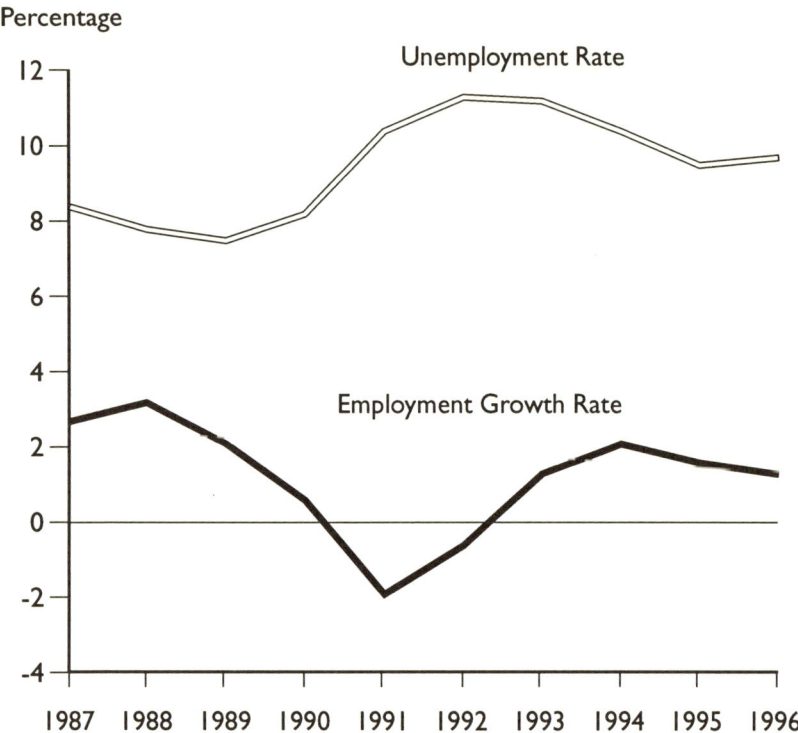

Employment growth rates and the unemployment rate apply to both sexes, 15 years and older, and are seasonally adjusted.

Source: *Historical Labour Force Statistics* (71-201), Statistics Canada, various years.

Figure A.8
Interest and Inflation Rates
1987-96

Percentage

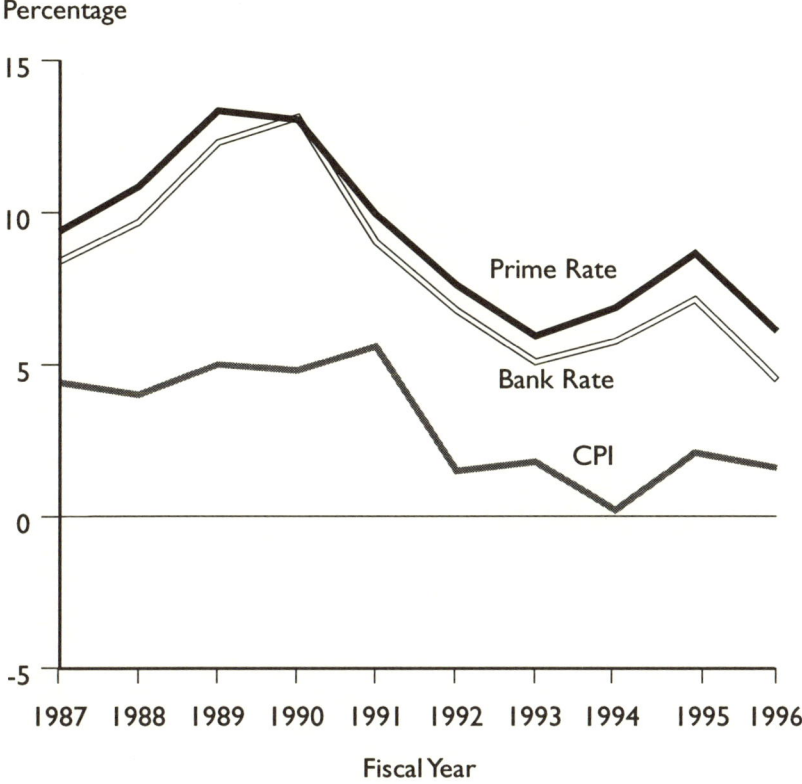

The Consumer Price Index is not seasonally adjusted. The CPI excludes food.
Energy is excluded from 1990 to 1994.
The prime rate refers to the prime business interest rate charged by the chartered
banks, and the Bank Rate refers to the rate charged by the Bank of Canada on
any loans to commercial banks.

Source: Bank of Canada Review, Table F1, various years; and Statistics Canada,
The Consumer Price Index, Cat. #62-001, various years.

Figure A.9
Productivity and Costs
1986-95

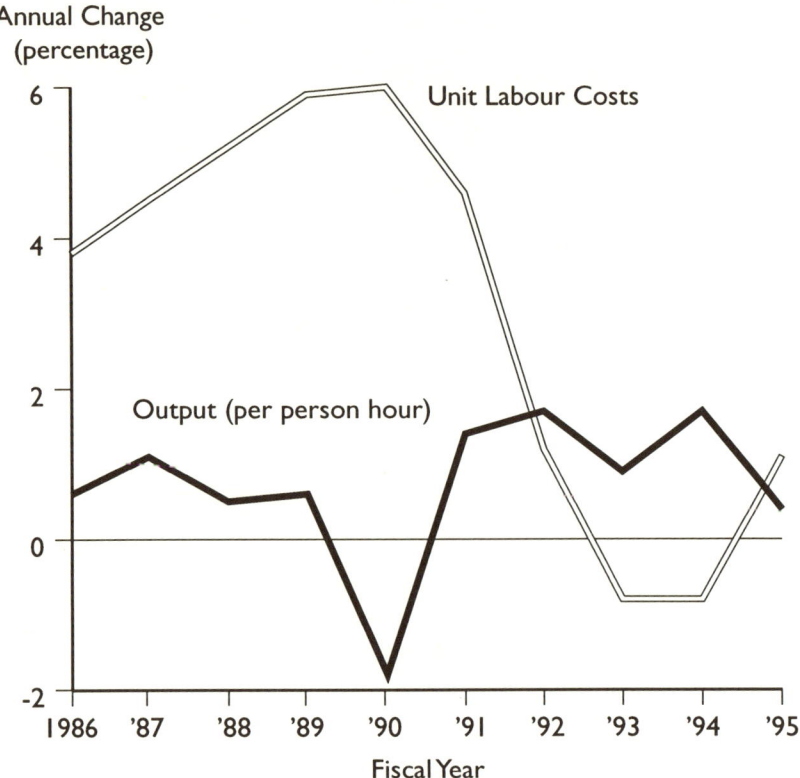

Source: Department of Finance, *Economic Reference Tables*, August 1996, Table 40.1, 74.

Figure A.10
Balance of Payments
1986-95

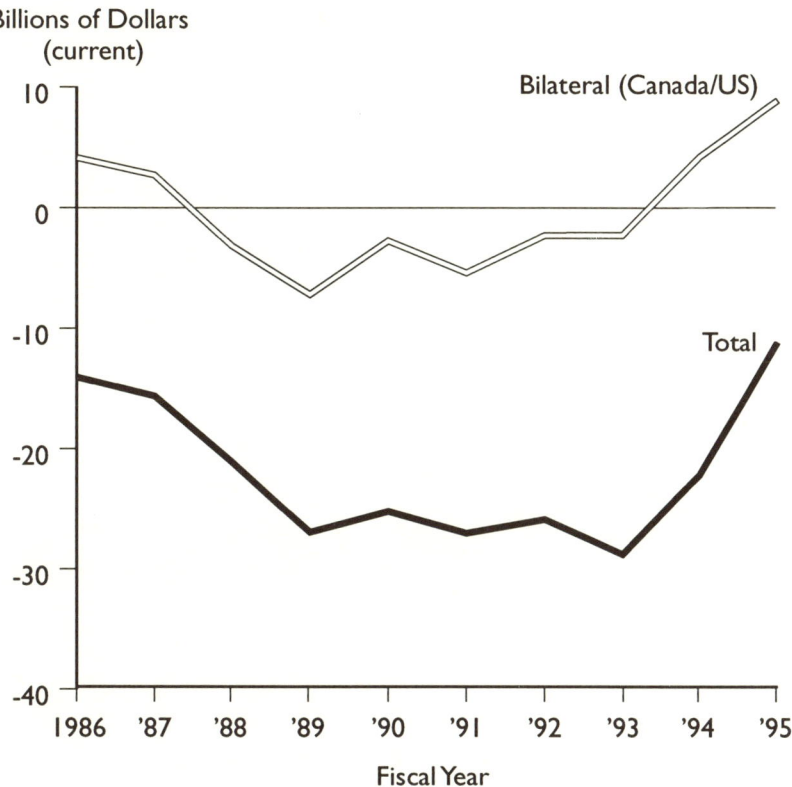

Source: Department of Finance, *Economic Reference Tables*, August 1996,
Tables 61 and 62, 109-10.

Figure A.11
Growth in Real GDP
Canada and Selected G7 Countries
1986-95

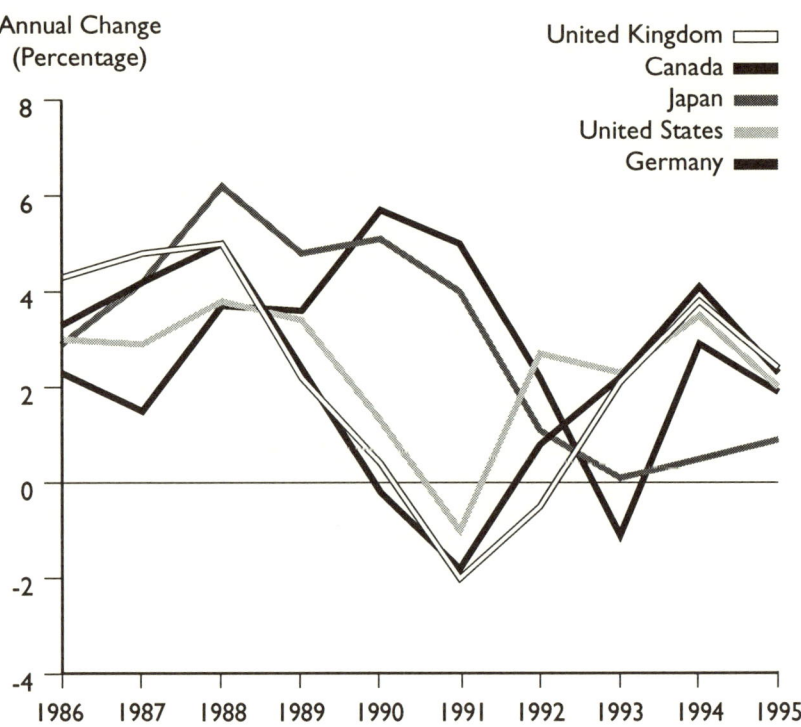

Source: Organization for Economic Co-operation and Development (OECD),
Economic Outlook, December 1996, Annex Table 1, A4.

Figure A.12
Unemployment Rates
Canada and Selected G7 Countries
1986-95

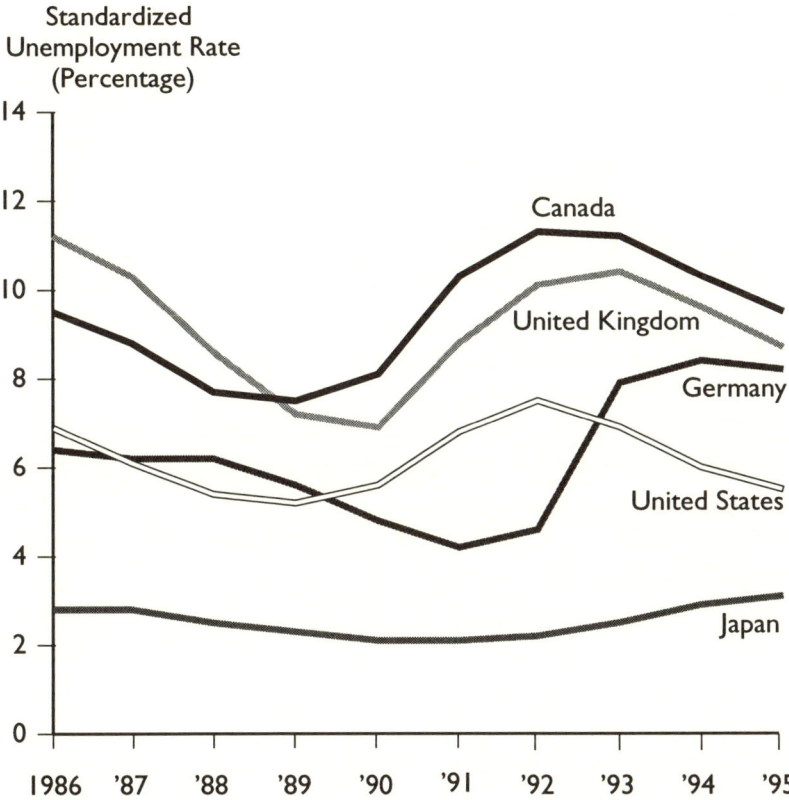

Source: *OECD Economic Outlook*, December 1996, Annex Table 22.

Figure A.13
Annual Inflation Rates
Canada and Selected G7 Countries
1986-95

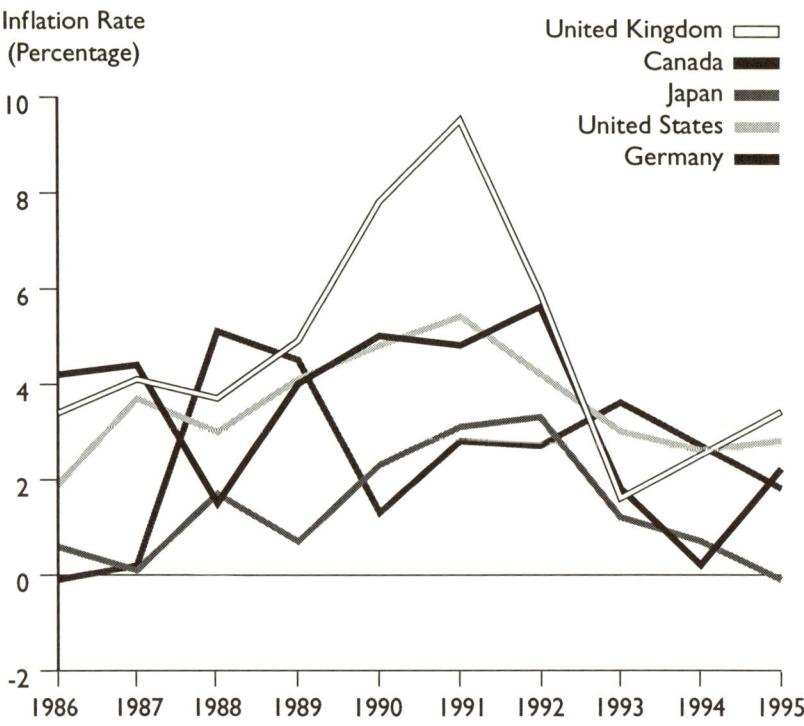

Source: *OECD Economic Outlook*, December 1996, Annex Table 16.

Figure A.14
Increase in Unit Labour Costs
Canada and Selected G7 Countries
1986-95

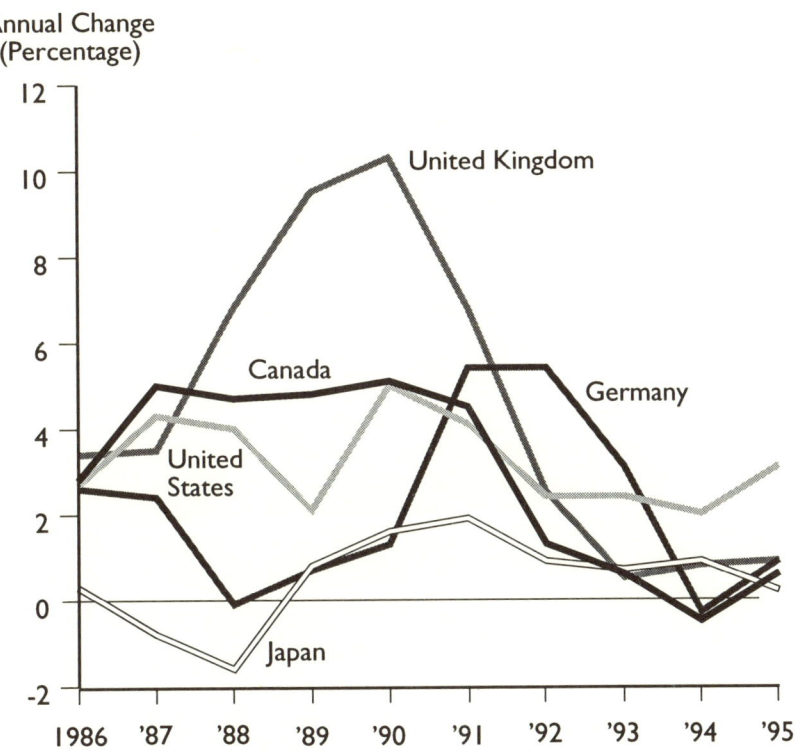

Source: *OECD Economic Outlook*, December 1996, Annex Table 13.

Table A.3
International Comparisons
1986-95

Percentage Change from Previous Period

Growth in Real GDP

	1986	1987	1988	1989	1990	1991	1992	1993	1994	1995
Canada	3.3	4.2	5.0	2.4	-0.2	-1.8	0.8	2.2	4.1	2.3
US	3.0	2.9	3.8	3.4	1.3	-1.0	2.7	2.3	3.5	2.0
Japan	2.9	4.2	6.2	4.8	5.1	4.0	1.1	0.1	0.5	0.9
Germany	2.3	1.5	3.7	3.6	5.7	5.0	2.2	-1.1	2.9	1.9
U.K.	4.3	4.8	5.0	2.2	0.4	-2.0	-0.5	2.1	3.8	2.4

Unemployment Rates

	1986	1987	1988	1989	1990	1991	1992	1993	1994	1995
Canada	9.5	8.8	7.7	7.5	8.1	10.3	11.3	11.2	10.3	9.5
US	6.9	6.1	5.4	5.2	5.6	6.8	7.5	6.9	6.0	5.5
Japan	2.8	2.8	2.5	2.3	2.1	2.1	2.2	2.5	2.9	3.1
Germany	6.4	6.2	6.2	5.6	4.8	4.2	4.6	7.9	8.4	8.2
U.K.	11.2	10.3	8.6	7.2	6.9	8.8	10.1	10.4	9.6	8.7

Increase in Unit Labour Costs

	1986	1987	1988	1989	1990	1991	1992	1993	1994	1995
Canada	2.8	5.0	4.7	4.8	5.1	4.5	1.3	0.6	-0.5	0.6
US	2.7	4.3	4.0	2.1	5.0	4.1	2.4	2.4	2.0	3.1
Japan	0.3	-0.8	-1.6	0.8	1.6	1.9	0.9	0.7	0.9	0.2
Germany	2.6	2.4	-0.1	0.7	1.3	5.4	5.4	3.1	-0.3	0.9
U.K.	3.4	3.5	6.8	9.5	10.3	6.8	2.5	0.5	0.8	0.9

Source: *OECD Economic Outlook*, December 1996, Annex Tables 1, 13, 22.

ABSTRACTS/RÉSUMÉS

Sandra Bach and Susan D. Phillips
Constructing a New Social Union: Child Care Beyond Infancy?

Child care is one of the Red Book's main unkept promises. The reasons given by the Chrétien government for failing to fulfil the commitment were a lack of provincial interest and insufficient economic growth. This chapter argues that these are inadequate explanations. A fuller explanation is that the federal government placed quasi-constitutional constraints on its spending power through the CHST and the 1996 Throne Speech, limiting both the federal and provincial ability to develop a national child care program. In a broader sense, child care can be seen as the first fatality of the construction by federal and provincial governments of a New Social Union, in which the federal government is withdrawing from direct support of social services in favour of providing tax assistance to individuals. The new emphasis is on fighting child poverty by funding an enhanced Child Tax Benefit. But this measure will do little to improve access to affordable quality care, and, indeed, may come at the expense of funding for child care spaces.

La garde d'enfants est une des principales promesses non tenues du Livre rouge. Les raisons données par le gouvernement Chrétien pour expliquer ce fait ont été un manque d'intérêt au niveau provincial et une croissance économique insuffisante. Ce chapitre soutient que ces explications ne suffisent pas. Une explication plus complète est que le gouvernement fédéral a mis des contraintes quasi constitutionnelles sur son pouvoir de dépenses par le TCSPS et le discours du trône de 1996, limitant la capacité des gouvernements fédéral et provinciaux d'élaborer un programme national de garde d'enfants. De façon plus générale, on peut voir la garde d'enfants comme la première victime de la construction par les deux paliers de gouvernement d'une nouvelle union sociale, où le gouvernement fédéral se retire du soutien direct des services sociaux pour donner une assistance fiscale aux particuliers. L'accent est mis sur la lutte contre la pauvreté infantile par le financement d'une meilleure prestation fiscale pour enfants. Mais cette mesure fera peu pour améliorer l'accès à une garde d'enfants de qualité et risque même de réduire le financement d'espaces pour la garde d'enfants.

Bruce Doern and Mark MacDonald

The Liberals' Internal Trade Agreement: The Beginning of a New Federal Assertiveness?

The chapter examines the 1994 Agreement on Internal Trade (AIT), one of the more surprising achievements of the Liberal government. The gestation and basic features of the AIT are examined in relation to the different provincial governing party views about the role of government, the meeting of trade versus regular federal-provincial policy communities, and the nature of the federal trade and commerce power. Contrary to some other assessments, which see the AIT as a weak first step, the authors argue that it represents a considerable example of federal assertiveness and constitutes a potentially very strong side-deal to the Constitution, which significantly disciplines the provincial governments in particular, and upon which various interests may now base renewed pressures to strengthen the Canadian economic union.

Ce chapitre examine l'Accord sur le commerce intérieur de 1994, une des réalisations plutôt surprenantes du gouvernement libéral. Les auteurs examinent la gestation et les traits fondamentaux de l'Accord par rapport aux différents points de vue des partis au pouvoir au niveau provincial sur le rôle du gouvernement, l'interaction des communautés s'intéressant au commerce et de celles s'occupant de politique fédéral-provinciale, et la nature du pouvoir fédéral en matière de commerce. Contrairement à d'autres évaluations qui voient dans l'Accord un premier pas plutôt faible, les auteurs soutiennent que c'est un exemple important de volonté fédérale et que cela constitue une entente potentiellement très forte parallèle à la Constitution, qui discipline de façon significative les gouvernements provinciaux en particulier, et qui pourra servir de base à des pressions renouvelées venant de divers intérêts et visant à renforcer l'union économique canadienne.

Ian Greene

Principle Versus Partisanship: The Chrétien Government's Record on Integrity Issues

This chapter argues that although the Chrétien government's record on ethics and integrity has been better than that of the Mulroney government, the Liberals missed a golden opportunity to implement major ethical reforms. This is because old habits of partisanship die hard, and because the Liberals failed to give due consideration to the higher expectations for democratic government that characterize an increasingly well-educated and attentive public. The chapter takes the principle of mutual respect as a reference point for ethical judgments in a liberal democratic political system. The major ethical issues present when the Chrétien government took office concerned conflicts of interest, patronage, party financing, undue influence by lobbyists, dishonest or "dirty-handed" political practices, and constraints on MPs caused by traditional party discipline. The Red Book promises of 1993 addressed only the least contentious of these issues. Thus, although most of the 1993 promises about integrity were kept, there is much unfinished business concerning a comprehensive regime for preventing conflicts of interest, the elimination of patronage, and the reform of party financing.

Ce chapitre soutient que si la fiche du gouvernement Chrétien en matière d'éthique et d'intégrité a été beaucoup meilleure que celle du gouvernement Mulroney, les libéraux ont raté une occasion pour réaliser des réformes majeures en matière d'éthique. C'est que les vieilles habitudes de politique partisane ont la vie dure. Les libéraux n'ont pas considéré comme il faut qu'un public de plus en plus instruit et attentif attend plus d'un gouvernement démocratique. Ce chapitre prend le principe de respect mutuel comme point de référence pour des jugements d'ordre éthique dans un système politique libéral et démocratique. Les questions principales d'ordre éthique présentes au moment de l'entrée en fonctions du gouvernement Chrétien étaient les conflits d'intérêt, le patronage, le financement des partis, une influence indue des lobbyistes, les pratiques politiques malhonnêtes, et les contraintes imposées aux députés par la discipline de parti traditionnelle. Les promesses du Livre rouge de 1993 n'abordaient que les moins controversées de ces questions. Il s'ensuit que si la plupart des promesses de 1993 en matière d'intégrité ont été tenues, il reste beaucoup à faire en vue d'un régime complet visant à empêcher les conflits d'intérêt, à éliminer le patronage et à réformer le financement des partis.

Luc Juillet and Glen Toner
From Great Leaps to Baby Steps: Environment and Sustainable Development Policy Under the Liberals
The Red Book indicated that environmental concerns would be high on a Liberal government's agenda. It spoke of the need for "a fundamental shift in values and public policy" to reconcile economic growth with the preservation of a healthy natural environment. This chapter provides a critical assessment of the Liberals' performance in five important areas of environmental policy-making: the control of toxic substances, environmental assessment of industrial projects, the establishment of a framework for the protection of biodiversity and endangered species, the fight against global warming, and the institutionalization of sustainable development in public administration. We find that in the transition from the campaign trail to the cabinet room the Liberals' environmental and sustainable development agenda was tamed by contact with the hard realities of Canadian politics in the 1990s. In explaining this shift, we emphasize the interplay among three factors: 1) the lack of political will within Cabinet and the opposition of economic departments with a traditional vision of economic development; 2) the overarching primacy given to an old-style economic agenda in the face of deficit problems and high unemployment; and 3) the desire of the government to avoid additional federal-provincial conflicts at a crucial period for national unity. The Liberals promised great leaps forward but took only baby steps. Although their policy documents indicate an understanding of what must be done, internal opposition within the bureaucracy and Cabinet and a growing divide between environmentalists and industrialists mean that the government is often at war with itself about what to do and how fast to move.

Le Livre rouge indiquait que les préoccupations environnementales auraient une place de choix dans le programme d'un gouvernement libéral. Il était question du besoin d'un changement fondamental des valeurs et de la politique pour réconcilier la croissance économique avec la préservation d'un environnement naturel sain. Ce chapitre fournit une évaluation critique de la fiche des libéraux dans cinq domaines importants de politique environnementale: le contrôle des substances toxiques, l'évaluation environnementale de projets industriels, l'établissement d'un cadre pour la protection de la biodiversité et des espèces menacées, la lutte contre le réchauffement de la planète, et l'institionnalisation du développement durable au sein de l'administration publique. Nous constatons que dans la transition de la campagne électorale aux réunions du Cabinet le programme des libéraux en matière d'environnement et de développement durable a été atténué au contact des dures réalités de la politique canadienne des années 1990. En expliquant ce changement, nous soulignons l'interaction de trois facteurs: 1) le manque de volonté politique au sein du Cabinet et l'opposition de la part de ministères économiques ayant une vision traditionnelle du développement économique; 2) la primauté absolue accordée à un programme économique de style ancien face aux problèmes de déficit et de chômage élevé; et 3) le désir de la part du gouvernement d'éviter des conflits fédéraux-provinciaux additionnels à une période cruciale pour l'unité nationale. Les libéraux ont promis des pas de géant, mais n'ont fait que trottiner. Si leurs documents en matière de politique indiquent une compréhension de ce qu'il faut faire, une opposition interne au sein de la bureaucratie et du Cabinet ainsi qu'une division croissante entre environnementalistes et industrialistes font que le gouvernement est souvent en guerre avec lui-même quand il s'agit de décisions sur des choses à faire ainsi que sur le rythme à suivre.

Fran Klodawsky and Aron Spector

Renovation or Abandonment?: Canadian Social Housing at a Crossroads

Nineteen ninety-seven is likely to mark the last year of direct federal involvement in social housing. Current federal policy echoes and continues the initiatives begun under the previous Conservative government to devolve to the provinces responsibility for producing and maintaining social housing. Social housing continues to be used as a convenient pawn in these governments' negotiations, which have been dominated by national unity and deficit reduction concerns. Given a long history of provincial reticence to encourage or produce social housing without strong federal urging, the probable outcome is a slow and steady erosion in its quantity and quality, and a return to reliance on the private market to produce housing for lower-income Canadians. This direction is concurrent with an increasing dependence on the private rental market for lower-income households and a sharp increase in the average proportion of income that they dedicate to shelter. We also note that this government has decoupled housing issues from most social policy debates, reversing past federal efforts to foster and strengthen the roles of communities and non-profit partners in creating supportive, empowering environments for low- and moderate-income Canadians.

L'année 1997 risque de marquer la dernière année d'engagement fédéral direct dans le logement social. La politique fédérale actuelle reflète et continue les initiatives amorcées sous le gouvernement conservateur précédant visant à déléguer aux provinces la responsabilité de produire et de maintenir le logement social. Celui-ci continue à servir de pion dans les négociations entre ces gouvernements, qui sont dominées par des préoccupations en matière d'unité nationale et de réduction de déficit. Étant donné la longue histoire de réticence de la part des provinces à encourager ou à produire le logement social sans incitation fédérale, le résultat probable de cette situation est une érosion lente et constante de la quantité et qualité de celui-ci, et la reprise par le marché privé de la production de logement pour les Canadiens à faible revenu. Cette direction coïncide avec un recours accru au marché de location de la part de ménages à faible revenu et l'augmentation soudaine de la proportion du revenu de ceux-ci qui est consacré au logement. Nous constatons également que ce gouvernement a dissocié les questions de logement de la plupart des débats sur la politique sociale, renversant ainsi les efforts fédéraux antérieurs visant à favoriser et à renforcer les rôles des communautés et des partenaires sans but lucratif dans la création d'environnements positifs et permettant une prise en charge de soi pour les Canadiens à faible et à moyen revenus.

Allan Maslove and Kevin Moore
From Red Books to Blue Books: Repairing Ottawa's Fiscal House
Despite the Red Book position that a Liberal government would deal with the deficit and unemployment in a balanced fashion, shortly after assuming office the Liberal government focused almost entirely upon deficit reduction. In doing so they became much like the predecessor

Conservative government, but the Liberals were much more success-ful deficit-busters. Among the reasons for this were changed public opinion in support of deficit reduction, a clear Liberal determination to cut spending, and a shift in the forecasting/goal-setting of the De-partment of Finance to post modest targets, which have been regularly surpassed. Whether this successful attack on the deficit was necessary or advisable is still open to debate. As they approach the end of their first mandate, the Liberals are, as a result of their successful deficit-cutting, approaching something of a crossroads. Public debate is be-ginning to shift from deficit reduction to what happens next: debt reduction, tax cuts, or new spending, particularly on social programs. It is likely that choosing among these alternatives will be a fundamen-tal task facing the next government. Meanwhile, the sea change in public opinion and budgetary politics brought about during their first term may be the Liberals' most important fiscal policy legacy.

Malgré la position prise par le Livre rouge qu'un gouvernement libéral s'occuperait du déficit et du chômage de façon équilibrée, peu après son entrée en fonctions le gouvernement libéral s'est concentré presque entièrement sur la réduction du déficit. En faisant cela, il se rapprochait de son prédécesseur conservateur, mais les libéraux ont beaucoup mieux réussi à réduire le déficit. Parmi les raisons de ce succès il y a un changement dans l'opinion publique en faveur d'une telle réduction, une décision ferme de la part des libéraux de réduire les dépenses, et un changement dans les prévisions et les établissements d'objectifs au sein du ministère des Finances, qui fait qu'on publie des cibles modestes, qui sont régulièrement dépassées. La question de savoir si cette attaque du déficit était nécessaire ou opportune est toujours à discuter. À l'approche de la fin de leur premier mandat, les libéraux, ayant réussi à réduire le déficit, s'approchent d'une sorte de carrefour. Le débat public passe de la réduction du déficit à ce qui arrive après: réduction de la dette, réduction des impôts, ou de nouvelles dépenses, en particulier en matière de programmes sociaux. Le choix parmi ces alternatives risque de constituer une tâche fondamentale du prochain gouvernement. Entre-temps, le profond changement dans l'opinion publique, ainsi que la politique budgétaire élaborée au cours de leur premier mandat, peuvent bien être le legs le plus important des libéraux en matière de politique fiscale.

Vincent Mosco

Marketable Commodity or Public Good: The Conflict Between Domestic and Foreign Communication Policy

Red Book promises in culture and communication are assessed and situated within a wider tension between domestic and international policy. The Liberals did not deliver on their promise to provide stable, multi-year funding for the CBC and other national cultural institutions. They did provide financial support for video and film production and advanced copyright legislation, and they promoted cultural exports. Promise and performance aside, the Liberal years have seen a growing division between a domestic policy of treating culture, communication, and information as market commodities like any other products, and an international policy that justifies protecting them because of their special status for Canadian identity and sovereignty. Growing domestic and international pressures make this division unsustainable and call for a fundamental rethinking of national communication and cultural policy.

Ce chapitre évalue les promesses du Livre rouge en matière de culture et communication et les situe dans le cadre d'une tension plus large entre la politique intérieure et la politique internationale. Les libéraux n'ont pas tenu leur promesse quant au financement stable, sur plusieurs années, de Radio-Canada et d'autres institutions culturelles du pays. Par contre ils ont appuyé financièrement la production de vidéos et de films et une législation avancée sur le copyright, et ils ont favorisé les exportations culturelles. De plus, pendant les années des libéraux, on a assisté à une division croissante entre une politique intérieure qui traite la culture, la communication et l'information comme des produits du marché comme tout autre produit, et une politique internationale qui justifie le fait de les protéger vu leur statut spécial pour l'identité et la souveraineté canadiennes. Des pressions intérieures et internationales croissantes rendent insoutenable cette division et nécessitent une refonte fondamentale de la politique nationale en matière de communication et culture.

Michael J. Prince

Lowering the Boom on the Boomers: Replacing Old Age Security with the New Seniors Benefit and Reforming the Canada Pension Plan

The proposed Seniors Benefit, to take effect in 2001, and reforms to the Canada Pension Plan to phase in over the 1998-2003 period, are the most significant policy development in retirement benefits in the past 30 years. The Seniors Benefit will replace the Old Age Security and Guaranteed Income Supplement programs as well as the Age and Pension Income tax credits. Benefits will be targeted, based on family income, and fully indexed and non-taxable. The chapter examines how past Conservative policies and pensions politics have shaped this policy reform by the Liberals. The promised full indexing of the Seniors Benefit is a social policy first in the 1990s in Canada. However, the new program will do little new to reduce poverty among seniors. The basic value of elderly benefits is frozen until 2001, and then will be raised by a puny amount of $10 a month. Thus, the large majority of today's seniors have little to fear or hope from the Seniors Benefit. The pattern of generational winners and losers is similar with respect to the latest reforms to the Canada Pension Plan. Since the main intent of the reform is to restrain future costs, it will be seniors of the next generation, the baby boomers, who will experience the cuts, and federal governments in the new millennium that will reap the savings.

La proposition de la Prestation aux aînés, que doit entrer en vigueur en 2001, et les réformes au Régime de pensions du Canada, qui doivent être introduites progressivement au cours de la période 1998-2003, constituent le changement le plus important en matière de prestations aux retraités depuis 30 ans. La Prestation aux aînés remplacera les prestations de sécurité de la vieillesse et le supplément de revenu garanti, ainsi que les crédits fiscaux en raison de l'âge et pour revenu de pension. Les prestations seront ciblées, basées sur le revenu familial, entièrement indexées et non imposables. Ce chapitre examine la façon dont certaines politiques des conservateurs du passé, et la *politique des pensions ont influencé cette réforme des libéraux. La promesse de l'indexation complète de la Prestation pour aînés est une première dans la politique sociale des années 90 au Canada. Le nouveau programme contribuera peu, cependant, à la réduction de la pauvreté chez les personnes âgées. La valeur de base des prestations aux aînés est gelée jusqu'en 2001, année où elle sera majorée de la petite somme de 10$ par mois. La grande majorité des personnes âgées d'aujourd'hui ont donc peu à craindre ou à espérer de la Prestation aux aînés. La répartition des gagnants et perdants, par génération, correspond à celle qui se dessine pour le Régime des pensions du Canada. Le but principal de la réforme étant la restriction des coûts futurs, les aînés de la génération suivante, ceux du baby boom, subiront ces réductions, et les gouvernements fédéraux du nouveau millénaire en récolteront les économies.*

Peter Stoyko
Creating Opportunity or Creative Opportunism?: Liberal Labour Market Policy
The keynote of the Red Book—the creation of employment opportunities—has come to haunt the Chrétien government as unemployment rates remain high. Yet, paradoxically, the Liberals remain extremely popular. While assessing the fulfilment of the Red Book's labour market commitments, this chapter offers an explanation of both the government's shortcomings and its enduring popularity. The Red Book agenda failed to fully account for a new set of policy constraints, particularly global competition, deficit reduction, and the intensification of federal politics. Instead of pressing forward with full implementation, the Liberals opted for a damage control strategy characterized by political calculation, cutback management tactics, cosmetic marketing, and high-tech fetishism. The result is breathtaking in its irony. While the Red Book promised an alternative to the laissez-faire policies of the Conservative party, the Liberal's political technique has helped make less interventionist government more politically palatable.

La clef de voûte du Livre rouge—la création de perspectives d'emploi—a fini par hanter le gouvernement Chrétien puisque les taux de chômage restent élevés. Paradoxalement, les libéraux restent extrêmement populaires. Tout en évaluant à quel point les libéraux ont tenu les engagements du Livre rouge en matière de marché du travail, ce chapitre tente une explication des défauts du gouvernement et de sa popularité durable. Le programme du Livre rouge ne tenait pas bien compte d'un nouvel ensemble de contraintes politiques, en particulier celles de la concurrence mondiale, la réduction des déficits, et l'intensification de la politique fédérale. Plutôt que de procéder à une mise en oeuvre complète, les libéraux ont opté pour une stratégie visant à limiter les dégâts et caractérisée par le calcul politique, les tactiques en gestion de réductions, le marketing cosmétique et le fétichisme de la haute technologie. Le résultat en est stupéfiant par son ironie. Alors que le Livre rouge promettait une alternative aux politiques de laissez-faire du parti conservateur, la technique politique des libéraux a contribué à rendre plus acceptable au plan politique un interventionnisme amoindri de la part du gouvernement.

Gene Swimmer
Seeing Red: A Liberal Report Card

In the run-up to the 1993 federal election, the Liberals distributed a detailed blueprint of how they would govern if elected. The publication, which became known as the Red Book, included about 200 specific commitments. Three years into their mandate, the Liberals issued a self-assessment indicating that 78 percent of the promises have been fulfilled and 12 percent are in progress. Opposition parties issued their own counting exercises, giving the Liberals much lower grades. None of these analyses represent an effective evaluation of the Liberal government's first term in office, because not all commitments were equally important to the public, and the Red Book was silent on many crucial public policy areas.

This edition of *How Ottawa Spends* attempts a more comprehensive assessment of the government, through analyses of eleven policy areas. The authors generally find that Liberals' policies, once they are in office, bear a much stronger resemblance to Tory Blue philosophy than to the Red Book. The Liberals have performed well in economic management areas, such as deficit control and trade promotion, with the important exception of employment policies. In the national unity field, they are barely passing, with another major test yet to come. Their record is weak in social areas, such as labour markets, child care, communications, and social housing, where the twin obsessions of deficit control and responding to decentralist pressures are driving the policy agenda. Finally, in environmental protection and integrity agendas, Liberal performance has been mixed, but falls far short of the expectations created by the Red Book.

Dans la période précédant les élections fédérales de 1993, les libéraux ont distribué un plan détaillé exposant la façon dont ils gouverneraient s'ils étaient élus. Cette publication, qu'on a fini par appeler le Livre rouge, comprenait à peu près 200 engagements précis. Au bout de trois ans au pouvoir, les libéraux ont publié une auto-évaluation indiquant que 78 pour cent des promesses ont été tenues et que 12 pour cent sont en voie d'exécution. Les partis d'opposition ont publié leurs propres exercices de comptage, qui donnaient des notes beaucoup moins bonnes aux libéraux. Aucune de ces analyses ne représente une évaluation utile du premier mandat du gouvernement libéral, puisque les engagements n'étaient pas tous d'une importance égale pour le public, et que le Livre rouge ne disait rien sur de nombreux domaines cruciaux de la politique.

Cette édition de How Ottawa Spends *tente une évaluation plus complète du gouvernement en analysant onze domaines politiques. En général, les auteurs constatent que les politiques des libéraux, une fois qu'ils sont au pouvoir, ressemblent beaucoup plus à la philosophie bleue des conservateurs qu'au rouge du Livre. Les libéraux ont eu du succès dans les domaines de la gestion de l'économie, tels que le contrôle du déficit et la promotion du commerce, avec l'exception importante de la politique d'emploi. Dans le domaine de l'unité nationale, ils réussissent tout juste, mais un autre test important va venir. Leur fiche est faible dans les domaines sociaux, tels que les marchés du travail, la garde d'enfants, les communications et le logement social, où les deux obsessions que représentent le déficit et la réponse aux pressions décentralisatrices mènent le programme politique. Finalement, dans le domaine de la protection de l'environnement et de l'intégrité, la fiche des libéraux montre des succès mitigés, mais est loin de répondre aux attentes créées par le Livre rouge.*

Claire Turenne Sjolander
International Trade as Foreign Policy: "Anything for a Buck"

Jean Chrétien came to office in 1993 having made few explicit promises with respect to international trade, other than to assist Canadian firms to become more aggressive international traders. At the same time, the Liberal Red Book proclaimed the need to adopt a more internationalist and independent orientation in Canadian foreign policy. Trade policy, however, is never presented as an element of Canadian foreign policy, and this chapter argues that there are two main consequences to this. First, while trade policy is only one element in the orbit of responsibilities that fall under the Department of Foreign Affairs and International Trade, trade policy is now the "tail" that has begun to wag the foreign policy "dog." Broad foreign policy objectives have in large part been made secondary to the requirements of international trade promotion, with attendant consequences for the "internationalist values" applauded in the Red Book. Second, in the priority given to international trade initiatives such as "Team Canada," the Chrétien government appears to be adopting the policies of the 1970 Trudeau government foreign policy paper, which argued that "Canada's 'traditional' middle-power role in the world seemed doomed to disappear." While the Trudeau government in reality contributed to the maintenance of the internationalist legacy of Canadian foreign policy, the Chrétien government appears ready by default if not intent to uphold the original "anti-internationalist" intentions of his predecessor.

Jean Chrétien a pris le pouvoir en 1993 ayant fait peu de promesses explicites en matière de commerce international, à part celle d'aider les entreprises canadiennes à devenir plus agressives dans ce domaine. En même temps, le Livre rouge proclamait qu'il fallait adopter une orientation plus internationaliste et plus indépendante dans la politique étrangère canadienne. La politique commerciale, cependant, n'est jamais présentée comme un élément de la politique étrangère canadienne. Ce chapitre soutient que cette situation a eu deux conséquences principales. Premièrement, si la politique commerciale n'est qu'un élément parmi toutes les responsabilités du ministère des

Affaires étrangères et du commerce international, cet élément a commencé à l'emporter sur la politique étrangère. Les objectifs généraux de la politique étrangère sont en grande partie devenus secondaires aux exigences de la promotion du commerce international, ce qui se répercute sur les valeurs internationalistes applaudies dans le Livre rouge. Deuxièmement, en donnant la priorité aux initiatives en matière de commerce international telles qu' « Équipe Canada,» le gouvernement Chrétien semble adopter les politiques du document de 1970 du gouvernement Trudeau sur la politique étrangère qui soutenait que le rôle traditionnel du Canada comme moyenne puissance dans le monde semblait voué à la disparition. Alors que le gouvernement Trudeau a contribué en réalité au maintien de la tradition internationaliste de la politique étrangère canadienne, le gouvernement Chrétien semble prêt, faute d'agir sinon de propos délibéré, à poursuivre les intentions « anti-internationalistes » originales de son prédécesseur.

Reg Whitaker

Cruising at 30,000 Feet with a Missing Engine: The Chrétien Government in the Aftermath of the Quebec Referendum

The near defeat for federalism in the Quebec referendum in 1995 represents the most serious failure of the Chrétien government. Even with the chill of a razor-thin No margin, and the clear prospect of another referendum to follow, the Liberals have found the challenge of enacting promises of constitutional change extraordinarily risky. Recognition of Quebec as a distinct society and a Quebec veto are strongly opposed by many Canadians outside Quebec, and rejected by Quebec sovereigntists. These elements of a so-called Plan A (positive constitutional inducements to Quebec) will not be promoted by the Liberals before the next federal election. The third element—devolution of powers to Quebec and to all other provinces—has more public supporters in English Canada, but the Liberals have good political reasons for not going too far down that path (although transfer of manpower training to the provinces will take place). The Chrétien government has also been under pressure to develop a "Plan B," which would spell out in advance the terms upon which the rest of Canada would agree to negotiate Quebec"s secession after a Yes vote, and the conditions that would be imposed. This raises the very volatile issue of the refusal of Quebec's

Aboriginal peoples to accept separation, and the potential partition of a secessionist Quebec. The Liberals have adroitly sidestepped this political landmine by the reference to the Supreme Court of the legality of a unilateral secession. The Liberals have shown political skill in avoiding the potential political risks in pushing both Plan A and Plan B, but after the election—and before the next referendum—they will require more decisiveness and willingness to take risks than Mr. Chrétien has so far shown himself capable of.

La victoire serrée du fédéralisme lors du référendum de 1995 représente l'échec le plus sérieux du gouvernement Chrétien. Même à la suite d'une marge de victoire à faire frissonner, et devant la nette perspective d'un autre référendum, les libéraux ont trouvé extraordinairement hasardeux le défi que représente la réalisation des changements constitutionnels promis. La reconnaissance du Québec comme société distincte et le droit de veto du Québec suscitent une opposition farouche chez de nombreux Canadiens en dehors du Québec, tout en étant rejetés par les souverainistes québécois. Ces éléments du soi-disant Plan A (incitations constitutionnelles positives à l'intention du Québec) ne seront pas promus par les libéraux avant les prochaines élections fédérales. Le troisième élément—la délégation des pouvoirs au Québec et à toutes les autres provinces— jouit de plus d'appui au Canada anglais, mais les libéraux ont de bonnes raisons politiques pour ne pas trop avancer sur ce chemin (il est vrai que le transfert de la formation de la main-d'oeuvre va se réaliser). Le gouvernement Chrétien a également subi des pressions pour qu'il élabore un « Plan B,» qui préciserait à l'avance les modalités selon lesquelles le reste du Canada accepterait de négocier la sécession du Québec à la suite d'un Oui, et les conditions qui seraient imposées. Cela soulève la question très explosive du refus des peuples autochtones du Québec d'accepter la séparation, et la partition potentielle du Québec sécessionniste. Les libéraux ont évité de façon adroite ce piège politique en référant à la Cour suprême la question de la légalité d'une sécession unilatérale. Les libéraux ont fait preuve d'habileté politique en évitant les risques politiques potentiels des deux Plans, mais après les élections—et avant le prochain référendum—ils devront dépasser le niveau de résolution, et de volonté de courir des risques, dont M. Chrétien s'est montré capable jusqu'ici.

Sandra Bach is a doctoral candidate in the School of Public Administration at Carleton University.

Bruce Doern is a Professor in the School of Public Administration at Carleton University and is Visiting Joint Professor of Public Policy at the University of Exeter.

Ian Greene is an Associate Professor of Political Science at York University.

Luc Juillet is a doctoral candidate in the School of Public Administration at Carleton University.

Fran Klodawsky is an Assistant Professor of Geography and Women's Studies at Carleton University.

Mark MacDonald is a doctoral candidate in the School of Public Administration at Carleton University.

Allan Maslove is a Professor in the School of Public Administration at Carleton University.

Kevin Moore is a doctoral candidate in the School of Public Administration at Carleton University.

Vincent Mosco is a Professor in the School of Journalism and Communication at Carleton University.

Susan Phillips is an Associate Professor in the School of Public Administration at Carleton University.

Michael Prince is the Lansdowne Professor of Social Policy, Faculty of Human and Social Development, at the University of Victoria.

Aron Spector is Chief Consultant with Ark Research Associates and an Adjunct Professor of Geography at Carleton University.

Peter Stoyko is a doctoral candidate in Political Science at Carleton University.

Gene Swimmer is a Professor in the School of Public Administration at Carleton University.

Glen Toner is an Associate Professor in the School of Public Administration at Carleton University.

Claire Turenne Sjolander is an Associate Professor of Political Science at the University of Ottawa.

Reg Whitaker is a Professor of Political Science at York University.

THE SCHOOL OF PUBLIC ADMINISTRATION
at Carleton University is a national centre for the study of public
policy and public management
in Canada.

The School's Centre for Policy and Program Assessment provides research services and courses to interest groups, businesses, unions and governments in the evaluation of public policies, programs and activities.

The *How Ottawa Spends* series is available from
Carleton University Press, Suite 1400, CTTC,
1125 Colonel By Drive, Ottawa, Ontario K1S 5B6

How Ottawa Spends 1996-97: Life Under the Knife
edited by Gene Swimmer
ISBN 0-88629-285-9 pbk. $29.95

How Ottawa Spends 1995-96: Mid-Life Crises
edited by Susan D. Phillips
ISBN 0-88629-263-8 pbk. $22.95

How Ottawa Spends 1994-95: Making Change
edited by Susan D. Phillips
ISBN 0-88629-229-8 pbk. $22.95

How Ottawa Spends 1993-94: A More Democratic Canada
edited by Susan D. Phillips
ISBN 0-88629-201-8 pbk. $22.95

How Ottawa Spends 1992-93: The Politics of Competitiveness
edited by Frances Abele
ISBN 0-88629-165-8 pbk. $21.95

How Ottawa Spends 1991-92: The Politics of Fragmentation
edited by Frances Abele
ISBN 0-88629-146-1 pbk. $21.95

How Ottawa Spends 1990-91: Tracking the Second Agenda
edited by Katherine A. Graham
ISBN 0-88629-107-0 pbk. $19.95

How Ottawa Spends 1989-90: The Buck Stops Where?
edited by Katherine A. Graham
ISBN 0-88629-085-6 pbk. $19.95

How Ottawa Spends 1988-89: The Conservatives Heading Into the Stretch
edited by Katherine A. Graham
ISBN 0-88629-071-6 pbk. $19.95

Order by phone (613) 520-3740 or by fax (613) 520-2893
(email orders: jsloan@ccs.carleton.ca)